KEY TO ATLAS MAPS

NATIONAL GEOGRAPHIC

Concise Atlas of the World

SECOND EDITION

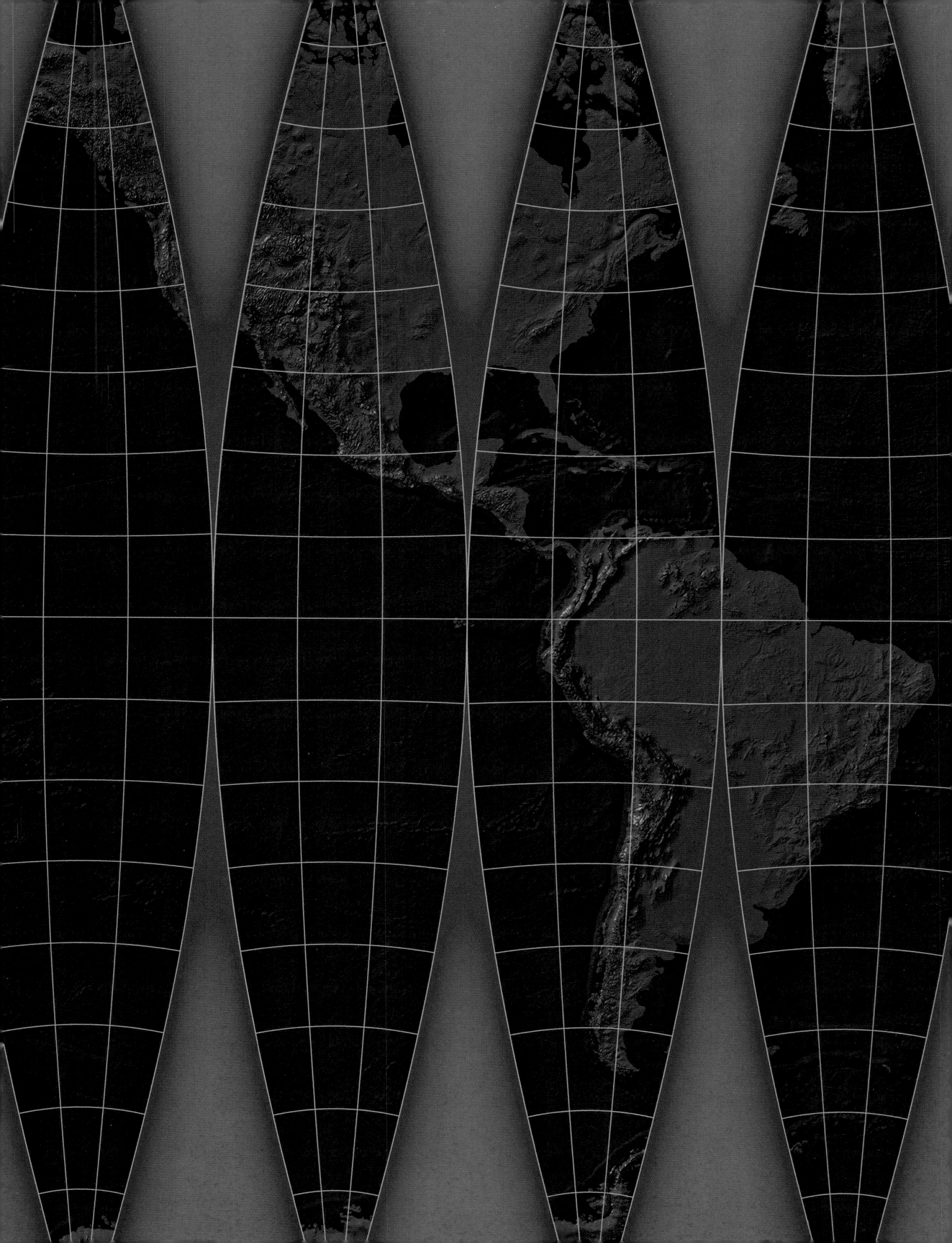

NATIONAL GEOGRAPHIC

Concise Atlas of the WORLD

SECOND EDITION

NATIONAL GEOGRAPHIC
WASHINGTON, D.C.

Founded in 1888, the National Geographic Society is one of the largest nonprofit scientific and educational organizations in the world. It reaches more than 285 million people worldwide each month through its official journal, NATIONAL GEOGRAPHIC, and its four other magazines; the National Geographic Channel; television documentaries; radio programs; films; books; videos and DVDs; maps; and interactive media. National Geographic has funded more than 8,000 scientific research projects and supports an education program combating geographic illiteracy.

For more information, please call
1-800-NGS LINE (647-5463)
or write to the following address:

National Geographic Society
1145 17th Street N.W.
Washington, D.C. 20036-4688 U.S.A.

Visit us online at www.nationalgeographic.com/books

For rights or permissions inquiries, please contact National Geographic Books Subsidiary Rights: ngbookrights@ngs.org

First Edition, 2003
Second Edition, 2008

This 2008 edition printed for Barnes & Noble, Inc., by National Geographic

ISBN-13: 978-1-4262-0445-6

Printed in Italy

This atlas was made possible by the contributions of numerous experts and organizations around the world, including the following:

Boston University Department of Geography and Environment Global Land Cover Project

Center for International Earth Science Information Network (CIESIN), Columbia University

Center for Systemic Peace and Center for Global Policy, George Mason University

Central Intelligence Agency (CIA)

National Aeronautics and Space Administration (NASA)
NASA Ames Research Center,
NASA Goddard Space Flight Center,
NASA Jet Propulsion Laboratory (JPL),
NASA Marshall Space Flight Center

National Geospatial-Intelligence Agency (NGA)

National Oceanic and Atmospheric Administration (NOAA) (see listing under U.S. Department of Commerce, below)

National Science Foundation

Population Reference Bureau

Scripps Institution of Oceanography

Smithsonian Institution

United Nations (UN)
UN Conference on Trade and Development,
UN Development Programme,
UN Educational, Scientific, and Cultural Organization (UNESCO),
UN Environment Programme (UNEP),
UN Population Division,
Food and Agriculture Organization (FAO),
International Telecommunication Union (ITU),
World Conservation Monitoring Centre (WCMC)

U.S. Board on Geographic Names

U.S. Department of Agriculture

U.S. Department of Commerce: Bureau of the Census, National Oceanic and Atmospheric Administration (NOAA)
National Climatic Data Center,
National Environmental Satellite, Data, and Information Service,
National Geophysical Data Center,
National Ocean Service

U.S. Department of Energy and Oak Ridge National Laboratory

U.S. Department of the Interior: Bureau of Indian Affairs, Bureau of Land Management, Fish and Wildlife Service, National Park Service, U.S. Geological Survey

U.S. Department of State: Office of the Geographer

World Bank

World Health Organization/Pan American Health Organization (WHO/PAHO)

World Resources Institute (WRI)

World Trade Organization (WTO)

For a complete listing of contributors, see pages 158 – 159.

Introduction

THE NATIONAL GEOGRAPHIC SOCIETY was born of a vision—that geography is key to understanding all aspects of life on Earth, from microscopic organisms to cultural traditions and world views to the push-pull of geopolitics. Like all strong visions, that original idea for the Society has had the flexibility to expand and evolve over the past century, as technologies advance and circumstances unfold. What strikes me today is how very essential to the well-being of the planet our mission of diffusing geographic knowledge has become. This updated Second Edition of our *Concise Atlas of the World* is one vital way in which we can help you participate in our critical mission.

In this age of global citizenry, no natural disaster, climatic event, economic success or collapse remains local. Virtually everything has a planetary consequence: The loss of ice and the melting of permafrost around Inuit villages in the Arctic have implications for all of us, as does the economic rise of China and India; the growing global trend toward urbanization in the developing world, which contributes to the incubation and spread of diseases, has worldwide repercussions, as does the insidious growth of fanaticism and terrorism. But there is good news to counter the bad. We now have sophisticated tools to track and share information on these changes that we can use to help alleviate tension at the world's pressure points.

In the pages that follow, the *Concise Atlas of the World* brings together such state-of-the-art technologies as enhanced satellite imagery, digital databases, and Geographic Information Systems (GIS) to overlay information and give you an expansive picture of conditions on the planet. In addition to political and physical maps, each continent has its own thematic spread on human and natural topics, with maps that allow you to understand at a glance how population density, economic resources, energy consumption, climatic zones, natural events, and water availability are distributed across the continent. Other spreads track worldwide climate change, trade, health and education, conflict and terrorism, and environmental stresses. And, of course, the topography of the ocean floor is mapped and the movement of all major tectonic plates charted.

We here at the Geographic send into the field the world's finest scientists—environmentalists, anthropologists, archaeologists, mammalogists, oceanographers. Governments and research institutions all over the world open their doors to us. Such access is a rare privilege, and we hope to pass on the information we amass in volumes like this one.

Spreading geographic knowledge is our way of building and strengthening a concerned global community. So, as you pursue your personal quest to make sense of and contribute to your own community and to the planet, keep the *Concise Atlas of the World* at hand. We hope you turn to it often to broaden your understanding and commitment to our shared world.

JOHN M. FAHEY, JR.

PRESIDENT AND
CHIEF EXECUTIVE OFFICER

Table of Contents

Located in the inner solar system, Earth is the third planet from the sun—after Mercury and Venus. Earth's oceans and continents join to form nearly 197 million square miles of surface area. Seventy-one percent of its surface is water. Although different terms are used to describe ocean depths (bathymetry) and the lay of the land (topography), Earth's surface is a continuum. Similar features, such as mountains, ridges, volcanoes, plateaus, valleys, and canyons, give texture to the lands both above and below sea level. See pages 16–17 to view the entire surface of the Earth.

Using This Atlas

MAP POLICIES

Maps are a rich, useful, and—to the extent humanly possible—accurate means of depicting the world. Yet maps inevitably make the world seem a little simpler than it really is. A neatly drawn boundary may in reality be a hotly contested war zone. The government-sanctioned, "official" name of a provincial city in an ethnically diverse region may bear little resemblance to the name its citizens routinely use. These cartographic issues often seem obscure and academic. But maps arouse passions. Despite our carefully reasoned map policies, users of National Geographic maps write us strongly worded letters when our maps are at odds with their worldviews.

How do National Geographic cartographers deal with these realities? With constant scrutiny, considerable discussion, and help from many outside experts.

EXAMPLES

Nations: Issues of national sovereignty and contested borders often boil down to "de facto versus de jure" discussions. Governments and international agencies frequently make official rulings about contested regions. These de jure decisions, no matter how legitimate, are often at odds with the wishes of individuals and groups, and they often stand in stark contrast to real-world situations. The inevitable conclusion: It is simplest and best to show the world as it is—de facto—rather than as we or others wish it to be.

Africa's Western Sahara, for example, was divided by Morocco and Mauritania after the Spanish government withdrew in 1976. Although Morocco now controls the entire territory, the United Nations does not recognize Morocco's sovereignty over this still disputed area. This atlas shows the de facto Moroccan rule but includes an explanatory note.

Place-names: Ride a barge down the Danube, and you'll hear the river called Donau, Duna, Dunaj, Dunarea, Dunav, Dunay. These are local names. This atlas uses the conventional name, "Danube," on physical maps. On political maps, local names are used, with the conventional name in parentheses where space permits. Usage conventions for both foreign and domestic place-names are established by the U.S. Board on Geographic Names, a group with representatives from several federal agencies.

Political Maps

Political maps portray features such as international boundaries, the locations of cities, road networks, and other important elements of the world's human geography. Most index entries are keyed to the political maps, listing the page numbers and then the specific locations on the pages. (See page 138 for details on how to use the index.)

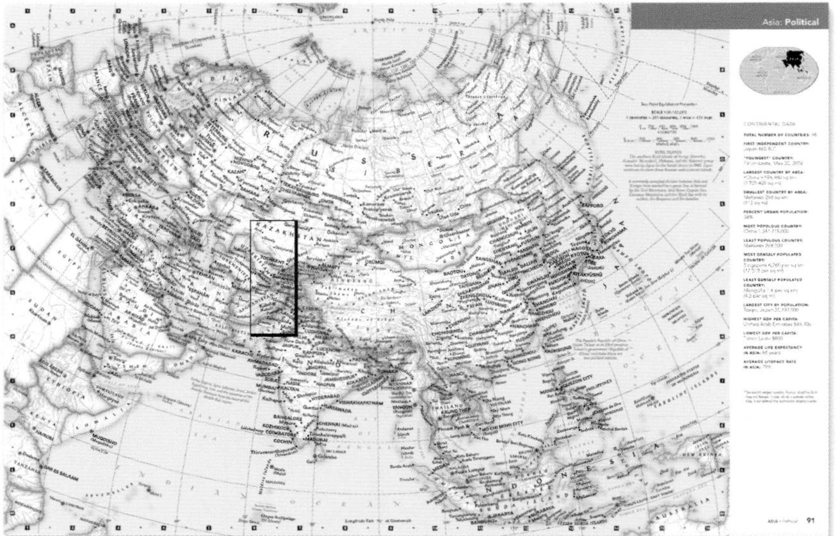

Asia Political, pp. 90–91

Physical features: Gray relief shading depicts surface features such as mountains, hills, and valleys.

Water features are shown in blue. Solid lines and filled-in areas indicate perennial water features; dashed lines and patterns indicate intermittent features.

Boundaries and political divisions are defined with both lines and colored bands; they vary according to whether a boundary is internal or international (for details, see map symbols key at right).

Cities: The regional political maps that form the bulk of this atlas depict four categories of cities or towns. The largest cities are shown in all capital letters (e.g., LONDON).

Physical Maps

Physical maps of the world, the continents, and the ocean floor reveal landforms and vegetation in stunning detail. Painted by relief artists John Bonner and Tibor Tóth, the maps have been edited for accuracy. Although painted maps are human interpretations, these depictions can emphasize subtle features that are sometimes invisible in satellite imagery.

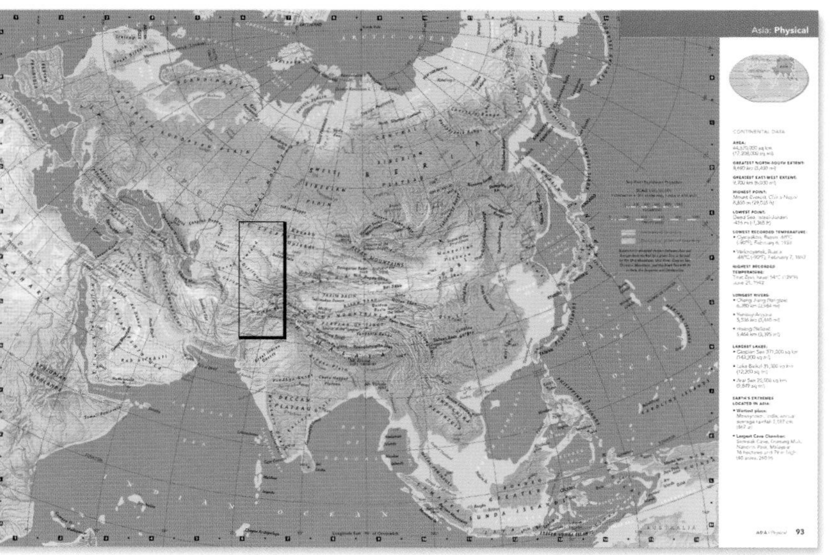

Asia Physical, pp. 92–93

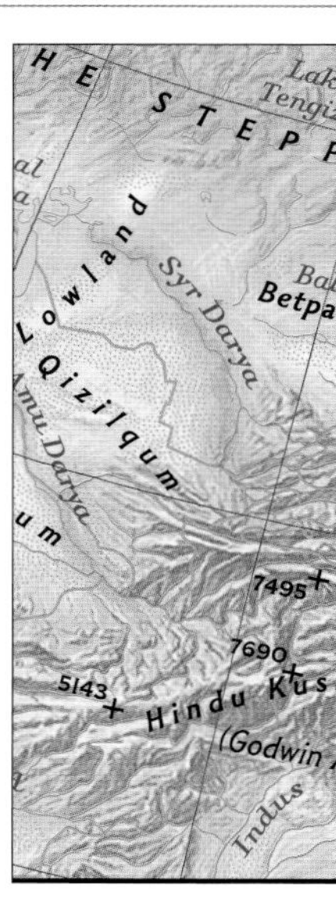

Physical features: Colors and shading illustrate variations in elevation, landforms, and vegetation. Patterns indicate specific landscape features, such as sand, glaciers, and swamps.

Water features: Blue lines indicate rivers; other water bodies are shown as areas of blue. Lighter shading reflects a depth of 200 meters or less.

Boundaries and political divisions are shown in red. Dotted lines indicate disputed or uncertain boundaries.

World Thematic Maps

Thematic maps reveal the rich patchwork and infinite interrelationships of our changing planet. The thematic section at the beginning of the atlas charts human patterns, with information on population, religions, and the world economy. In this section, maps are coupled with charts, diagrams, photographs, and tabular information, which together create a very useful framework for studying geographic patterns.

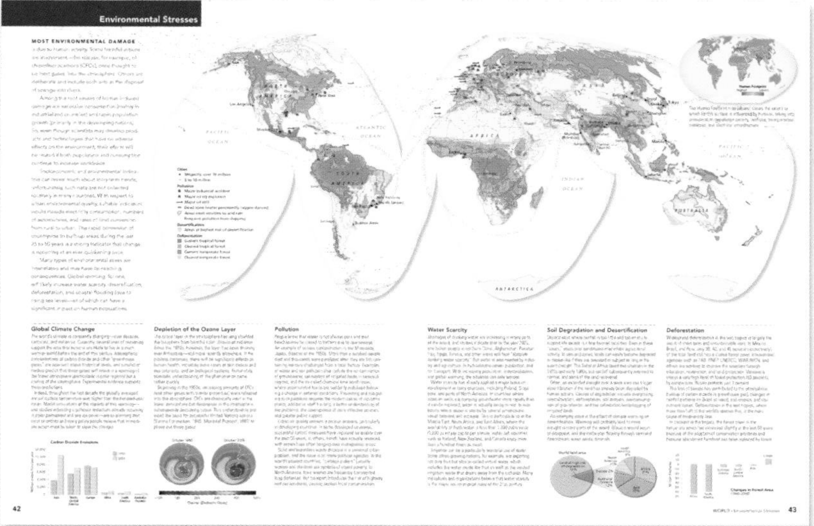

World Environmental Stresses, pp. 42–43

Flags and Facts

This atlas recognizes 193 independent nations. All of these countries, along with dependencies and U.S. states, are profiled in the continental sections of the atlas. Accompanying each entry are highlights of geographic, demographic, and economic data. These details provide a brief overview of each country, state, or territory; they are not intended to be comprehensive. A detailed description of the sources and policies used in compiling the listings is included in the Key to Flags and Facts on page 159.

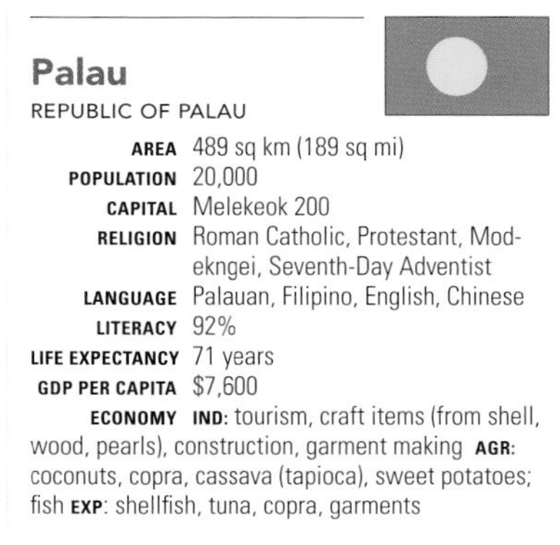

Palau
REPUBLIC OF PALAU

AREA 489 sq km (189 sq mi)
POPULATION 20,000
CAPITAL Melekeok 200
RELIGION Roman Catholic, Protestant, Modekngei, Seventh-Day Adventist
LANGUAGE Palauan, Filipino, English, Chinese
LITERACY 92%
LIFE EXPECTANCY 71 years
GDP PER CAPITA $7,600
ECONOMY **IND:** tourism, craft items (from shell, wood, pearls), construction, garment making **AGR:** coconuts, copra, cassava (tapioca), sweet potatoes; fish **EXP:** shellfish, tuna, copra, garments

Index and Grid

Beginning on page 138 is a full index of place-names found in this atlas. The edge of each map is marked with letters (in rows) and numbers (in columns), to which the index entries are referenced. As an example, "Cartagena, Col. 68 A2" (see inset below) refers to the grid section on page 68 where row A and column 2 meet. More examples and additional details about the index are included on page 138.

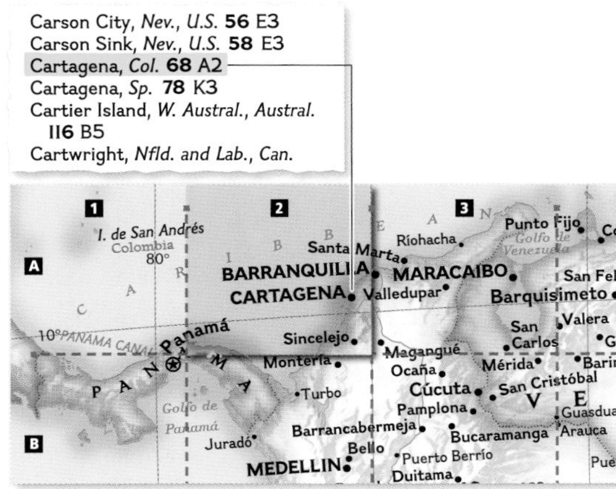

Carson City, *Nev., U.S.* **56** E3
Carson Sink, *Nev., U.S.* **58** E3
Cartagena, *Col.* **68** A2
Cartagena, *Sp.* **78** K3
Cartier Island, *W. Austral., Austral.* **116** B5
Cartwright, *Nfld. and Lab., Can.*

Map Symbols

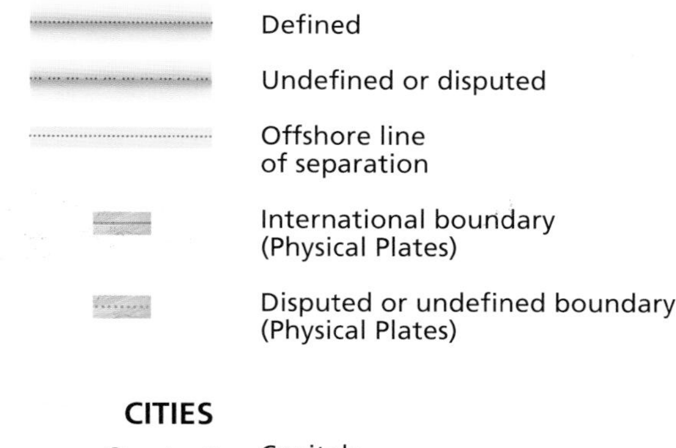

BOUNDARIES

Defined
Undefined or disputed
Offshore line of separation
International boundary (Physical Plates)
Disputed or undefined boundary (Physical Plates)

CITIES

Capitals
Towns

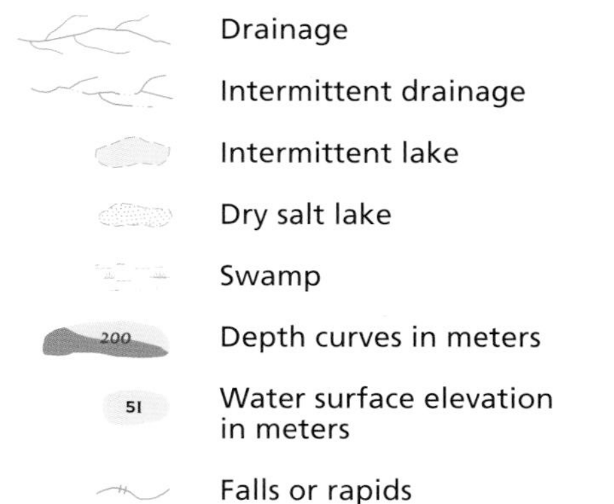

WATER FEATURES

Drainage
Intermittent drainage
Intermittent lake
Dry salt lake
Swamp
Depth curves in meters
Water surface elevation in meters
Falls or rapids

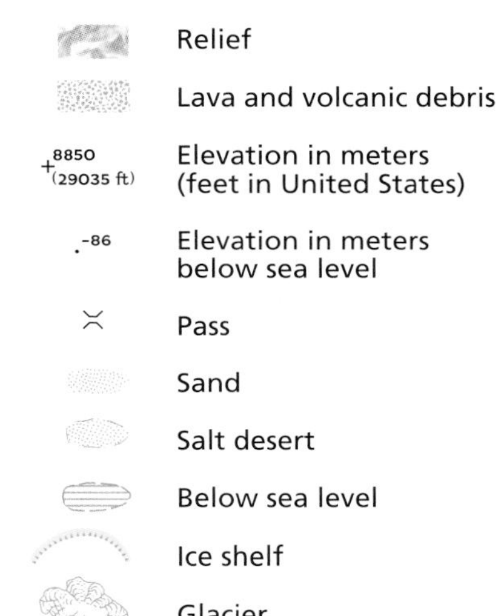

PHYSICAL FEATURES

Relief
Lava and volcanic debris
+8850 (29035 ft) Elevation in meters (feet in United States)
-86 Elevation in meters below sea level
Pass
Sand
Salt desert
Below sea level
Ice shelf
Glacier

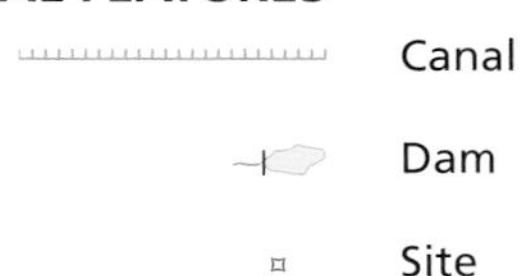

CULTURAL FEATURES

Canal
Dam
Site

MAP SCALE ***(Sample)***

SCALE 1:9,957,000
1 CENTIMETER = 100 KILOMETERS; 1 INCH = 157 MILES

0 100 200 300 400
KILOMETERS

0 100 200 300 400
STATUTE MILES

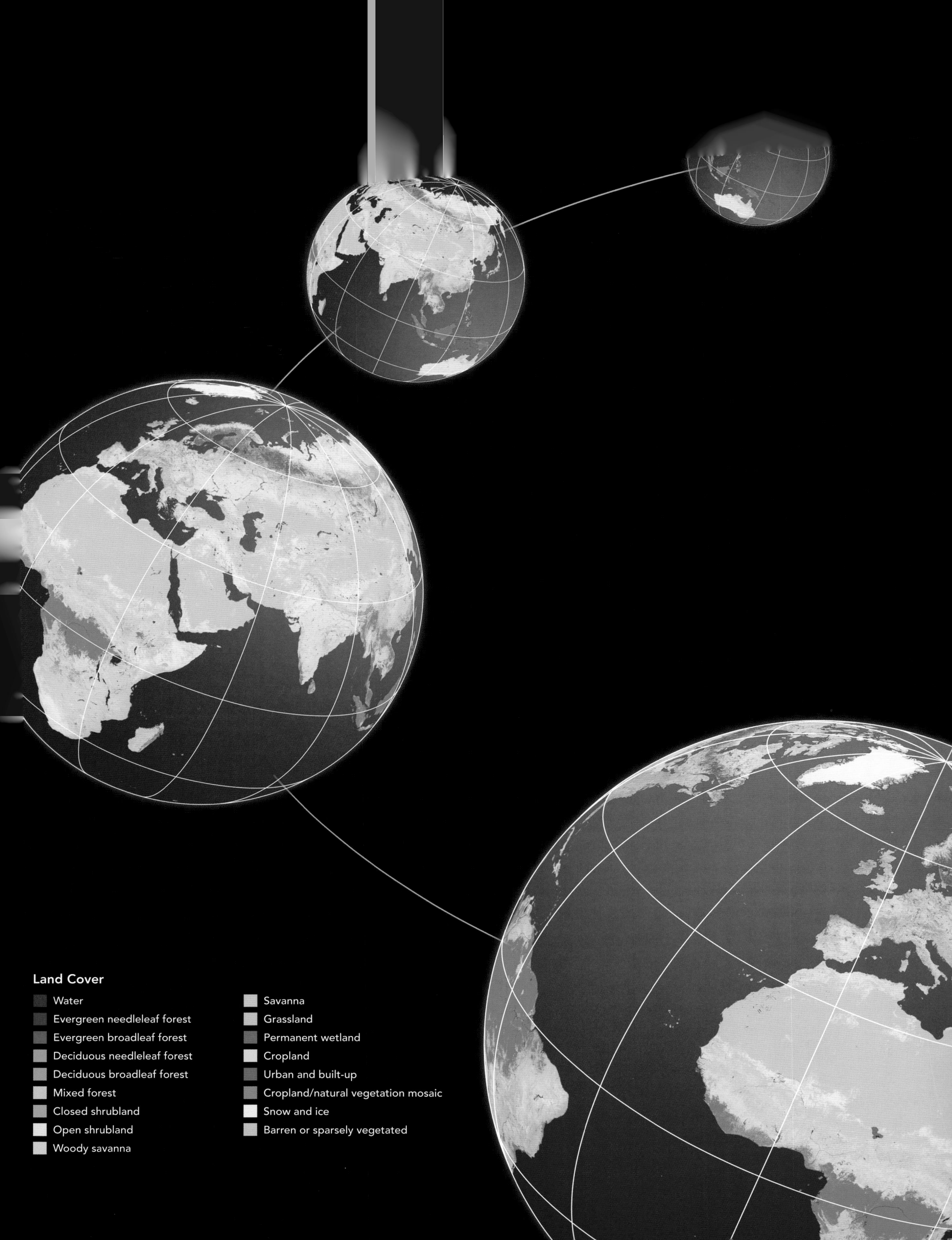
Land Cover
Water
Evergreen needleleaf forest
Evergreen broadleaf forest
Deciduous needleleaf forest
Deciduous broadleaf forest
Mixed forest
Closed shrubland
Open shrubland
Woody savanna
Savanna
Grassland
Permanent wetland
Cropland
Urban and built-up
Cropland/natural vegetation mosaic
Snow and ice
Barren or sparsely vegetated

World

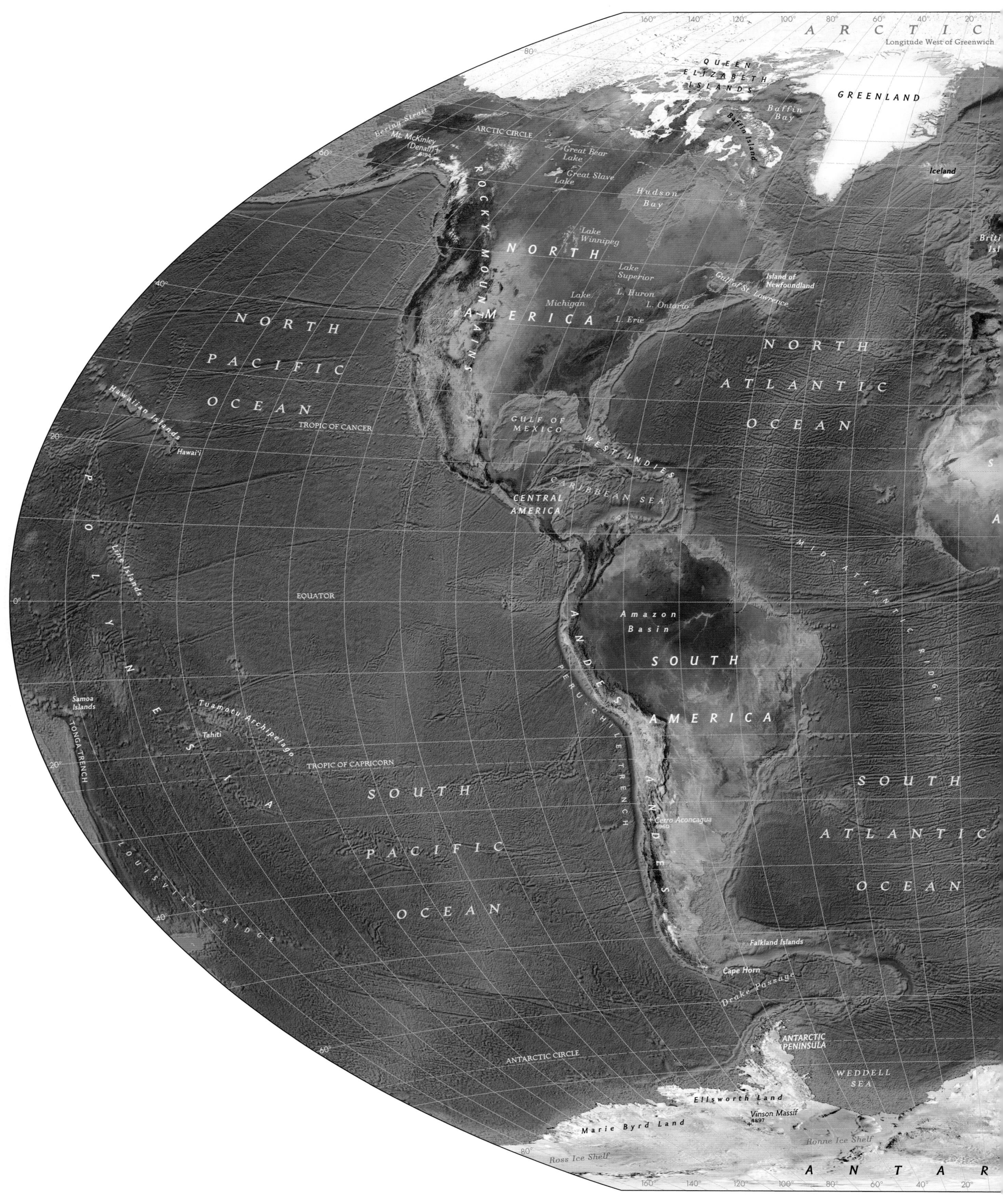
ARCTIC
Longitude West of Greenwich
QUEEN ELIZABETH ISLANDS
GREENLAND
Baffin Bay
Baffin Island
Iceland
Bering Strait
Mt. McKinley (Denali)
6194
ARCTIC CIRCLE
Great Bear Lake
Great Slave Lake
Hudson Bay
ROCKY MOUNTAINS
Lake Winnipeg
NORTH AMERICA
Lake Superior
Island of Newfoundland
Gulf of St. Lawrence
Lake Michigan
L. Huron
L. Ontario
L. Erie
NORTH PACIFIC OCEAN
NORTH ATLANTIC OCEAN
Hawaiian Islands
Hawai'i
TROPIC OF CANCER
GULF OF MEXICO
WEST INDIES
CARIBBEAN SEA
CENTRAL AMERICA
POLYNESIA
Line Islands
MID-ATLANTIC RIDGE
EQUATOR
Amazon Basin
SOUTH AMERICA
ANDES
PERU-CHILE TRENCH
Samoa Islands
TONGA TRENCH
Tuamotu Archipelago
Tahiti
TROPIC OF CAPRICORN
SOUTH PACIFIC OCEAN
SOUTH ATLANTIC OCEAN
Cerro Aconcagua
6960
LOUISVILLE RIDGE
Falkland Islands
Cape Horn
Drake Passage
ANTARCTIC PENINSULA
ANTARCTIC CIRCLE
WEDDELL SEA
Ellsworth Land
Vinson Massif
4897
Marie Byrd Land
Ronne Ice Shelf
Ross Ice Shelf
ANTAR
160° 140° 120° 100° 80° 60° 40° 20°
80° 60° 40° 20° 0° 20° 40° 60° 80°

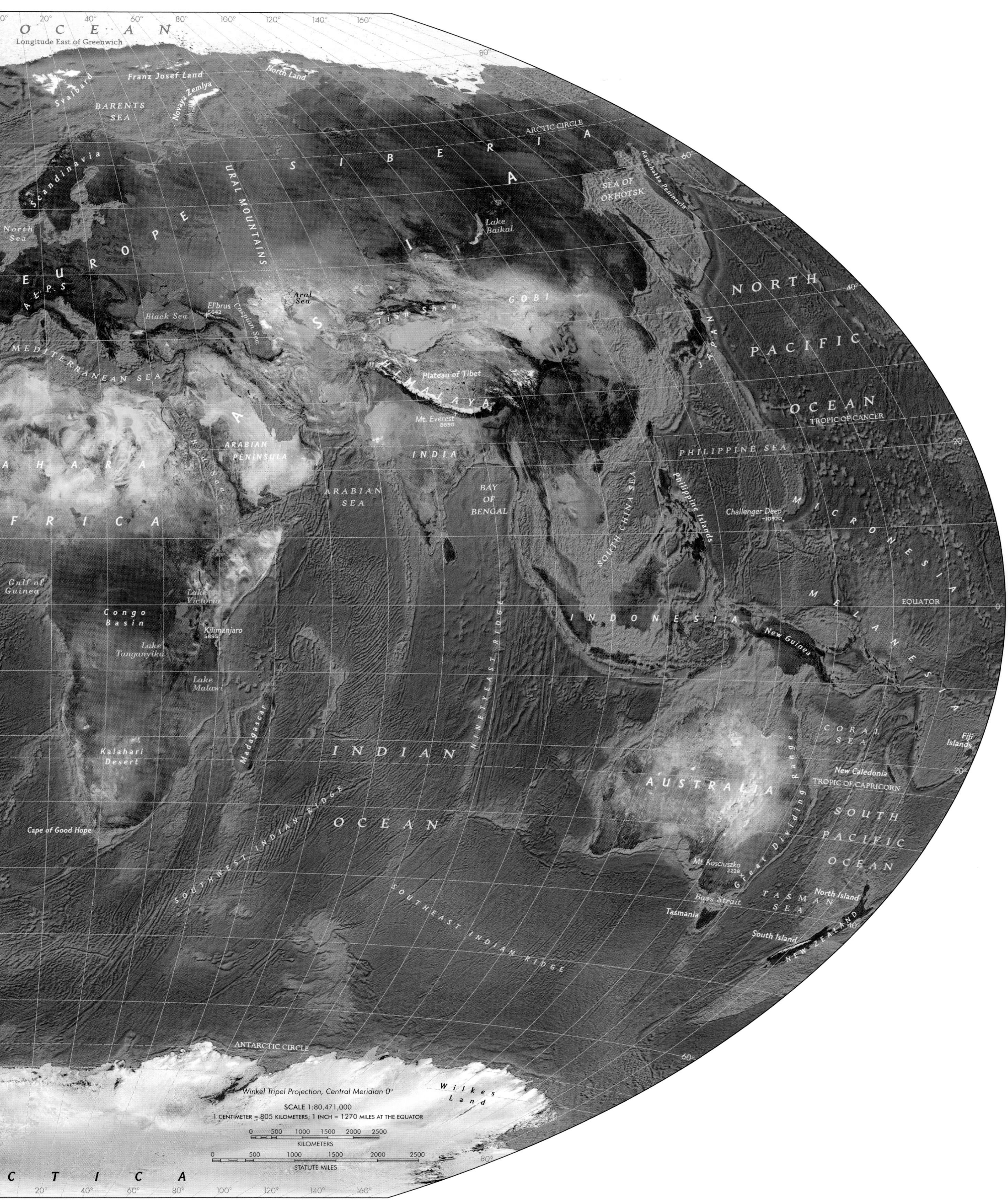
OCEAN
Longitude East of Greenwich
Svalbard
Franz Josef Land
North Land
Novaya Zemlya
BARENTS SEA
ARCTIC CIRCLE
SIBERIA
ASIA
Scandinavia
SEA OF OKHOTSK
Kamchatka Peninsula
Lake Baikal
URAL MOUNTAINS
North Sea
EUROPE
ALPS
Aral Sea
El'brus 5642
Caspian Sea
Black Sea
Tian Shan
GOBI
NORTH PACIFIC OCEAN
JAPAN
MEDITERRANEAN SEA
Plateau of Tibet
HIMALAYA
Mt. Everest 8850
TROPIC OF CANCER
ARABIAN PENINSULA
Red Sea
INDIA
PHILIPPINE SEA
SAHARA
AFRICA
ARABIAN SEA
BAY OF BENGAL
SOUTH CHINA SEA
Philippine Islands
Challenger Deep -10920
MICRONESIA
Gulf of Guinea
Lake Victoria
Congo Basin
Kilimanjaro 5895
Lake Tanganyika
Lake Malawi
NINETYEAST RIDGE
INDONESIA
New Guinea
MELANESIA
EQUATOR
Madagascar
Kalahari Desert
INDIAN OCEAN
CORAL SEA
Fiji Islands
New Caledonia
TROPIC OF CAPRICORN
AUSTRALIA
Great Dividing Range
SOUTH PACIFIC OCEAN
Cape of Good Hope
SOUTHWEST INDIAN RIDGE
SOUTHEAST INDIAN RIDGE
Mt. Kosciuszko 2228
Bass Strait
TASMAN SEA
North Island
Tasmania
South Island
NEW ZEALAND
ANTARCTIC CIRCLE
Wilkes Land
ANTARCTICA
Winkel Tripel Projection, Central Meridian 0°
SCALE 1:80,471,000
1 CENTIMETER = 805 KILOMETERS; 1 INCH = 1270 MILES AT THE EQUATOR
0 500 1000 1500 2000 2500
KILOMETERS
0 500 1000 1500 2000 2500
STATUTE MILES

A R C T I C
North Magnetic Pole 2007
QUEEN ELIZABETH ISLANDS
PARRY ISLANDS
ELLESMERE ISLAND
Knud Rasmussen Land
GREENLAND
(KALAALLIT NUNAAT)
Denmark
Longitude West of Greenwich
Wrangel I.
Monday
Sunday
BEAUFORT SEA
Barrow
RUSSIA
ARCTIC CIRCLE
Brooks Range
ALASKA
U.S.
Date Line
Nome
Mt. McKinley (Denali) 6194 (20320 ft)
Fairbanks
Bethel
Anchorage
Valdez
BERING SEA
Aleutian Islands
Alaska Peninsula
Cold Bay
Kodiak
Alexander Archipelago
Juneau
Skagway
Whitehorse
Inuvik
Great Bear Lake
Deline
Great Slave Lake
Yellowknife
Hay River
Fort Smith
VICTORIA ISLAND
Cambridge Bay
Taloyoak
Resolute
Qaanaaq (Thule)
BAFFIN BAY
BAFFIN ISLAND
Pond Inlet
Igloolik
Upernavik
Bathurst Inlet
Chesterfield Inlet
Whale Cove
Arviat
HUDSON BAY
Iqaluit
DAVIS STRAIT
Nuuk (Godthåb)
Narsarsuaq
Denmark Strait
ICELAND
Reykjavík
Jan Mayen Norway
Faroe Is. Denmark
Shetland Is.
Orkney Is.
UNITED KINGDOM
Dublin
IRELAND
London
Celtic Sea
English Channel
FRANCE
C A N A D A
ROCKY MOUNTAINS
Prince Rupert
Queen Charlotte Islands
Fort St. John
Peace River
Fort McMurray
Thompson
Fort Severn
Sanikiluaq
Kuujjuaq
Nain
LABRADOR SEA
Prince George
Edmonton
Saskatoon
Regina
Calgary
Lake Winnipeg
Winnipeg
Fort Albany
Chisasibi
LABRADOR
Labrador City
Vancouver I.
Victoria
Vancouver
Seattle
Chibougamau
Sept-Îles
ISLAND OF NEWFOUNDLAND
St. John's
Timmins
Thunder Bay
Québec
Montréal
Ottawa
Charlottetown
Halifax
St.-Pierre & Miquelon France
N O R T H
Portland
Helena
Billings
Fargo
Eugene
Boise
Minneapolis
Milwaukee
Detroit
Toronto
Buffalo
Boston
Salt Lake City
Chicago
Omaha
Sacramento
San Francisco
Reno
Denver
Kansas City
Indianapolis
Columbus
New York
Philadelphia
Washington
UNITED STATES
Las Vegas
Santa Fe
Albuquerque
Oklahoma City
Tulsa
Nashville
Charlotte
Memphis
Atlanta
Los Angeles
San Diego
Tijuana
Mexicali
Phoenix
El Paso
Dallas
Mississippi
Birmingham
Ciudad Juárez
Chihuahua
San Antonio
Austin
Houston
New Orleans
Jacksonville
Tampa
Orlando
Miami
Bermuda Islands U.K.
Portugal
Azores (Açores)
PORTUGAL
Lisbon
Madrid
SPAIN
Seville
Zaragoza
GIBRALTAR U.K.
Rabat
Fès
Casablanca
MOROCCO
Marrakech
Madeira Islands Portugal
A T L A N T I C
Midway Is. U.S.
P A C I F I C
Isla Guadalupe Mexico
Baja California
Nuevo Laredo
Laredo
Monterrey
GULF OF MEXICO
Nassau
BAHAMAS
Canary Islands (Islas Canarias) Spain
Santa Cruz
Laayoune
WESTERN SAHARA
Morocco
Tindouf
Tropic of Cancer
HAWAII United States
Kaua'i
Honolulu
Maui
Hilo
Hawai'i
Mazatlán
Tampico
Mérida
Havana
CUBA
Cancún
Cayman Is. U.K.
Turks and Caicos Is. U.K.
Port-au-Prince
DOMINICAN REP.
Santo Domingo
PUERTO RICO U.S.
HAITI
GREATER ANTILLES
Virgin Is. U.S. & U.K.
Guadalajara
Islas Revillagigedo Mexico
Isla Clarión
Puebla
Veracruz
Mexico
MEXICO
Yucatán
Belmopan
BELIZE
JAMAICA
Kingston
San Juan
ST. KITTS AND NEVIS
ANTIGUA AND BARBUDA
Guadeloupe France
DOMINICA
Martinique France
ST. LUCIA
BARBADOS
ST. VINCENT AND THE GRENADINES
GRENADA
Port-of-Spain
TRINIDAD AND TOBAGO
LESSER ANTILLES
CARIBBEAN SEA
Acapulco
Tuxtla Gutiérrez
GUATEMALA
HONDURAS
Tegucigalpa
Guatemala
San Salvador
EL SALVADOR
NICARAGUA
Managua
San José
COSTA RICA
Panama
PANAMA
Neth.
Aruba
Curaçao
Maracaibo
Barranquilla
Cartagena
Caracas
Mérida
VENEZUELA
Georgetown
Paramaribo
SURINAME
Cayenne
FRENCH GUIANA France
GUYANA
Puerto Ayacucho
Cotticá
Johnston Atoll U.S.
O C E A N
Clipperton France
Isla del Coco Costa Rica
Isla de Malpelo Colombia
Medellín
Bogotá
Cali
COLOMBIA
Palmyra Atoll U.S.
LINE ISLANDS
Kiritimati (Christmas I.)
Howland Island
Baker Island U.S.
EQUATOR
Jarvis I. U.S.
GALÁPAGOS ISLANDS (ARCHIPIÉLAGO DE COLÓN) Ecuador
Quito
ECUADOR
Guayaquil
Cuenca
Piura
Trujillo
Iquitos
Leticia
Mitú
Boa Vista
Macapá
Belém
São Luís
Fortaleza
Natal
Recife
Barcelos
Manaus
Óbidos
Santarém
Itaituba
Amazon
Caxias
Marabá
Carolina
Juàzeiro do Norte
Manicoré
Eirunepé
Cruzeiro do Sul
Rio Branco
Prainha
Arquipélago de Fernando de Noronha Brazil
St. Peter and St. Paul Rocks Brazil
Ascension U.K.
B R A Z I L
PERU
Lima
Ayacucho
Ica
Cusco
Ji-Paraná (Rondônia)
Guajará Mirim
Vilhena
Porangatu
Peixe
Feira de Santana
Aracaju
Salvador (Bahia)
Ilhéus
Montes Claros
BOLIVIA
La Paz
Trinidad
Cuiabá
Cáceres
Brasília
Goiânia
Corumbá
Santa Cruz
Sucre
Cochabamba
Tacna
Arica
Iquique
Campo Grande
Belo Horizonte
Vitória
Bauru
Rio de Janeiro
São Paulo
Curitiba
Florianópolis
PHOENIX ISLANDS
KIRIBATI
TOKELAU N.Z.
MARQUESAS ISLANDS France
COOK ISLANDS New Zealand
SAMOA
AMERICAN SAMOA U.S.
Apia
Pago Pago
Wallis France
SAMOA IS.
Lau Group
Niue N.Z.
TONGA IS.
Fiji Islands
TONGA
Nuku'alofa
Rarotonga
TUAMOTU ARCHIPELAGO
Rangiroa
Papeete
Tahiti
SOCIETY IS.
FRENCH POLYNESIA France
Tubuai
Îles Gambier
AUSTRAL ISLANDS (TUBUAI ISLANDS)
Rapa
United Kingdom
Ducie Island
Pitcairn Island
TROPIC OF CAPRICORN
S O U T H
P A C I F I C
Isla Sala y Gómez Chile
Easter Island (Isla de Pascua) Chile
Isla San Félix Chile
Isla San Ambrosio
Antofagasta
San Salvador de Jujuy
San Miguel de Tucumán
Salta
PARAGUAY
Asunción
Posadas
Porto Alegre
Pelotas
La Rioja
Cerro Aconcagua 6960 (22834 ft)
Córdoba
Salto
URUGUAY
Montevideo
Buenos Aires
Mar del Plata
Mendoza
Santiago
Río Cuarto
Archipiélago Juan Fernández Chile
Concepción
Santa Rosa
PAMPAS
ARGENTINA
CHILE
Bahía Blanca
Neuquén
Viedma
Península Valdés
Puerto Madryn
Valdivia
Puerto Montt
PATAGONIA
Comodoro Rivadavia
Balmaceda
Puerto Deseado
Península de Taitao
Ilha de Trindade
Ilhas Martin Vaz Brazil
Tristan da Cunha Group U.K.
Kermadec Islands N.Z.
Date Line
Sunday
Monday
Chatham Is. N.Z.
O C E A N
Stanley
FALKLAND ISLANDS (ISLAS MALVINAS) U.K.
Shag Rocks U.K.
South Georgia U.K.
South Sandwich Islands U.K.
Rio Gallegos
Punta Arenas
TIERRA DEL FUEGO
Ushuaia
Islas Diego Ramírez Chile
SCOTIA SEA
Drake Passage
S. Shetland Is.
S. Orkney Is.
ANTARCTIC PENINSULA
ANTARCTIC CIRCLE
WEDDELL SEA
Riiser-Larsen Ice Shelf
Ronne Ice Shelf
Filchner Ice Shelf
Berkner Island
ELLSWORTH LAND
Vinson Massif 4897 (16067 ft)
Scott I.
ROSS SEA
Ross Ice Shelf
MARIE BYRD LAND
TRANSANTARCTIC MOUNTAINS
A N T A R
Cap Barbas
Fdérik
Atar
MAURITANIA
Nouakchott
Taoudenni
Tombouctou (Timbuktu)
CAPE VERDE
Praia
SENEGAL
Dakar
Rosso
Banjul
GAMBIA
Bamako
Ouagadougou
Bissau
GUINEA-BISSAU
GUINEA
BURKINA FASO
Conakry
Freetown
SIERRA LEONE
Monrovia
LIBERIA
CÔTE D'IVOIRE
Yamoussoukro
Abidjan
Accra
St. Helena U.K.

Longitude East of Greenwich
Meridian of Greenwich (London)
RUSSIA
KAZAKHSTAN
CHINA
INDIA
MONGOLIA
AUSTRALIA
INDONESIA
NORTH PACIFIC OCEAN
INDIAN OCEAN
SOUTH PACIFIC OCEAN
ARCTIC CIRCLE
TROPIC OF CANCER
EQUATOR
TROPIC OF CAPRICORN
ANTARCTIC CIRCLE
Date Line
Winkel Tripel Projection, Central Meridian 0°
SCALE 1:80,471,000
1 CENTIMETER = 805 KILOMETERS; 1 INCH = 1270 MILES AT THE EQUATOR
KILOMETERS
STATUTE MILES
International boundaries and disputed territories, where scale permits, reflect de facto status at the time of publication.

A R C T I C
LOMONOSOV RIDGE
MAKAROV BASIN
MENDELEYEV PLAIN
CANADA BASIN
North Magnetic Pole 2007
Axel Heiberg Island
QUEEN ELIZABETH ISLANDS
Ellesmere Island
Lincoln Sea
Knud Rasmussen Land
GREENLAND
CHUKCHI PLAIN
CHUKCHI PLATEAU
NORTHWIND ESCARPMENT
CANADA PLAIN
CONTINENTAL SHELF
Prince Patrick Island
Melville I.
Banks Island
Victoria Island
Devon I.
Hayes Peninsula
Wrangel I.
Point Barrow
North Slope
Brooks Range
ARCTIC CIRCLE
SIBERIA
Chukchi Pen.
Seward Pen.
ALASKA
Beaufort Sea
Amundsen Gulf
Baffin Bay
Baffin Island
Boothia Pen.
Melville Pen.
Foxe Basin
Southampton Island
Great Bear Lake
Great Slave Lake
BERING SEA
Mt. McKinley (Denali) 6194
Alaska Range
Mt. Logan 5959
Yukon
Mackenzie
Thelon
Peace
Hudson Bay
James Bay
Churchill
Nelson
Lake Winnipeg
Aleutian Islands
ALEUTIAN TRENCH
Gulf of Alaska
Alexander Archipelago
Queen Charlotte Is.
Vancouver Island
Gilbert Seamount
TUFTS PLAIN
CASCADIA BASIN
Harris Seamount
Ice thickness 3410
Gunnbjørn
3700
ICELAND PLATEAU
Iceland
Jan Mayen
GREENLAND SEA
CONTINENTAL SLOPE
Faroe Is.
Shetland Is.
Orkney Is.
British Isles
Ireland
Great Britain
Cape Farewell
IRMINGER BASIN
REYKJANES RIDGE
MAURY SEACHANNEL
ROCKALL RISE
ROCKALL TROUGH
NORTHWEST ATLANTIC MID-OCEAN CANYON
LABRADOR SEA
Labrador
Ungava Bay
Hudson Strait
CHARLIE-GIBBS FRACTURE ZONE
FARADAY FRACTURE ZONE
Celtic Sea
Bay of Biscay
BISCAY PLAIN
Cape Finisterre
Iberian Peninsula
Anticosti I.
Island of Newfoundland
Gulf of St. Lawrence
Grand Banks of Newfoundland
Flemish Cap
Nova Scotia
Gulf of Maine
Cape Cod
Long Island
Laurentian Fan
Canadian Shield
NORTH AMERICA
ROCKY MOUNTAINS
Great Plains
Missouri
Source of the Mississippi
L. Superior
L. Michigan
L. Huron
Lake Ontario
Lake Erie
St. Lawrence
Ohio
Mississippi
Ozark Plateau
Mt. Mitchell 2037
Appalachian Mountains
Chesapeake Bay
Cape Hatteras
Coastal Plain
Great Salt Lake
Great Basin
Mt. Whitney 4418
Death Valley
Mt. Elbert 4399
Cascade Range
Snake
Colorado
Sierra Nevada
Cape Mendocino
MENDOCINO FRACTURE ZONE
PIONEER FRACTURE ZONE
MURRAY FRACTURE ZONE
MOLOKAI FRACTURE ZONE
NORTH PACIFIC OCEAN
NORTHEAST PACIFIC BASIN
NORTHWEST HAWAIIAN RIDGE
Musicians Seamounts
Midway Is.
Hawaiian Islands
Mendelssohn Seamount
Moonless Mts.
Fieberling Tablemount
PATTON ESCARPMENT
Guadalupe I.
Baja California
Gulf of California
CEDROS TRENCH
Sierra Madre Occidental
Sierra Madre Oriental
Rio Grande
Henderson Seamount
TROPIC OF CANCER
NECKER RIDGE
Kauai
Oahu
Maui
Hawai'i
Johnston Atoll
SOHM PLAIN
Kelvin Seamount
Bermuda Islands
BERMUDA RISE
Corner Seamounts
NORTH AMERICAN BASIN
HATTERAS PLAIN
BLAKE PLATEAU
CONTINENTAL SHELF
Florida
Bahama Is.
GULF OF MEXICO
Mississippi Fan
MEXICO BASIN
Campeche Bank
Yucatan Peninsula
Cuba
WEST INDIES
Greater Antilles
Hispaniola
Puerto Rico
PUERTO RICO TRENCH
CAYMAN TRENCH
Jamaica
CARIBBEAN SEA
COLOMBIAN BASIN
Pt. Gallinas
AVES RIDGE
Lesser Antilles
Trinidad
Pico de Orizaba 5747
CENTRAL AMERICA
MIDDLE AMERICA TRENCH
Isthmus of Panama
NORTH ATLANTIC OCEAN
Azores
OCEANOGRAPHER FRACTURE ZONE
Josephine Seamount
Strait of Gibraltar
Madeira Is.
Canary Islands
Atlas
Great Meteor Tablemount
CAPE VERDE PLAIN
ATLANTIS FRACTURE ZONE
MID-ATLANTIC RIDGE
Krylov Seamount
Cape Verde Islands
Cape Verde
Sénégal
GAMBIA PLAIN
VEMA FRACTURE ZONE
DEMERARA PLAIN
DOLDRUMS FRACTURE ZONE
SIERRA LEONE RISE
SIERRA LEONE BASIN
Cape Palmas
GUINEA BASIN
ROMANCHE FRACTURE ZONE
Romanche Gap
CHAIN FRACTURE ZONE
CLARION FRACTURE ZONE
Mathematicians Seamounts
CLIPPERTON FRACTURE ZONE
Clipperton
CENTRAL PACIFIC BASIN
MAGELLAN RISE
Palmyra Atoll
Kiritimati (Christmas I.)
EQUATOR
Howland I.
Baker I.
Jarvis I.
Phoenix Islands
GALÁPAGOS FRACTURE ZONE
GUATEMALA BASIN
Cocos Island
COCOS RIDGE
COLON RIDGE
PANAMA BASIN
Galápagos Islands
Carnegie Ridge
Gulf of Guayaquil
Pariñas Point
Maracaibo
Orinoco
Llanos
Angel Falls
Mt. Roraima
Guiana Highlands
Pico da Neblina
CONTINENTAL SHELF
Amazon Fan
Marajó I.
CEARA PLAIN
Amazon Basin
Point Calcanhar
Point Coqueiros
PERNAMBUCO PLAIN
ASCENSION FRACTURE ZONE
Ascension
Nevado Huascarán 6768
La Montaña
SOUTH AMERICA
Brazilian Highlands
ANDES
PERU BASIN
PERU-CHILE TRENCH
Source of the Amazon
Lake Titicaca
Atacama Desert
Salar de Uyuni
Gran Chaco
Iguazú Falls
Paraná
Cape Frio
Santos Plateau
Stocks Seamount
BRAZIL BASIN
Hotspur Seamount
Martin Vaz Islands
Columbia Seamount
Vitória Seamount
ST. HELENA FRACTURE ZONE
St. Helena
MARTIN VAZ FRACTURE ZONE
RIO GRANDE FRACTURE ZONE
RIO GRANDE RISE
SOUTH ATLANTIC OCEAN
Walvis Ridge
Wüst Seamount
TRISTAN DA CUNHA FRACTURE ZONE
GOUGH FRACTURE ZONE
Marquesas Islands
MARQUESAS FRACTURE ZONE
Caroline I.
Flint I.
Atafu
Tokelau
Swains I.
Samoa
Nassau
Wallis Islands
Upolu
Savai'i
Rose Atoll
Cook Islands
Pukapuka
Tuamotu Archipelago
Society Islands
Tahiti
Scilly
Rarotonga
Maria
Mangaia
Morane
Niue
TONGA TRENCH
LAU BASIN
Fiji Is.
TROPIC OF CAPRICORN
President Thiers Bank
Rapa
Marotiri
Austral Islands
Pitcairn I.
Isla Sala y Gómez
Easter Island
EAST PACIFIC RISE
GALÁPAGOS RISE
NASCA RIDGE
CHILE BASIN
San Félix I.
San Ambrosio I.
Juan Fernández Islands
Salinas Grandes
Cerro Aconcagua 6960
Pampas
SOUTH PACIFIC OCEAN
Kermadec Islands
KERMADEC TRENCH
LOUISVILLE RIDGE
CHALLENGER FRACTURE ZONE
AGASSIZ FRACTURE ZONE
CHILE RISE
VALDIVIA FRACTURE ZONE
Isla Grande de Chiloé
Taitao Peninsula
Wellington I.
SOUTHEAST PACIFIC BASIN
SOUTHWEST PACIFIC BASIN
Chatham Islands
CHATHAM RISE
MENARD FRACTURE ZONE
HEEZEN FRACTURE ZONE
ELTANIN FRACTURE ZONE
THARP FRACTURE ZONE
UDINTSEV FRACTURE ZONE
PACIFIC-ANTARCTIC RIDGE
HUMBOLDT PLAIN
Valdés Peninsula
ARGENTINE PLAIN
Gulf of San Jorge
Patagonia
CONTINENTAL SHELF
CONTINENTAL SLOPE
CONTINENTAL RISE
FALKLAND ESCARPMENT
FALKLAND PLATEAU
Falkland Islands
Strait of Magellan
Tierra del Fuego
Cape Horn
Drake Passage
Scotia Sea
SOUTH GEORGIA RIDGE
South Georgia
ISLAS ORCADAS RISE
SOUTH SANDWICH TRENCH
South Sandwich Islands
AMERICA-ANTARCTICA RIDGE
South Shetland Islands
South Orkney Islands
BELLINGSHAUSEN PLAIN
De Gerlache Seamounts
ANTARCTIC PENINSULA
Adelaide Island
Alexander Island
WEDDELL SEA
WEDDELL PLAIN
Cape Norvegia
AMUNDSEN PLAIN
ANTARCTIC CIRCLE
AMUNDSEN RIDGES
Marie Byrd Seamount
Peter I I.
Bellingshausen Sea
Thurston I.
Amundsen Sea
Scott Island
Carney I.
Siple Island
Wrigley Gulf
Ellsworth Land
Ronne Ice Shelf
Berkner Island
Filchner Ice Shelf
Sulzberger Bay
Ross Sea
Edward VII Pen.
Roosevelt I.
Ross Ice Shelf
Mt. Sidley 4181
Marie Byrd Land
Bentley Subglacial Trench -2550
Ice thickness 4342
Vinson Massif 4897
Ellsworth Mountains
TRANSANTARCTIC MOUNTAINS
ANTAR
Longitude West of Greenwich
Meridian of Greenwich (London)

Winkel Tripel Projection, Central Meridian 0°
SCALE 1:80,471,000
1 CENTIMETER = 805 KILOMETERS; 1 INCH = 1270 MILES AT THE EQUATOR
0 500 1000 1500 2000 2500
KILOMETERS
0 500 1000 1500 2000 2500
STATUTE MILES
Longitude East of Greenwich
20° 40° 60° 80° 100° 120° 140° 160° 90° 180°
NANSEN RIDGE
NANSEN BASIN
POLE PLAIN
MAKAROV BASIN
OCEAN
North East Land
Franz Josef Land
Spitsbergen
Svalbard
Molloy Hole
Edge Island
Bear Island
BARENTS SEA
KARA SEA
Novaya Zemlya
NORWEGIAN SEA
North Cape
CONTINENTAL SHELF
Komsomolets Island
October Revolution Island
Bol'shevik Island
Cape Chelyuskin
North Land
Taymyr Peninsula
LAPTEV SEA
New Siberian Islands
EAST SIBERIAN SEA
CONTINENTAL SLOPE
Wrangel I.
Chukchi Range
ARCTIC CIRCLE
North Siberian Lowland
Gyda Peninsula
Yamal Pen.
Kolguyev I.
Central Siberian Plateau
SIBERIA
Verkhoyansk Range
Chersky Range
Kolyma
Koryak Range
Kolyma Range
VORING PLATEAU
Halten Bank
Scandinavia
Kola Pen.
White Sea
Timan Ridge
Ural Mountains
West Siberian Plain
Lake Onega
Lake Ladoga
Gulf of Finland
North Sea
Jutland
Baltic Sea
Source of the Volga
Volga
Northern European Plain
EUROPE
Central Russian Upland
Pinsk Marshes
Carpathian Mts.
Danube
Don
Alps
Mont Blanc 4810
Corsica
Sardinia
Apennines
Sicily
Adriatic Sea
Balkan Peninsula
Black Sea
Bosporus
Crimea
Sea of Azov
Caucasus Mts.
El'brus 5642
Caspian Depression
Caspian Sea
Aral Sea
Ustyurt Plateau
The Steppes
Kazakh Uplands
Lake Balkhash
Dzungarian Basin
Tian Shan
Victory Peak 7439
Turpan Depression
Taklimakan Desert
Altun Shan Mountains
Kunlun Mountains
Muztag 6987
Qinghai Hu
Plateau of Tibet
Source of the Yangtze
HIMALAYA
Mt. Everest 8850 (29035 ft)
Brahmaputra
Ganges
Indus
Hindu Kush
K2 8611
Great Indian Desert
ANATOLIA (ASIA MINOR)
Mt. Ararat 5137
Elburz Mts. 5671
Zagros Mountains
Mesopotamia
Syrian Desert
Dead Sea -416 (-1365 ft)
Cyprus
Crete
Ionian Sea
MEDITERRANEAN SEA
Nile Fan
Sinai
An Nafūd
ARABIAN PENINSULA
Persian Gulf
Gulf of Oman
Rub al Khali (Empty Quarter)
Great Eastern Dunes
Qattara Depression -133
Western Desert
Libyan Desert
Eastern Desert
Nubian Desert
Ahaggar Mts.
Mt. Tahat 3003
Tibesti Mts. 3415
Aïr Massif 2022
SAHARA
SAHEL
Lake Chad
Niger
Marra Mts. 3088
AFRICA
Guinea
Blue Nile
White Nile
Ethiopian Highlands
Danakil
Socotra
Somali Peninsula
Lake Turkana (L. Rudolf)
Cameroon Mt. 4100
Bioko
Gulf of Guinea
São Tomé
Congo
Congo Basin
Ruwenzori 5109
Lake Albert
Lake Victoria
Sources of the Nile
Kilimanjaro 5895
Lake Tanganyika
Zanzibar I.
Mitumba Mts.
Congo Canyon
Lower Guinea
Katanga Plateau
Lake Malawi
Aldabra Is.
Comoro Is.
Zambezi
Victoria Falls
Lake Kariba
Madagascar
Mozambique Channel
Maromokotro 2876
ANGOLA PLAIN
Namib Desert
Kalahari Desert
Thabana Ntlenyana 3482
Drakensberg
Great Karroo
Cape of Good Hope
Cape Agulhas
CAPE PLAIN
WALVIS RIDGE
Vema Seamount
Wyandot Seamount
Discovery Tablemount
AGULHAS RIDGE
AGULHAS BASIN
AGULHAS PLATEAU
MOZAMBIQUE PLATEAU
NATAL BASIN
MADAGASCAR PLATEAU
MADAGASCAR BASIN
Meteor Seamount
PRINCE EDWARD FRACTURE ZONE
Prince Edward Islands
Crozet Islands
CROZET BASIN
SOUTHWEST INDIAN RIDGE
ATLANTIC-INDIAN RIDGE
Ob Tablemount
Lena Tablemount
ENDERBY PLAIN
Cosmonaut Sea
Riiser-Larsen Peninsula
Cape Ann
Enderby Land
Prydz Bay
Queen Maud Land
ANTARCTICA
Amsterdam St. Paul
Kerguelen Islands
KERGUELEN PLATEAU
Heard Island
SOUTHEAST INDIAN RIDGE
SOUTH INDIAN BASIN
INDIAN OCEAN
ARABIAN SEA
ARABIAN BASIN
OWEN FRACTURE ZONE
CARLSBERG RIDGE
SOMALI BASIN
Coco-de-Mer Seamounts
Seychelles
Amirante Isles
MASCARENE PLATEAU
MASCARENE BASIN
Mascarene Islands
Mauritius
Réunion
Rodrigues
MASCARENE PLAIN
CHAGOS-LACCADIVE PLATEAU
Maldive Islands
Chagos Archipelago
Diego Garcia
CHAGOS TRENCH
MID-INDIAN RIDGE
MID-INDIAN BASIN
CEYLON PLAIN
Nikitin Seamount
NINETYEAST RIDGE
COCOS BASIN
Cocos Islands
OSBORN PLATEAU
INVESTIGATOR RIDGE
Christmas I.
JAVA TRENCH
WHARTON BASIN
Wallaby Plateau
EXMOUTH PLATEAU
North West Cape
Cape Inscription
PERTH BASIN
BROKEN RIDGE
EAST INDIAN RIDGE
DIAMANTINA FRACTURE ZONE
Cape Naturaliste
INDIA
Deccan Plateau
Western Ghats
Eastern Ghats
Indus Fan
Ganges Fan
BAY OF BENGAL
Andaman Islands
Nicobar Islands
Sri Lanka (Ceylon)
Andaman Sea
Gulf of Thailand
Indochina Peninsula
Malay Pen.
Strait of Malacca
Sumatra
INDONESIA
Greater Sunda Islands
Java Sea
Java
Lesser Sunda Islands
Timor
Timor Sea
Flores
Celebes
Buru
Banda Sea
Arafura Sea
Borneo
Kinabalu 4101
CELEBES BASIN
Mindanao
SULU BASIN
Palawan
PALAWAN TROUGH
Philippine Islands
PHILIPPINE TRENCH
Luzon
Mt. Pinatubo 1486
SOUTH CHINA SEA
Hainan
Gulf of Tonkin
Mekong
Yangtze
Qin Ling
North China Plain
Yellow Sea
EAST CHINA SEA
Taiwan
Ryukyu Islands
RYUKYU TRENCH
Kyushu
Shikoku
Honshu
Hokkaido
SEA OF JAPAN (EAST SEA)
Korea
JAPAN TRENCH
KURIL TRENCH
Kuril Islands
Sakhalin
SEA OF OKHOTSK
Kamchatka Peninsula
Manchurian Plain
Greater Khingan Range
Sikhote Alin Range
Mongolian Plateau
GOBI
Lake Baikal
Yablonovyy Range
Stanovoy Range
Eastern Sayan Mts.
Altay Mountains
Belukha 4506
Ob
Yenisey
Lena
Amur
ALEUTIAN BASIN
BERING SEA
Aleutian Is.
Attu
ALEUTIAN TRENCH
Detroit Tablemount 1857
EMPEROR TROUGH
EMPEROR SEAMOUNTS
HESS RISE
NORTHWEST PACIFIC BASIN
NORTH PACIFIC
SHATSKY RISE
Isakov Seamount
Makarov Seamount
Grosvenor Seamount
MAPMAKER SEAMOUNTS
TROPIC OF CANCER
MID-PACIFIC MOUNTAINS
OCEAN
Wake I.
BONIN TRENCH
IZU TRENCH
Nampo Shoto
KYUSHU-PALAU RIDGE
PHILIPPINE SEA
PHILIPPINE BASIN
WEST MARIANA BASIN
MARIANA TROUGH
Mariana Islands
MARIANA TRENCH
Guam
Challenger Deep -10920
YAP TRENCH
PALAU TRENCH
MAGELLAN SEAMOUNTS
EAST MARIANA BASIN
Bikini Atoll
Enewetak Atoll
Kwajalein Atoll
Marshall Islands
Taongi Atoll
MICRONESIA
Caroline Islands
Chuuk
Pohnpei (Ponape)
WEST CAROLINE BASIN
EAST CAROLINE BASIN
CENTRAL PACIFIC BASIN
EQUATOR
Nauru
Banaba
Gilbert Islands
Beru
Admiralty Is.
Bismarck Archipelago
New Ireland
New Britain
Bougainville
Solomon Islands
Solomon Sea
Guadalcanal
Nanumea
Tuvalu
VITYAZ TRENCH
NORTH NEW HEBRIDES TRENCH
Vanuatu
New Guinea
Jaya Peak 4884
MELANESIA
Cape York Pen.
Gulf of Carpentaria
Great Barrier Reef
CORAL SEA BASIN
CORAL SEA
NORTH FIJI BASIN
Fiji Islands
New Caledonia
NEW HEBRIDES TRENCH
TROPIC OF CAPRICORN
SOUTH FIJI BASIN
SOUTH PACIFIC OCEAN
LORD HOWE RISE
NEW CALEDONIA BASIN
Lord Howe I.
NORTH AUSTRALIAN BASIN
Kimberley Plateau
Great Sandy Desert
Western Plateau
Macdonnell Ranges
AUSTRALIA
Great Artesian Basin
Central Lowlands
Great Victoria Desert
Lake Eyre -16
Nullarbor Plain
Great Australian Bight
Darling
Murray
Great Dividing Range
Mt. Kosciuszko 2228
CONTINENTAL SLOPE
SOUTH AUSTRALIAN BASIN
Bass Strait
Tasmania
TASMAN PLAIN
TASMAN BASIN
TASMAN SEA
Gascoyne Tablemount
EAST TASMAN PLATEAU
SOUTH TASMAN RISE
NEW ZEALAND
North Island
South Island
Aoraki/Mt. Cook 3754
Stewart Island
CAMPBELL PLATEAU
Auckland
MACQUARIE RIDGE
Macquarie I.
South Magnetic Pole
Cape Poinsett
ANTARCTIC CIRCLE
Balleny Is.
Ice thickness 4776
TRANSANTARCTIC MOUNTAINS
Victoria Land
Ross Sea
Ross Ice Shelf

Poles and Hemispheres

North Pole

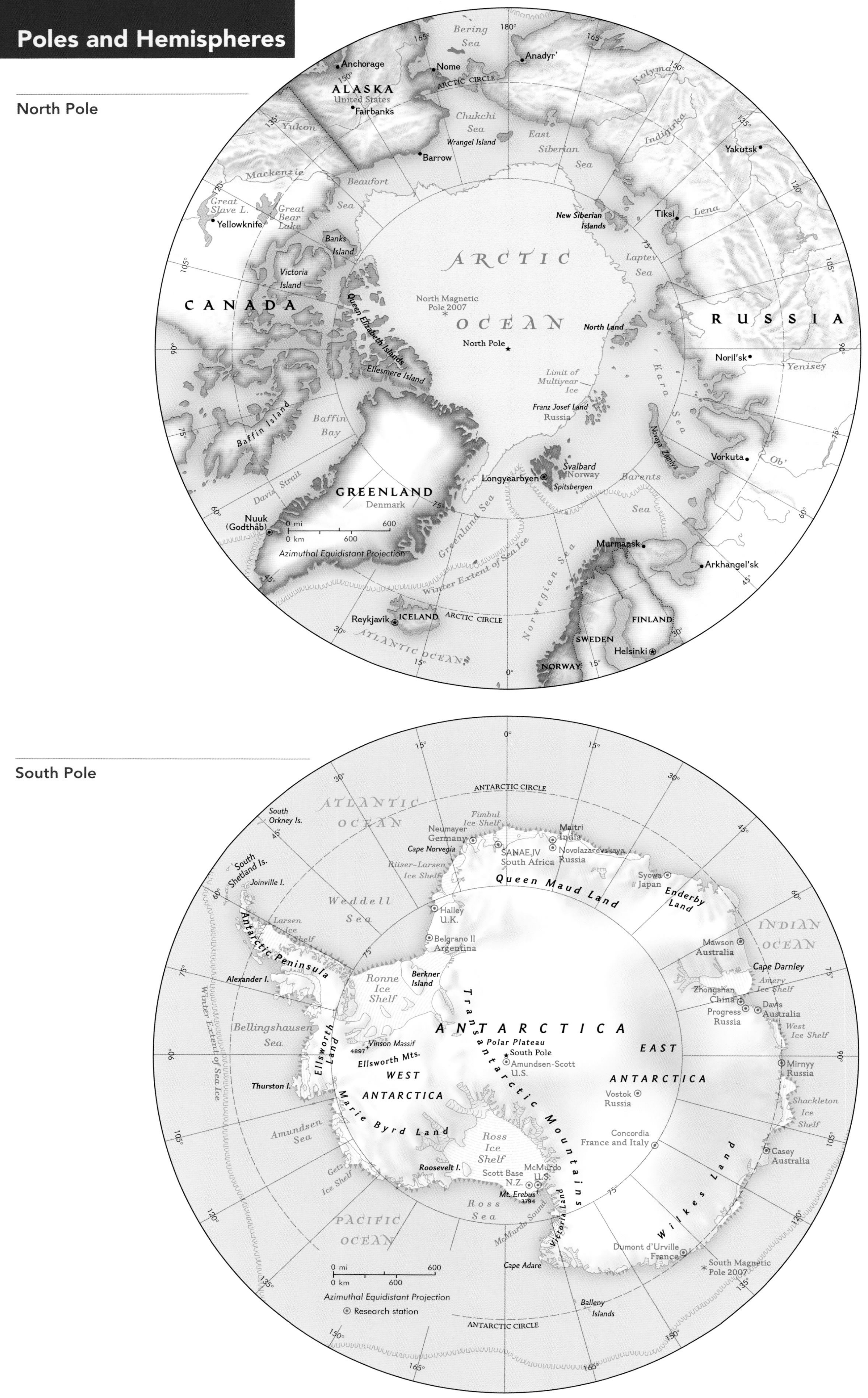

South Pole

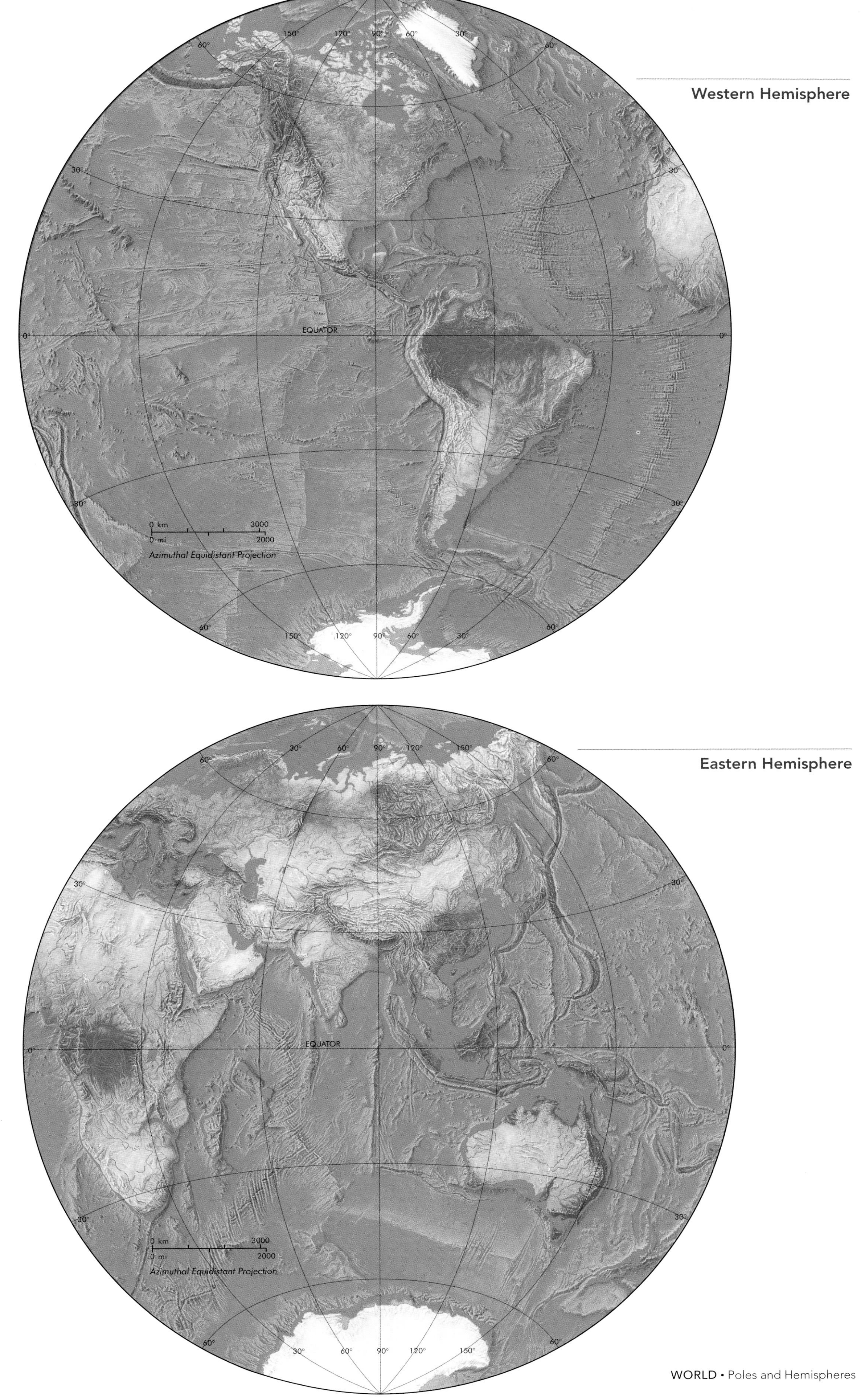
Western Hemisphere
150°
120°
90°
60°
30°
60°
30°
EQUATOR
0°
0 km
3000
0 mi
2000
Azimuthal Equidistant Projection
Eastern Hemisphere
EQUATOR

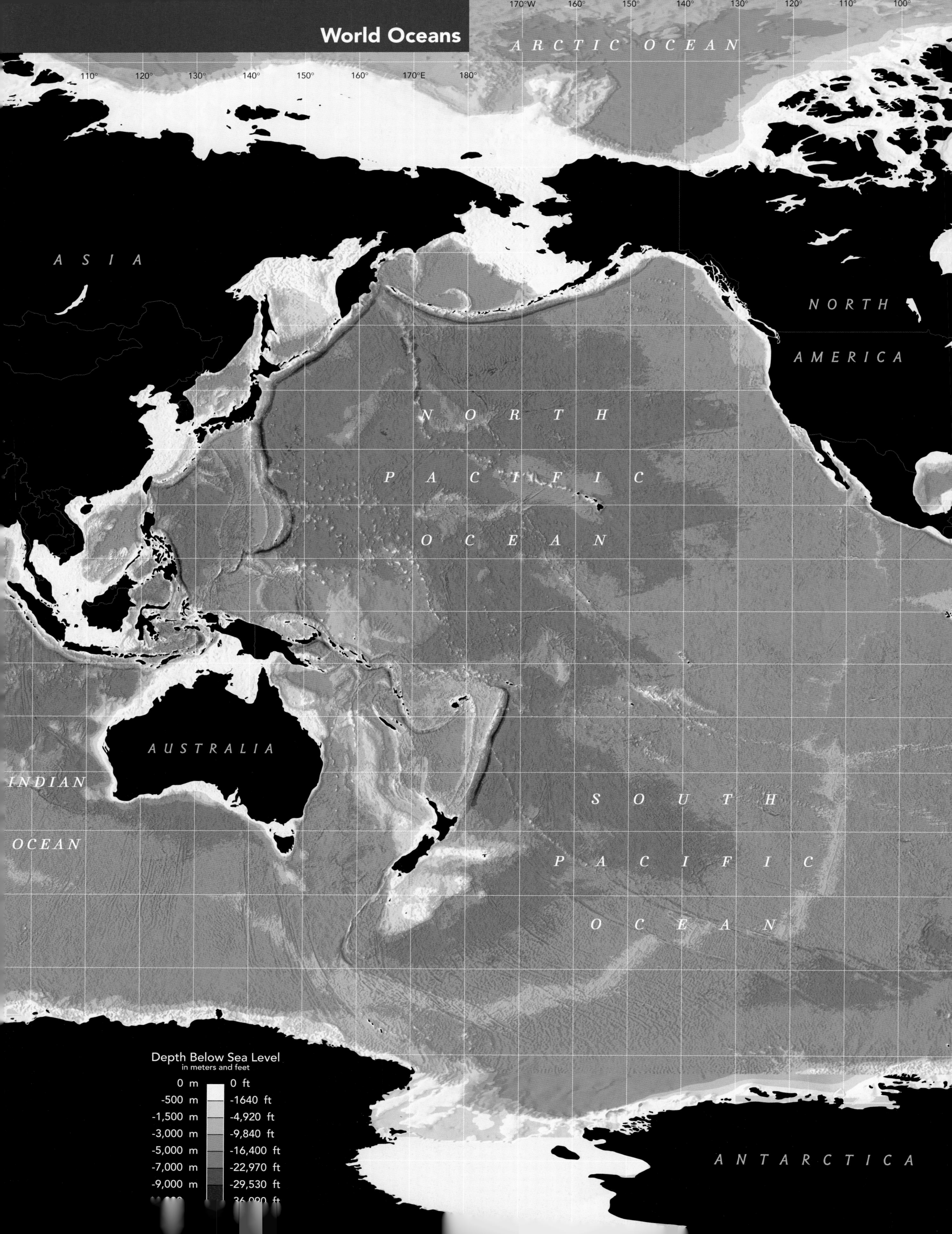
ARCTIC OCEAN
ASIA
NORTH AMERICA
NORTH PACIFIC OCEAN
AUSTRALIA
INDIAN OCEAN
SOUTH PACIFIC OCEAN
ANTARCTICA
170°W
160°
150°
140°
130°
120°
110°
100°
110°
120°
130°
140°
150°
160°
170°E
180°
Depth Below Sea Level
in meters and feet
0 m
-500 m
-1,500 m
-3,000 m
-5,000 m
-7,000 m
-9,000 m
0 ft
-1640 ft
-4,920 ft
-9,840 ft
-16,400 ft
-22,970 ft
-29,530 ft

ARCTIC OCEAN
Greenland
EUROPE
ASIA
NORTH ATLANTIC OCEAN
AFRICA
SOUTH AMERICA
SOUTH ATLANTIC OCEAN
INDIAN OCEAN
World Bathymetry
Kilometers
0 1,000 2,000 3,000
Statute Miles
0 1,000 2,000 3,000
Nautical Miles
80° 70° 60° 50° 40° 30° 20° 10°W 0° 10°E 20° 30° 40° E 50° 60° 70° 80° E
80°N 70° 60° 50° 40° 30° 20° 10°N 0°

LIKE ICE ON A GREAT LAKE, the Earth's crust, or the lithosphere, floats over the planet's molten innards, is cracked in many places, and is in slow but constant movement. Earth's surface is broken into 16 enormous slabs of rock, called plates, averaging thousands of miles wide and having a thickness of several miles. As they move and grind against each other, they push up mountains, spawn volcanoes, and generate earthquakes.

Although these often cataclysmic events capture our attention, the movements that cause them are imperceptible, a slow waltz of rafted rock that continues over eons. How slow? The Mid-Atlantic Ridge (see "spreading" diagram, opposite) is being built by magma oozing between two plates, separating North America and Africa at the speed of a growing human fingernail.

The dividing lines between plates often mark areas of high volcanic and earthquake activity as plates strain against each other or one dives beneath another. In the Ring of Fire around the Pacific Basin, disastrous earthquakes have occurred in Kobe, Japan, and in Los Angeles and San Francisco, California. Volcanic eruptions have taken place at Pinatubo in the Philippines and Mount St. Helens in Washington State.

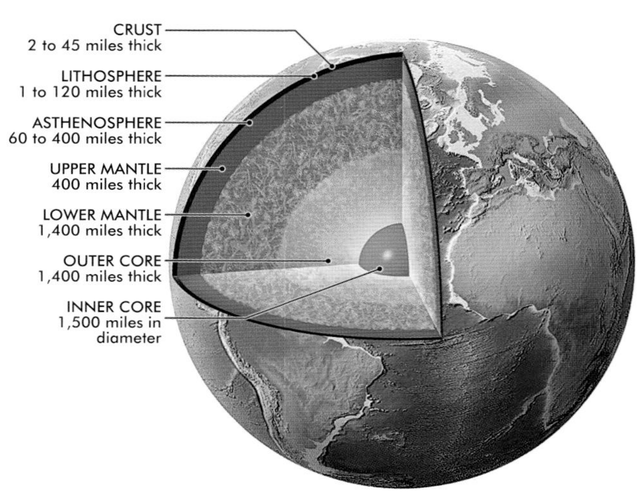

Continents Adrift in Time

With unceasing movement of Earth's tectonic plates, continents "drift" over geologic time—breaking apart, reassembling, and again fragmenting to repeat the process. Three times during the past billion years, Earth's drifting landmasses have merged to form so-called supercontinents. Rodinia, a supercontinent in the late Precambrian, began breaking apart about 750 million years ago. In time, its pieces reassembled to form another supercontinent, which in turn later split into smaller landmasses during the Paleozoic. The largest of these were called Euramerica (ancestral Europe and North America) and Gondwana (ancestral Africa, Antarctica, Arabia, India, and Australia). More than 250 million years ago, these two landmasses recombined, forming Pangaea. In the Mesozoic era, Pangaea split and the Atlantic and Indian Oceans began forming. Though the Atlantic is still widening today, scientists predict it will close as the seafloor recycles back into Earth's mantle. A new supercontinent, Pangaea Ultima, will eventually form.

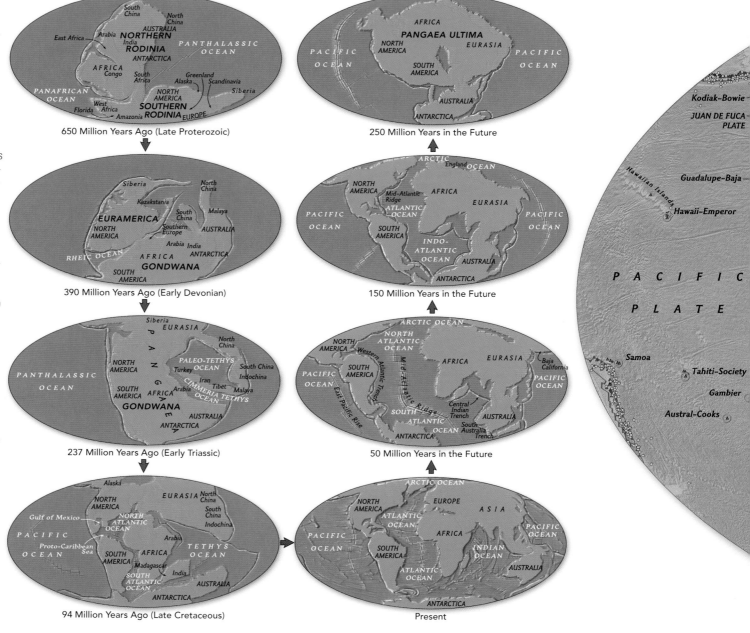

650 Million Years Ago (Late Proterozoic)

390 Million Years Ago (Early Devonian)

237 Million Years Ago (Early Triassic)

94 Million Years Ago (Late Cretaceous)

Present

50 Million Years in the Future

150 Million Years in the Future

250 Million Years in the Future

KEY TO PALEO-GEOGRAPHIC MAPS

- Seafloor spreading ridge
- Subduction zone
- Ancient landmass
- Continental shelf

Geologic Time

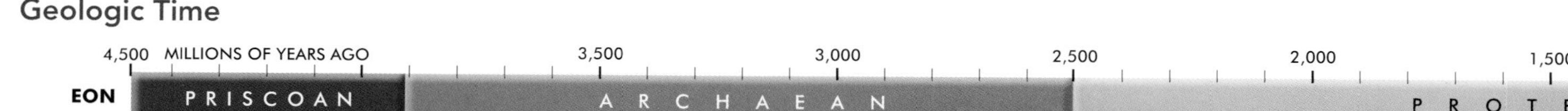

Geologic Forces Change the Face of the Planet

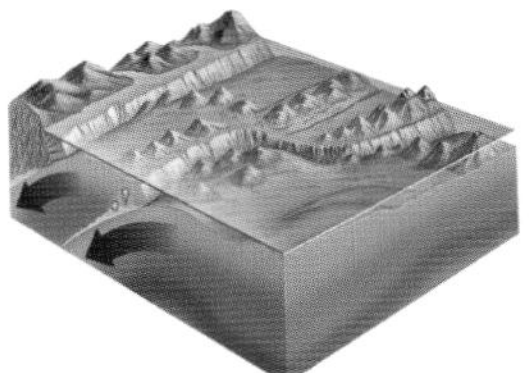

ACCRETION
As ocean plates move toward the edges of continents or island arcs and slide under them, seamounts are skimmed off and piled up in submarine trenches. The resulting buildup can cause continents to grow.

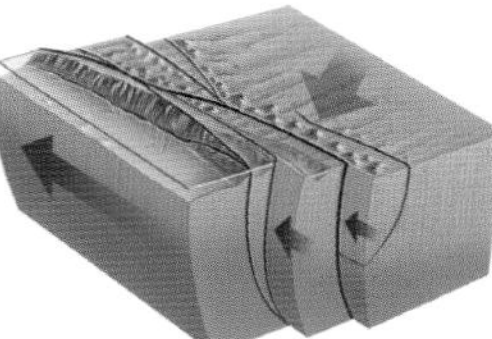

FAULTING
Enormous crustal plates do not slide smoothly. Strain built up along their edges may release in a series of small jumps, felt as minor tremors on land. Extended buildup can cause a sudden jump, producing an earthquake.

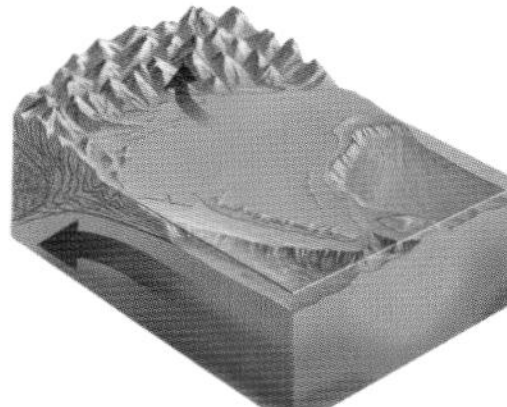

COLLISION
When two continental plates converge, the result can be the most dramatic mountain-building process on Earth. The Himalaya mountain range rose when the Indian subcontinent collided with Eurasia, driving the land upward.

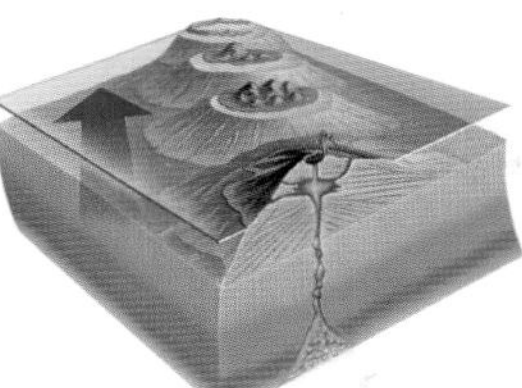

HOT SPOTS
In the cauldron of inner Earth, some areas burn hotter than others and periodically blast through their crustal covering as volcanoes. Such a "hot spot" built the Hawaiian Islands, leaving a string of oceanic protuberances.

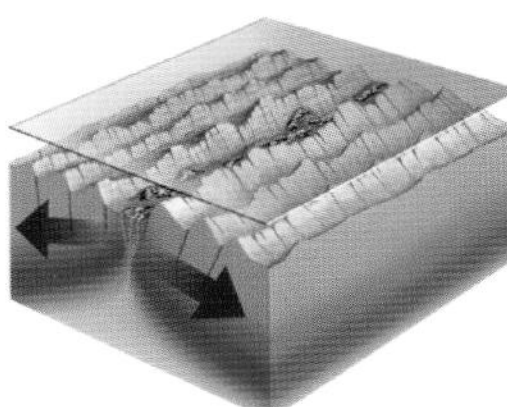

SPREADING
At the divergent boundary known as the Mid-Atlantic Ridge, oozing magma forces two plates apart by as much as eight inches a year. If that rate had been constant, the ocean could have reached its current width in 30 million years.

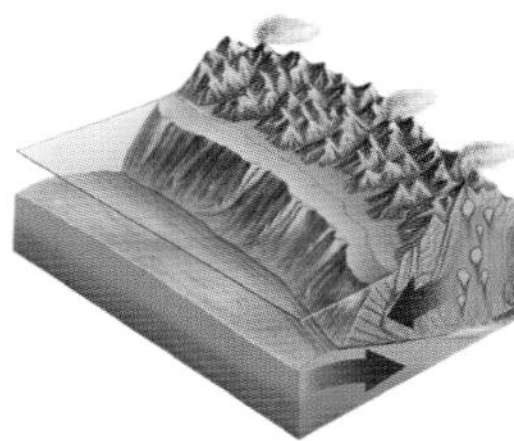

SUBDUCTION
When an oceanic plate and a continental plate converge, the older and heavier sea plate takes a dive. Plunging back into the interior of the Earth, it is transformed into molten material, only to rise again as magma.

Plate Tectonics

Tectonic boundaries mark areas of geologic change in ocean floors, on the margins of continents, and even within continents, as seen in the Great Rift Valley of East Africa. Clusters of volcanoes and frequent earthquakes indicate unstable areas.

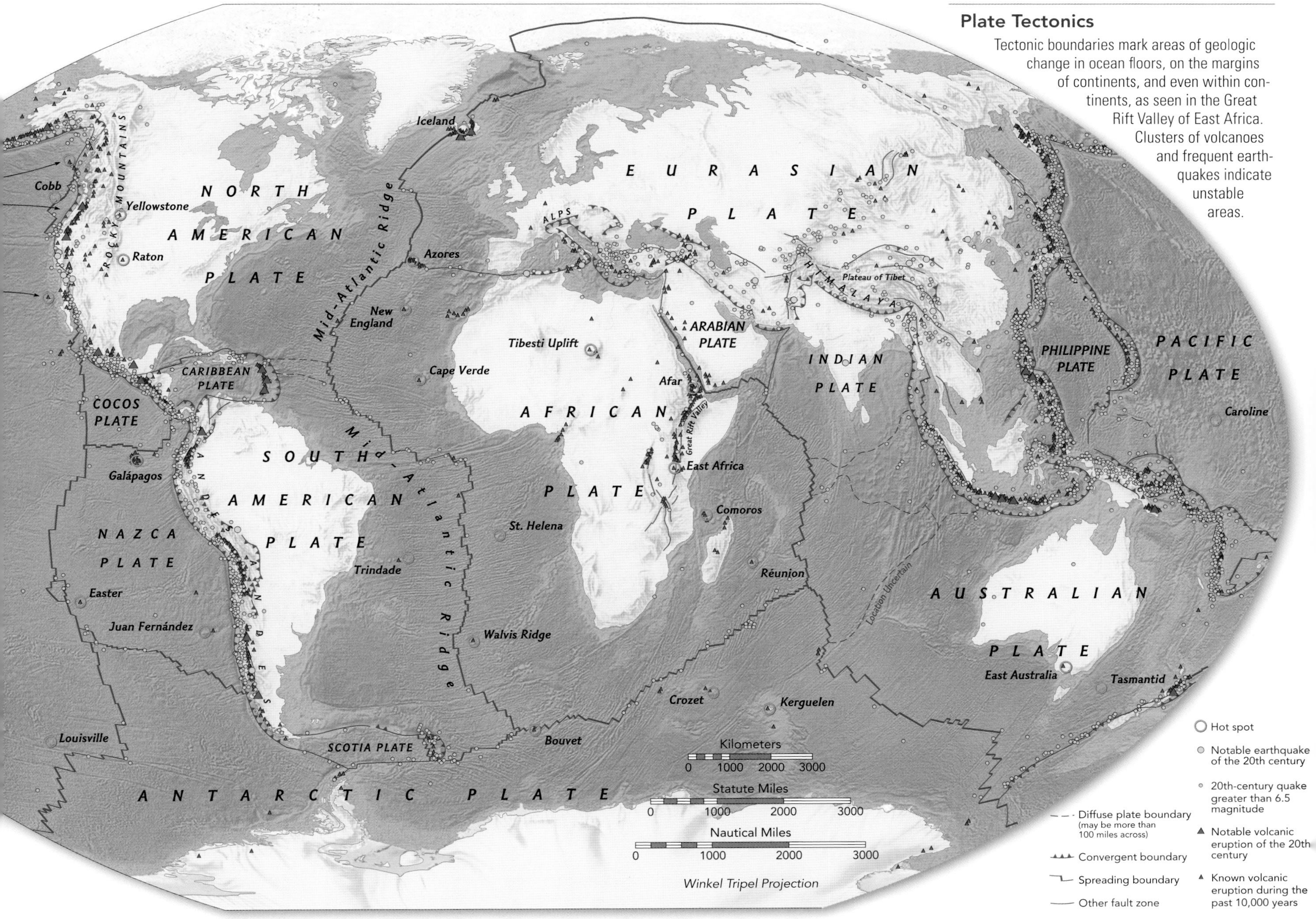

Hot spot
Notable earthquake of the 20th century
20th-century quake greater than 6.5 magnitude
Notable volcanic eruption of the 20th century
Known volcanic eruption during the past 10,000 years
Diffuse plate boundary (may be more than 100 miles across)
Convergent boundary
Spreading boundary
Other fault zone

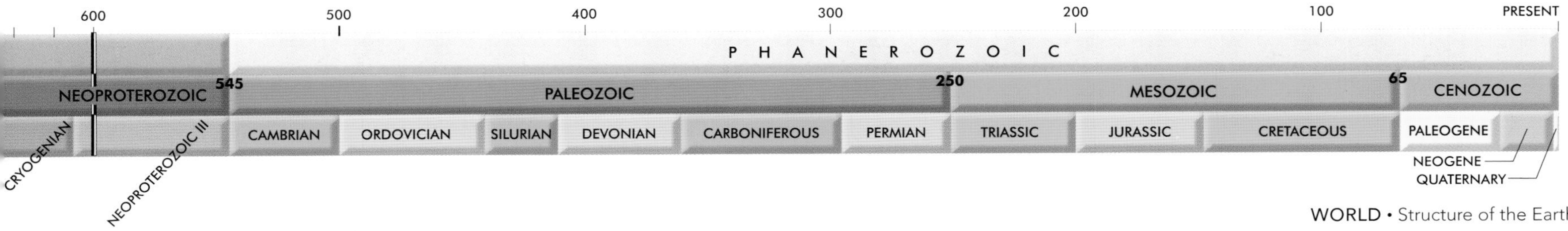

Kilometers 0 1000 2000 3000
Statute Miles 0 1000 2000 3000
Nautical Miles 0 1000 2000 3000

Winkel Tripel Projection

600 500 400 300 200 100 PRESENT

PHANEROZOIC

NEOPROTEROZOIC 545 PALEOZOIC 250 MESOZOIC 65 CENOZOIC

CRYOGENIAN NEOPROTEROZOIC III CAMBRIAN ORDOVICIAN SILURIAN DEVONIAN CARBONIFEROUS PERMIAN TRIASSIC JURASSIC CRETACEOUS PALEOGENE NEOGENE QUATERNARY

Climate

THE TERM "CLIMATE" describes the average "weather" conditions, as measured over many years, that prevail at any given point around the world at a given time of the year. Daily weather may differ dramatically from that expected on the basis of climatic statistics.

Energy from the sun drives the global climate system. Much of this incoming energy is absorbed in the tropics. Outgoing heat radiation, much of which exits at high latitudes, balances the absorbed incoming solar energy. To achieve a balance across the globe, huge amounts of heat are moved from the tropics to polar regions by both the atmosphere and the oceans.

The tilt of Earth's axis leads to shifting patterns of incoming solar energy throughout the year. More energy is transported to higher latitudes in winter than in summer, and hence the contrast in temperatures between the tropics and polar regions is greatest at this time of year—especially in the Northern Hemisphere.

Scientists present this data in many ways, using climographs (see page 26), which show information about specific places. Alternatively, they produce maps, which show regional and worldwide data.

The effects of the climatic contrasts are seen in the distribution of Earth's lifeforms. Temperature, precipitation, and the amount of sunlight all determine what plants can grow in a region and the animals that live there. People are more adaptable, but climate exerts powerful constraints on where we live.

Climatic conditions define planning decisions, such as how much heating oil we need for the winter, and the necessary rainfall for agriculture in the summer. Fluctuations from year to year (e.g., cold winters or summer droughts) make planning more difficult.

In the longer term, continued global warming may change climatic conditions around the world, which could dramatically alter temperature and precipitation patterns and lead to more frequent heat waves, floods, and droughts.

JANUARY SOLAR ENERGY

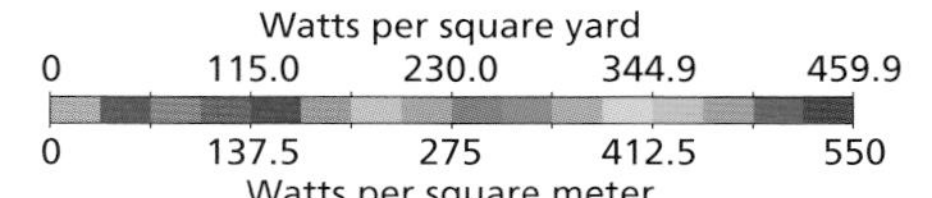

JULY SOLAR ENERGY

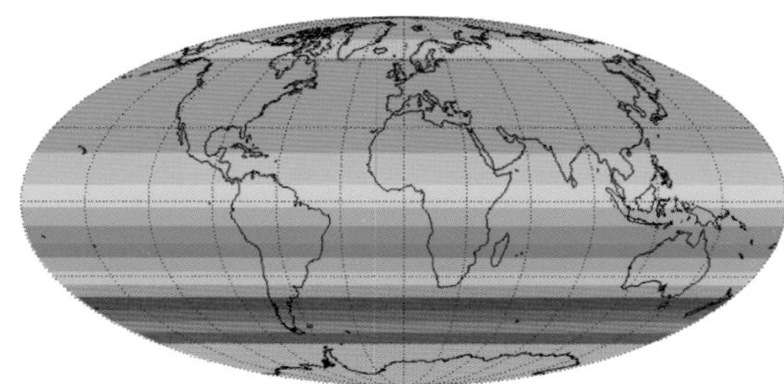

Watts per square yard
0 115.0 230.0 344.9 459.9
0 137.5 275 412.5 550
Watts per square meter

JANUARY AVERAGE TEMPERATURE

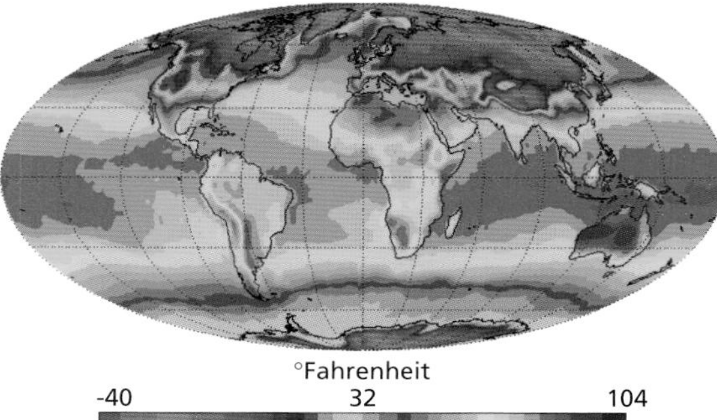

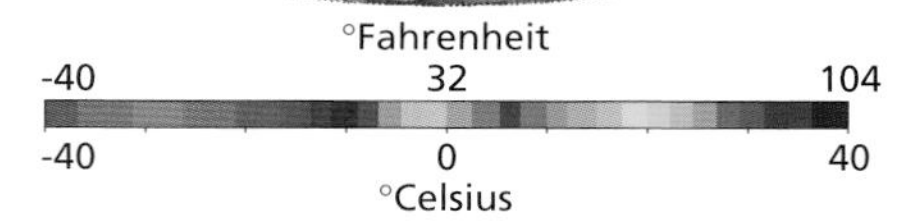

JULY AVERAGE TEMPERATURE

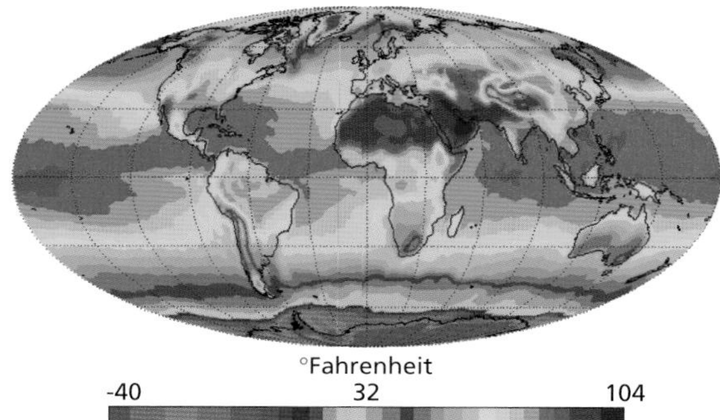

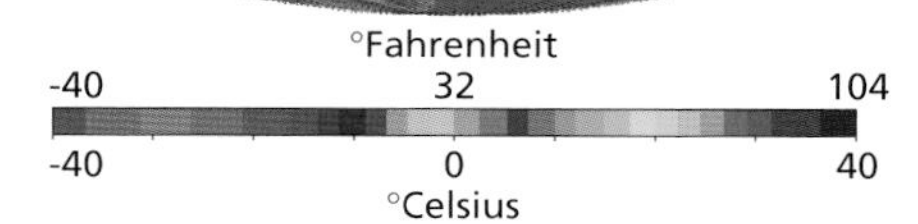

JANUARY CLOUD COVER

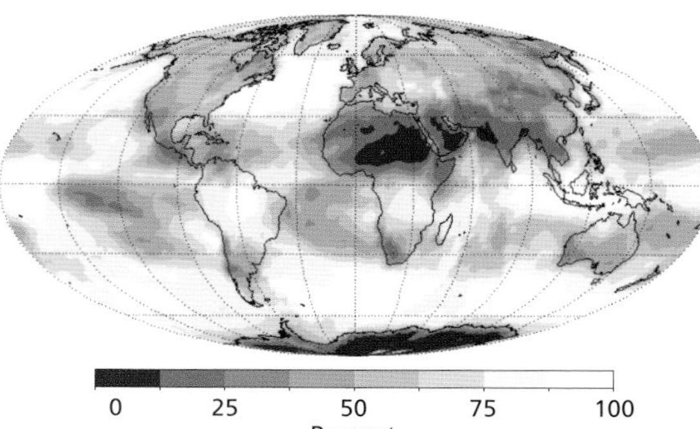

0 25 50 75 100
Percent

JULY CLOUD COVER

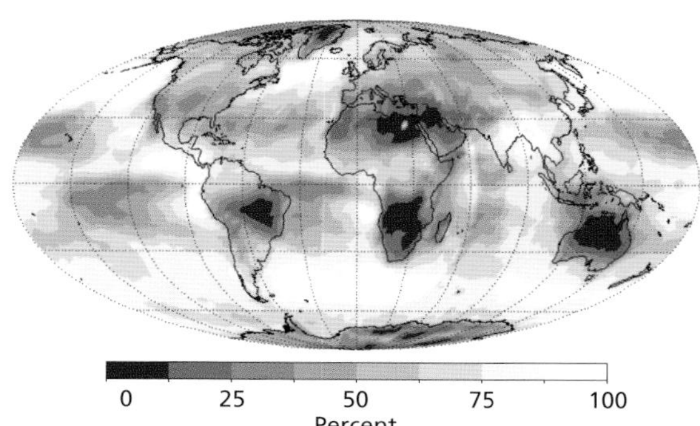

0 25 50 75 100
Percent

JANUARY PRECIPITATION

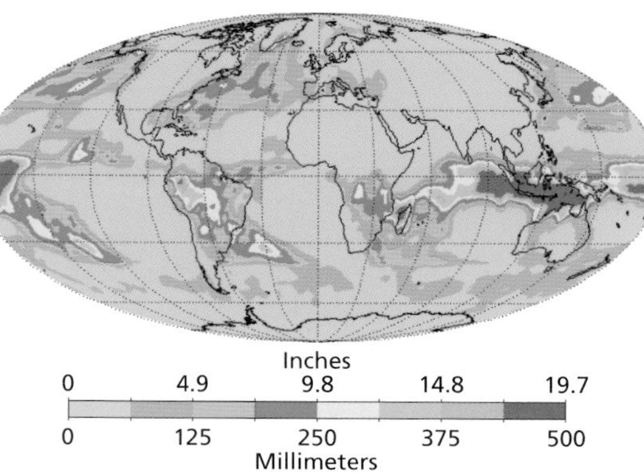

JULY PRECIPITATION

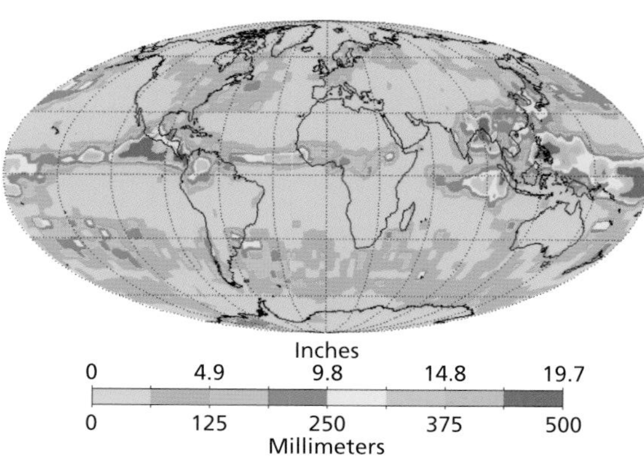

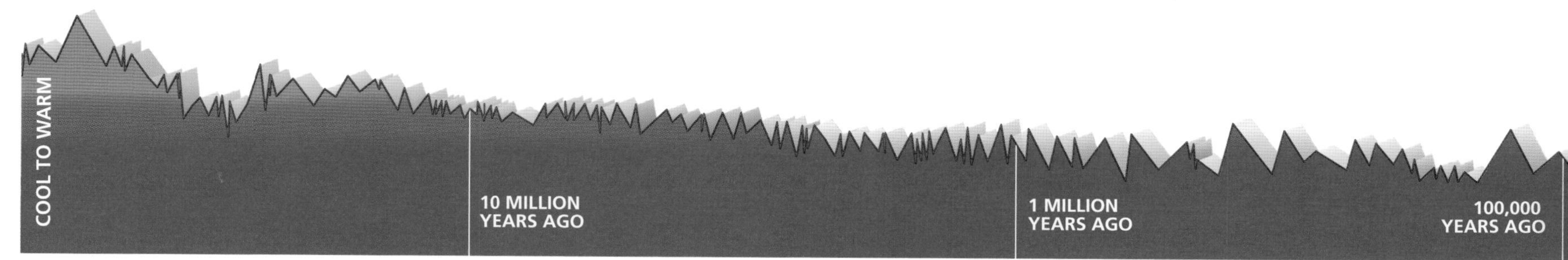

Major Factors that Influence Climate

LATITUDE AND ANGLE OF THE SUN'S RAYS

As Earth circles the sun, the tilt of its axis causes changes in the angle of the sun's rays and in the periods of daylight at different latitudes. Polar regions experience the greatest variation, with long periods of limited or no sunlight in winter and sometimes 24 hours of daylight in the summer.

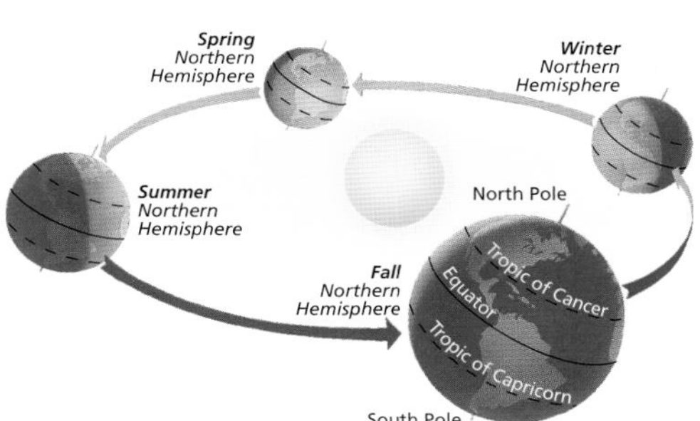

ELEVATION (ALTITUDE)

In general, climatic conditions become colder as elevation increases, just as they do when latitude increases. "Life zones" on a high mountain reflect the changes: Plants at the base are the same as those in surrounding countryside. Farther up, treed vegetation distinctly ends at the tree line; at the highest elevations, snow covers the mountain.

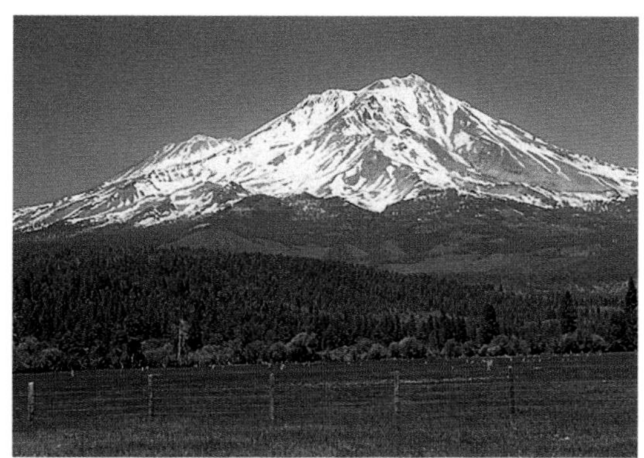

Mount Shasta, California

TOPOGRAPHY

Mountain ranges are natural barriers to air movement. In California (see diagram at right), winds off the Pacific carry moisture-laden air toward the coast. The Coast Ranges allow for some condensation and light precipitation. Inland, the taller Sierra Nevada range wrings more significant precipitation from the air. On the leeward slopes of the Sierra Nevada, sinking air warms from compression, clouds evaporate, and dry conditions prevail.

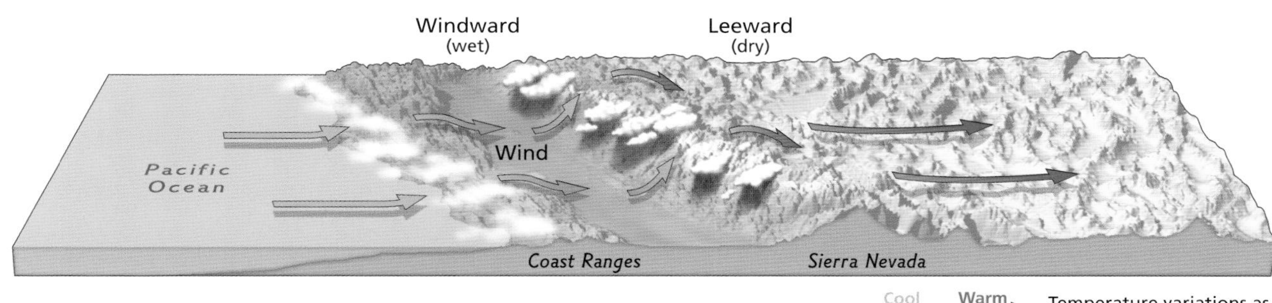

EFFECTS OF GEOGRAPHY

The location of a place and its distance from mountains and bodies of water help determine its prevailing wind patterns and what types of air masses affect it. Coastal areas may enjoy refreshing breezes in summer, when cooler ocean air moves ashore. Places south and east of the Great Lakes can expect "lake effect" snow in winter, when cold air travels over relatively warmer waters. In spring and summer, people living in "Tornado Alley" in the central United States watch for thunderstorms. Here, three types of air masses often converge: cold and dry from the north, warm and dry from the southwest, and warm and moist from the Gulf of Mexico. The colliding air masses often spawn tornadic storms.

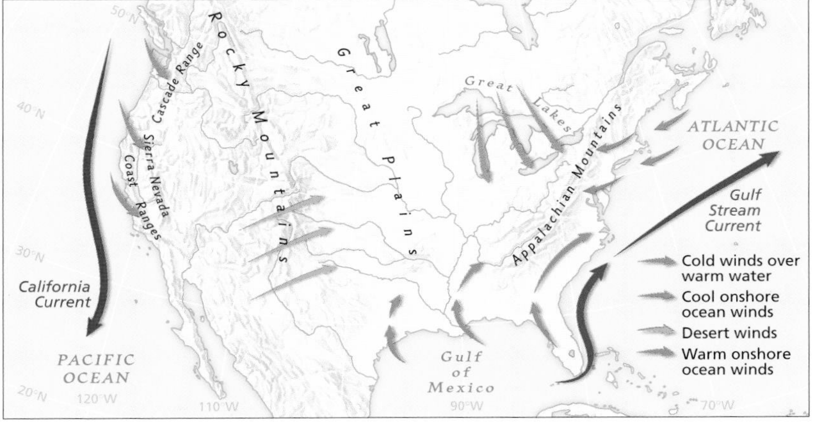

PREVAILING GLOBAL WIND PATTERNS

As shown at right, three large-scale wind patterns are found in the Northern Hemisphere and three are found in the Southern Hemisphere. These are average conditions and do not necessarily reflect conditions on a particular day. As seasons change, the wind patterns shift north or south. So does the intertropical convergence zone, which moves back and forth across the Equator. Sailors called this zone the doldrums because its winds are typically weak.

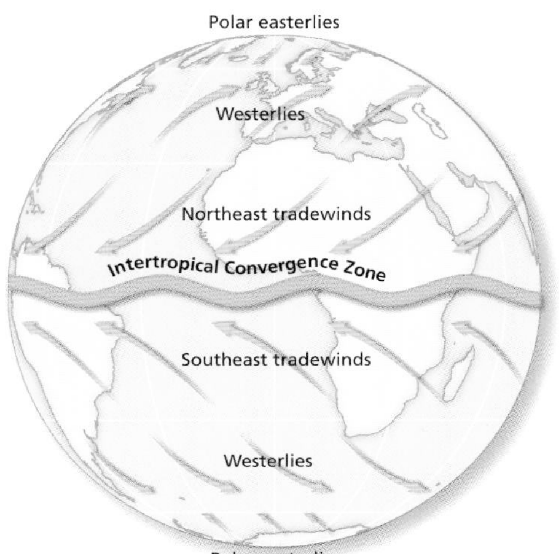

SURFACE OF THE EARTH

Just look at any globe or a world map showing land cover, and you will see another important influence on climate: Earth's surface. The amount of sunlight that is absorbed or reflected by the surface determines how much atmospheric heating occurs. Darker areas, such as heavily vegetated regions, tend to be good absorbers; lighter areas, such as snow- and ice-covered regions, tend to be good reflectors. Oceans absorb a high proportion of the solar energy falling upon them, but release it more slowly. Both the oceans and the atmosphere distribute heat around the globe.

Temperature Change over Time

Cold and warm periods punctuate Earth's long history. Some were fairly short (perhaps hundreds of years); others spanned hundreds of thousands of years. In some cold periods, glaciers grew and spread over large regions. In subsequent warm periods, the ice retreated. Each period profoundly affected plant and animal life. The most recent cool period, often called the little ice age, ended in western Europe around the year 1850.

Since the turn of the 20th century, temperatures have been rising steadily throughout the world. But it is not yet clear how much of this warming is due to natural causes and how much derives from human activities, such as the burning of fossil fuels and the clearing of forests.

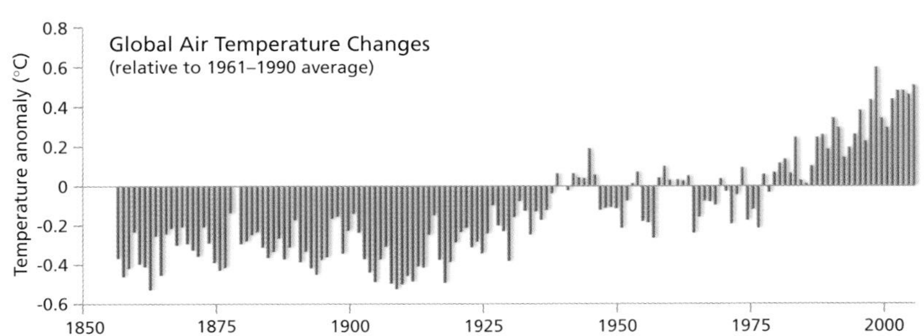

10,000 YEARS AGO

1,000 YEARS AGO

PRESENT

CLIMATE ZONES ARE PRIMARILY CONTROLLED by latitude—which governs the prevailing winds, the angle of the sun's rays, and the length of day throughout the year—and by geographical location with respect to mountains and oceans. Elevation, surface attributes, and other variables modify the primary controlling factors. Latitudinal banding of climate zones is most pronounced over Africa and Asia, where fewer north-south mountain ranges mean less disruption of prevailing winds. In the Western Hemisphere, the high, almost continuous mountain range that extends from western Canada to southern South America helps create dry regions on its leeward slopes. Over the United States, where westerly winds prevail, areas to the east of the range lie in a "rain shadow" and are therefore drier. In northern parts of South America, where easterly trade winds prevail, the rain shadow lies west of the mountains. Ocean effects dominate much of western Europe and southern parts of Australia.

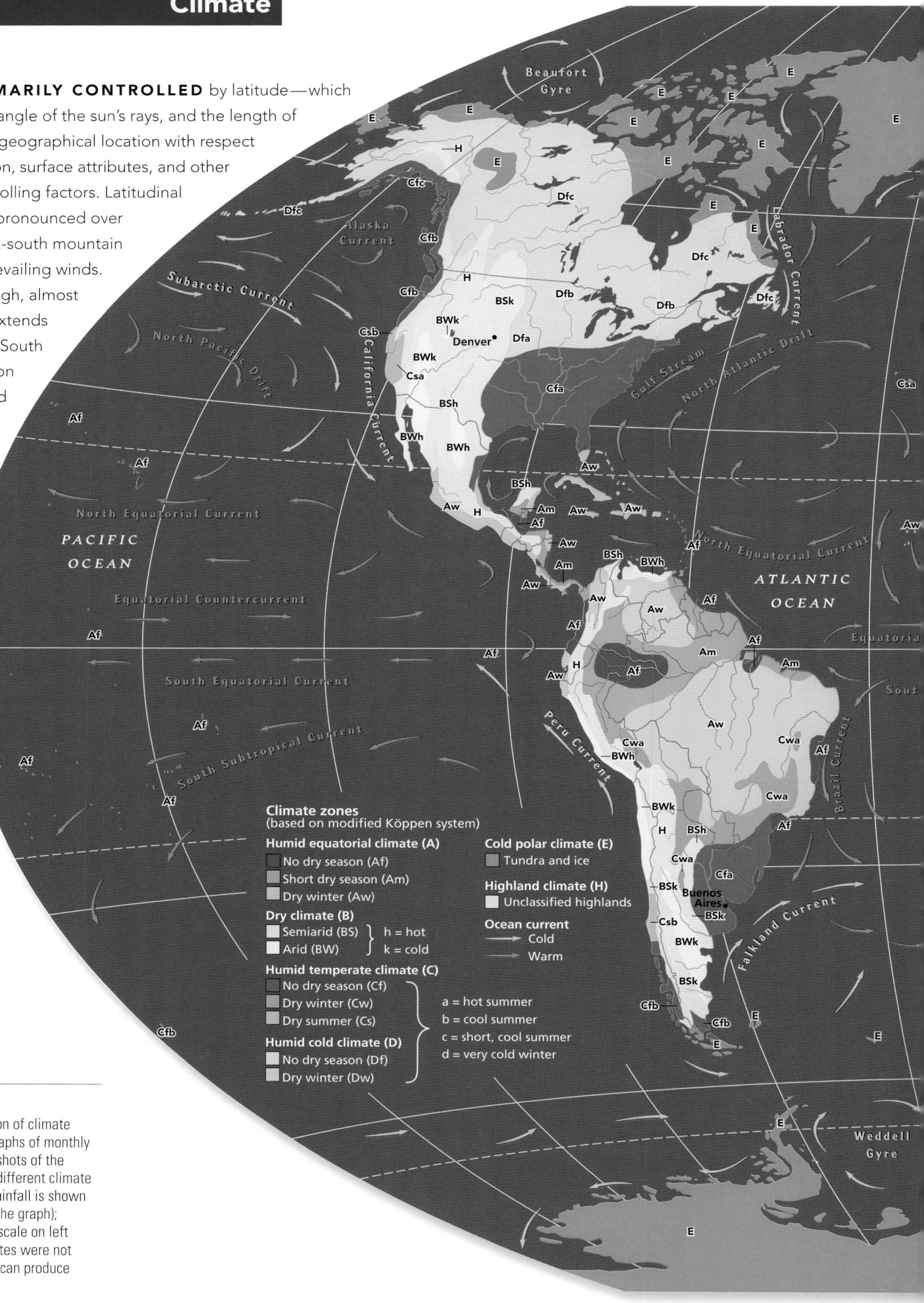

Climate zones
(based on modified Köppen system)

Humid equatorial climate (A)
- No dry season (Af)
- Short dry season (Am)
- Dry winter (Aw)

Dry climate (B)
- Semiarid (BS)
- Arid (BW)

h = hot
k = cold

Humid temperate climate (C)
- No dry season (Cf)
- Dry winter (Cw)
- Dry summer (Cs)

Humid cold climate (D)
- No dry season (Df)
- Dry winter (Dw)

a = hot summer
b = cool summer
c = short, cool summer
d = very cold winter

Cold polar climate (E)
- Tundra and ice

Highland climate (H)
- Unclassified highlands

Ocean current
- Cold
- Warm

Climographs

The map at right shows the global distribution of climate zones, while the following 8 climographs (graphs of monthly temperature and precipitation) provide snapshots of the climate at specific places. Each place has a different climate type, which is described in general terms. Rainfall is shown in a bar graph format (scale on right side of the graph); temperature is expressed with a line graph (scale on left side). Places with highland and upland climates were not included because local changes in elevation can produce significant variations in local conditions.

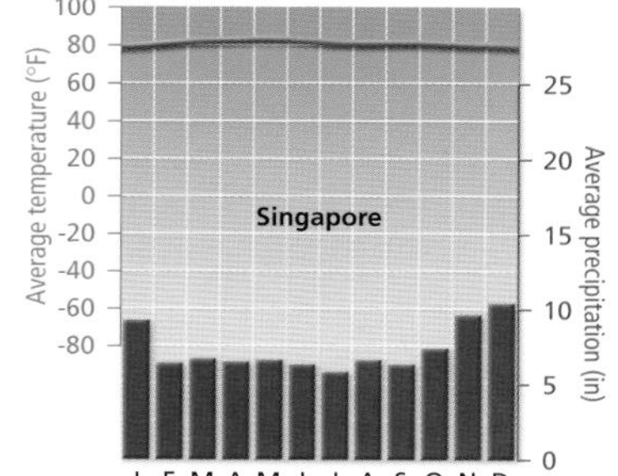

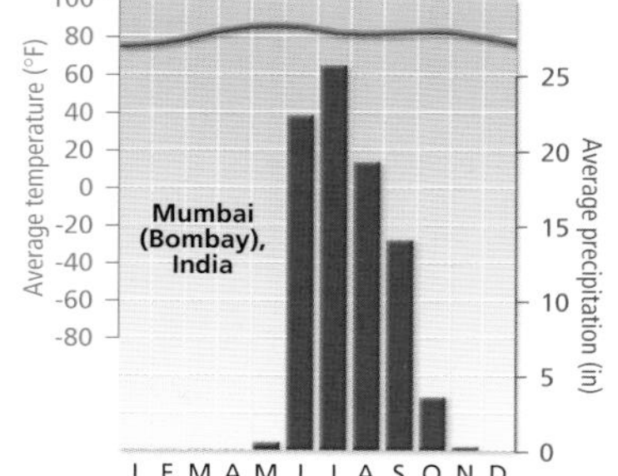

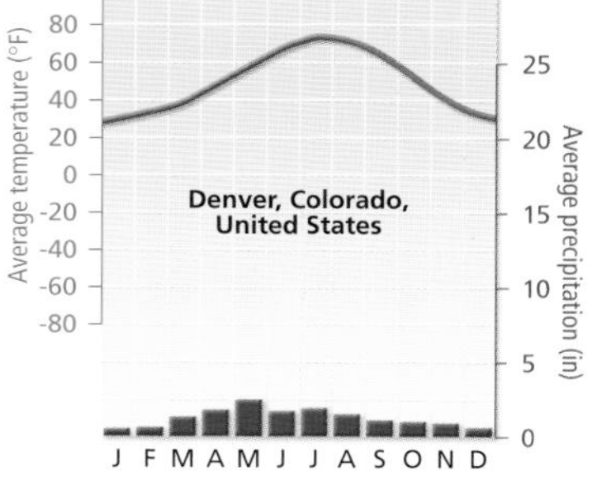

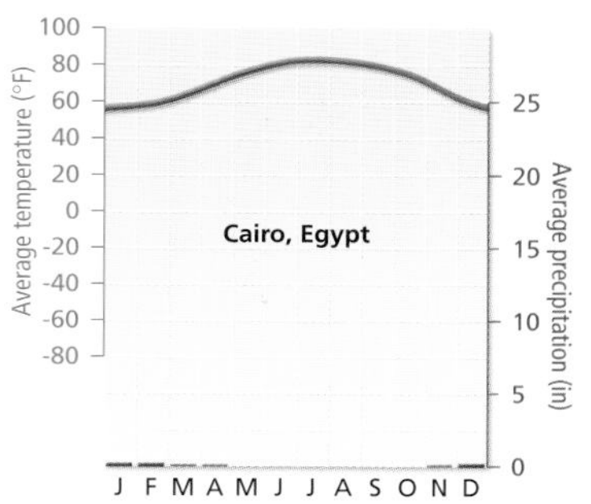

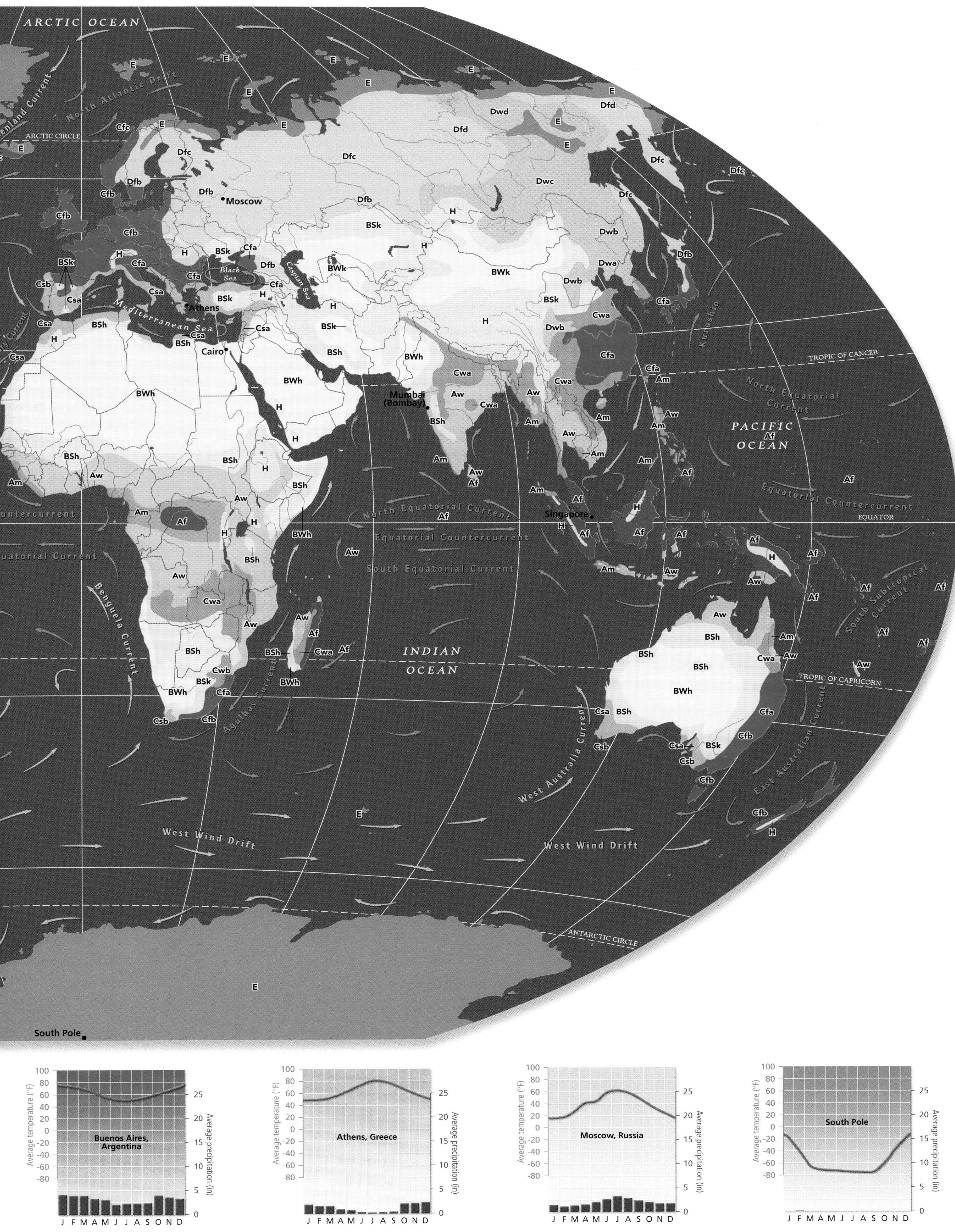

ARCTIC OCEAN
North Atlantic Drift
Greenland Current
ARCTIC CIRCLE
Moscow
Black Sea
Caspian Sea
Athens
Mediterranean Sea
Cairo
Mumbai (Bombay)
Singapore
Kuroshio
TROPIC OF CANCER
North Equatorial Current
PACIFIC OCEAN
Equatorial Countercurrent
EQUATOR
North Equatorial Current
Equatorial Countercurrent
South Equatorial Current
Equatorial Current
Countercurrent
Benguela Current
Agulhas Current
INDIAN OCEAN
South Subtropical Current
TROPIC OF CAPRICORN
West Australia Current
East Australian Current
West Wind Drift
West Wind Drift
ANTARCTIC CIRCLE
South Pole
Buenos Aires, Argentina
Athens, Greece
Moscow, Russia
South Pole
Average temperature (°F)
Average precipitation (in)
J F M A M J J A S O N D

WHILE POPULATIONS IN MANY PARTS of the world are expanding, those of Europe—along with some other rich industrial areas such as Japan—show little to no growth, or may actually be shrinking. Many such countries must bring in immigrant workers to keep their economies thriving. A clear correlation exists between wealth and low fertility: the higher the incomes and educational levels, the lower the rates of reproduction.

Many governments keep vital statistics, recording births and deaths, and count their populations regularly to try to plan ahead. The United States has taken a census every ten years since 1790, recording the ages, the occupations, and other important facts about its people. The United Nations helps less developed countries carry out censuses and improve their demographic information.

Governments of some poor countries may find that half their populations are under the age of 20. They are faced with the overwhelming tasks of providing adequate education and jobs while encouraging better family-planning programs. Governments of nations with low birthrates find themselves with growing numbers of elderly people but fewer workers able to provide tax money for health care and pensions.

In a mere 150 years, world population has grown fivefold, at an ever increasing pace. The industrial revolution helped bring about improvements in food supplies and advances in both medicine and public health, which allowed people to live longer and to have more healthy babies. Today, 15,000 people are born into the world every hour, and nearly all of them are in poor African, Asian, and South American nations. This situation concerns planners, who look to demographers (professionals who study all aspects of population) for important data.

Lights of the World

Satellite imagery offers a surprising view of the world at night. Bright lights in Europe, Asia, and the United States give a clear picture of densely populated areas with ample electricity. Reading this map requires great care, however. Some totally dark areas, like most of Australia, do in fact have very small populations, but other light-free areas—in China and Africa, for example—may simply hide dense populations with not enough electricity to be seen by a satellite. Wealthy areas with fewer people, such as Florida, may be using their energy wastefully. Ever since the 1970s, demographers have supplemented census data with information from satellite imagery.

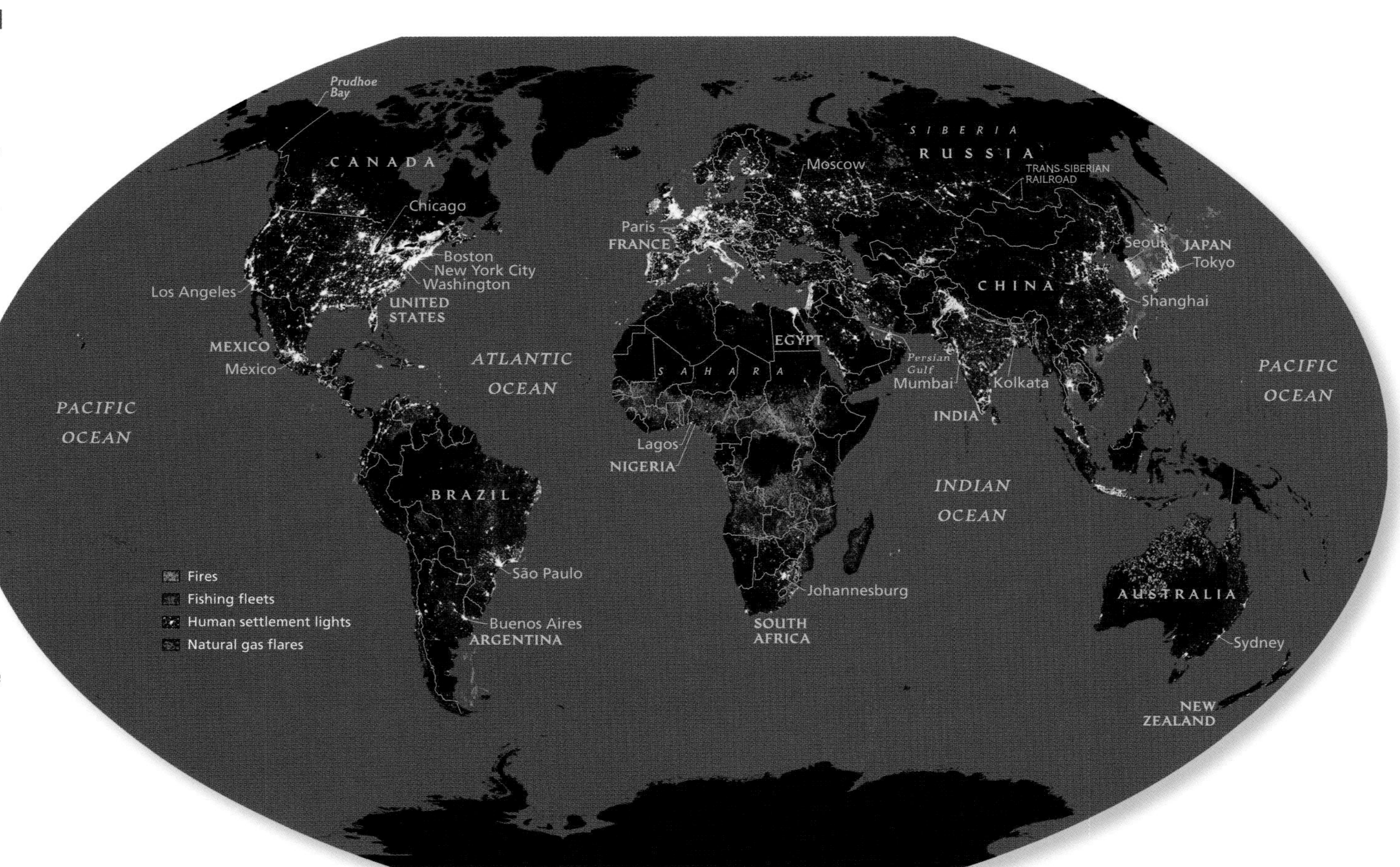

Population Pyramids

A population pyramid shows the number of males and females in every age group of a population. A pyramid for Nigeria reveals that over half—about 55 percent—of the population is under 20, while only 19 percent of Italy's population is younger than 20.

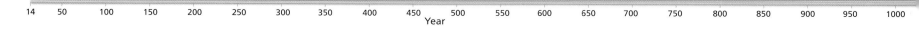

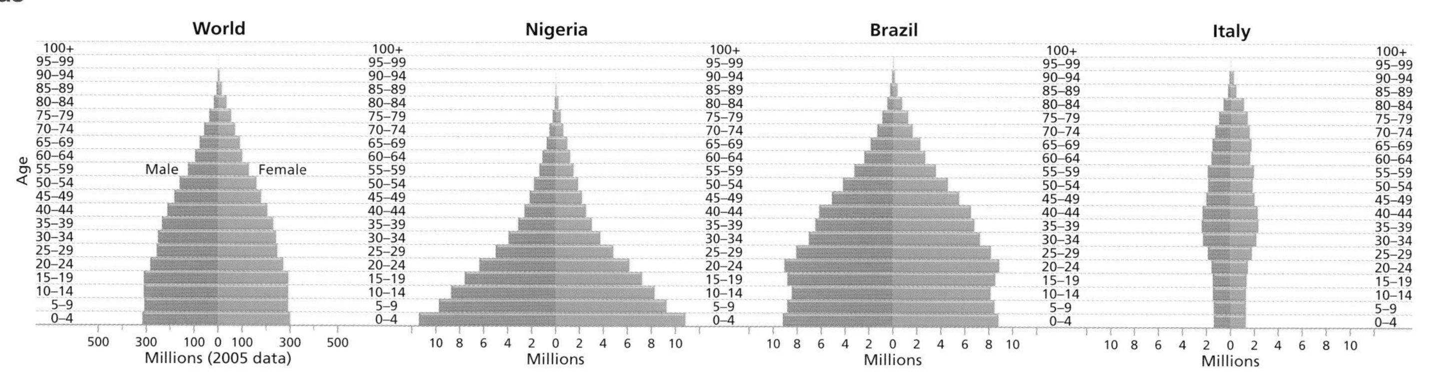

14 50 100 150 200 250 300 350 400 450 500 550 600 650 700 750 800 850 900 950 1000
Year

Population Growth

The population of the world is not distributed evenly. In this cartogram Canada is almost invisible, while India looks enormous because its population is 34 times greater than Canada's. In reality, Canada is 3 times larger than India, in size. The shape of almost every country looks distorted when populations are compared in this way.

Population sizes are constantly changing, however. In countries that are experiencing many more births than deaths, population totals are ballooning. In others, too few babies are born to replace the number of people who die, and populations are shrinking. A cartogram devoted solely to growth rates around the world would look quite different from this one.

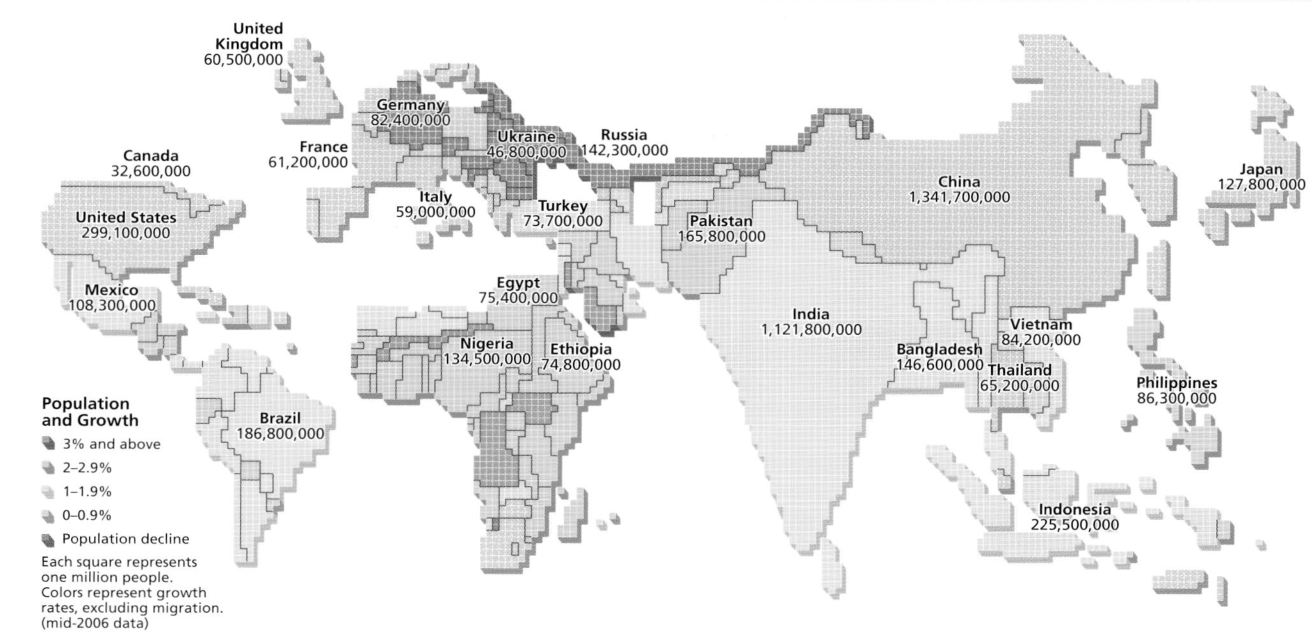

Population Density

A country's population density is estimated by figuring out how many people would occupy one square mile if they were all spread out evenly. In reality, people live together most closely in cities, on seacoasts, and in river valleys. Singapore, a tiny country largely composed of a single city, has a high population density—more than 17,000 people per square mile. Greenland, by comparison, has less than one person per square mile because it is mostly covered by ice. Its people mainly fish for a living and dwell in small groups near the shore.

Regional Population Growth Disparities

Two centuries ago, the population of the world began a phenomenal expansion. Even so, North America and Australia still have a long way to go before their population numbers equal those of Asia and Africa. China and India now have more than a billion people each, making Asia the most populous continent. Africa, which has the second greatest growth, does not yet approach Asia in numbers. According to some experts, the world's population, now totaling more than six and a half billion, will not start to level off until about the year 2200, when it could reach eleven billion. Nearly all the new growth will take place in Asia, Africa, and Latin America; however, Africa's share will be almost double that of its present level and China's share will decline.

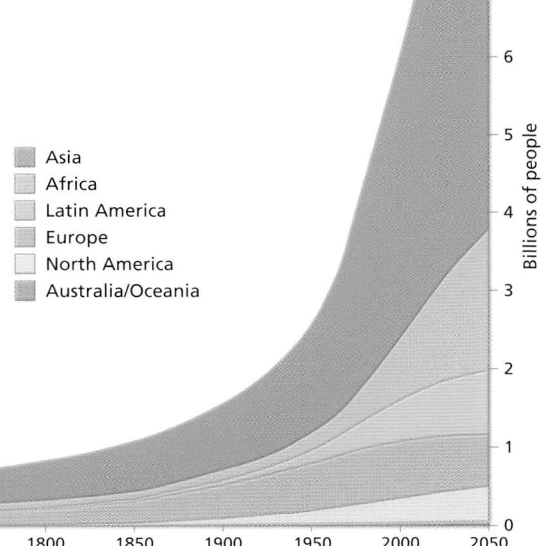

Fertility

Fertility, or birthrate, measures the average number of children born to women in a given population. It can also be expressed as the number of live births per thousand people in a population per year. In low-income countries with limited educational opportunities for girls and women, birthrates reach their highest levels.

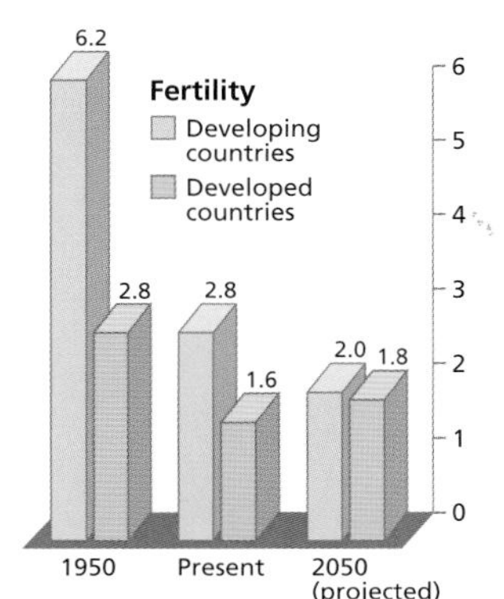

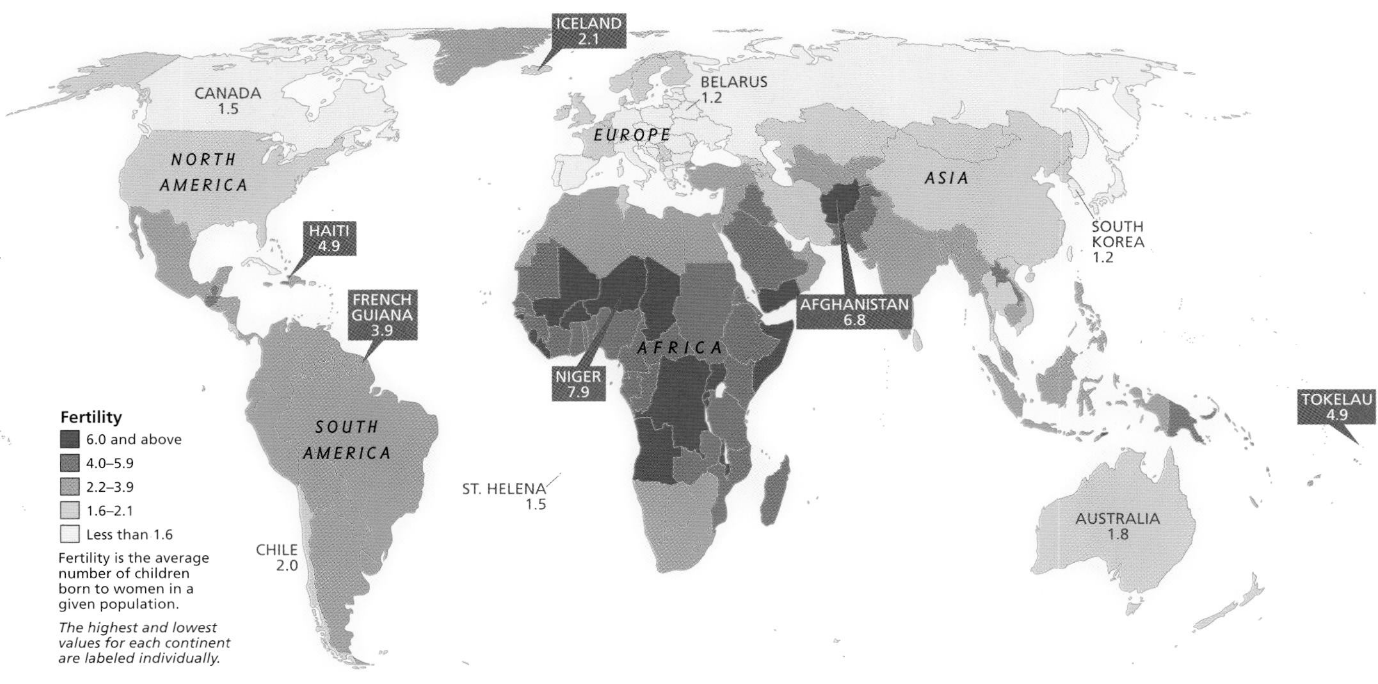

Urban Population Densities

People around the world are leaving farms and moving to cities, where jobs and opportunities are better. In 2000 almost half the world's people lived in towns or cities. The shift of population from the countryside to urban centers will probably continue in less developed countries for many years to come.

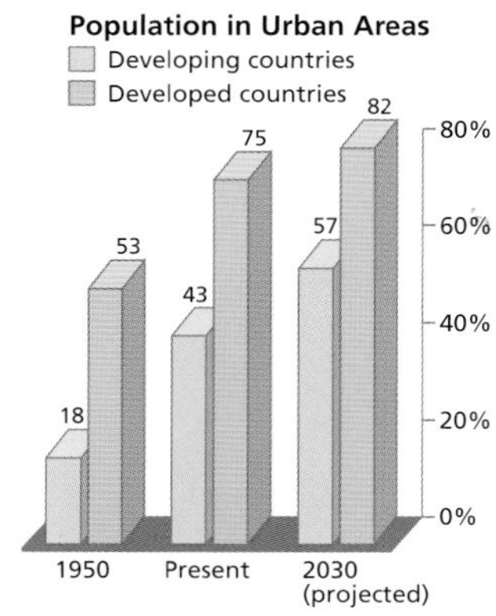

Urban Population Growth

Urban populations are growing more than twice as fast as populations as a whole. Soon, the world's city dwellers will outnumber its rural inhabitants as towns become cities and cities merge into megacities with more than ten million people. Globalization speeds the process. Although cities generate wealth and provide better health care along with electricity, clean water, sewage treatment, and other benefits, they can also cause great ecological damage. Squatter settlements and slums may develop if cities cannot keep up with millions of new arrivals. Smog, congestion, pollution, and crime are other dangers. Good city management is a key to future prosperity.

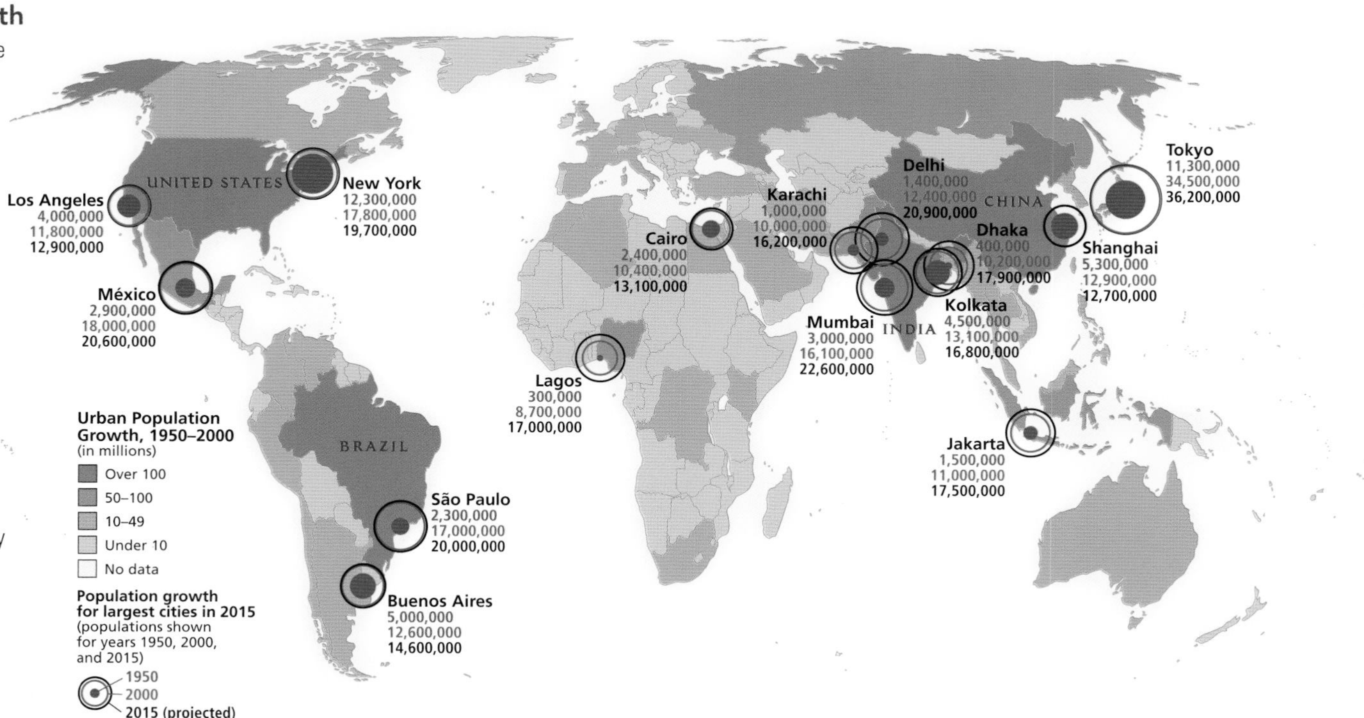

Life Expectancy

Life expectancy for population groups does not mean that all people die by a certain age. It is an average of death statistics. High infant mortality results in low life expectancy: People who live to adulthood will probably reach old age; there are just fewer of them.

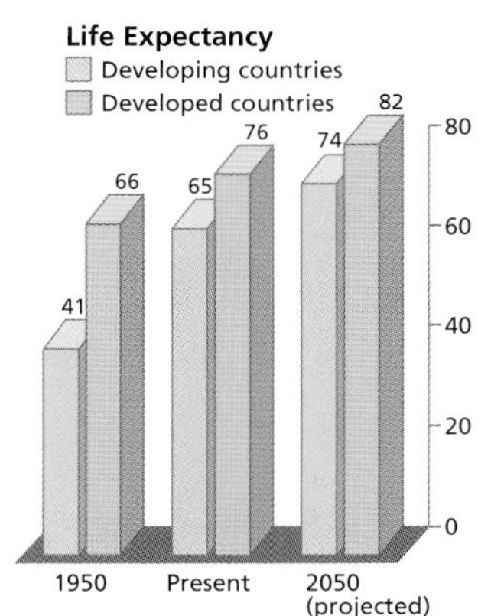

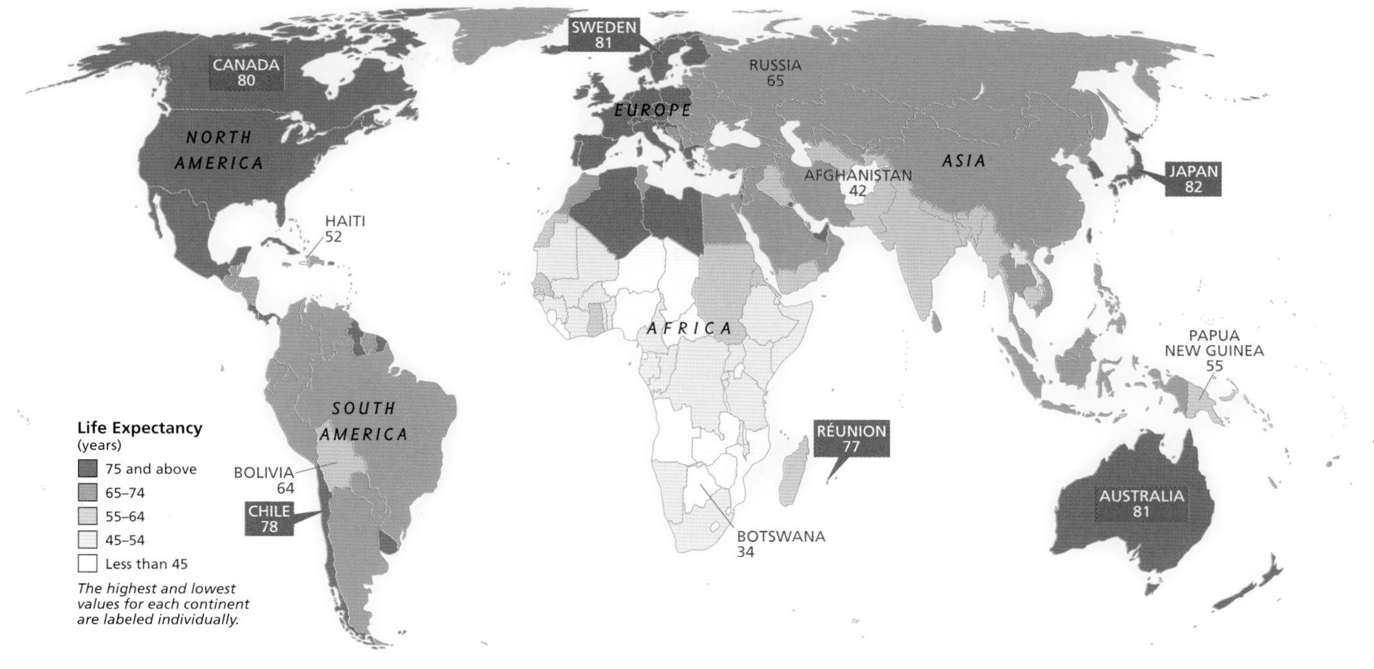

Migration

International migration has reached its highest level, with foreign workers now providing the labor in several Middle Eastern nations and immigrant workers proving essential to rich countries with low birthrates. Refugees continue to escape grim political and environmental conditions, while businesspeople and tourists keep many economies spinning.

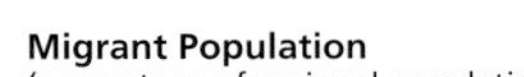

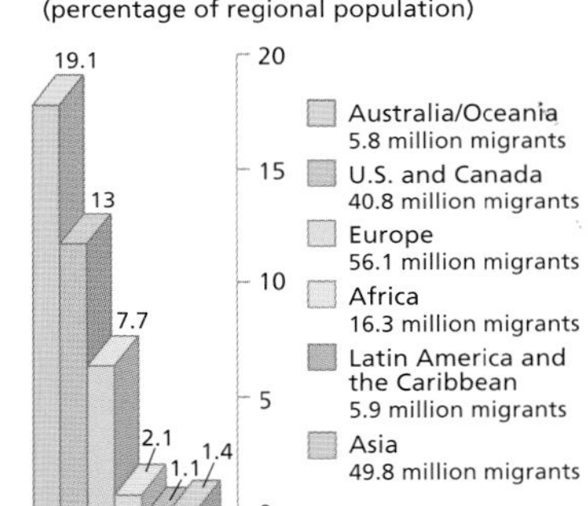

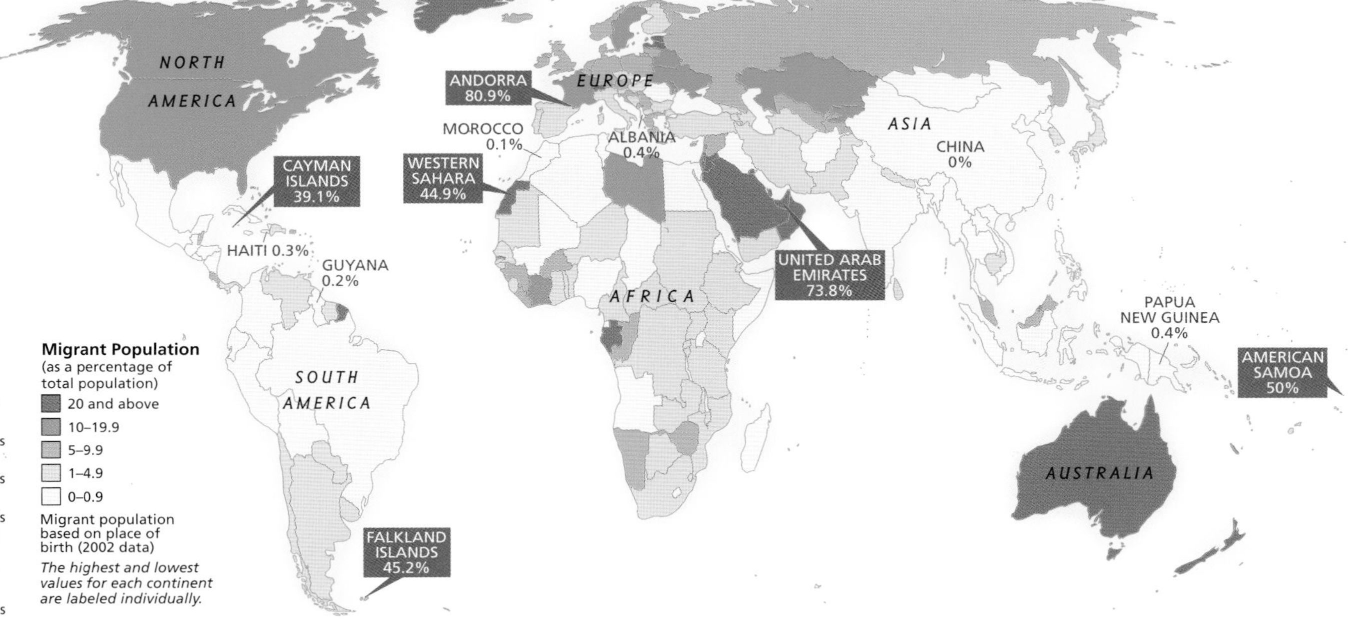

Most Populous Places

(MID-2006 DATA)

1. China 1,341,700,000
2. India 1,121,800,000
3. United States 299,100,000
4. Indonesia 225,500,000
5. Brazil 186,800,000
6. Pakistan 165,800,000
7. Bangladesh 146,600,000
8. Russia 142,300,000
9. Nigeria 134,500,000
10. Japan 127,800,000
11. Mexico 108,300,000
12. Philippines 86,300,000
13. Vietnam 84,200,000
14. Germany 82,400,000
15. Egypt 75,400,000
16. Ethiopia 74,800,000
17. Turkey 73,700,000
18. Iran 70,300,000
19. Thailand 65,200,000
20. Dem. Rep. of Congo 62,700,000

Most Crowded Places

POPULATION DENSITY (POP/SQ. MI.)

1. Monaco 44,000
2. Singapore 17,510
3. Gibraltar (U.K.) 11,600
4. Vatican City 4,000
5. Malta 3,320
6. Bermuda (U.K.) 2,952
7. Bahrain 2,686
8. Maldives 2,591
9. Bangladesh 2,573
10. Channel Islands (U.K.) 1,987
11. Taiwan 1,642
12. Barbados 1,627
13. Nauru 1,625
14. Palestinian Areas 1,609
15. Mauritius 1,591
16. Aruba (Neth.) 1,307
17. Mayotte (Fr.) 1,306
18. San Marino 1,292
19. South Korea 1,266
20. Puerto Rico (U.S.) 1,120

Demographic Extremes

LIFE EXPECTANCY

LOWEST (FEMALE, IN YEARS):

33 Botswana
35 Swaziland
36 Lesotho
37 Zambia, Zimbabwe

LOWEST (MALE, IN YEARS):

33 Swaziland
35 Botswana, Lesotho
38 Zambia, Zimbabwe
39 Angola, Sierra Leone

HIGHEST (FEMALE, IN YEARS):

86 Japan
84 France, San Marino, Spain, Switzerland
83 Australia, Iceland, Italy, Norway, Sweden

HIGHEST (MALE, IN YEARS):

79 Iceland, Japan, Liechtenstein, Switzerland
78 Australia, Israel, Italy, Norway San Marino, Singapore, Sweden
77 Anguilla (U.K.), Canada, Cayman Islands (U.K.), Costa Rica, Faroe Islands (Den.), France, Greece, Kuwait, Malta, Netherlands, New Zealand, Spain

POPULATION AGE STRUCTURE

HIGHEST % POPULATION UNDER AGE 15

53% Guinea-Bissau
50% Uganda
49% Niger
48% Dem. Rep. of Congo , Mali
47% Angola, Chad, Liberia, Malawi, Rwanda

HIGHEST % POPULATION AGE 65 AND OVER

22% Monaco
20% Japan
19% Germany, Italy
18% Greece

THE GREAT POWER OF RELIGION comes from its ability to speak to the heart of individuals and societies. Since earliest human times, honoring nature spirits or the belief in a supreme being has brought comfort and security in the face of fundamental questions of life and death.

Billions of people are now adherents of Hinduism, Buddhism, Judaism, Christianity, and Islam, all of which began in Asia. Universal elements of these faiths include ritual and prayer, sacred sites and pilgrimage, saints and martyrs, ritual clothing and implements, dietary laws and fasting, festivals and holy days, and special ceremonies for life's major moments. Sometimes otherworldly, most religions have moral and ethical guidelines that attempt to make life better on Earth as well. Their tenets and goals are taught not only at the church, synagogue, mosque, or temple but also through schools, storytelling, parables, painting, sculpture, and even dance and drama.

The world's major religions blossomed from the teachings and revelations of individuals who heeded and transmitted the voice of God or discovered a way to salvation that could be understood by others. Abraham and Moses for Jews, the Buddha for Buddhists, Jesus Christ for Christians, and Muhammad for Muslims fulfilled the roles of divine teachers who experienced essential truths of existence.

Throughout history, priests, rabbis, clergymen, and imams have recited, interpreted, and preached the holy words of sacred texts and writings to the faithful. Today the world's religions, with their guidance here on Earth and hopes and promises for the afterlife, continue to exert an extraordinary force on billions of people.

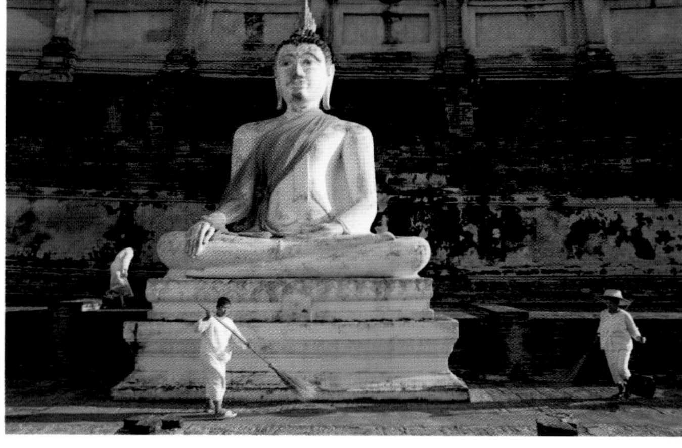

BUDDHISM
Founded about 2,500 years ago by Shakyamuni Buddha (or Gautama Buddha), Buddhism teaches liberation from suffering through the threefold cultivation of morality, meditation, and wisdom. Buddhists revere the Three Jewels: Buddha (the Awakened One), Dharma (the Truth), and Sangha (the community of monks and nuns).

CHRISTIANITY
Christian belief in eternal life is based on the example of Jesus Christ, a Jew born some 2,000 years ago. The New Testament tells of his teaching, persecution, crucifixion, and resurrection. Today Christianity is found around the world in three main forms: Roman Catholicism, Eastern Orthodox, and Protestantism.

HINDUISM
Hinduism began in India more than 4,000 years ago and is still flourishing. Sacred texts known as the Vedas form the basis of Hindu faith and ritual.

Adherents Worldwide

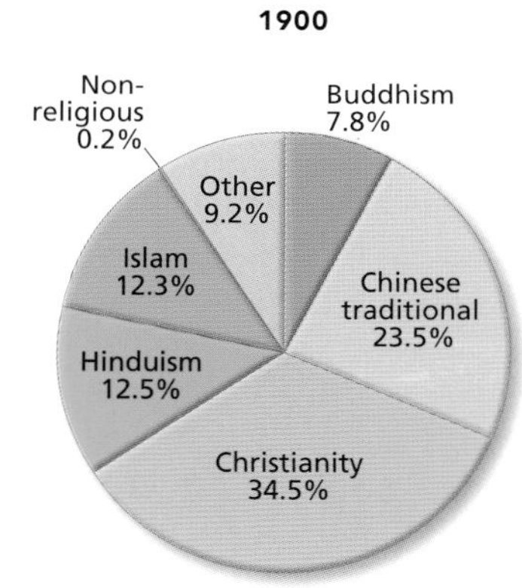

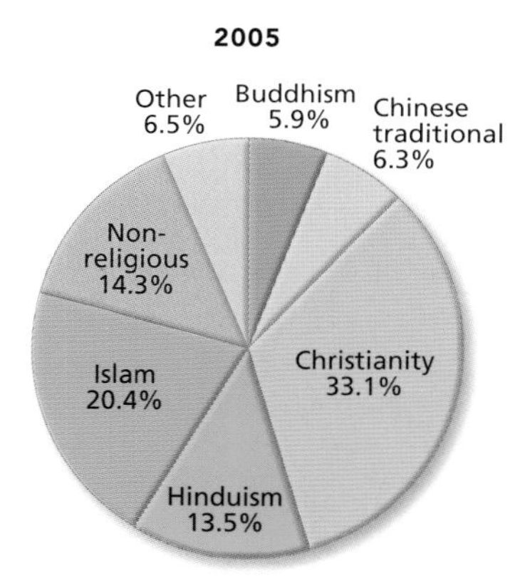

The growth of Islam and the decline of Chinese traditional religion stand out as significant changes over the past hundred years. Christianity, the largest of the world's main faiths, has remained fairly stable in its number of adherents. Today more than one in six people claim to be atheistic or nonreligious.

Adherents by Continent

In terms of the total number of religious adherents, Asia ranks first. This is not only because half the world's people live on that continent, but also because three of the five major faiths are practiced there: Hinduism in South Asia; Buddhism in East and Southeast Asia; and Islam from Indonesia to the Central Asian republics to Turkey. Oceania, Europe, North America, and South America are overwhelmingly Christian. Africa, with many millions of Muslims and Christians, also retains large numbers of animists.

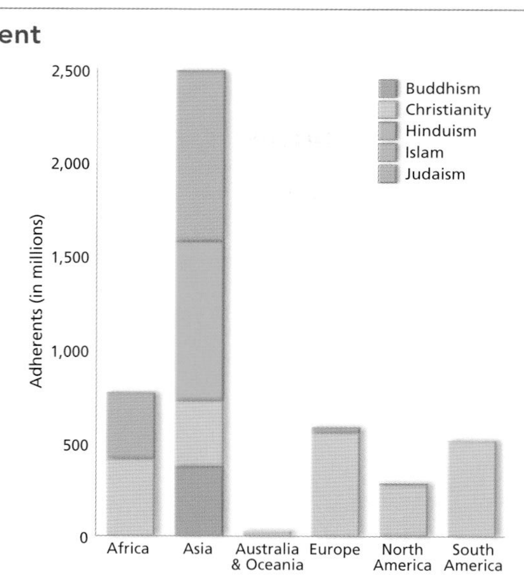

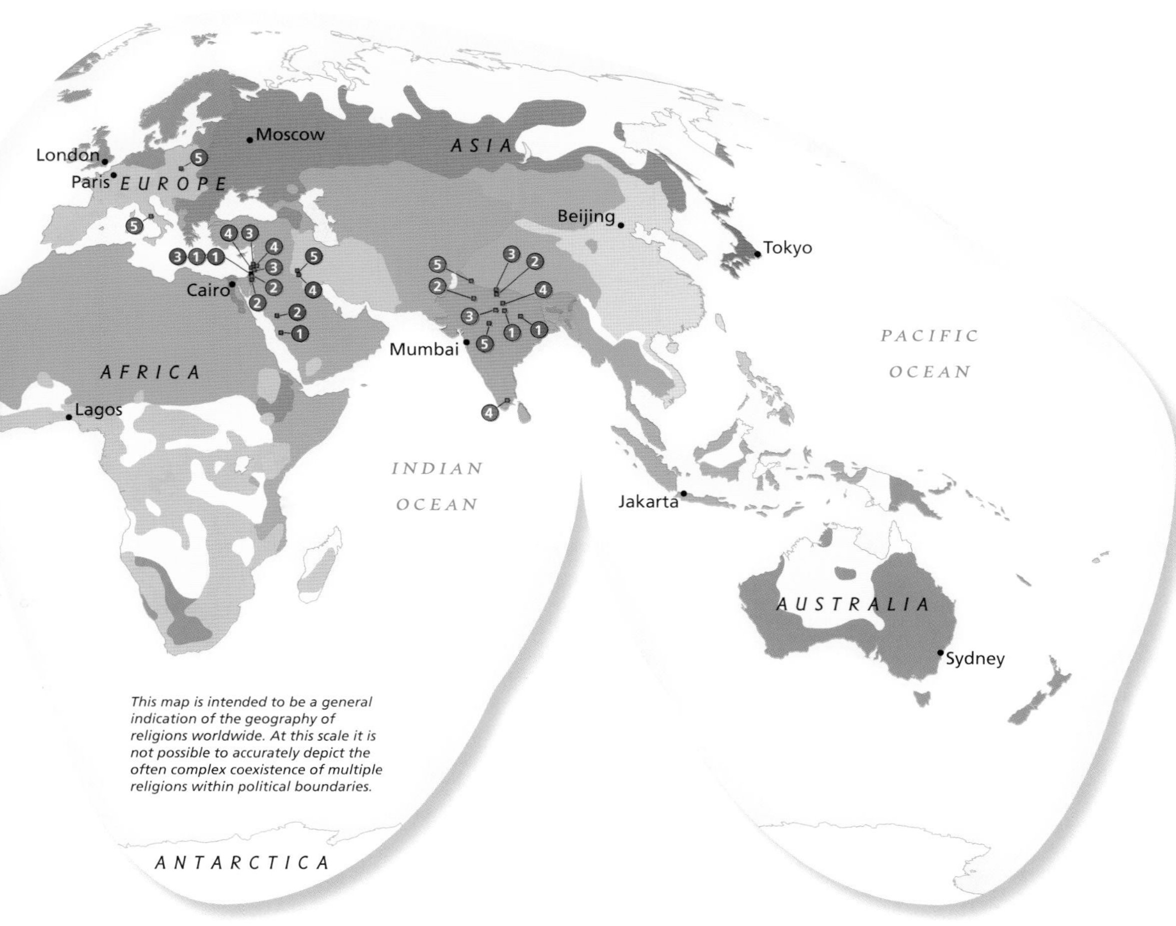
London
Paris
EUROPE
Moscow
ASIA
Beijing
Tokyo
Cairo
Mumbai
AFRICA
Lagos
PACIFIC
OCEAN
INDIAN
OCEAN
Jakarta
AUSTRALIA
Sydney
ANTARCTICA
This map is intended to be a general indication of the geography of religions worldwide. At this scale it is not possible to accurately depict the often complex coexistence of multiple religions within political boundaries.

Sacred Places

BUDDHISM
1. Bodhgaya: Where Buddha attained awakening
2. Kusinagara: Where Buddha entered nirvana
3. Lumbini: Place of Buddha's last human birth
4. Sarnath: Place where Buddha delivered his first sermon
5. Sanchi: Location of famous stupa containing relics of Buddha

CHRISTIANITY
1. Jerusalem: Church of the Holy Sepulchre, Jesus's crucifixion
2. Bethlehem: Jesus's birthplace
3. Nazareth: Where Jesus grew up
4. Shore of the Sea of Galilee: Where Jesus gave the Sermon on the Mount
5. Rome and the Vatican: Tombs of St. Peter and St. Paul

HINDUISM
1. Varanasi (Benares): Most holy Hindu site, home of Shiva
2. Vrindavan: Krishna's birthplace
3. Allahabad: At confluence of Ganges and Yamuna rivers, purest place to bathe
4. Madurai: Temple of Minakshi, great goddess of the south
5. Badrinath: Vishnu's shrine

ISLAM
1. Mecca: Muhammad's birthplace
2. Medina: City of Muhammad's flight, or hegira
3. Jerusalem: Dome of the Rock, Muhammad's stepping-stone to heaven
4. Najaf (Shiite): Tomb of Imam Ali
5. Kerbala (Shiite): Tomb of Imam Hoseyn

JUDAISM
1. Jerusalem: Location of the Western Wall and first and second temples
2. Hebron: Tomb of the patriarchs and their wives
3. Safed: Where Kabbalah (Jewish mysticism) flourished
4. Tiberias: Where Talmud (source of Jewish law) first composed
5. Auschwitz: Symbol of six million Jews who perished in the Holocaust

The main trinity of gods comprises Brahma the creator, Vishnu the preserver, and Shiva the destroyer. Hindus believe in reincarnation.

ISLAM
Muslims believe that the Koran, Islam's sacred book, accurately records the spoken word of God (Allah) as revealed to the Prophet Muhammad, born in Mecca around A.D. 570. Strict adherents pray five times a day, fast during the holy month of Ramadan, and make at least one pilgrimage to Mecca, Islam's holiest city.

JUDAISM
The 4,000-year-old religion of the Jews stands as the oldest of the major faiths that believe in a single god. Judaism's traditions, customs, laws, and beliefs date back to Abraham, the founder, and to the Torah, the first five books of the Old Testament, believed to have been handed down to Moses on Mount Sinai.

Adherents by Country

COUNTRIES WITH THE MOST BUDDHISTS

COUNTRY	BUDDHISTS
1. China	111,359,000
2. Japan	70,723,000
3. Thailand	53,294,000
4. Vietnam	40,781,000
5. Myanmar	37,152,000
6. Sri Lanka	13,235,000
7. Cambodia	12,698,000
8. India	7,597,000
9. South Korea	7,281,000
10. Taiwan*	4,823,000

COUNTRIES WITH THE MOST CHRISTIANS

COUNTRY	CHRISTIANS
1. United States	252,394,000
2. Brazil	166,847,000
3. China	110,956,000
4. Mexico	102,012,000
5. Russia	84,495,000
6. Philippines	73,987,000
7. India	68,190,000
8. Germany	61,833,000
9. Nigeria	61,438,000
10. Congo, Dem. Rep.	53,371,000

COUNTRIES WITH THE MOST HINDUS

COUNTRY	HINDUS
1. India	810,387,000
2. Nepal	19,020,000
3. Bangladesh	17,029,000
4. Indonesia	7,633,000
5. Sri Lanka	2,173,000
6. Pakistan	2,100,000
7. Malaysia	1,855,000
8. United States	1,144,000
9. South Africa	1,079,000
10. Myanmar	1,007,000

COUNTRIES WITH THE MOST MUSLIMS

COUNTRY	MUSLIMS
1. Indonesia	171,569,000
2. Pakistan	154,563,000
3. India	134,150,000
4. Bangladesh	132,868,000
5. Turkey	71,323,000
6. Iran	67,724,000
7. Egypt	63,503,000
8. Nigeria	54,666,000
9. Algeria	31,859,000
10. Morocco	31,001,000

COUNTRIES WITH THE MOST JEWS

COUNTRY	JEWS
1. United States	5,764,000
2. Israel	4,772,000
3. France	607,000
4. Argentina	520,000
5. Palestine*	451,000
6. Canada	414,000
7. Brazil	384,000
8. United Kingdom	312,000
9. Russia	245,000
10. Germany	226,000

**Non-sovereign nation*

All figures are estimates based on data for the year 2005.
Countries with the highest reported nonreligious populations include China, Russia, United States, Germany, India, Japan, North Korea, Vietnam, France, and Italy.

A GLOBAL ECONOMIC ACTIVITY MAP (right) reveals striking differences in the composition of output in advanced economies (such as the United States, Japan, and western Europe) compared with less developed countries (such as Nigeria and China). Advanced economies tend to have high proportions of their GDP in services, while developing economies have relatively high proportions in agriculture and industry.

There are different ways of looking at the distribution of manufacturing industry activity. When examined by country, the United States leads in production in many industries, but Western European countries are also a major manufacturing force. Western Europe outpaces the U.S. in the production of cars, chemicals, and food.

The world's sixth largest economy is found in China, and it has been growing quite rapidly. Chinese workers take home only a fraction of the cash pocketed each week by their economic rivals in the West, but are quickly catching up to the global economy with their purchase of cell phones and motor vehicles—two basic consumer products of the modern age.

The Middle East—a number of whose countries enjoy relatively high per-capita GDP values—produces more fuel than any other region, but it has virtually no other economic output besides that single commodity.

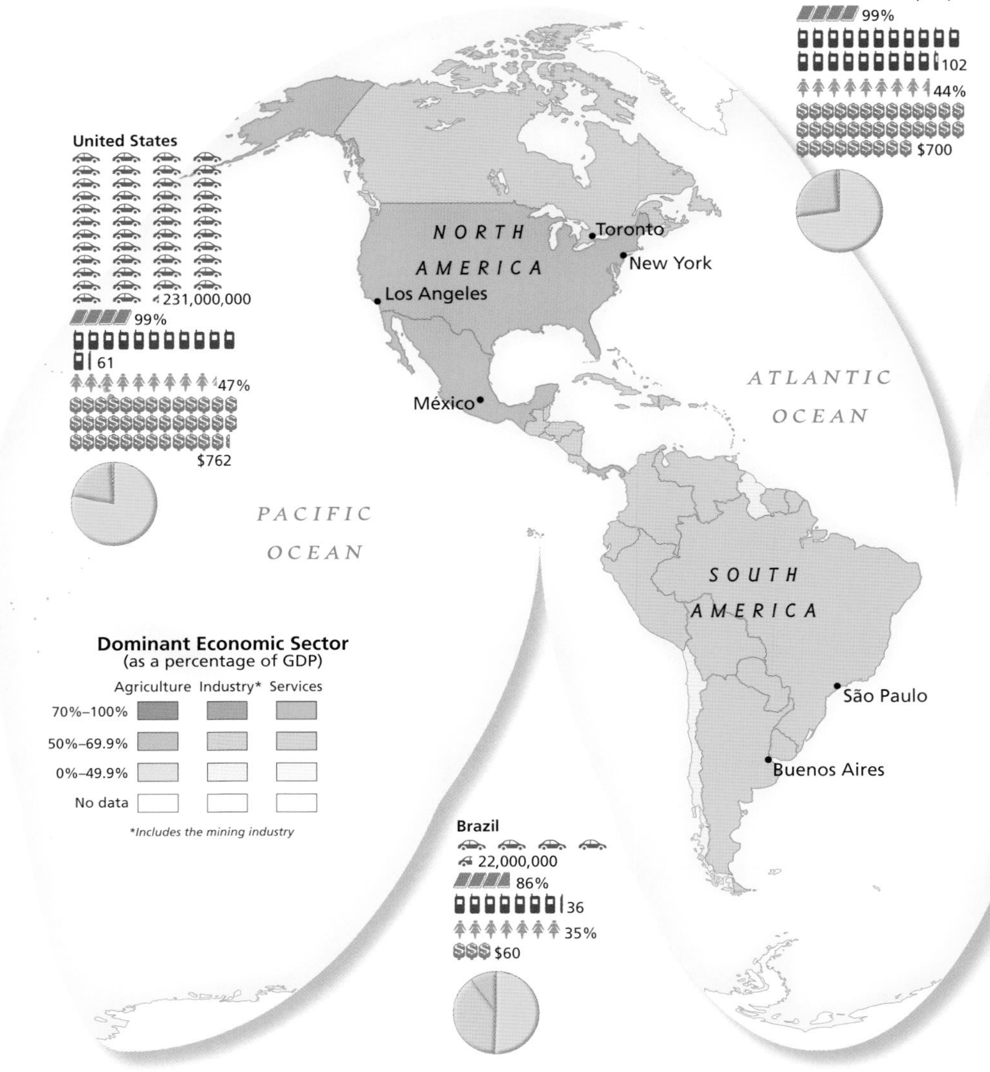

Labor Migration

People in search of jobs gravitate toward the higher-income economies, unless immigration policies prevent them from doing so. Japan, for instance, has one of the world's most restrictive immigration policies and a population that is more than 99 percent Japanese. Some nations are "labor importers," while others are "labor exporters." In the mid-1990s, Malaysia was the largest Asian importer (close to a million workers) and the Philippines was the largest Asian exporter (4.2 million). The largest share of foreign workers in domestic employment is found in the Persian Gulf and Singapore.

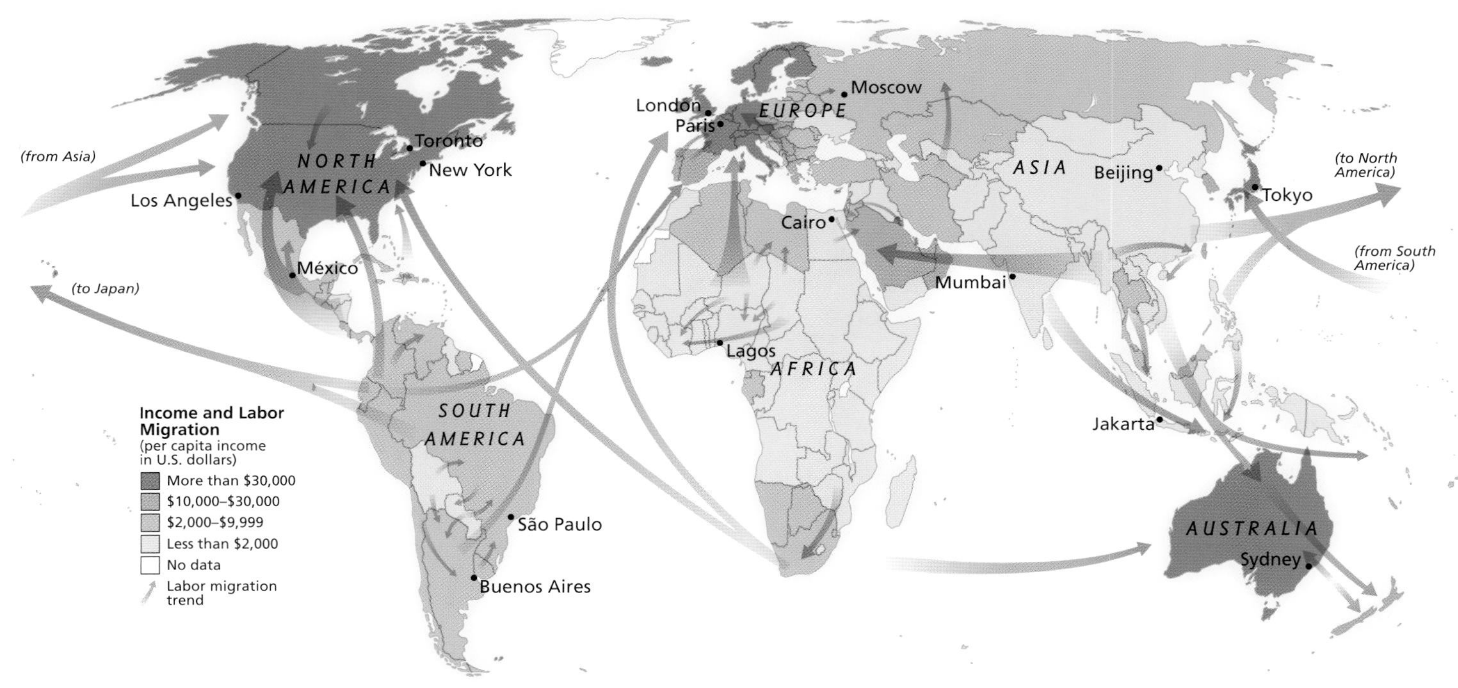

Top GDP Growth Rates
(based on PPP, or purchasing power parity)*

(2000–2005 AVERAGE)

1.	Equatorial Guinea	13%
2.	Turkmenistan	12%
3.	Sierra Leone	12%
4.	Chad	12%
5.	Armenia	11%
6.	Azerbaijan	11%
7.	Kazakhstan	11%
8.	Tajikistan	11%
9.	China	11%
10.	Myanmar	11%

*For more information on PPP, please see map on page 35.

The World's Richest and Poorest Countries

RICHEST		GDP PER CAPITA (PPP) (2005)
1.	Luxembourg	$68,800
2.	Equatorial Guinea	$50,200
3.	United Arab Emirates	$49,700
4.	Norway	$47,800
5.	Ireland	$43,600
6.	United States	$43,500
7.	Andorra	$38,800
8.	Iceland	$38,100
9.	Denmark	$37,000
10.	Austria	$35,500

POOREST		GDP PER CAPITA (PPP) (2005)
1.	Comoros	$600
2.	Malawi	$600
3.	Solomon Islands	$600
4.	Somalia	$600
5.	Burundi	$700
6.	Dem. Rep. of the Congo	$700
7.	Afghanistan	$800
8.	Tanzania	$800
9.	Timor-Leste	$800
10.	Guinea-Bissau, Madagascar, Sierra Leone, Yemen	$900

Figures are listed in U.S. dollars.

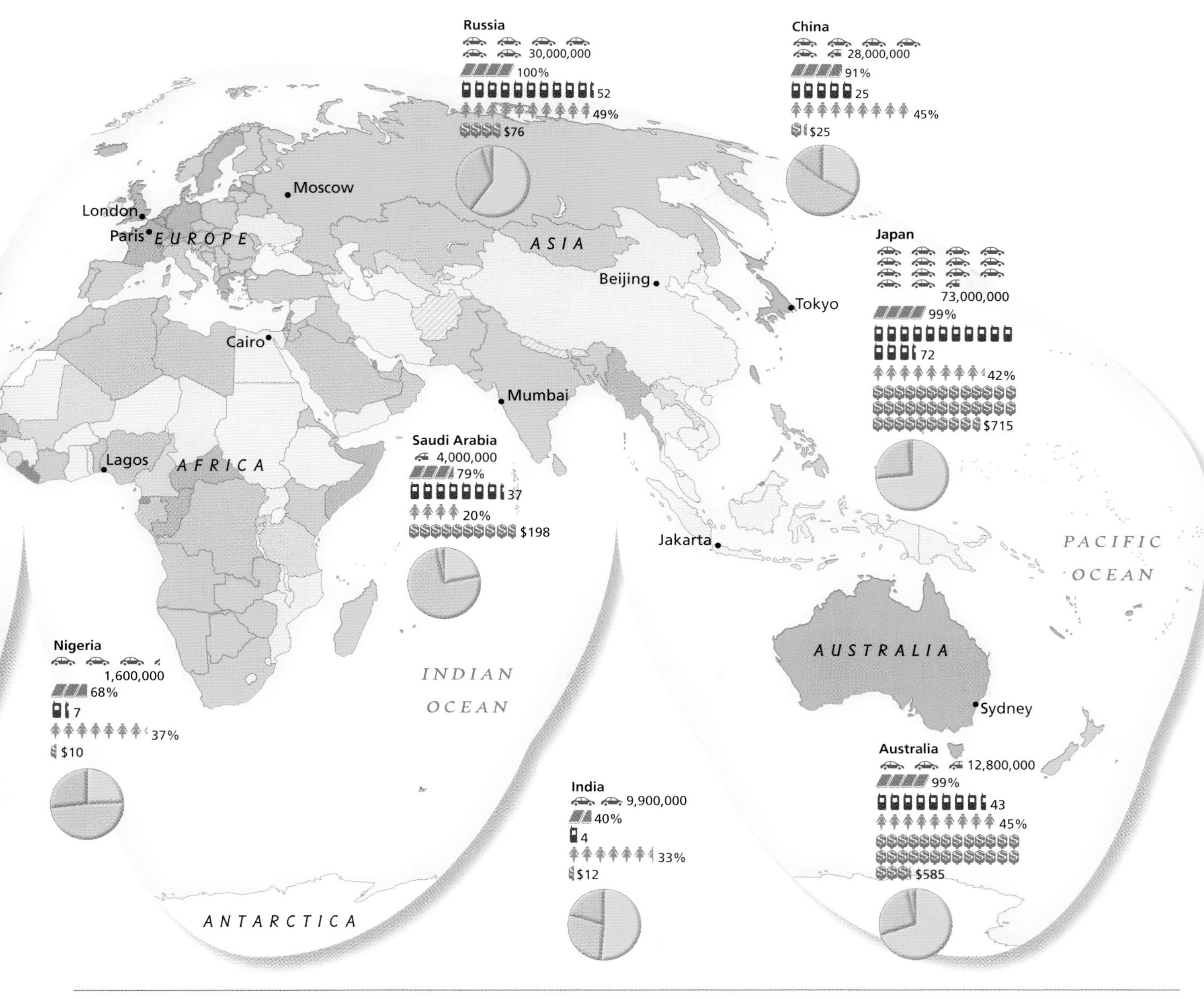

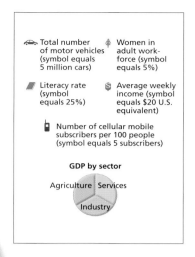

Total number of motor vehicles (symbol equals 5 million cars)

Women in adult work-force (symbol equals 5%)

Literacy rate (symbol equals 25%)

Average weekly income (symbol equals $20 U.S. equivalent)

Number of cellular mobile subscribers per 100 people (symbol equals 5 subscribers)

GDP by sector

Agriculture Services Industry

Major Manufacturers

(All figures in billions of U.S. dollars, 2005)

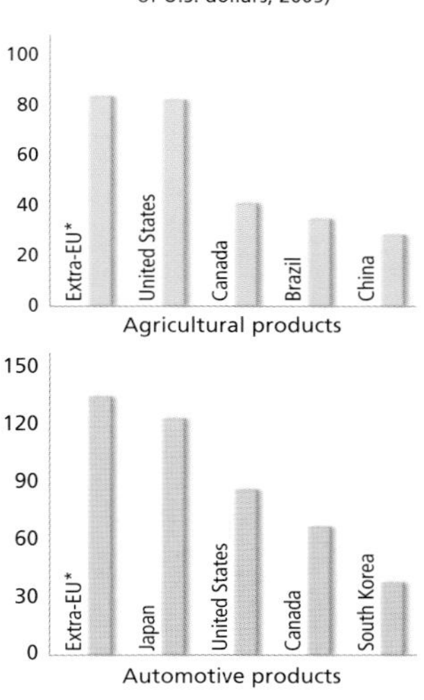

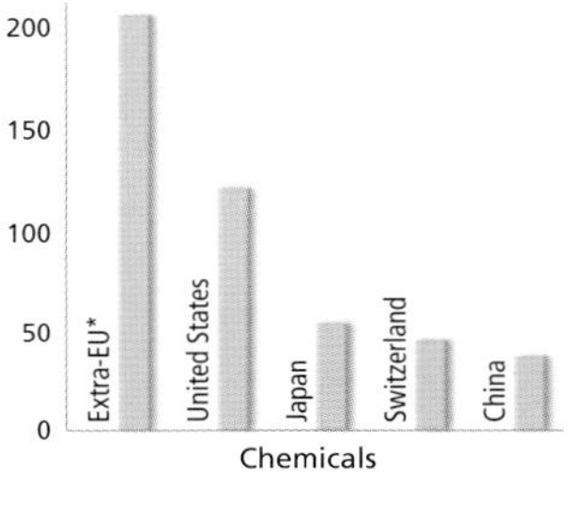

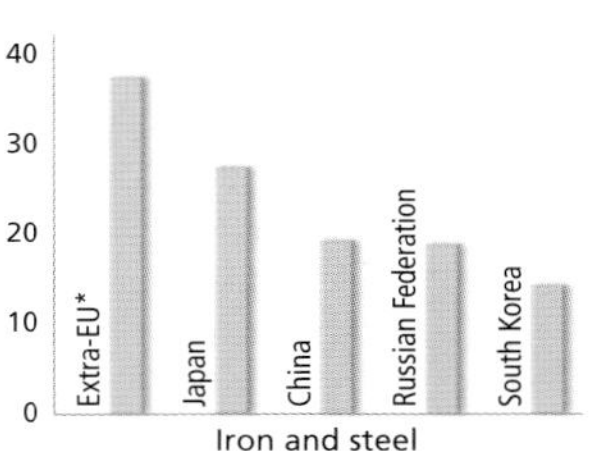

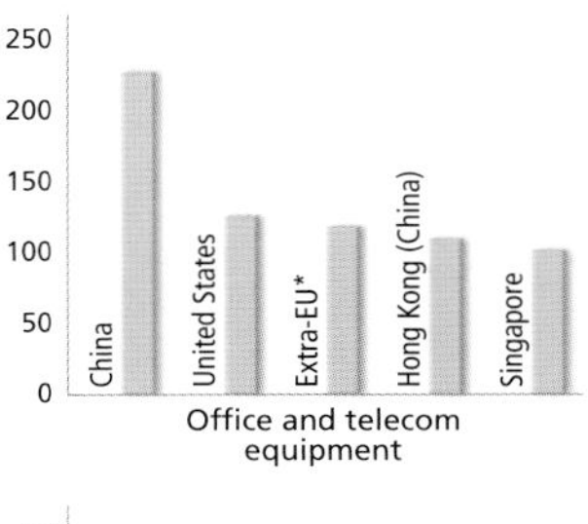

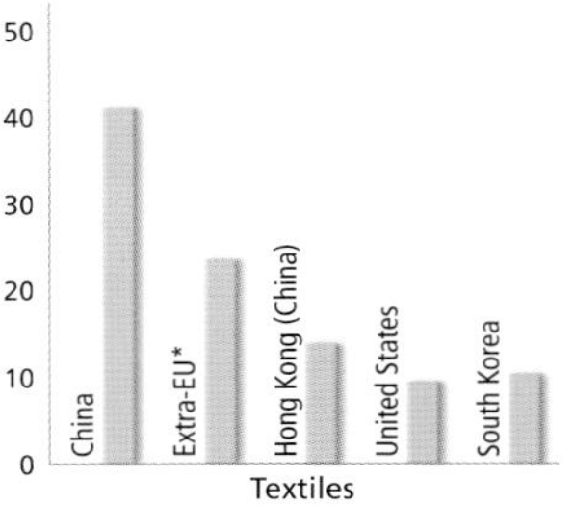

*Extra-EU trade statistics record goods imported and exported between European Union members and non-European Union members.

Gross Domestic Product

The gross domestic product (GDP) is the total market value of goods and services produced by a nation's economy in a given year using global currency exchange rates. It is a convenient way of calculating the level of a nation's international purchasing power and economic strength, but it does not show average wealth of individuals or measure standard of living. For example, a country could have high exports in products, but still have a low standard of living.

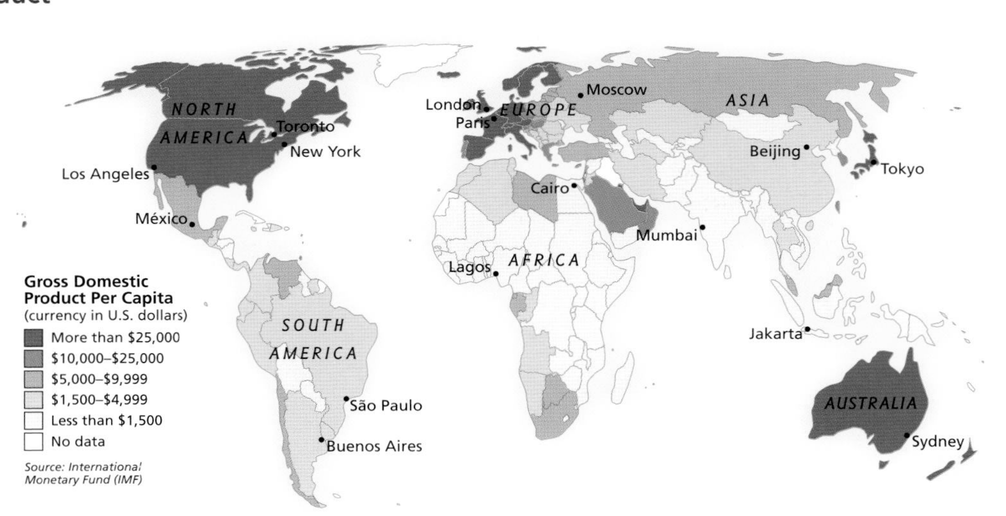

Gross Domestic Product: Purchasing Power Parity (PPP)

The PPP method calculates the relative value of currencies based on what each currency will buy in its country of origin–providing a good comparison between national economies. Per capita GDP at PPP is a very good but not perfect indicator of living standards. For instance, although workers in China earn only a fraction of the wage of American workers, (measured at current dollar rates) they also spend it in a lower-cost environment.

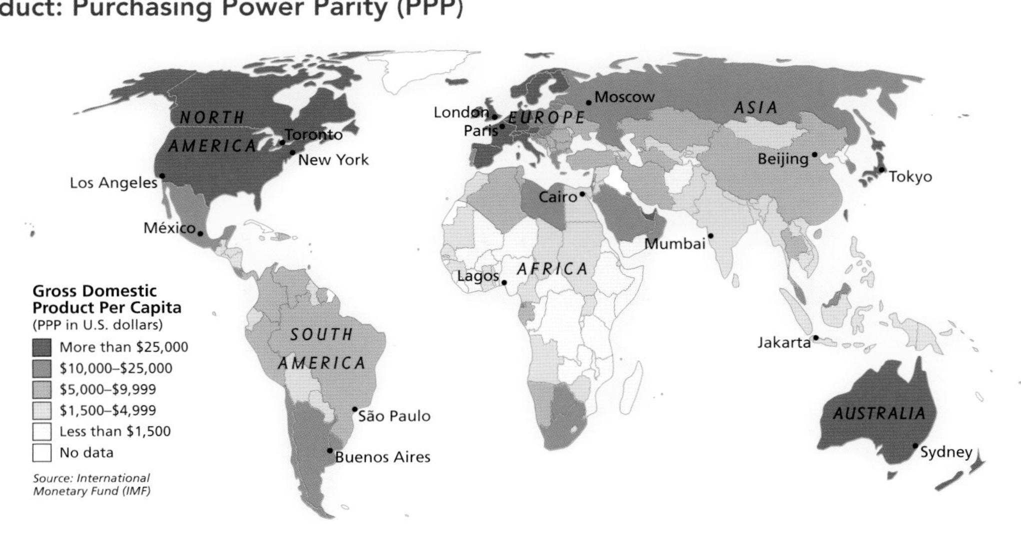

WORLD TRADE HAS EXPANDED at a dizzying pace in the decades following World War II. The dollar value of world merchandise exports rose from $61 billion in 1950 to $10.1 trillion in 2005. Adjusted for price changes, world trade grew 30 times over the last 55 years, much faster than world output. Trade in manufactures expanded much faster than that of mining products (including fuels) and agricultural products. In the last decades many developing countries have become important exporters of manufactures (e.g. China, South Korea, Mexico). However, there are still many less-developed countries—primarily in Africa and the Middle East—that are dependent on a few primary commodities for their export earnings. Commercial services exports have expanded rapidly over the past two decades, and amounted to $2.4 trillion in 2005. While developed countries account for more than two-thirds of world services trade, some developing countries now gain most of their export earnings from services exports. Earnings from tourism in the Caribbean and that from software exports in India are prominent examples of developing countries' dynamic services exports.

Capital flows and worker remittances have gained in importance worldwide and are another important aspect of globalization. The stock of worldwide foreign direct investment was estimated to be close to $9 trillion at the end of 2004, $2.2 trillion of which was invested in developing countries. Capital markets in many developing countries remain small, fragile, and underdeveloped, which hampers household savings and the funding of local enterprises.

Growth of World Trade

After World War II the export growth of manufactured goods greatly outstripped other exports. This graph shows the volume growth on a semi-log scale (a straight line represents constant growth) rather than a standard scale (a straight line indicates a constant increase in the absolute values in each year).

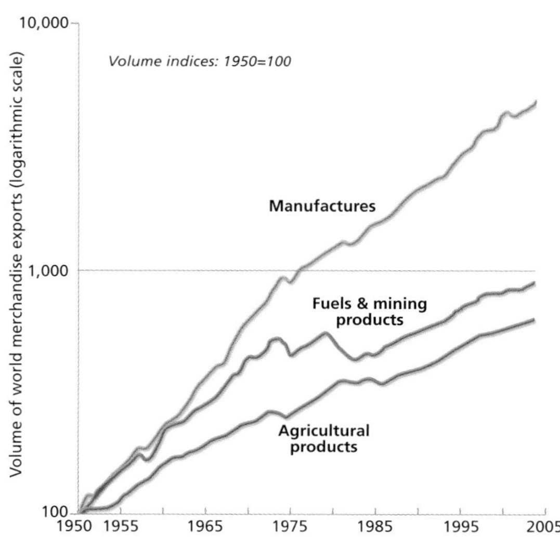

Merchandise Exports

Manufactured goods account for three-quarters of world merchandise exports. Export values of two subtypes—machinery and office/telecom equipment—exceed the total export value of mining products; world exports in chemicals and automotive products exceed the export value of all agricultural products.

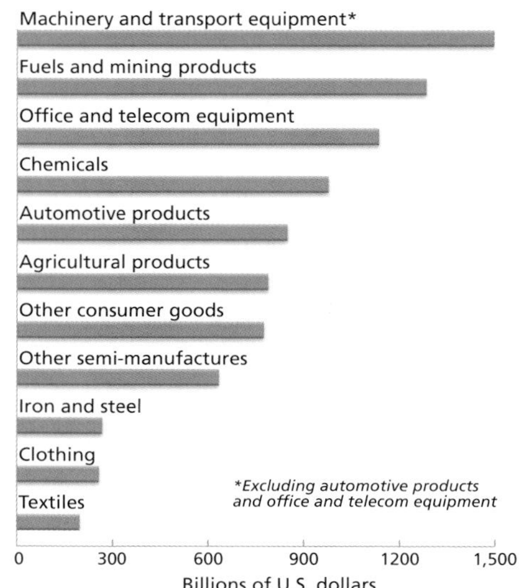

Main Trading Nations

The U.S., Germany, and Japan account for nearly 30 percent of total world merchandise trade. Ongoing negotiations among the 144 member nations of the World Trade Organization are tackling market-access barriers in agriculture, textiles, and clothing—areas where many developing countries hope to compete.

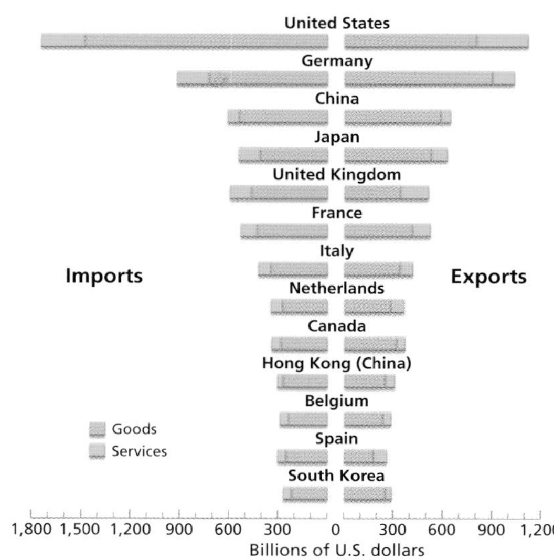

World Debt

Measuring a nation's outstanding foreign debt in relation to its GDP indicates the size of future income needed to pay back the debt; it also shows how much a nation has relied in the past on foreign savings to finance investment and consumption expenditures. A high external debt ratio can pose a financial risk if debt service payments are not assured.

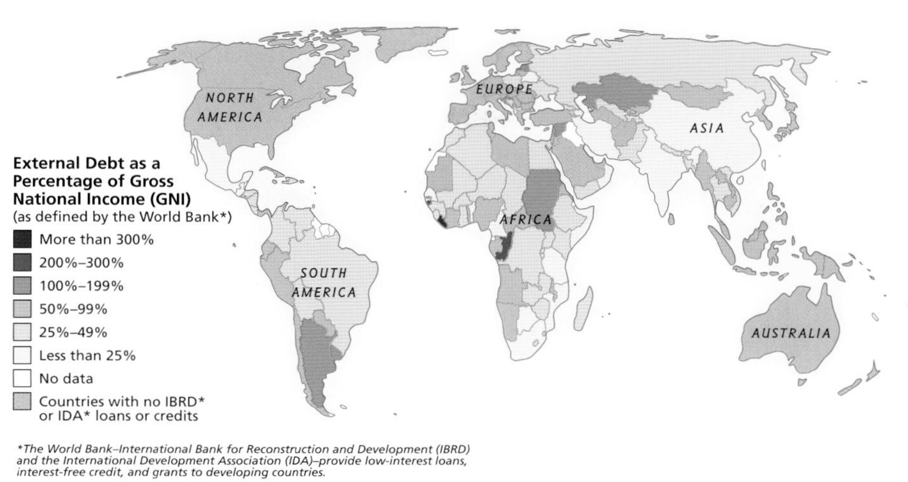

*The World Bank–International Bank for Reconstruction and Development (IBRD) and the International Development Association (IDA)–provide low-interest loans, interest-free credit, and grants to developing countries.

Trade Blocs

Regional trade is on the rise. Agreements between neighboring countries to offer each other trade benefits can create larger markets and improve the economy of the region as a whole. But they can also lead to discrimination, especially when more efficient suppliers outside the regional agreements are prevented from supplying their goods and services.

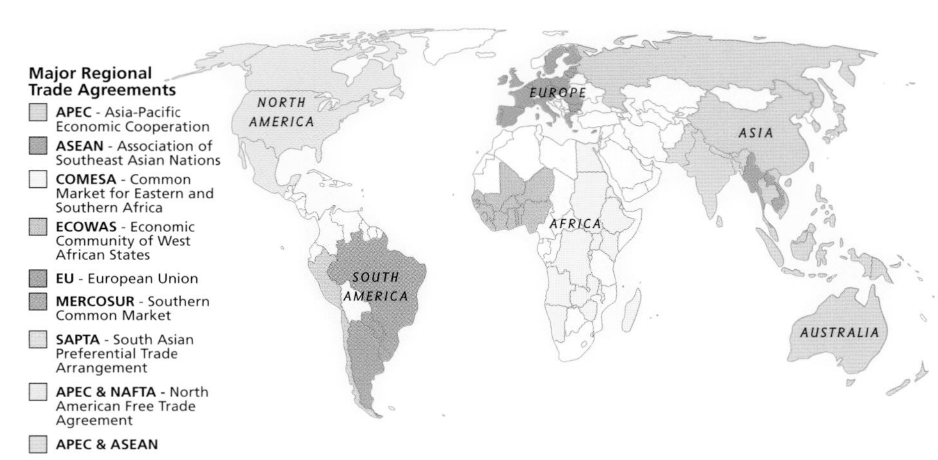

Trade Flow: Fuels

The leading exporters of fuel products are countries in the Middle East, Africa, Russia, and central and western Asia; all export more fuel than they consume. But intraregional energy trade is growing, with some of the key producers—Canada, Indonesia, Norway, and the United Kingdom, for example—located in regions that are net energy importers.

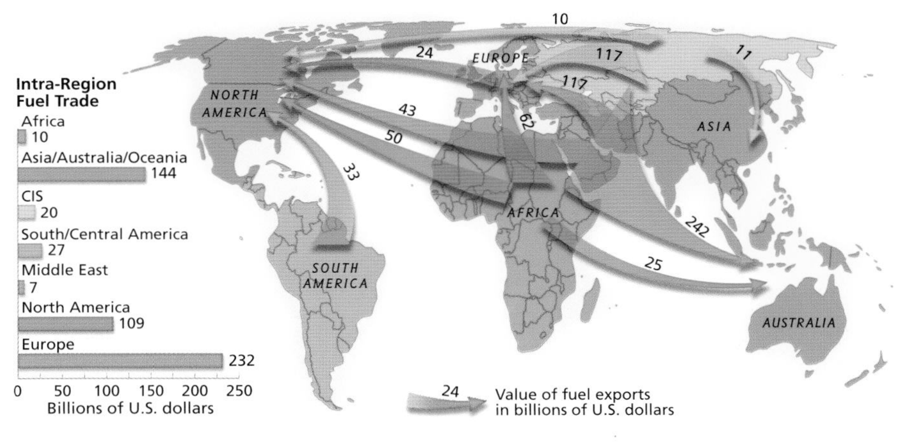

Trade Flow: Agricultural Products

The world trade in agricultural products is less concentrated than trade in fuels, with processed goods making up the majority. Agricultural products encounter high export barriers, which limit the opportunities for some exporters to expand into foreign markets. Reducing such barriers is a major challenge for governments that are engaged in agricultural trade negotiations.

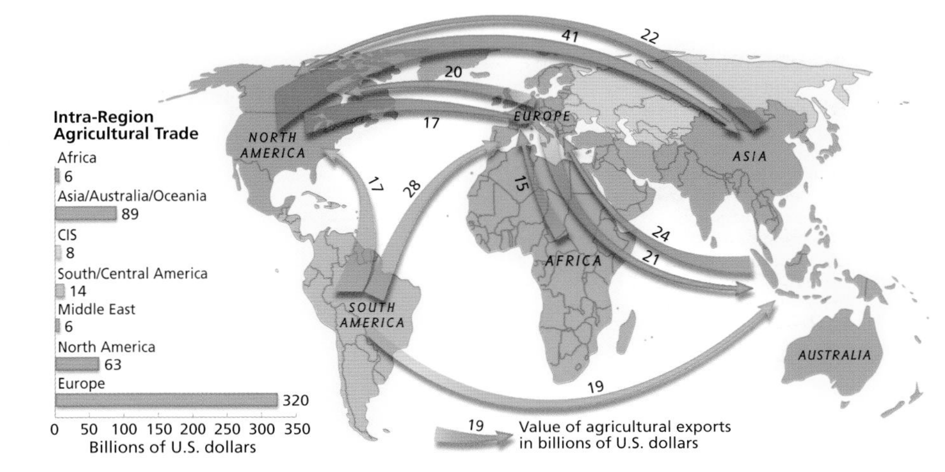

Top Merchandise Exporters and Importers

	PERCENTAGE OF WORLD TOTAL	VALUE (BILLIONS)
TOP EXPORTERS		
Germany	9.3	$970
United States	8.7	$904
China	7.3	$762
Japan	5.7	$595
France	4.4	$460
Netherlands	3.9	$402
United Kingdom	3.7	$383
Italy	3.5	$367
Canada	3.4	$359
Belgium	3.2	$334
Hong Kong (China)	2.8	$292
South Korea	2.7	$284
Russia	2.3	$244
Singapore	2.2	$230
Mexico	2.0	$214
TOP IMPORTERS		
United States	16.1	$1,732
Germany	7.2	$774
China	6.1	$660
Japan	4.8	$515
United Kingdom	4.7	$510
France	4.6	$498
Italy	3.5	$380
Netherlands	3.3	$359
Canada	3.0	$320
Belgium	3.0	$319
Hong Kong (China)	2.8	$300
Spain	2.6	$279
South Korea	2.4	$261
Mexico	2.1	$232
Singapore	1.9	$200

Top Commercial Services Exporters and Importers

(includes transportation, travel, and other services)

	PERCENTAGE OF WORLD TOTAL	VALUE (BILLIONS)
TOP EXPORTERS		
United States	14.6	$353
United Kingdom	7.6	$183
Germany	5.9	$143
France	4.7	$114
Japan	4.4	$107
Italy	3.9	$93
Spain	3.8	$91
China	3.4	$81
Netherlands	3.1	$75
India	2.8	$68
Hong Kong (China)	2.5	$60
Ireland	2.3	$55
Austria	2.2	$54
Belgium	2.2	$53
Canada	2.1	$51
TOP IMPORTERS		
United States	12.2	$289
Germany	8.4	$199
United Kingdom	6.4	$150
Japan	5.8	$136
France	4.4	$103
Italy	3.9	$92
China	3.6	$85
Netherlands	2.9	$69
Ireland	2.9	$68
India	2.9	$67
Spain	2.8	$65
Canada	2.6	$62
South Korea	2.5	$58
Austria	2.2	$52
Belgium	2.2	$51

IN THE PAST 50 YEARS, health conditions have improved dramatically. With better economic and living conditions and access to immunization and other basic health services, global life expectancy has risen from 40 to 65 years; the death rate for children under five years old has fallen by half; and diseases that once killed and disabled millions have been eradicated, eliminated, or greatly reduced in impact. Today, fully three-quarters of the world's children benefit from protection against six infectious diseases that were responsible in the past for many millions of infant and child deaths.

Current efforts to improve health face new and daunting challenges, however. Infant and child mortality from infectious diseases remains relatively high in many poor countries. Each year, more than ten million children under five years old die—41 percent of them in sub-Saharan Africa and 34 percent in South Asia. Improvement in children's health has slowed dramatically in the past 20 years, particularly where child death rates have historically been highest.

The HIV/AIDS pandemic has erased decades of steady improvements in sub-Saharan Africa. An estimated 24 million people are HIV-positive in Africa alone—and AIDS is taking a toll in India, China, and Eastern Europe. The death toll in Africa is contributing to reversals in life expectancy—just 47 years instead of the estimated 62 years without AIDS. An estimated 15 million children have lost one or both their parents to the disease.

Vast gaps in health outcomes between rich and poor persist. About 99 percent of global childhood deaths occur in poor countries, with the poorest within those countries having the highest child-mortality rates. In Indonesia, for example, a child born in a poor household is four times as likely to die by her fifth birthday than a child born to a well-off family.

In many high- and middle-income countries, chronic, lifestyle-related diseases such as cardiovascular disease, diabetes, and others are becoming the predominant cause of disability and death. Because the focus of policymakers has been on treatment rather than prevention, the costs of dealing with these ailments contributes to high (and rapidly increasing) health-care spending. Tobacco-related illnesses are major problems worldwide. In developed countries, smoking is the cause of more than one-third of male deaths in middle age, and about one in eight female deaths. It is estimated that due to trends of increasing tobacco use, of all the people aged under 20 alive today in China, 50 million will die prematurely from tobacco use.

Health Care Availability

Regional differences in health care resources are striking. While countries in Europe and the Americas have relatively large numbers of physicians and nurses, nations with far higher burdens of disease (particularly African countries) are experiencing severe deficits in both health workers and health facilities.

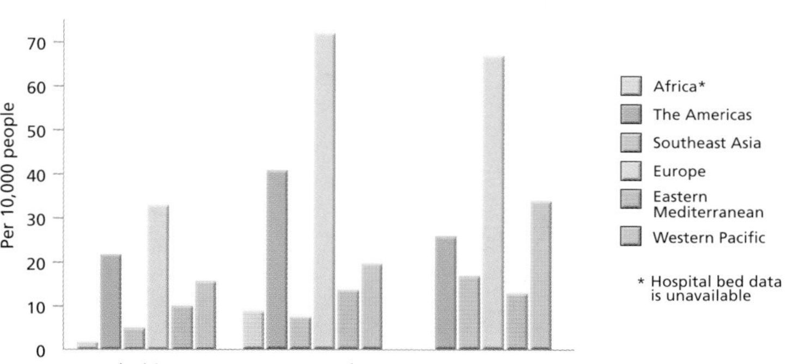

Income Levels: Indicators of Health and Literacy

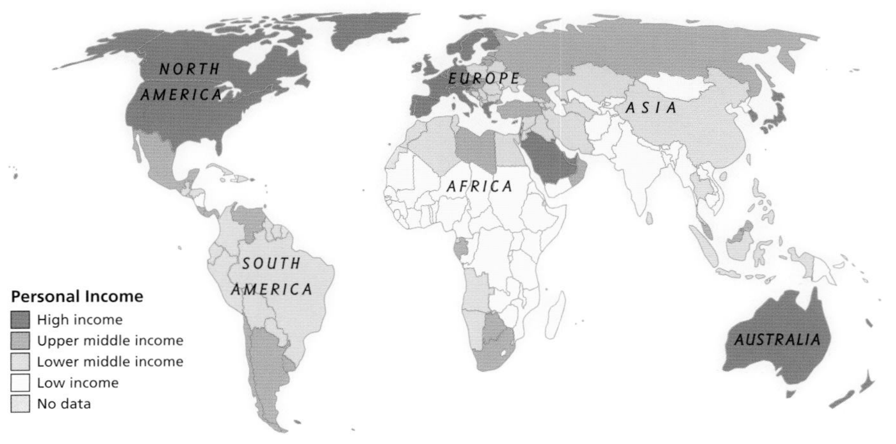

Access to Improved Sanitation

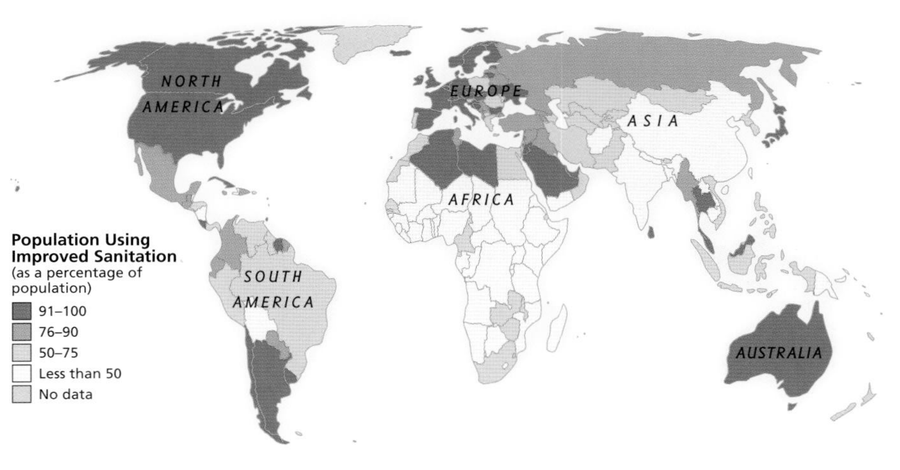

Nutrition

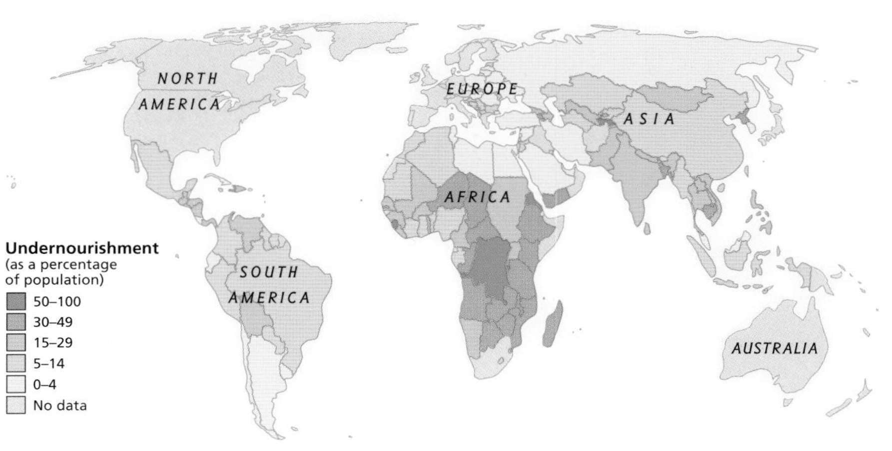

HIV

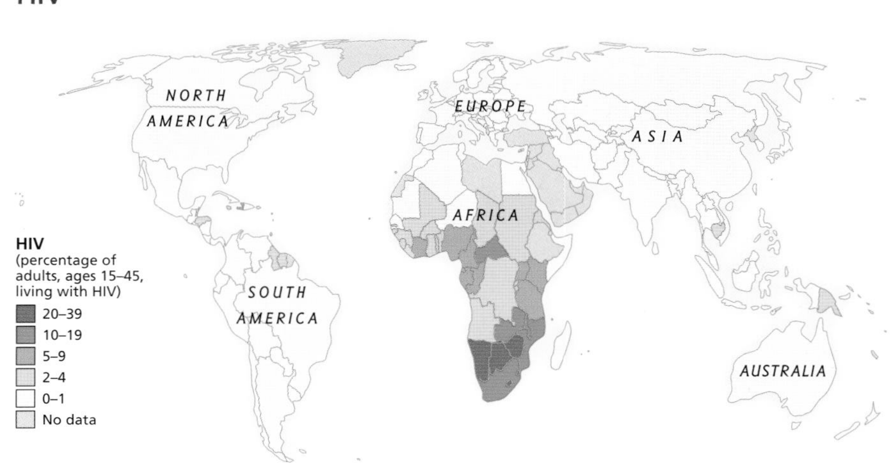

Global Disease Burden

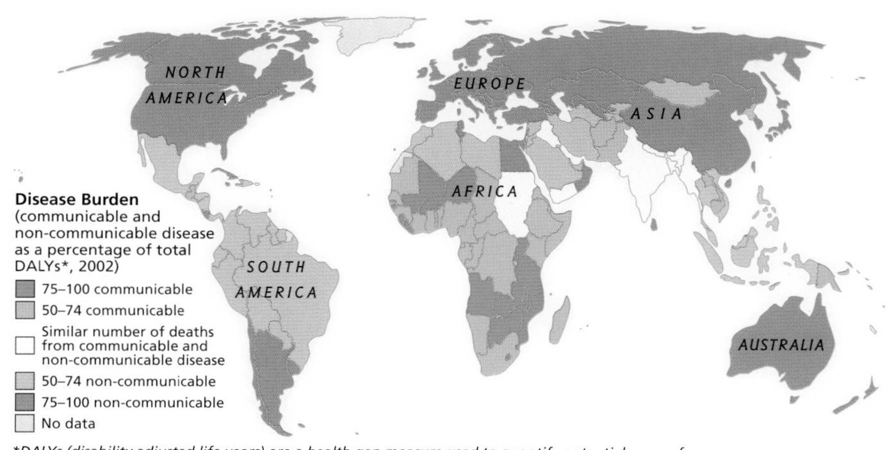

DALYs (disability adjusted life years) are a health gap measure used to quantify potential years of life lost to illness or premature death. One DALY can be thought of as one lost year of "healthy" life.

While infectious and parasitic diseases account for nearly one-quarter of total deaths in developing countries, they result in relatively few deaths in wealthier nations. In contrast, cardiovascular diseases and cancer are more significant causes of death in industrialized countries. Over time, as fertility rates fall, social and living conditions improve, the population ages, and further advances are made against infectious diseases in poorer countries, the distribution of causes of death between developed and developing nations may converge.

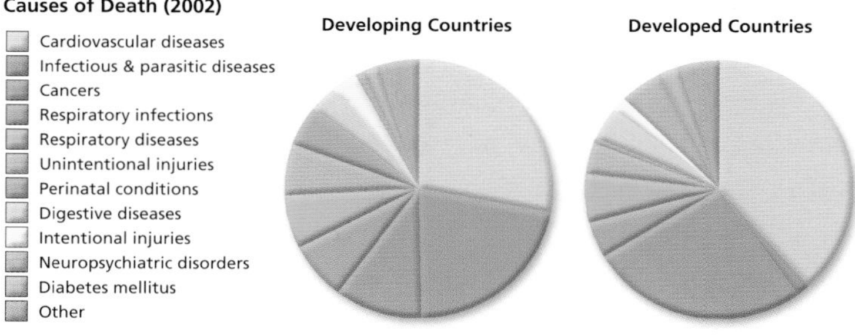

Under-Five Mortality

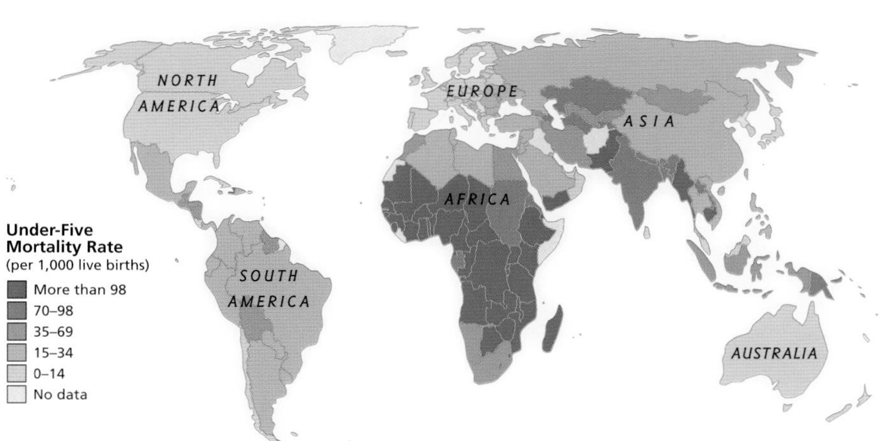

Maternal Mortality

MATERNAL MORTALITY RATIO PER 100,000 LIVE BIRTHS*

COUNTRIES WITH THE HIGHEST MATERNAL MORTALITY RATES:

1.	Sierra Leone	2,000
2.	Malawi	1,800
3.	Angola	1,700
4.	Niger	1,600
5.	Tanzania	1,500
6.	Rwanda	1,400
7.	Mali	1,200
8.	Zimbabwe	1,100
9.	Central African Republic	1,100
10.	Guinea-Bissau	1,100

COUNTRIES WITH THE LOWEST MATERNAL MORTALITY RATES:

1.	Iceland	0
2.	Sweden	2
3.	Slovakia	3
4.	Spain	4
5.	Austria	4
6.	Kuwait	5
7.	Portugal	5
8.	Italy	5
9.	Denmark	5
10.	Ireland	5

**Adjusted for underreporting and misclassification*

Education and Literacy

NORTH AMERICA
EUROPE
ASIA
AFRICA
SOUTH AMERICA
AUSTRALIA

Adult Literacy
(as a percentage of population)
- More than 93
- 80–93
- 60–79
- 20–59
- 0–19
- No data

Basic education is an investment for the long-term prosperity of a nation, generating individual, household, and social benefits. Some countries (e.g., Eastern and Western Europe, the U.S.) have long traditions of high educational attainment among both genders, and now have well-educated populations of all ages. In contrast, many low-income countries have only recently expanded access to primary education; girls still lag behind boys in enrollment and completion of primary school, and then in making the transition to secondary school. These countries will have to wait many years before most individuals in the productive ages have even minimal levels of reading, writing, and basic arithmetic skills.

The expansion of secondary schooling tends to lag even further behind, so countries with low educational attainment will likely be at a disadvantage for at least a generation. Although no one doubts that the key to long-term economic growth and poverty reduction lies in greater education opportunities for all, many poor countries face the tremendous challenge of paying for schools and teachers today, while having to wait 20 years for the economic return on the investment.

School Enrollment for Girls

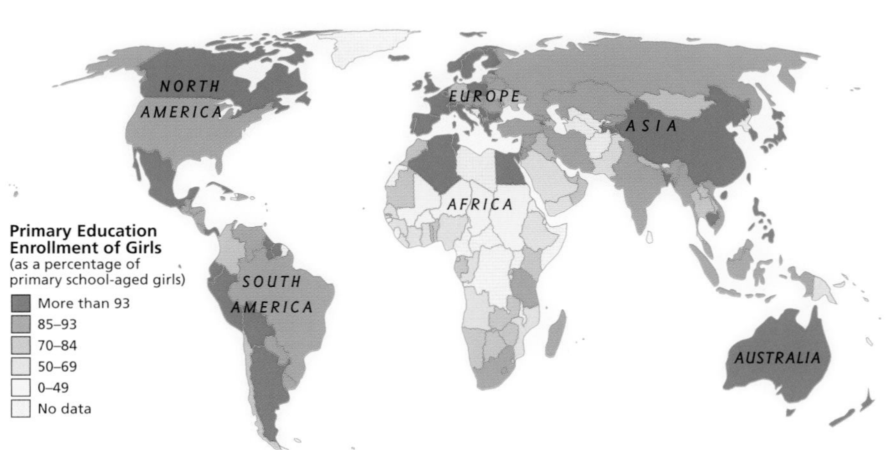

Developing Human Capital

In the pyramids below, more red and blue in the bars indicates a higher level of educational attainment, or "human capital," which contributes greatly to a country's potential for future economic growth. These two countries are similar in population size, but their human capital measures are significantly different.

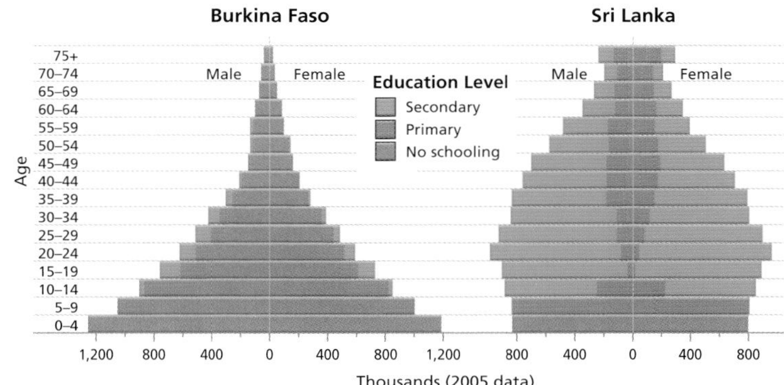

POLITICAL VIOLENCE, WAR, AND TERROR continue to plague many areas of the world in the early 21st century, despite dramatic decreases in major armed conflict since 1991. The 20th century is often described as the century of "total war" as modern weapons technologies made every facet of society a potential target in warfare. The globe was rocked by two world wars, self-determination wars in developing countries, and the threat of nuclear annihilation during the Cold War. Whereas the first half of the century was torn by interstate wars among the most powerful states, the latter half was consumed by protracted civil wars in the weakest states. The end of the Cold War emboldened international engagement, and concerted efforts toward peace had reduced armed conflicts more than half by early 2007.

While long-standing wars still smolder in Africa and Asia in the early 21st century, global apprehension is riveted on super-powerful states, super-empowered individuals, and the proliferation of "weapons of mass disruption." Globalization is both bringing people closer together and making us ever more vulnerable. Though violence is generally subsiding and democracy spreading, tensions appear to be increasing across the world's oil-producing regions. A little-understood "war on terror" punctuates the hard-won peace and prods us toward an uncertain future. Prospects for an increasingly peaceful world are good, yet much work remains to be done.

Political Violence

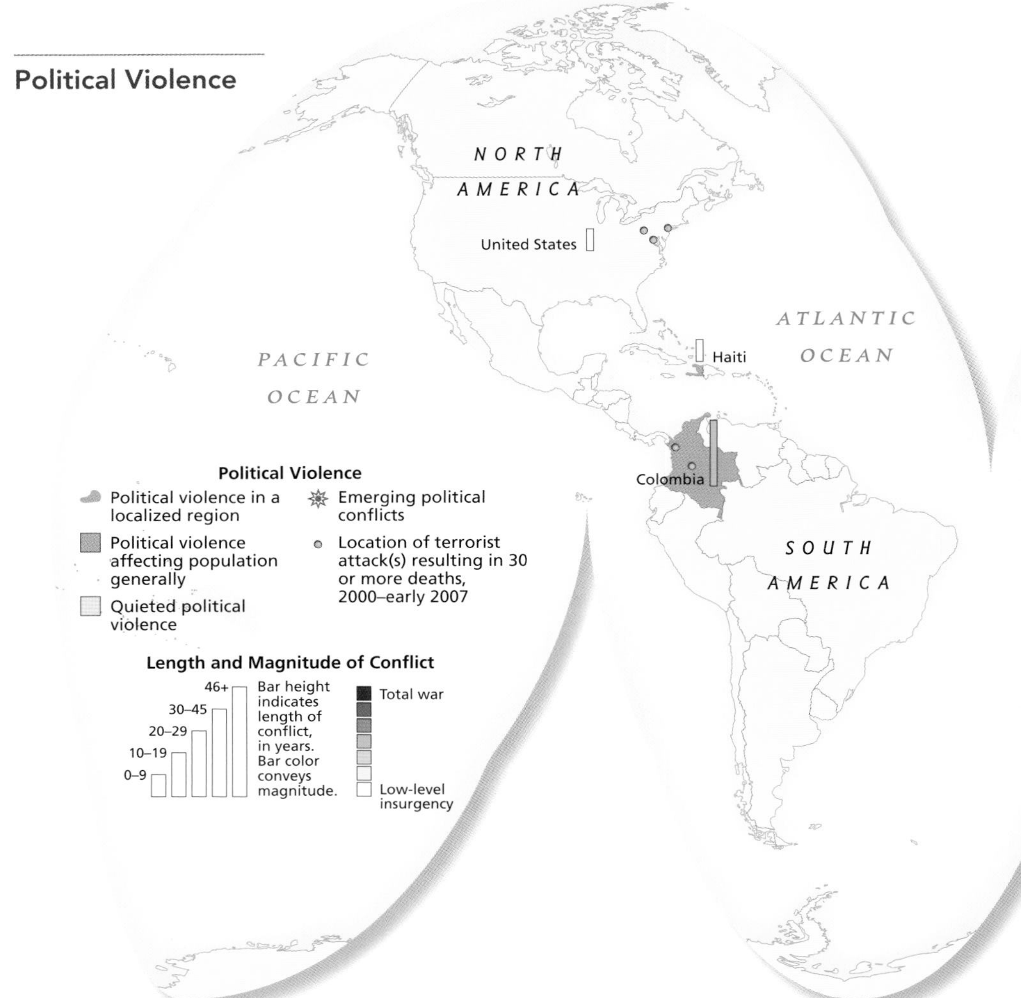

State Fragility

The quality of a government's response to rising tensions is the most crucial factor in the management of political conflict. "State fragility" gauges a country's vulnerability to civil disorder and political violence by evaluating government effectiveness and legitimacy in its four functions: security, political, economic, and social. Fragility is most serious when a government cannot provide reasonable levels of security; engages in brutal repression; lacks political accountability and responsiveness; excludes or marginalizes social groups; suffers poverty and inadequate development; fails to manage growth or reinvest; and neglects the well-being and key aspirations of its citizens. State fragility has lessened since the end of the Cold War, but remains a serious challenge in many African and Muslim countries.

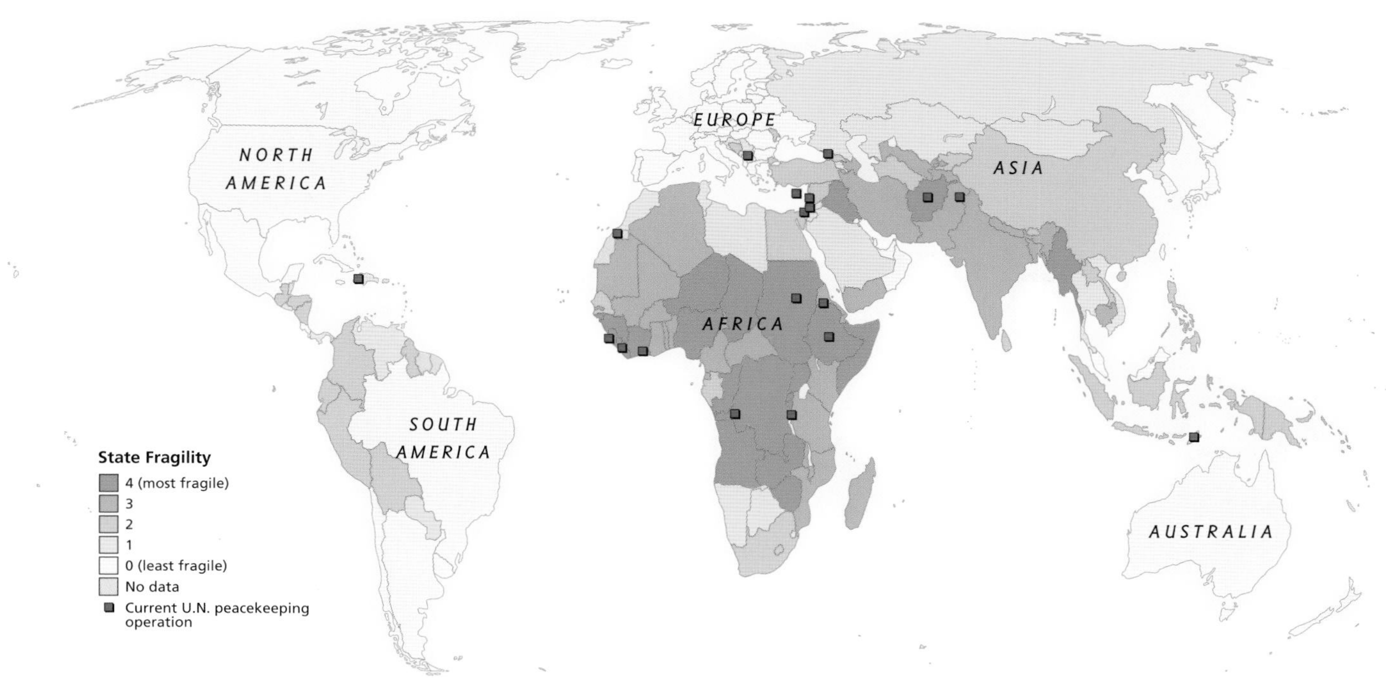

Change in Magnitude of Ongoing Conflicts

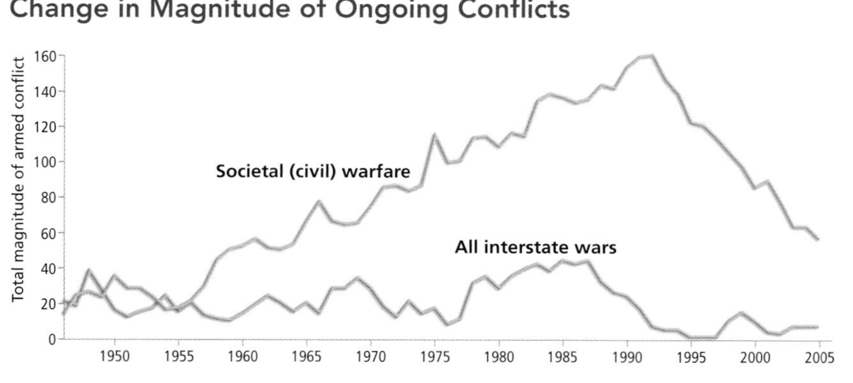

Global Regimes by Type

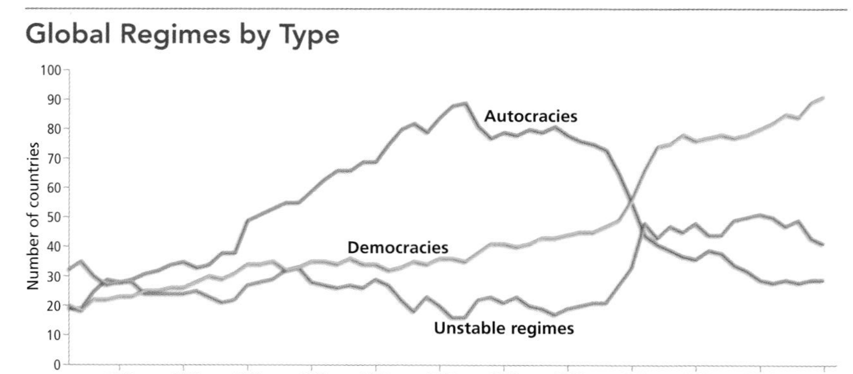

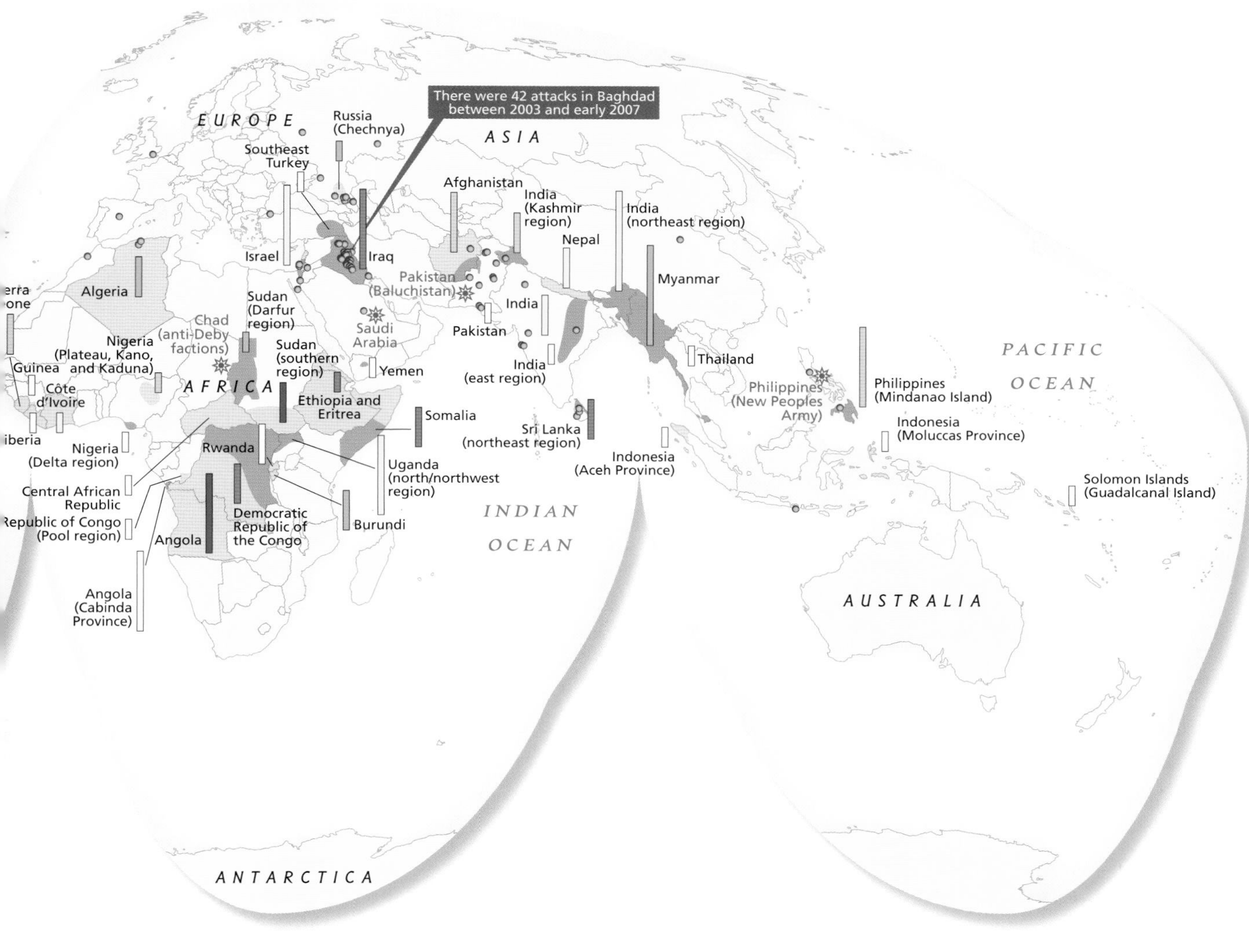

Terrorist Attacks

"Terrorism" has a special connotation with violent attacks on civilians. The vast majority of such attacks are domestic; both state and non-state actors can engage in terror tactics. "International terrorism" is a special subset of attacks linked to globalization in which militants go abroad to strike their targets, select domestic targets linked to a foreign state, or attack international transports such as planes or ships. The intentional bombing of civilian targets has become a common tactic in the wars of the early 21st century.

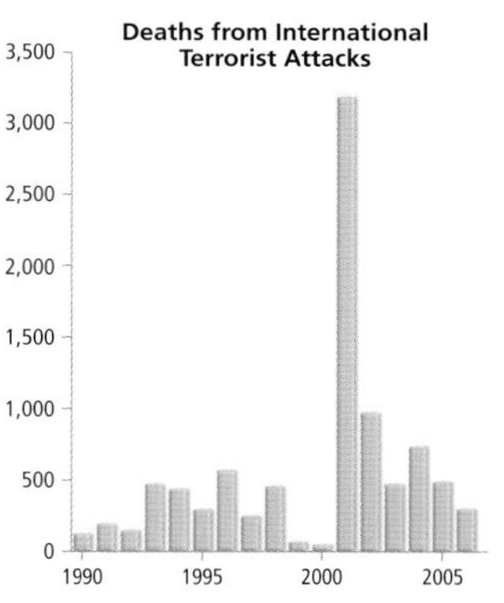

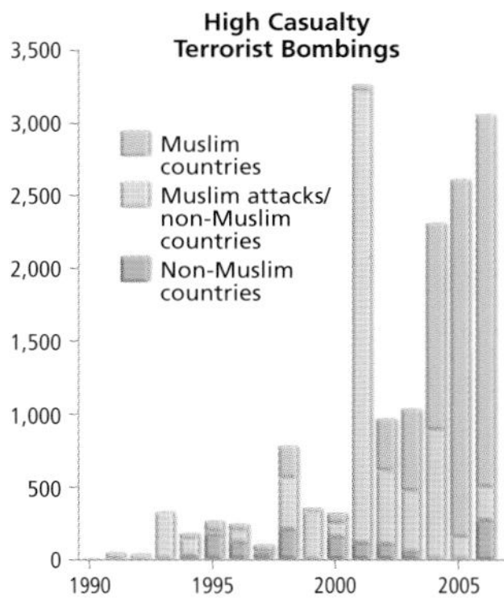

Genocides and Politicides Since 1955

Our worst fears are realized when governments are directly involved in killing their own, unarmed citizens. Lethal repression is most often associated with autocratic regimes; its most extreme forms are termed genocide and politicide. These policies involve the intentional destruction, in whole or in part, of a communal or ethnic group (genocide) or opposition group (politicide). "Death squads" and "ethnic cleansing" have brutalized populations in 29 countries at various times since 1955.

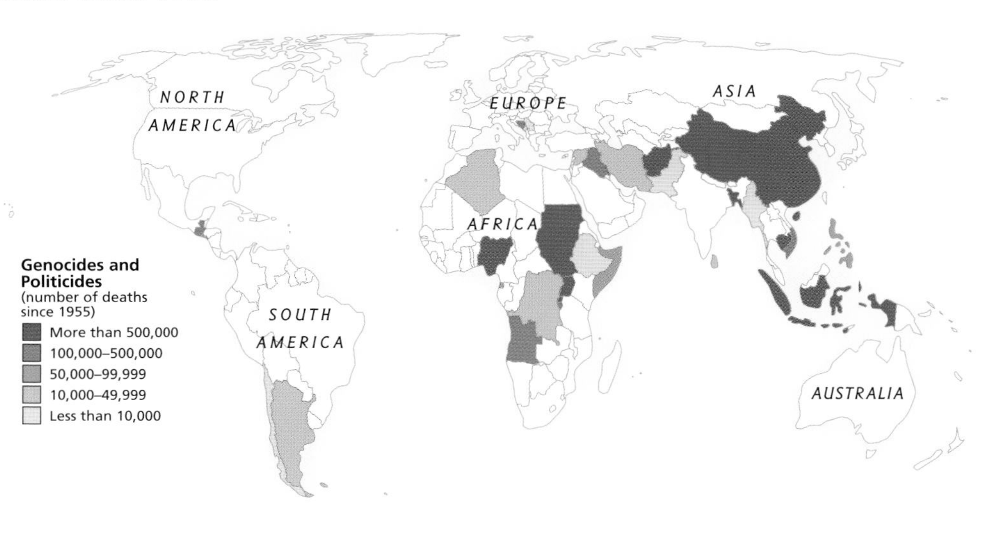

Weapons Possessions

	Nuclear: Declared stockpile	Nuclear: Suspected or undeclared program	Chemical: Declared stockpile now being destroyed	Chemical: Undeclared stockpile or development program	Biological: Suspected offensive development program
Albania			●		
China	●			●	●
Egypt				●	●
France	●				
India	●		●		
Iran		●		●	●
Israel	●			●	●
Libya			●		
North Korea		●		●	●
Pakistan	●				
Russia	●		●		●
South Korea			●		
Syria				●	●
United Kingdom	●				
United States	●		●		

The proliferation of weapons of mass destruction (WMD) is a principal concern in the 21st century. State fragility and official corruption increase the possibilities that these modern technologies might fall into the wrong hands and be a source of terror, extortion, or war.

Refugees

Refugees are persons who have fled their country of origin due to fear of persecution for reasons of, for example, race, religion, or political opinion. IDPs (internally displaced persons) are often displaced for the same reasons as refugees, but they still reside in their country of origin. By the end of 2005, the global number of refugees was nearly 12 million persons; the number of IDPs worldwide was just under 21 million.

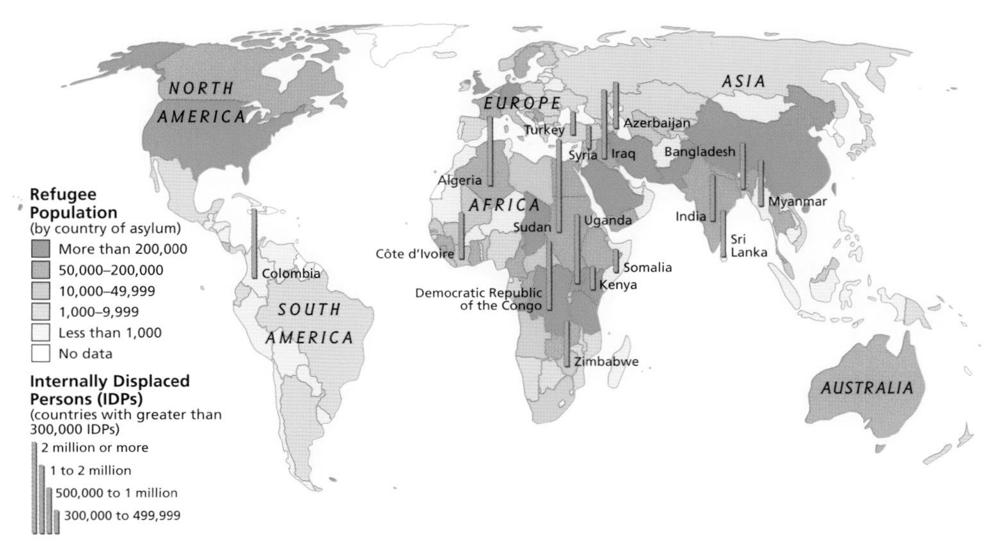

MOST ENVIRONMENTAL DAMAGE is due to human activity. Some harmful actions are inadvertent—the release, for example, of chlorofluorocarbons (CFCs), once thought to be inert gases, into the atmosphere. Others are deliberate and include such acts as the disposal of sewage into rivers.

Among the root causes of human-induced damage are excessive consumption (mainly in industrialized countries) and rapid population growth (primarily in the developing nations). So, even though scientists may develop products and technologies that have no adverse effects on the environment, their efforts will be muted if both population and consumption continue to increase worldwide.

Socioeconomic and environmental indicators can reveal much about long-term trends; unfortunately, such data are not collected routinely in many countries. With respect to urban environmental quality, suitable indicators would include electricity consumption, numbers of automobiles, and rates of land conversion from rural to urban. The rapid conversion of countryside to built-up areas during the last 25 to 50 years is a strong indicator that change is occurring at an ever-quickening pace.

Many types of environmental stress are interrelated and may have far-reaching consequences. Global warming, for one, will likely increase water scarcity, desertification, deforestation, and coastal flooding (due to rising sea level)—all of which can have a significant impact on human populations.

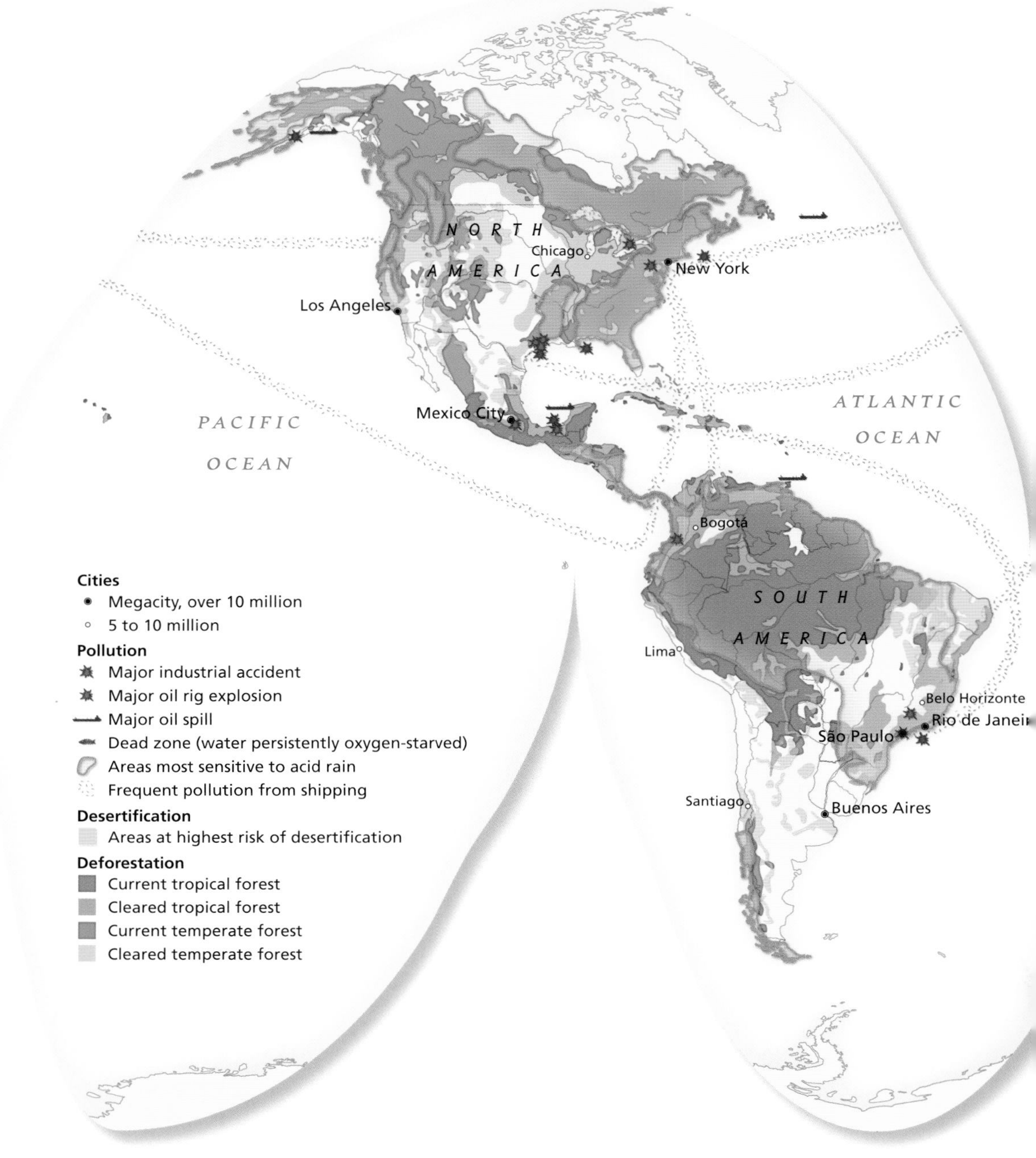

Global Climate Change

The world's climate is constantly changing—over decades, centuries, and millennia. Currently, several lines of reasoning support the idea that humans are likely to live in a much warmer world before the end of this century. Atmospheric concentrations of carbon dioxide and other "greenhouse gases" are now well above historical levels, and simulation models predict that these gases will result in a warming of the lower atmosphere (particularly in polar regions) but a cooling of the stratosphere. Experimental evidence supports these predictions.

Indeed, throughout the last decade the globally averaged annual surface temperature was higher than the hundred-year mean. Model simulations of the impacts of this warming—and studies indicating significant reductions already occurring in polar permafrost and sea ice cover—are so alarming that most scientists and many policy people believe that immediate action must be taken to slow the changes.

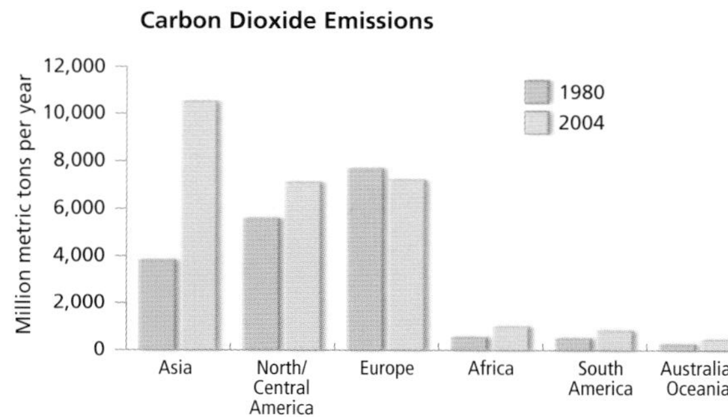

Depletion of the Ozone Layer

The ozone layer in the stratosphere has long shielded the biosphere from harmful solar ultraviolet radiation. Since the 1970s, however, the layer has been thinning over Antarctica—and more recently elsewhere. If the process continues, there will be significant effects on human health, including more cases of skin cancer and eye cataracts, and on biological systems. Fortunately, scientific understanding of the phenomenon came rather quickly.

Beginning in the 1950s, increasing amounts of CFCs (and other gases with similar properties) were released into the atmosphere. CFCs are chemically inert in the lower atmosphere but decompose in the stratosphere, subsequently destroying ozone. This understanding provided the basis for successful United Nations actions (Vienna Convention, 1985; Montréal Protocol, 1987) to phase out these gases.

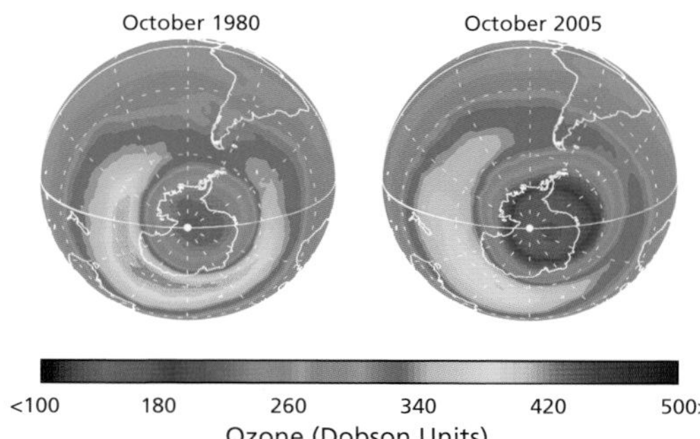

Pollution

People know that water is not always pure and that beaches may be closed to bathers due to raw sewage. An example of serious contamination is the Minamata, Japan, disaster of the 1950s. More than a hundred people died and thousands were paralyzed after they ate fish containing mercury discharged from a local factory. Examples of water and soil pollution also include the contamination of groundwater, salinization of irrigated lands in semiarid regions, and the so-called chemical time bomb issue, where accumulated toxins are suddenly mobilized following a change in external conditions. Preventing and mitigating such problems requires the modernization of industrial plants, additional staff training, a better understanding of the problems, the development of more effective policies, and greater public support.

Urban air quality remains a serious problem, particularly in developing countries. In some developed countries, successful control measures have improved air quality over the past 50 years; in others, trends have actually reversed, with brown haze often hanging over metropolitan areas.

Solid and hazardous waste disposal is a universal urban problem, and the issue is on many political agendas. In the world's poorest countries, "garbage pickers" (usually women and children) are symbols of abject poverty. In North America, toxic wastes are frequently transported long distances. But transport introduces the risk of highway and rail accidents, causing serious local contamination.

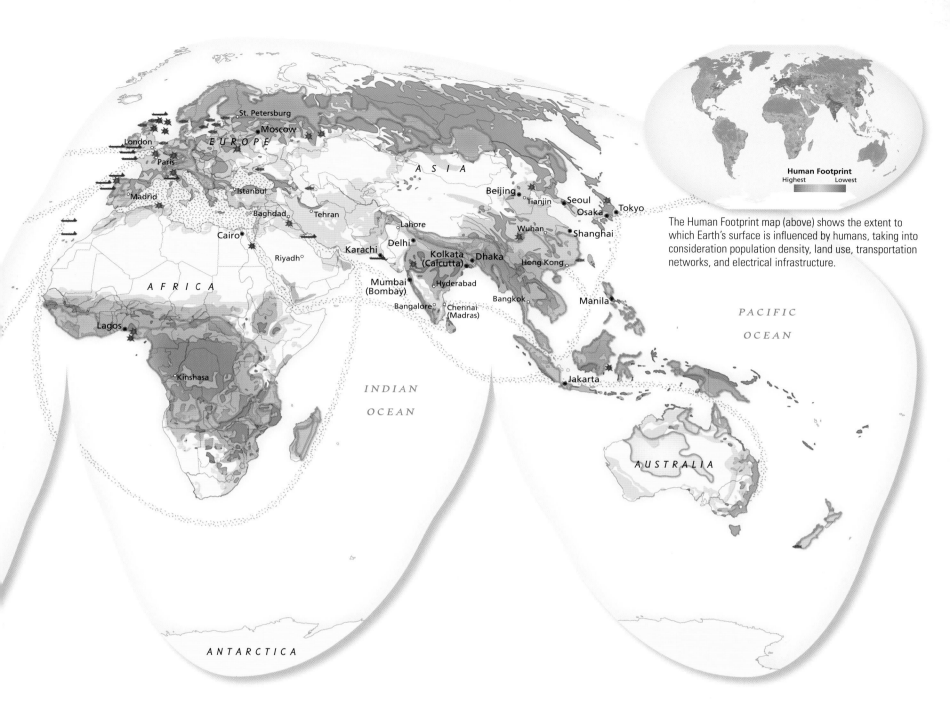

The Human Footprint map (above) shows the extent to which Earth's surface is influenced by humans, taking into consideration population density, land use, transportation networks, and electrical infrastructure.

Water Scarcity

Shortages of drinking water are increasing in many parts of the world, and studies indicate that by the year 2025, one billion people in northern China, Afghanistan, Pakistan, Iraq, Egypt, Tunisia, and other areas will face "absolute drinking water scarcity." But water is also needed by industry and agriculture, in hydroelectric-power production, and for transport. With increasing population, industrialization, and global warming, the situation can only worsen.

Water scarcity has already applied a major brake on development in many countries, including Poland, Singapore, and parts of North America. In countries where artesian wells are pumping groundwater more rapidly than it can be replaced, water is actually being mined. In river basins where water is shared by several jurisdictions, social tensions will increase. This is particularly so in the Middle East, North Africa, and East Africa, where the availability of fresh water is less than 1,300 cubic yards (1,000 cu m) per capita per annum; water-rich countries such as Iceland, New Zealand, and Canada enjoy more than a hundred times as much.

Irrigation can be a particularly wasteful use of water. Some citrus-growing nations, for example, are exporting not only fruit but also so-called virtual water, which includes the water inside the fruit as well as the wasted irrigation water that drains away from the orchards. Many individuals and organizations believe that water scarcity is the major environmental issue of the 21st century.

Soil Degradation and Desertification

Deserts exist where rainfall is too little and too erratic to support life except in a few favored localities. Even in these "oases," occasional sandstorms may inhibit agricultural activity. In semiarid zones, lands can easily become degraded or desert-like if they are overused or subject to long or frequent drought. The Sahel of Africa faced this situation in the 1970s and early 1980s, but rainfall subsequently returned to normal, and some of the land recovered.

Often, an extended drought over a wide area can trigger desertification if the land has already been degraded by human actions. Causes of degradation include overgrazing, overcultivation, deforestation, soil erosion, overconsumption of groundwater, and the salinization/waterlogging of irrigated lands.

An emerging issue is the effect of climate warming on desertification. Warming will probably lead to more drought in more parts of the world. Glaciers would begin to disappear, and the meltwater flowing through semiarid downstream areas would diminish.

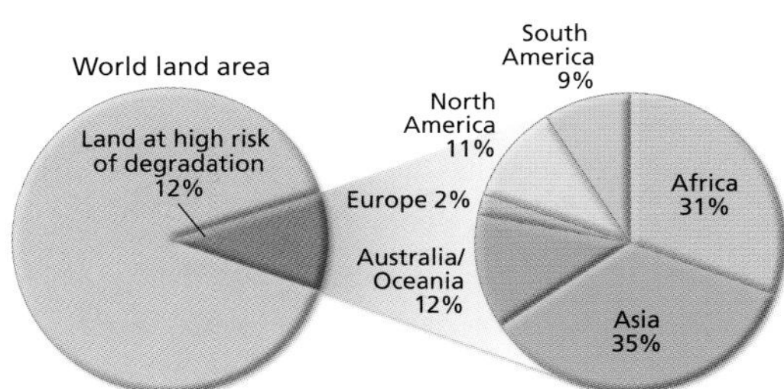

Deforestation

Widespread deforestation in the wet tropics is largely the result of short-term and unsustainable uses. In Mexico, Brazil, and Peru, only 30, 42, and 45 percent (respectively) of the total land still has a closed forest cover. International agencies such as FAO, UNEP, UNESCO, WWF/IUCN, and others are working to improve the situation through education, restoration, and land protection. Venezuela enjoys a very high level of forest protection (63 percent); by comparison, Russia protects just 2 percent.

The loss of forests has contributed to the atmospheric buildup of carbon dioxide (a greenhouse gas), changes in rainfall patterns (in Brazil at least), soil erosion, and soil nutrient losses. Deforestation in the wet tropics, where more than half of the world's species live, is the main cause of biodiversity loss.

In contrast to the tropics, the forest cover in the temperate zones has increased slightly in the last 50 years because of the adoption of conservation practices and because abandoned farmland has been replaced by forest.

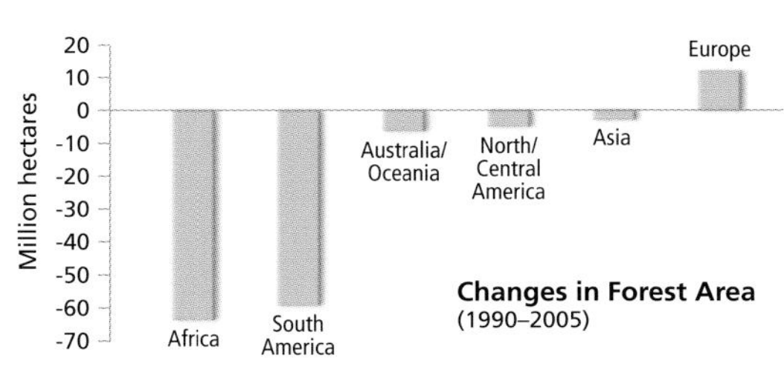

World Geographic Comparisons

THE EARTH

Mass: 5,974,000,000,000,000,000,000 (5.974 sextillion) metric tons

Total Area: 510,066,000 sq km (196,938,000 sq mi)

Land Area: 148,647,000 sq km (57,393,000 sq mi), 29.1% of total

Water Area: 361,419,000 sq km (139,545,000 sq mi), 70.9% of total

Population: 6,555,336,000

THE EARTH'S EXTREMES

Hottest Place: Dalol, Danakil Depression, Ethiopia, annual average temperature 34°C (93°F)

Coldest Place: Plateau Station, Antarctica, annual average temperature -56.7°C (-70°F)

Hottest Recorded Temperature: Al Aziziyah, Libya 58°C (136.4°F), September 3, 1922

Coldest Recorded Temperature: Vostok, Antarctica -89.2°C (-128.6°F), July 21, 1983

Wettest Place: Mawsynram, Assam, India, annual average rainfall 1,187 cm (467 in)

Driest Place: Arica, Atacama Desert, Chile, rainfall barely measurable

Highest Waterfall: Angel Falls, Venezuela 979 m (3,212 ft)

Largest Hot Desert: Sahara, Africa 9,000,000 sq km (3,475,000 sq mi)

Largest Ice Desert: Antarctica 13,209,000 sq km (5,100,000 sq mi)

Largest Canyon: Grand Canyon, Colorado River, Arizona 446 km (277 mi) long along river, 180 m (600 ft) to 29 km (18 mi) wide, about 1.8 km (1.1 mi) deep

Largest Cave Chamber: Sarawak Cave, Gunung Mulu National Park, Malaysia 16 hectares and 79 meters high (40.2 acres and 260 feet)

Largest Cave System: Mammoth Cave, Kentucky, over 530 km (330 mi) of passageways mapped

Most Predictable Geyser: Old Faithful, Wyoming, annual average interval 66 to 80 minutes

Longest Reef: Great Barrier Reef, Australia 2,300 km (1,429 mi)

Greatest Tidal Range: Bay of Fundy, Canadian Atlantic Coast 16 m (52 ft)

AREA OF EACH CONTINENT

	SQ KM	SQ MI	PERCENT OF EARTH'S LAND
Asia	44,570,000	17,208,000	30.0
Africa	30,065,000	11,608,000	20.2
North America	24,474,000	9,449,000	16.5
South America	17,819,000	6,880,000	12.0
Antarctica	13,209,000	5,100,000	8.9
Europe	9,947,000	3,841,000	6.7
Australia	7,687,000	2,968,000	5.2

HIGHEST POINT ON EACH CONTINENT

	METERS	FEET
Mount Everest, Asia	8,850	29,035
Cerro Aconcagua, South America	6,960	22,834
Mount McKinley (Denali), N. America	6,194	20,320
Kilimanjaro, Africa	5,895	19,340
El'brus, Europe	5,642	18,510
Vinson Massif, Antarctica	4,897	16,067
Mount Kosciuszko, Australia	2,228	7,310

LOWEST SURFACE POINT ON EACH CONTINENT

	METERS	FEET
Dead Sea, Asia	-416	-1,365
Lake Assal, Africa	-156	-512
Laguna del Carbón, South America	-105	-344
Death Valley, North America	-86	-282
Caspian Sea, Europe	-28	-92
Lake Eyre, Australia	-16	-52
Bentley Subglacial Trench, Antarctica	-2,555	-8,383

LARGEST ISLANDS

	AREA SQ KM	AREA SQ MI
1 Greenland	2,166,000	836,000
2 New Guinea	792,500	306,000
3 Borneo	725,500	280,100
4 Madagascar	587,000	226,600
5 Baffin Island	507,500	196,000
6 Sumatra	427,300	165,000
7 Honshu	227,400	87,800
8 Great Britain	218,100	84,200
9 Victoria Island	217,300	83,900
10 Ellesmere Island	196,200	75,800
11 Sulawesi (Celebes)	178,700	69,000
12 South Island (New Zealand)	150,400	58,100
13 Java	126,700	48,900
14 North Island (New Zealand)	113,700	43,900
15 Island of Newfoundland	108,900	42,000

LARGEST DRAINAGE BASINS

	AREA SQ KM	AREA SQ MI
1 Amazon, South America	7,050,000	2,721,000
2 Congo, Africa	3,700,000	1,428,000
3 Mississippi-Missouri, North America	3,250,000	1,255,000
4 Paraná, South America	3,100,000	1,197,000
5 Yenisey-Angara, Asia	2,700,000	1,042,000
6 Ob-Irtysh, Asia	2,430,000	938,000
7 Lena, Asia	2,420,000	934,000
8 Nile, Africa	1,900,000	733,400
9 Amur, Asia	1,840,000	710,000
10 Mackenzie-Peace, North America	1,765,000	681,000
11 Ganges-Brahmaputra, Asia	1,730,000	668,000
12 Volga, Europe	1,380,000	533,000
13 Zambezi, Africa	1,330,000	513,000
14 Niger, Africa	1,200,000	463,000
15 Chang Jiang (Yangtze), Asia	1,175,000	454,000

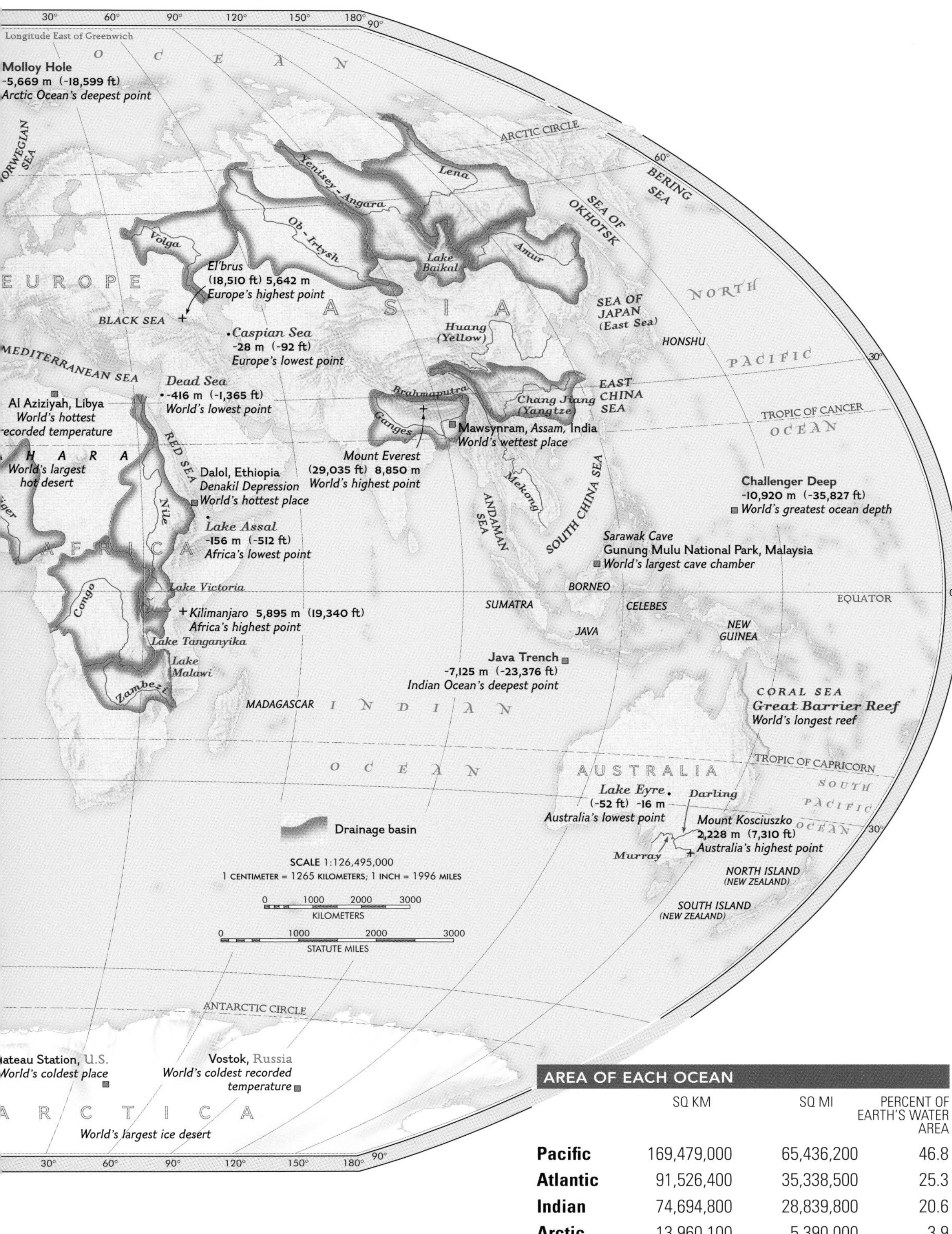

GEOPOLITICAL EXTREMES

Largest Country: Russia 17,075,400 sq km (6,592,850 sq mi)

Smallest Country: Vatican City 0.4 sq km (0.2 sq mi)

Most Populous Country: China 1,341,715,000 people

Least Populous Country: Vatican City 800 people

Most Crowded Country: Monaco 16,923 per sq km (44,000 per sq mi)

Least Crowded Country: Mongolia 1.6 per sq km (4.3 per sq mi)

Largest Metropolitan Area: Tokyo 35,197,000 people

Country with the Greatest Number of Bordering Countries: China 14, Russia 14

ENGINEERING WONDERS

Tallest Office Building: Taipei 101, Taipei, Taiwan 508 m (1,667 ft)

Tallest Tower (Freestanding): CN Tower, Toronto, Canada 553 m (1,815 ft)

Tallest Manmade Structure: KVLY TV tower, near Fargo, North Dakota 629 m (2,063 ft)

Longest Wall: Great Wall of China, approx. 3,460 km (2,150 mi)

Longest Road: Pan-American highway (not including gap in Panama and Colombia), more than 24,140 km (15,000 mi)

Longest Railroad: Trans-Siberian Railroad, Russia 9,288 km (5,772 mi)

Longest Road Tunnel: Laerdal Tunnel, Laerdal, Norway 24.5 km (15.2 mi)

Longest Rail Tunnel: Seikan submarine rail tunnel, Honshu to Hokkaido, Japan 53.9 km (33.5 mi)

Highest Bridge: Millau Viaduct, France 343 m (1,125 ft)

Longest Highway Bridge: Lake Pontchartrain Causeway, Louisiana 38.4 km (23.9 mi)

Longest Suspension Bridge: Akashi-Kaikyo Bridge, Japan 3,911 m (12,831 ft)

Longest Boat Canal: Grand Canal, China, over 1,770 km (1,100 mi)

Longest Irrigation Canal: Garagum Canal, Turkmenistan, nearly 1,100 km (700 mi)

Largest Artificial Lake: Lake Volta, Volta River, Ghana 9,065 sq km (3,500 sq mi)

Tallest Dam: Rogun Dam, Vakhsh River, Tajikistan 335 m (1,099 ft)

Tallest Pyramid: Great Pyramid of Khufu, Egypt 137 m (450 ft)

Deepest Mine: Savuka Mine, South Africa approx. 4 km (2.5 mi) deep

Longest Submarine Cable: Sea-Me-We 3 cable, connects 33 countries on four continents, 39,000 km (24,200 mi) long

AREA OF EACH OCEAN

	SQ KM	SQ MI	PERCENT OF EARTH'S WATER AREA
Pacific	169,479,000	65,436,200	46.8
Atlantic	91,526,400	35,338,500	25.3
Indian	74,694,800	28,839,800	20.6
Arctic	13,960,100	5,390,000	3.9

LONGEST RIVERS

	KM	MI
1 **Nile, Africa**	6,825	4,241
2 **Amazon, South America**	6,437	4,000
3 **Chang Jiang (Yangtze), Asia**	6,380	3,964
4 **Mississippi-Missouri, North America**	5,971	3,710
5 **Yenisey-Angara, Asia**	5,536	3,440
6 **Huang (Yellow), Asia**	5,464	3,395
7 **Ob-Irtysh, Asia**	5,410	3,362
8 **Amur, Asia**	4,416	2,744
9 **Lena, Asia**	4,400	2,734
10 **Congo, Africa**	4,370	2,715
11 **Mackenzie-Peace, North America**	4,241	2,635
12 **Mekong, Asia**	4,184	2,600
13 **Niger, Africa**	4,170	2,591
14 **Paraná-Río de la Plata, S. America**	4,000	2,485
15 **Murray-Darling, Australia**	3,718	2,310
16 **Volga, Europe**	3,685	2,290
17 **Purus, South America**	3,380	2,100

DEEPEST POINT IN EACH OCEAN

	METERS	FEET
Challenger Deep, Pacific Ocean	-10,920	-35,827
Puerto Rico Trench, Atlantic Ocean	-8,605	-28,232
Java Trench, Indian Ocean	-7,125	-23,376
Molloy Hole, Arctic Ocean	-5,669	-18,599

LARGEST LAKES BY AREA

	AREA SQ KM	AREA SQ MI	MAXIMUM DEPTH METERS	MAXIMUM DEPTH FEET
1 **Caspian Sea**	371,000	143,200	1,025	3,363
2 **Lake Superior**	82,100	31,700	406	1,332
3 **Lake Victoria**	69,500	26,800	82	269
4 **Lake Huron**	59,600	23,000	229	751
5 **Lake Michigan**	57,800	22,300	281	922
6 **Lake Tanganyika**	32,600	12,600	1,470	4,823
7 **Lake Baikal**	31,500	12,200	1,637	5,371
8 **Great Bear Lake**	31,300	12,100	446	1,463
9 **Lake Malawi**	28,900	11,200	695	2,280
10 **Great Slave Lake**	28,600	11,000	614	2,014

LARGEST SEAS BY AREA

	AREA SQ KM	AREA SQ MI	AVGERAGE DEPTH METERS	AVGERAGE DEPTH FEET
1 **Coral Sea**	4,183,510	1,615,260	2,471	8,107
2 **South China Sea**	3,596,390	1,388,570	1,180	3,871
3 **Caribbean Sea**	2,834,290	1,094,330	2,596	8,517
4 **Bering Sea**	2,519,580	972,810	1,832	6,010
5 **Mediterranean Sea**	2,469,100	953,320	1,572	5,157
6 **Sea of Okhotsk**	1,625,190	627,490	814	2,671
7 **Gulf of Mexico**	1,531,810	591,430	1,544	5,066
8 **Norwegian Sea**	1,425,280	550,300	1,768	5,801
9 **Greenland Sea**	1,157,850	447,050	1,443	4,734
10 **Sea of Japan**	1,008,260	389,290	1,647	5,404
11 **Hudson Bay**	1,005,510	388,230	119	390
12 **East China Sea**	785,990	303,470	374	1,227
13 **Andaman Sea**	605,760	233,890	1,061	3,481
14 **Red Sea**	436,280	168,450	494	1,621

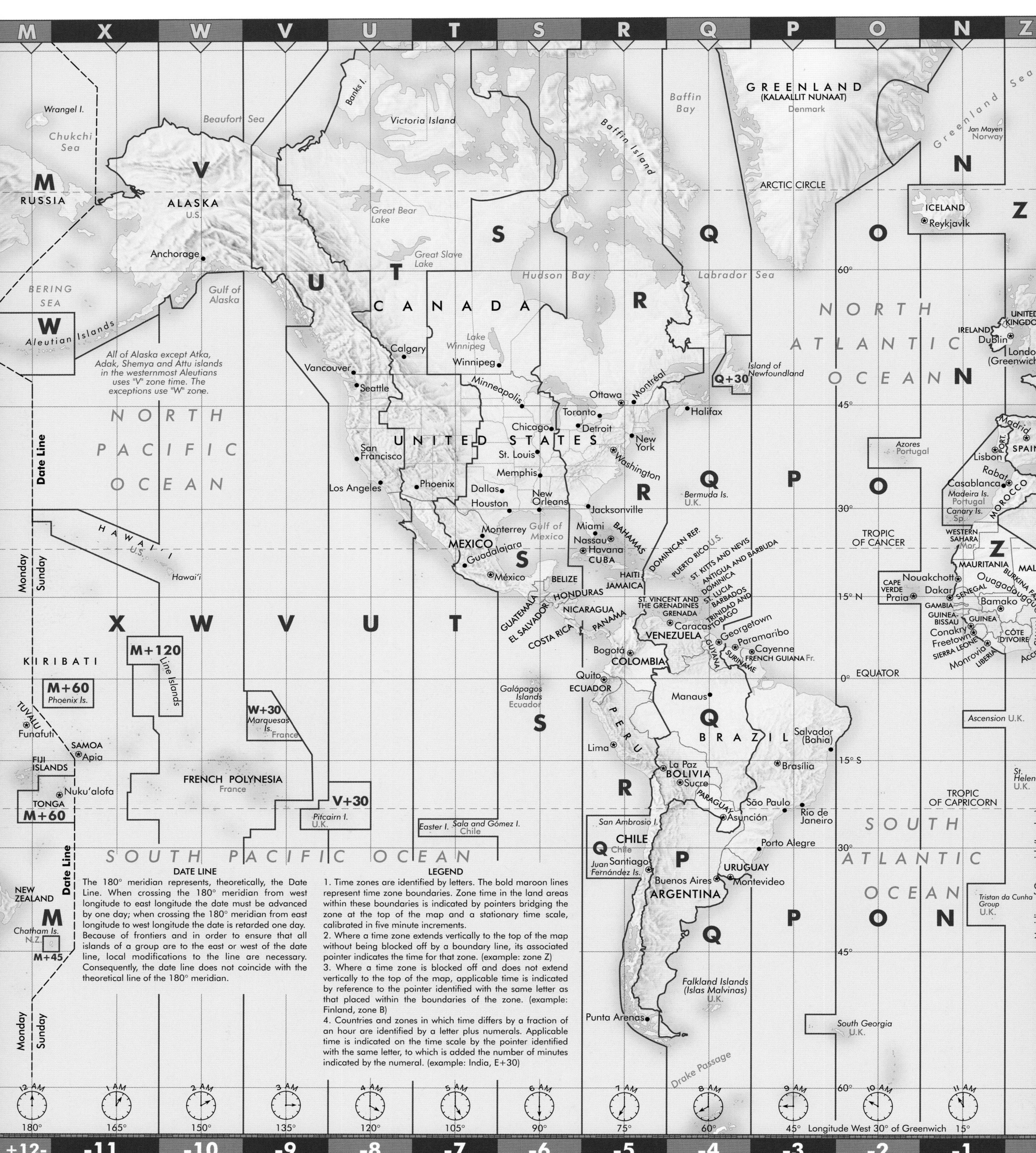

DATE LINE

The 180° meridian represents, theoretically, the Date Line. When crossing the 180° meridian from west longitude to east longitude the date must be advanced by one day; when crossing the 180° meridian from east longitude to west longitude the date is retarded one day. Because of frontiers and in order to ensure that all islands of a group are to the east or west of the date line, local modifications to the line are necessary. Consequently, the date line does not coincide with the theoretical line of the 180° meridian.

LEGEND

1. Time zones are identified by letters. The bold maroon lines represent time zone boundaries. Zone time in the land areas within these boundaries is indicated by pointers bridging the zone at the top of the map and a stationary time scale, calibrated in five minute increments.
2. Where a time zone extends vertically to the top of the map without being blocked off by a boundary line, its associated pointer indicates the time for that zone. (example: zone Z)
3. Where a time zone is blocked off and does not extend vertically to the top of the map, applicable time is indicated by reference to the pointer identified with the same letter as that placed within the boundaries of the zone. (example: Finland, zone B)
4. Countries and zones in which time differs by a fraction of an hour are identified by a letter plus numerals. Applicable time is indicated on the time scale by the pointer identified with the same letter, to which is added the number of minutes indicated by the numeral. (example: India, E+30)

The numeral in each tab directly above shows the number of hours to be added to, or subtracted from, Coordinated Universal Time (UTC), formerly Greenwich Mean Time (GMT).

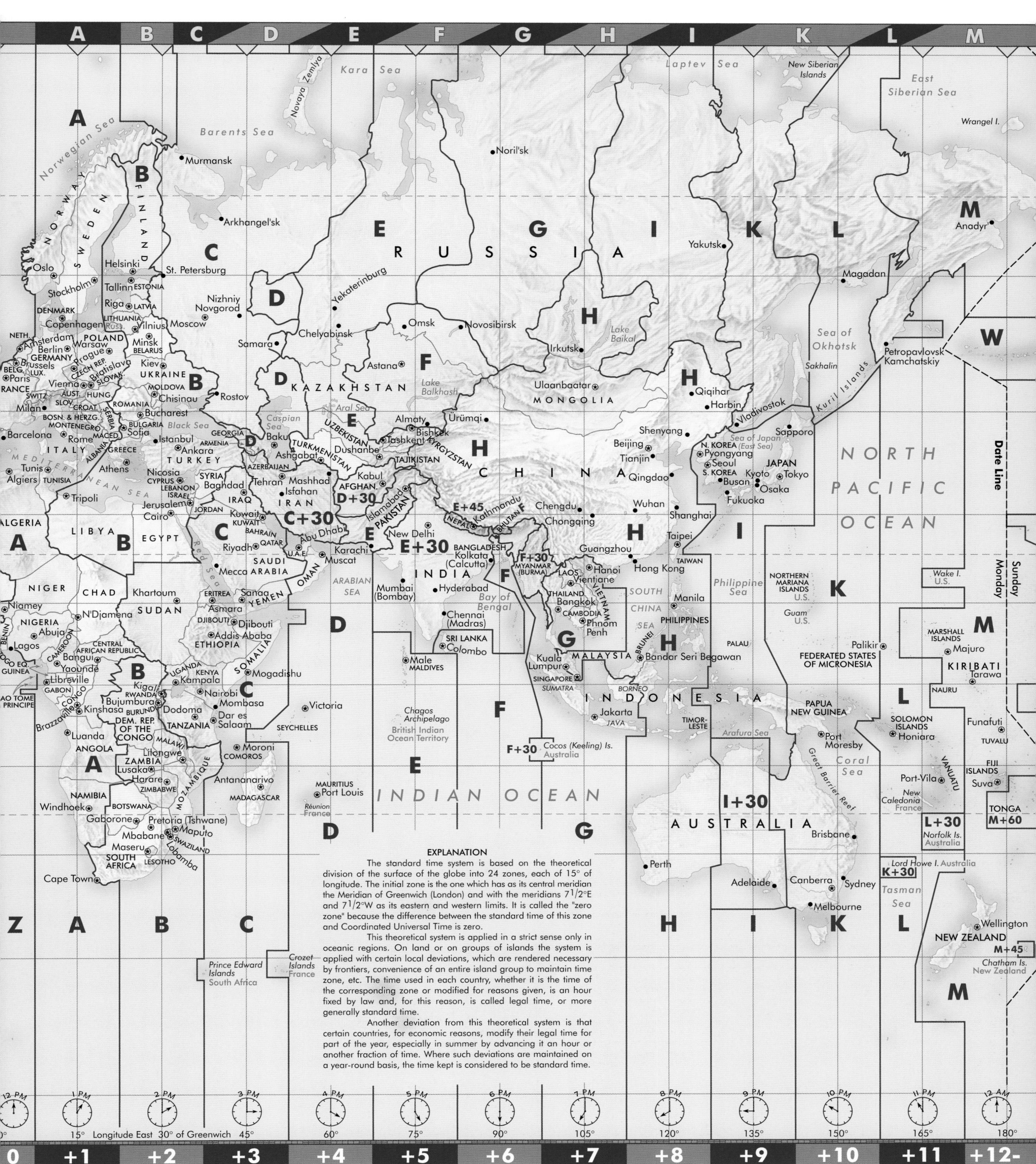

EXPLANATION

The standard time system is based on the theoretical division of the surface of the globe into 24 zones, each of 15° of longitude. The initial zone is the one which has as its central meridian the Meridian of Greenwich (London) and with the meridians $7^1/2$°E and $7^1/2$°W as its eastern and western limits. It is called the "zero zone" because the difference between the standard time of this zone and Coordinated Universal Time is zero.

This theoretical system is applied in a strict sense only in oceanic regions. On land or on groups of islands the system is applied with certain local deviations, which are rendered necessary by frontiers, convenience of an entire island group to maintain time zone, etc. The time used in each country, whether it is the time of the corresponding zone or modified for reasons given, is an hour fixed by law and, for this reason, is called legal time, or more generally standard time.

Another deviation from this theoretical system is that certain countries, for economic reasons, modify their legal time for part of the year, especially in summer by advancing it an hour or another fraction of time. Where such deviations are maintained on a year-round basis, the time kept is considered to be standard time.

Mercator Projection

Land Cover
Water
Evergreen needleleaf forest
Evergreen broadleaf forest
Deciduous broadleaf forest
Mixed forest
Closed shrubland
Open shrubland
Woody savanna
Savanna
Grassland
Permanent wetland
Cropland
Urban and built-up
Cropland/natural vegetation mosaic
Snow and ice
Barren or sparsely vegetated

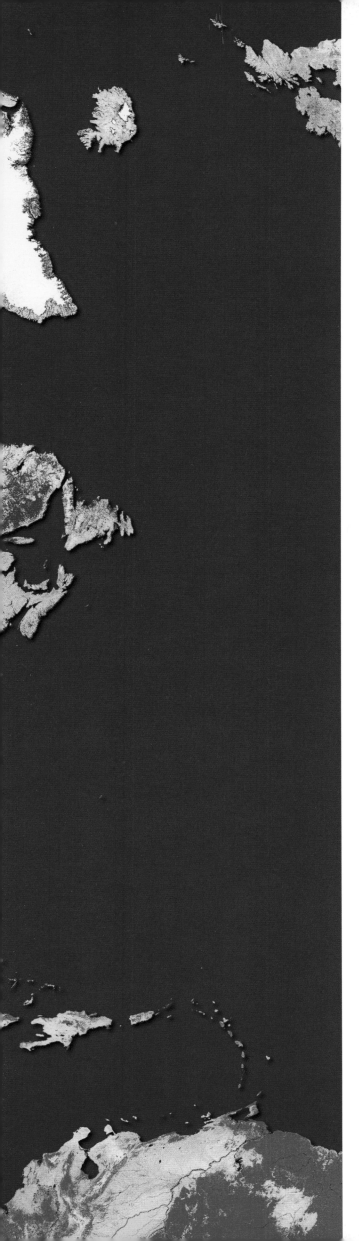

North America

LOCATED BETWEEN THE ATLANTIC, Pacific, and Arctic Oceans, North America is almost an island unto itself, connected to the rest of the world only by the tenuous thread running through the Isthmus of Panama. Geologically old in some places, young in others, and diverse throughout, the continent sweeps from Arctic tundra in the north through the plains, prairies, and deserts of the interior to the tropical rain forests of Central America. Its eastern coastal plain is furrowed by broad rivers that drain worn and ancient mountain ranges, while in the West younger and more robust ranges thrust their still-growing high peaks skyward. Though humans have peopled the continent for perhaps as long as 40,000 years, political boundaries were unknown there until some 400 years ago when European settlers imprinted the land with their ideas of ownership. Despite, or perhaps because of, its relative youth—and its geographic location—most of North America has remained remarkably stable. In the past century, when country borders throughout much of the rest of the world have altered dramatically, they have changed little in North America, while the system of government by democratic rule, first rooted in this continent's soil in the 18th century, has spread to many corners of the globe.

Third largest of the Earth's continents, North America seems made for human habitation. Its waterways—the inland seas of Hudson Bay and the Great Lakes, the enormous Mississippi system draining its midsection, and the countless navigable rivers of the East—have long provided natural corridors for human commerce. In its vast interior, the nurturing soils of plains and prairies have offered up bountiful harvests, while rich deposits of oil and gas have fueled industrial growth, making this continent's mainland one of the world's economic powerhouses.

Just in the past couple of centuries, North America has experienced dramatic changes in its population, landscapes, and environment, an incredible transformation brought about by waves of immigration, booming economies, and relentless development. During the 20th century, the United States and Canada managed to propel themselves into the ranks of the world's richest nations. But success has brought a host of concerns, not the least of which involves the continued exploitation of natural resources. North America is home to roughly eight percent of the planet's people, yet its per capita consumption of energy is almost six times as great as the average for all other continents.

The United States ended the 20th century as the only true superpower, with a military presence and political, economic, and cultural influences that extend around the globe. But the rest of the continent south of the U.S. failed to keep pace, plagued by poverty, despotic governments, and social unrest. Poverty has spurred millions of Mexicans, Central Americans, and Caribbean islanders to migrate northward (legally and illegally) in search of better lives. Finding ways to integrate these disenfranchised masses into the continent's economic miracle is one of the greatest challenges facing North America in the 21st century.

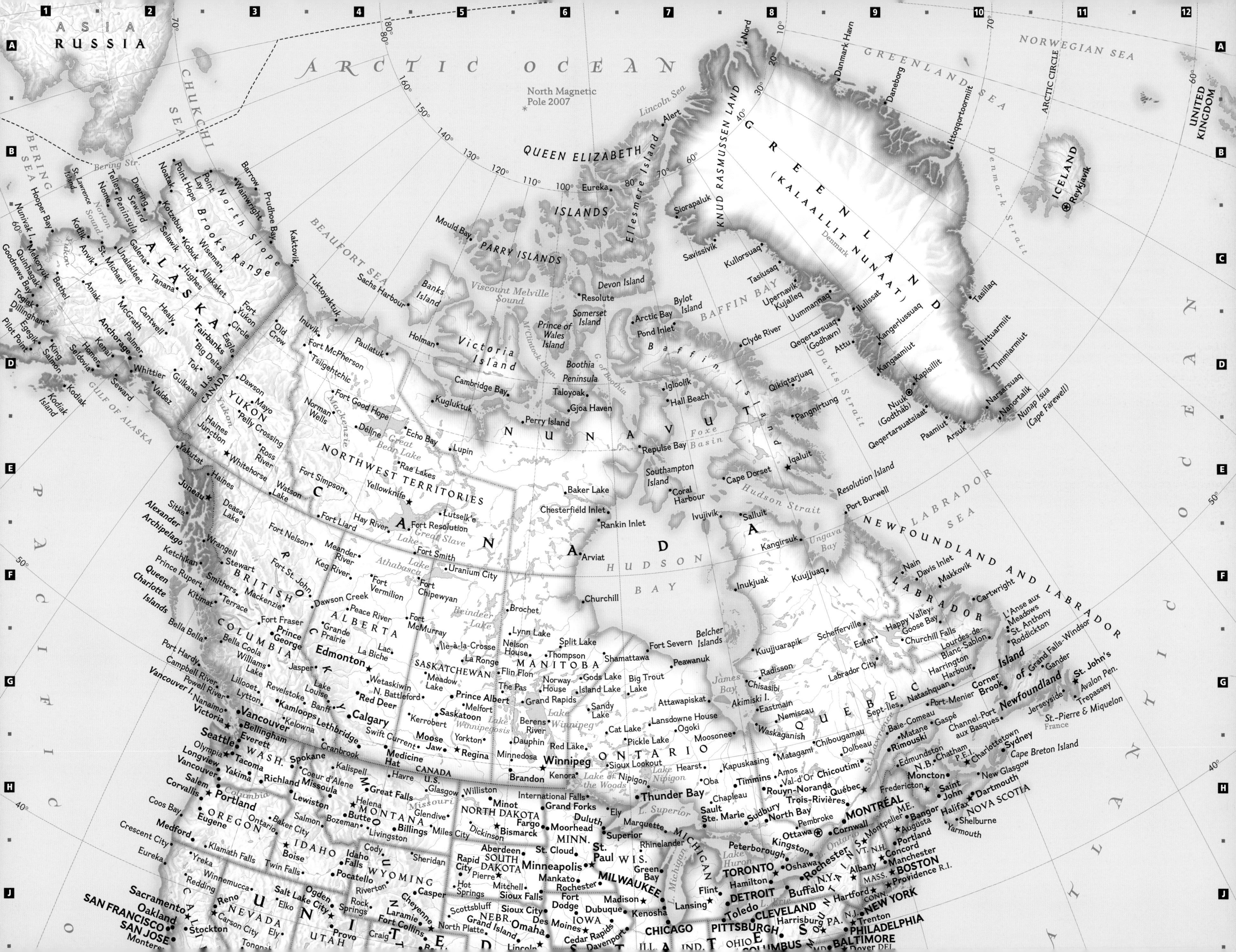

ASIA
RUSSIA
ARCTIC OCEAN
ATLANTIC OCEAN
PACIFIC OCEAN
North Magnetic Pole 2007
CHUKCHI SEA
BERING SEA
Bering Str.
BEAUFORT SEA
Lincoln Sea
QUEEN ELIZABETH ISLANDS
PARRY ISLANDS
Ellesmere Island
Victoria Island
Banks Island
Baffin Island
BAFFIN BAY
Davis Strait
Foxe Basin
Hudson Strait
HUDSON BAY
James Bay
Ungava Bay
LABRADOR SEA
GREENLAND (KALAALLIT NUNAAT)
Denmark
KNUD RASMUSSEN LAND
GREENLAND SEA
NORWEGIAN SEA
Denmark Strait
ARCTIC CIRCLE
ICELAND
Reykjavík
UNITED KINGDOM
ALASKA
Brooks Range
North Slope
GULF OF ALASKA
U.S.
CANADA
YUKON
NORTHWEST TERRITORIES
NUNAVUT
BRITISH COLUMBIA
ALBERTA
SASKATCHEWAN
MANITOBA
ONTARIO
QUEBEC
LABRADOR
NEWFOUNDLAND AND LABRADOR
Island of Newfoundland
N.B.
P.E.I.
NOVA SCOTIA
St.-Pierre & Miquelon
France
WASH.
OREGON
IDAHO
MONTANA
WYOMING
NEVADA
UTAH
NORTH DAKOTA
SOUTH DAKOTA
NEBR.
MINN.
IOWA
WIS.
MICHIGAN
Anchorage
Fairbanks
Juneau
Whitehorse
Yellowknife
Iqaluit
Nuuk (Godthåb)
Edmonton
Calgary
Regina
Winnipeg
Vancouver
Victoria
Seattle
Portland
TORONTO
Ottawa
MONTRÉAL
Québec
St. John's
Halifax
Fredericton
Charlottetown
BOSTON
NEW YORK
PHILADELPHIA
BALTIMORE
CHICAGO
DETROIT
CLEVELAND
PITTSBURGH
MILWAUKEE
Minneapolis
St. Paul
SAN FRANCISCO
SAN JOSE
Oakland
Sacramento
Salt Lake City

CONTINENTAL DATA

TOTAL NUMBER OF COUNTRIES: 23

FIRST INDEPENDENT COUNTRY:
United States, July 4, 1776

"YOUNGEST" COUNTRY:
St. Kitts and Nevis,
Sept. 19, 1983

LARGEST COUNTRY BY AREA:
Canada 9,984,670 sq km
(3,855,101 sq mi)

SMALLEST COUNTRY BY AREA:
St. Kitts and Nevis 269 sq km
(104 sq mi)

PERCENT URBAN POPULATION:
75%

MOST POPULOUS COUNTRY:
United States 299,112,000

LEAST POPULOUS COUNTRY:
St. Kitts and Nevis 47,000

MOST DENSELY POPULATED COUNTRY:
Barbados 628 per sq km
(1,627 per sq mi)

LEAST DENSELY POPULATED COUNTRY:
Canada 3.3 per sq km
(8.5 per sq mi)

LARGEST CITY BY POPULATION:
Mexico City, Mexico 19,411,000

HIGHEST GDP PER CAPITA:
United States $43,500

LOWEST GDP PER CAPITA:
Haiti $1,800

AVERAGE LIFE EXPECTANCY IN NORTH AMERICA: 76 years

AVERAGE LITERACY RATE IN NORTH AMERICA: 96%

ARCTIC OCEAN
ATLANTIC OCEAN
PACIFIC OCEAN
NORWEGIAN SEA
GREENLAND SEA
Meridian of Greenwich (London)
BRITISH ISLES
Faroe Islands
ICELAND
Jan Mayen
ARCTIC CIRCLE
Denmark Strait
GREENLAND
Peary Land
Crown Prince Christian Land
King Frederik VIII Land
King Wilhelm Land
King Christian X Land
King Christian IX Land
King Frederik VI Coast
KNUD RASMUSSEN LAND
Gunnbjørn 3700
Mont Forel 3360
3270
Ice thickness 3410
J.A.D. Jensen Nunatakker 1680
Cape Farewell
Cape Morris Jesup
Lincoln Sea
North Magnetic Pole 2007
QUEEN ELIZABETH ISLANDS
Axel Heiberg Island
Ellesmere Island
Hayes Pen.
Smith Bay
Cape York
Melville Bay
BAFFIN BAY
Qeqertarsuaq
Davis Strait
Jones Sd.
Devon I.
Lancaster Sd.
Bylot Island
Borden Pen.
Brodeur Pen.
Baffin Island
Somerset Island
Prince of Wales I.
Boothia Peninsula
G. of Boothia
Cornwallis I.
Bathurst I.
PARRY ISLANDS
Melville I.
Prince Patrick Island
M'Clure Str.
Viscount Melville Sound
M'Clintock Chan.
Banks Island
Victoria Island
Wollaston Peninsula
Collinson Peninsula
Queen Maud Gulf
Cape Prince Alfred
Amundsen Gulf
Franklin Bay
Melville Hills
BEAUFORT SEA
Mackenzie Bay
Point Barrow
Melville Pen.
Foxe Basin
Prince Charles I.
Cumberland Peninsula
Cumberland Sd.
Foxe Pen.
Meta Incognita Peninsula
Hudson Strait
Southampton Island
Cape Dobbs
Chesterfield Inlet
Coats I.
Mansel I.
HUDSON BAY
Cape Churchill
Cape Tatnam
Belcher Islands
James Bay
Akimiski I.
Killiniq Island
LABRADOR SEA
Ungava Bay
Ungava Peninsula
Torngat Mts.
Labrador
Cape Harrison
Leaf
Caniapiscau
Réservoir Caniapiscau
Smallwood Reservoir
Monts Otish 1135
Eastmain
Rés. Manicouagan
Laurentide Scarp
Str. of Belle Isle
Long Range Mts.
ISLAND OF NEWFOUNDLAND
Bonavista Bay
Avalon Peninsula
Anticosti I.
St. Lawrence R.
Gulf of St. Lawrence
Cabot Str.
Cape Breton Island
Gaspé Pen.
Prince Edward I.
Rés. Gouin
Lake Abitibi
Abitibi
NOVA SCOTIA
Sable I.
Cape Sable
Bay of Fundy
Mt. Katahdin 1606
Mt. Washington 1917
White Mts.
Adirondack Mts.
Gulf of Maine
Cape Cod
Long Island
Hudson
Delaware
Mont Tremblant 968
Laurentian Scarp
Ottawa
L. Champlain
Georgian Bay
L. Ontario
Niagara Falls
L. Erie
Ohio
Potomac
Plateau Mts.
MOUNTAINS
L. Huron
Lower Peninsula
L. Michigan
Upper Pen.
L. Superior
Lake Nipigon
Lake St. Joseph
Attawapiskat
Severn
CANADIAN SHIELD
Lake of the Woods
Lake Winnipeg
Trout Lake
Lake Winnipegosis
Lake Manitoba
Saskatchewan
N. Saskatchewan
Nelson
Churchill
Wollaston Lake
Reindeer Lake
Lac la Ronge
Lake Athabasca
Athabasca
Birch Mts.
Caribou Mts.
Peace
Hay
Great Slave Lake
Dubawnt Lake
Thelon
Back
Great Bear Lake
Franklin Mts.
Mackenzie
Mackenzie Mts.
Selwyn Mts.
Richardson Mts.
Virginia Falls
Laird
Source of the Mackenzie-Peace
Williston Lake
Lake Sakakawea
Source of the Mississippi (Lake Itasca)
St. Croix
Mississippi
Des Moines
Lake Oahe
Platte
CENTRAL LOWLAND
Badlands
Black Hills 2207
GREAT PLAINS
Missouri
Yellowstone
Source of the Missouri-Red Rock
Bighorn Mts.
Grand Teton 4197
Snake River Plain
Front Ra.
Wasatch Ra.
Great Salt Lake
Great Basin
Bitterroot Ra.
Snake
Columbia Plateau
Great Sandy Desert
Columbia
Columbia Mts.
Selkirk Mts.
ROCKY MOUNTAINS
Fraser
COAST MOUNTAINS
Cassiar Mts.
Source of the Yukon
YUKON PLATEAU
Ogilvie Mountains
Porcupine
Yukon
Davidson Mts.
North Slope
Brooks Range
ARCTIC CIRCLE
Noatak
Kobuk
Baird Mts.
White Mts.
Highest point in North America
Mt. McKinley (Denali) 6194 (20320 ft)
Alaska Range
Kuskokwim Mts.
Kuskokwim
Mt. Logan 5959
Chugach Mts.
Prince William Sd.
Kenai Peninsula
Cook Inlet
Kodiak Island
GULF OF ALASKA
Alexander Archipelago
Queen Charlotte Is.
Hecate Str.
Vancouver I.
Str. of Georgia
Cape Flattery
Mt. Rainier 4392
Mt. St. Helens 2550
CASCADE RANGE
Cape Blanco
Mt. Shasta 4317
Cape Mendocino
COAST RANGES
Sacramento Valley
Sierra
San
Farallon Islands
Monterey Bay
SIBERIA
ASIA
BERING SEA
Bering Strait
St. Lawrence Island
Nunivak I.
Norton Sound
Seward Peninsula

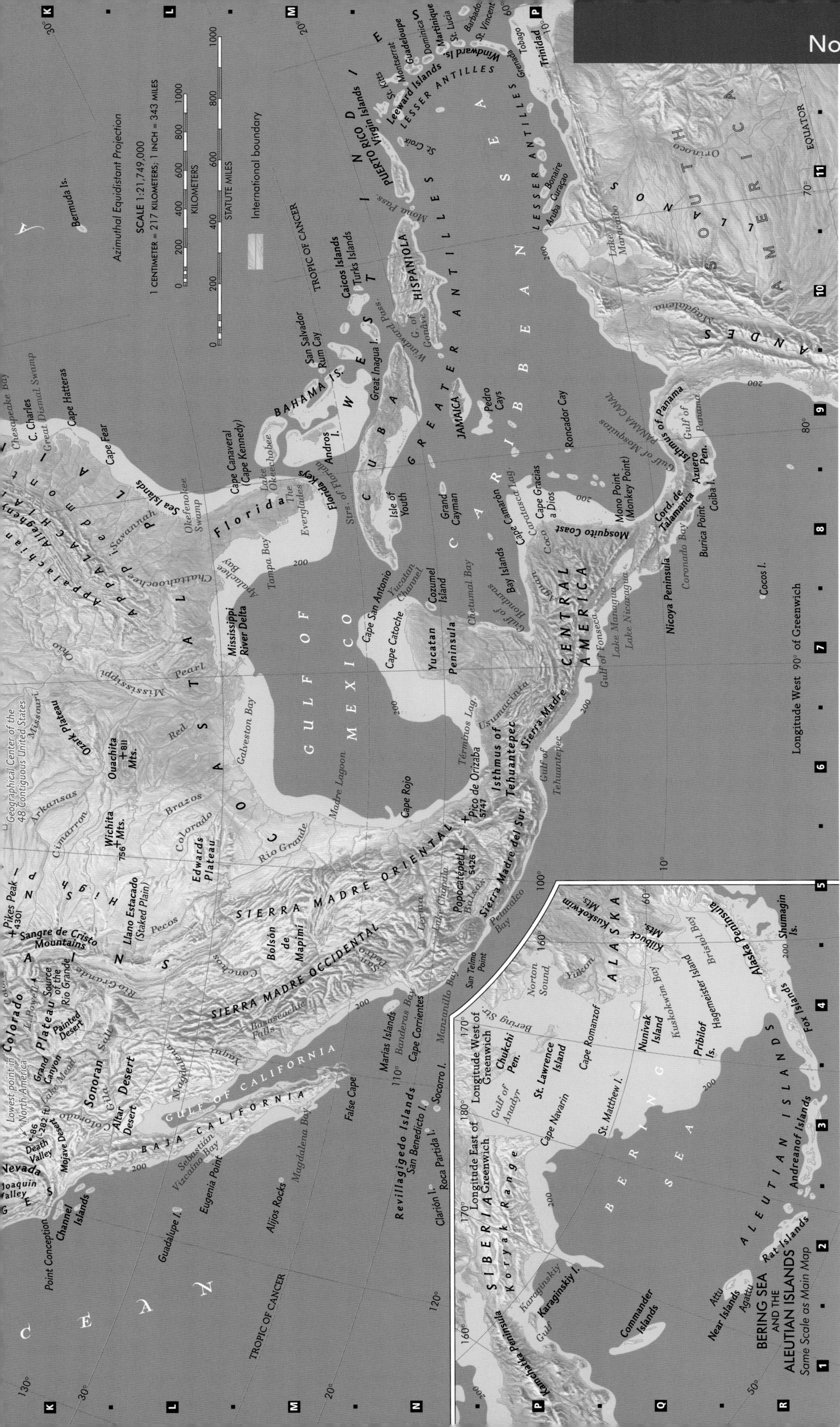

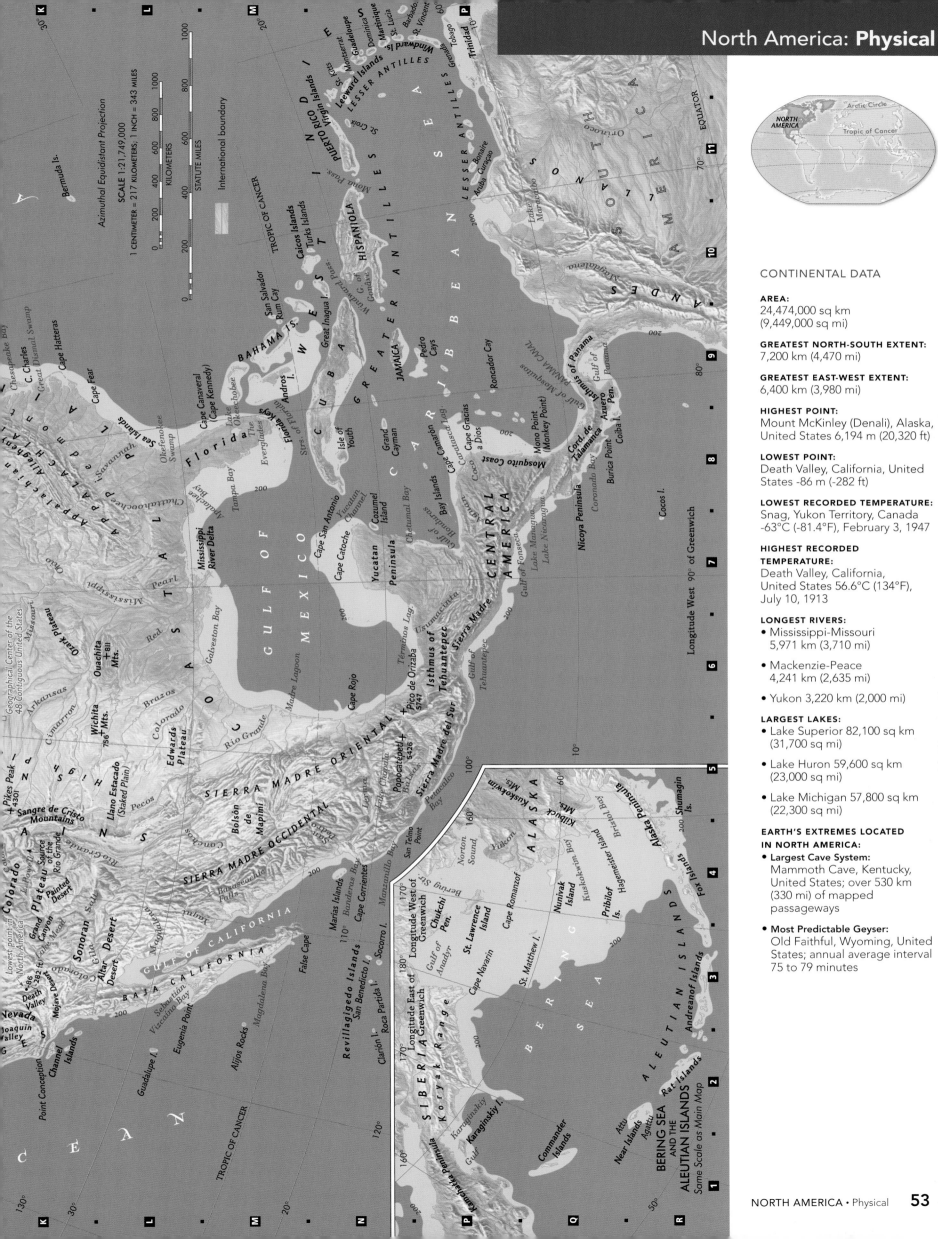

North America: **Physical**

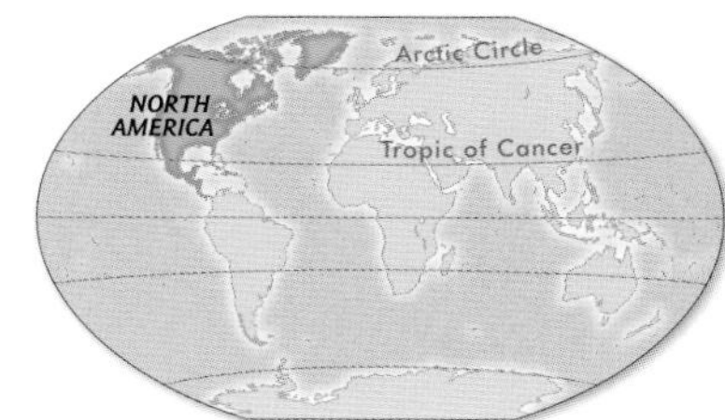

CONTINENTAL DATA

AREA:
24,474,000 sq km
(9,449,000 sq mi)

GREATEST NORTH-SOUTH EXTENT:
7,200 km (4,470 mi)

GREATEST EAST-WEST EXTENT:
6,400 km (3,980 mi)

HIGHEST POINT:
Mount McKinley (Denali), Alaska, United States 6,194 m (20,320 ft)

LOWEST POINT:
Death Valley, California, United States -86 m (-282 ft)

LOWEST RECORDED TEMPERATURE:
Snag, Yukon Territory, Canada -63°C (-81.4°F), February 3, 1947

HIGHEST RECORDED TEMPERATURE:
Death Valley, California, United States 56.6°C (134°F), July 10, 1913

LONGEST RIVERS:
- Mississippi-Missouri 5,971 km (3,710 mi)
- Mackenzie-Peace 4,241 km (2,635 mi)
- Yukon 3,220 km (2,000 mi)

LARGEST LAKES:
- Lake Superior 82,100 sq km (31,700 sq mi)
- Lake Huron 59,600 sq km (23,000 sq mi)
- Lake Michigan 57,800 sq km (22,300 sq mi)

EARTH'S EXTREMES LOCATED IN NORTH AMERICA:
- **Largest Cave System:** Mammoth Cave, Kentucky, United States; over 530 km (330 mi) of mapped passageways
- **Most Predictable Geyser:** Old Faithful, Wyoming, United States; annual average interval 75 to 79 minutes

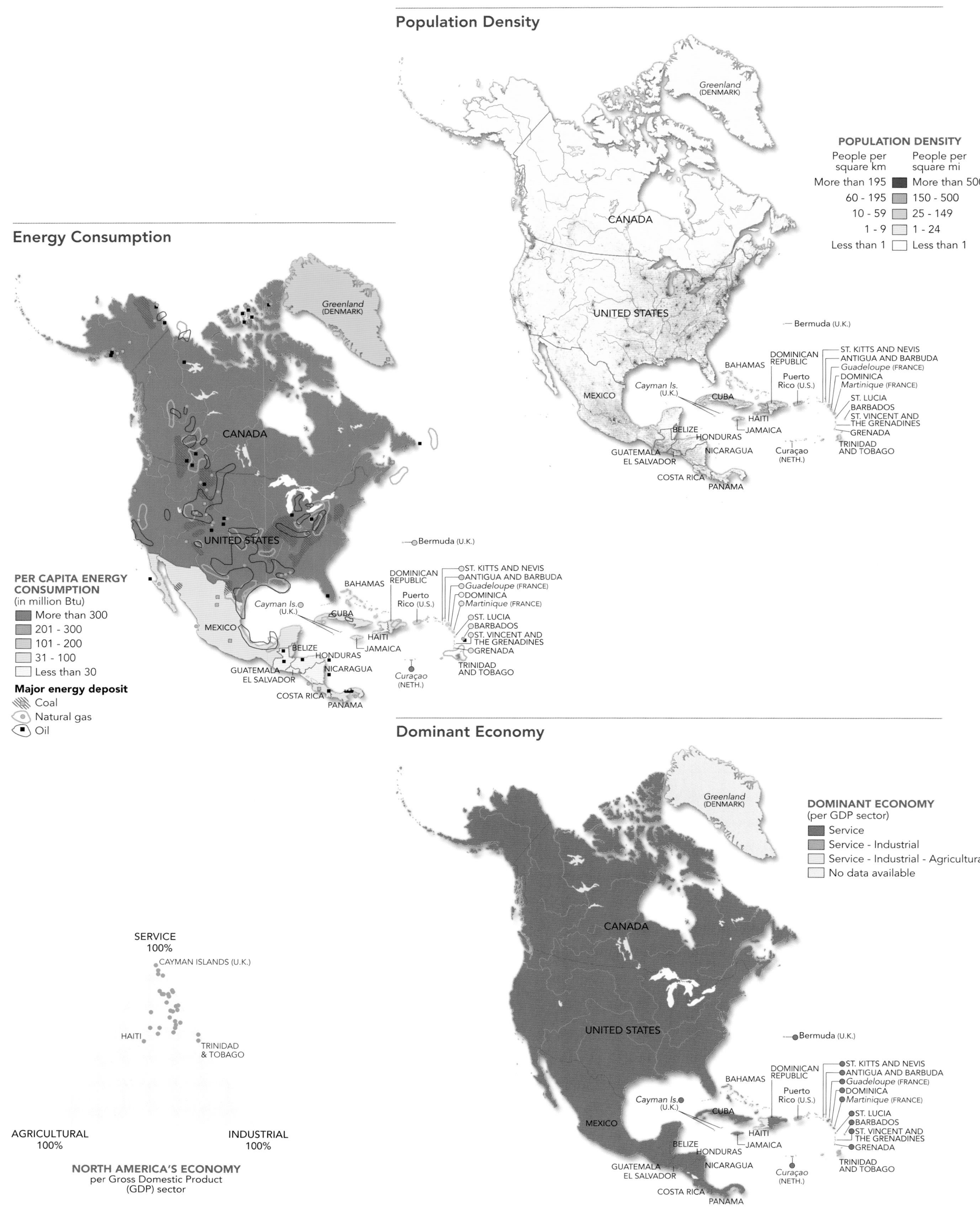
Population Density
Greenland (DENMARK)
CANADA
UNITED STATES
MEXICO
Bermuda (U.K.)
BAHAMAS
DOMINICAN REPUBLIC
Puerto Rico (U.S.)
Cayman Is. (U.K.)
CUBA
HAITI
JAMAICA
BELIZE
HONDURAS
GUATEMALA
EL SALVADOR
NICARAGUA
COSTA RICA
PANAMA
Curaçao (NETH.)
ST. KITTS AND NEVIS
ANTIGUA AND BARBUDA
Guadeloupe (FRANCE)
DOMINICA
Martinique (FRANCE)
ST. LUCIA
BARBADOS
ST. VINCENT AND THE GRENADINES
GRENADA
TRINIDAD AND TOBAGO
POPULATION DENSITY
People per square km
People per square mi
More than 195 More than 500
60 - 195 150 - 500
10 - 59 25 - 149
1 - 9 1 - 24
Less than 1 Less than 1
Energy Consumption
Greenland (DENMARK)
CANADA
UNITED STATES
MEXICO
Bermuda (U.K.)
BAHAMAS
DOMINICAN REPUBLIC
Puerto Rico (U.S.)
Cayman Is. (U.K.)
CUBA
HAITI
JAMAICA
BELIZE
HONDURAS
GUATEMALA
EL SALVADOR
NICARAGUA
COSTA RICA
PANAMA
Curaçao (NETH.)
ST. KITTS AND NEVIS
ANTIGUA AND BARBUDA
Guadeloupe (FRANCE)
DOMINICA
Martinique (FRANCE)
ST. LUCIA
BARBADOS
ST. VINCENT AND THE GRENADINES
GRENADA
TRINIDAD AND TOBAGO
PER CAPITA ENERGY CONSUMPTION
(in million Btu)
More than 300
201 - 300
101 - 200
31 - 100
Less than 30
Major energy deposit
Coal
Natural gas
Oil
Dominant Economy
Greenland (DENMARK)
CANADA
UNITED STATES
MEXICO
Bermuda (U.K.)
BAHAMAS
DOMINICAN REPUBLIC
Puerto Rico (U.S.)
Cayman Is. (U.K.)
CUBA
HAITI
JAMAICA
BELIZE
HONDURAS
GUATEMALA
EL SALVADOR
NICARAGUA
COSTA RICA
PANAMA
Curaçao (NETH.)
ST. KITTS AND NEVIS
ANTIGUA AND BARBUDA
Guadeloupe (FRANCE)
DOMINICA
Martinique (FRANCE)
ST. LUCIA
BARBADOS
ST. VINCENT AND THE GRENADINES
GRENADA
TRINIDAD AND TOBAGO
DOMINANT ECONOMY
(per GDP sector)
Service
Service - Industrial
Service - Industrial - Agricultural
No data available
SERVICE 100%
CAYMAN ISLANDS (U.K.)
HAITI
TRINIDAD & TOBAGO
AGRICULTURAL 100%
INDUSTRIAL 100%
NORTH AMERICA'S ECONOMY
per Gross Domestic Product (GDP) sector

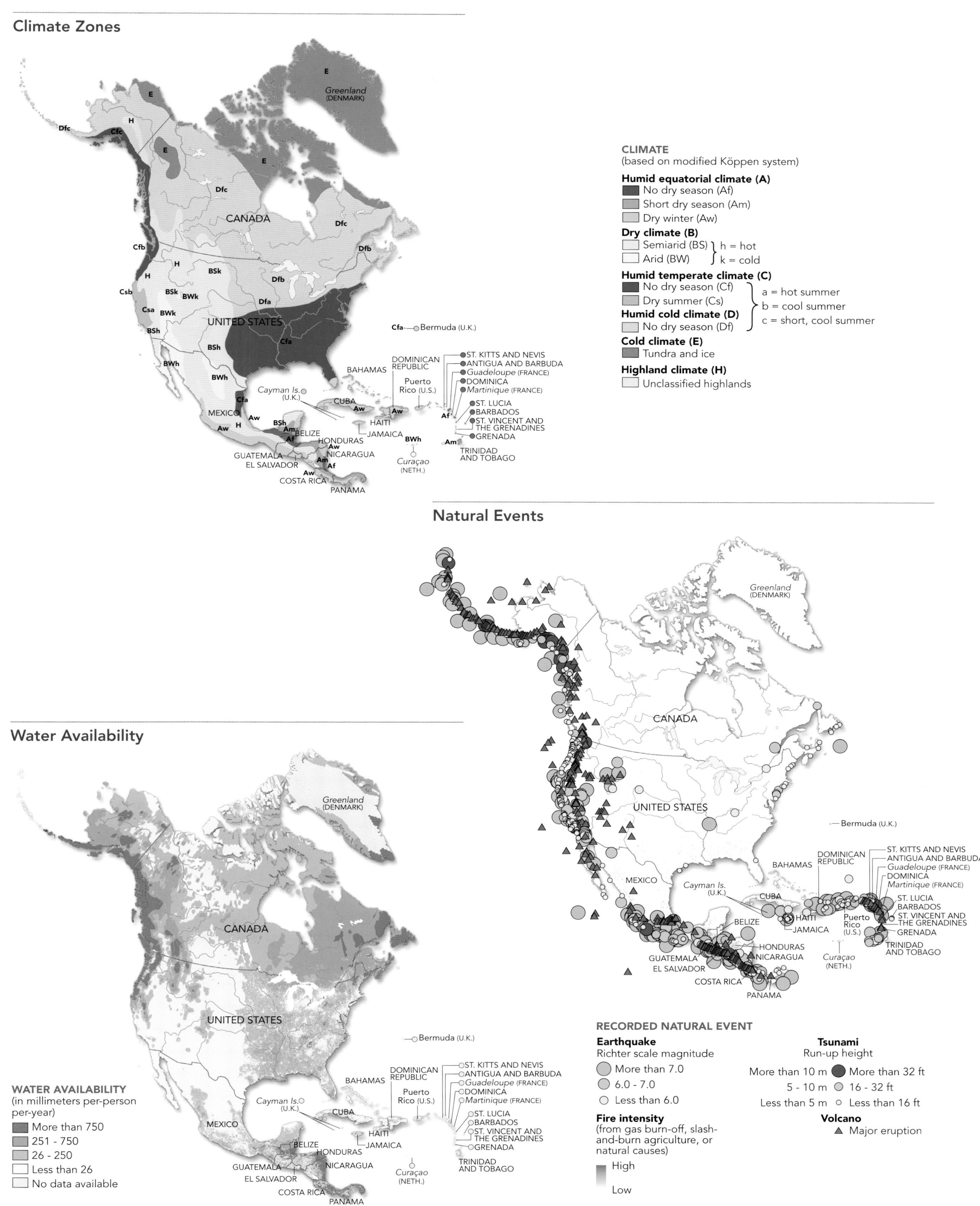

Climate Zones
Greenland (DENMARK)
CANADA
UNITED STATES
MEXICO
E
H
Dfc
Cfc
Cfb
Csb
Csa
BSk
BWk
BSh
BWh
Dfb
Dfa
Cfa
Aw
Am
Af
Cfa—Bermuda (U.K.)
BAHAMAS
DOMINICAN REPUBLIC
Puerto Rico (U.S.)
Cayman Is. (U.K.)
CUBA
HAITI
JAMAICA
BELIZE
HONDURAS
GUATEMALA
EL SALVADOR
NICARAGUA
COSTA RICA
PANAMA
Curaçao (NETH.)
ST. KITTS AND NEVIS
ANTIGUA AND BARBUDA
Guadeloupe (FRANCE)
DOMINICA
Martinique (FRANCE)
ST. LUCIA
BARBADOS
ST. VINCENT AND THE GRENADINES
GRENADA
TRINIDAD AND TOBAGO
CLIMATE
(based on modified Köppen system)
Humid equatorial climate (A)
No dry season (Af)
Short dry season (Am)
Dry winter (Aw)
Dry climate (B)
Semiarid (BS)
Arid (BW)
h = hot
k = cold
Humid temperate climate (C)
No dry season (Cf)
Dry summer (Cs)
Humid cold climate (D)
No dry season (Df)
a = hot summer
b = cool summer
c = short, cool summer
Cold climate (E)
Tundra and ice
Highland climate (H)
Unclassified highlands
Natural Events
Greenland (DENMARK)
CANADA
UNITED STATES
MEXICO
Bermuda (U.K.)
BAHAMAS
DOMINICAN REPUBLIC
Cayman Is. (U.K.)
CUBA
HAITI
JAMAICA
Puerto Rico (U.S.)
BELIZE
HONDURAS
GUATEMALA
EL SALVADOR
NICARAGUA
COSTA RICA
PANAMA
Curaçao (NETH.)
ST. KITTS AND NEVIS
ANTIGUA AND BARBUDA
Guadeloupe (FRANCE)
DOMINICA
Martinique (FRANCE)
ST. LUCIA
BARBADOS
ST. VINCENT AND THE GRENADINES
GRENADA
TRINIDAD AND TOBAGO
RECORDED NATURAL EVENT
Earthquake
Richter scale magnitude
More than 7.0
6.0 - 7.0
Less than 6.0
Fire intensity
(from gas burn-off, slash-and-burn agriculture, or natural causes)
High
Low
Tsunami
Run-up height
More than 10 m
More than 32 ft
5 - 10 m
16 - 32 ft
Less than 5 m
Less than 16 ft
Volcano
Major eruption
Water Availability
Greenland (DENMARK)
CANADA
UNITED STATES
MEXICO
Bermuda (U.K.)
BAHAMAS
DOMINICAN REPUBLIC
Puerto Rico (U.S.)
Cayman Is. (U.K.)
CUBA
HAITI
JAMAICA
BELIZE
HONDURAS
GUATEMALA
EL SALVADOR
NICARAGUA
COSTA RICA
PANAMA
Curaçao (NETH.)
ST. KITTS AND NEVIS
ANTIGUA AND BARBUDA
Guadeloupe (FRANCE)
DOMINICA
Martinique (FRANCE)
ST. LUCIA
BARBADOS
ST. VINCENT AND THE GRENADINES
GRENADA
TRINIDAD AND TOBAGO
WATER AVAILABILITY
(in millimeters per-person per-year)
More than 750
251 - 750
26 - 250
Less than 26
No data available

CANADA
BRITISH COLUMBIA
ALBERTA
SASKATCHEWAN
MANITOBA
ROCKY MOUNTAINS
PACIFIC OCEAN
Str. of Georgia
Str. of Juan de Fuca
WASHINGTON
Bellingham
Everett
Seattle
Bremerton
Mt. Olympus 7965
Olympia
Tacoma
Aberdeen
Centralia
Longview
Astoria
Kelso
Mt. Rainier 14411
Mt. St. Helens 8366
Wenatchee
Colville
Sandpoint
Coeur d'Alene
Spokane
Yakima
Richland
Pullman
Walla Walla
Vancouver
Columbia
OREGON
Portland
Salem
Albany
Corvallis
Eugene
Springfield
Newport
North Bend
Coos Bay
Roseburg
Grants Pass
Medford
Ashland
Klamath Falls
Crescent City
Mt. Hood 11239
The Dalles
Pendleton
La Grande
Baker City
John Day
Ontario
Burns
Crane
CASCADE RANGE
IDAHO
Bonners Ferry
Wallace
Lewiston
Snake
Salmon
Payette
Caldwell
Boise
Nampa
Mountain Home
Sun Valley
Borah Pk. 12662
Idaho Falls
Blackfoot
Pocatello
Jerome
Twin Falls
Rupert
Burley
Preston
Montpelier
MONTANA
Kalispell
Polson
Missoula
Deer Lodge
Helena
Butte
Dillon
Bozeman
Livingston
Great Falls
Fort Benton
Cut Bank
Shelby
Havre
Turner
Malta
Glasgow
Fort Peck Lake
Missouri
Wolf Point
Williston
Sidney
Lewistown
Roundup
Billings
Laurel
Forsyth
Miles City
Glendive
Hardin
Baker
NORTH DAKOTA
Portal
St. John
Stanley
Minot
Rugby
Grafton
Lake Sakakawea
Devils Lake
Thief River Falls
Harvey
Grand Forks
Crookston
Dickinson
Mandan
Bismarck
Jamestown
Valley City
Fargo
Moorhead
Mott
Fort Yates
Ashley
Oakes
SOUTH DAKOTA
Lemmon
Mobridge
Aberdeen
Milbank
Lake Oahe
Faith
Belle Fourche
Lead
Watertown
Pierre
Rapid City
Huron
Brookings
Mitchell
Hot Springs
Martin
Lake Francis Case
Sioux Falls
Yankton
WYOMING
Powell
Cody
Sheridan
Buffalo
Gillette
Grand Teton 13770
Worland
Thermopolis
Newcastle
Gannett Pk. 13804
Riverton
Lander
Casper
Douglas
Lusk
Kemmerer
Green River
Rock Springs
Rawlins
Evanston
Laramie
Cheyenne
NEBRASKA
Chadron
Valentine
Ainsworth
Sioux City
Alliance
Norfolk
Scottsbluff
Columbus
Fremont
Sidney
North Platte
Platte
Grand Island
Kearney
Lincoln
Hastings
McCook
Beatrice
CALIFORNIA
Yreka
Goose L.
Mt. Shasta 14162
Eureka
Redding
Susanville
Red Bluff
Fort Bragg
Ukiah
Yuba City
L. Tahoe
Sacramento
Santa Rosa
Vallejo
Oakland
SAN FRANCISCO
San Mateo
Stockton
Palo Alto
SAN JOSE
Modesto
Santa Cruz
Monterey
Salinas
Fresno
Visalia
Coalinga
Delano
Paso Robles
San Luis Obispo
Bakersfield
Santa Maria
Lompoc
Santa Barbara
Glendale
Pasadena
LOS ANGELES
Long Beach
Santa Ana
San Bernardino
Palm Springs
Riverside
Salton Sea
SAN DIEGO
National City
El Centro
Mojave
Ridgecrest
Needles
Bishop
Mt. Whitney 14494
Death Valley -282
SIERRA NEVADA
COAST RANGES
NEVADA
GREAT BASIN
Denio
McDermitt
Winnemucca
Wells
Elko
Carlin
Lovelock
Reno
Carson City
Hawthorne
Mt. Jefferson 11949
Tonopah
Goldfield
McGill
Ely
Pioche
Caliente
Beatty
Las Vegas
Boulder City
Lake Mead
UTAH
Great Salt Lake
Logan
Ogden
Salt Lake City
Tooele
Utah L.
Provo
Kings Pk. 13528
Vernal
Nephi
Price
Sevier Lake
Fillmore
Manti
Richfield
Green Junction
Moab
Parowan
Cedar City
Panguitch
St. George
Kanab
Monticello
Lake Powell
COLORADO
Craig
Fort Collins
Greeley
Longmont
Boulder
Fort Morgan
DENVER
Aurora
Glenwood Springs
Colorado
Grand Junction
Delta
Gunnison
Montrose
Pikes Pk. 14110
Colorado Springs
Salida
Canon City
Pueblo
Silverton
Lamar
La Junta
Cortez
Durango
Alamosa
Walsenburg
Trinidad
ARIZONA
COLORADO PLATEAU
Grand Canyon
Kingman
Williams
Flagstaff
Prescott
Winslow
Holbrook
Wickenburg
Scottsdale
PHOENIX
Mesa
Baldy Peak 11403
Globe
Gila Bend
Casa Grande
Morenci
Eloy
Safford
Ajo
Yuma
Tucson
Willcox
Benson
Tombstone
Bisbee
Nogales
Douglas
NEW MEXICO
Farmington
Raton
Wheeler Peak 13161
Los Alamos
Springer
Clayton
Santa Fe
Las Vegas
Gallup
Grants
Albuquerque
Tucumcari
Belen
Vaughn
Magdalena
Socorro
Fort Sumner
Clovis
Truth or Consequences
Roswell
Alamogordo
Silver City
Artesia
Hobbs
Lordsburg
Deming
Las Cruces
Carlsbad
El Paso
KANSAS
Norton
Colby
Goodland
Russell
Hays
Manhattan
Salina
Great Bend
Emporia
Hutchinson
Newton
Garden City
Arkansas
Dodge City
Wichita
Arkansas City
OKLAHOMA
Liberal
Guymon
Woodward
Ponca City
Enid
Stillwater
Shawnee
Oklahoma City
Chickasha
Lawton
Ada
Red
Ardmore
Durant
TEXAS
Dalhart
Dumas
Borger
Pampa
Amarillo
Hereford
Childress
Vernon
Wichita Falls
Denison
Sherman
Plainview
Lubbock
Brownfield
DALLAS
Fort Worth
Lamesa
Snyder
Sweetwater
Abilene
Cleburne
Corsicana
Midland
Big Spring
Odessa
Brownwood
Waco
Pecos
San Angelo
Temple
Van Horn
Fort Stockton
Bryan
Marfa
Alpine
Ozona
Sonora
Sanderson
Austin
Amistad Reservoir
New Braunfels
San Marcos
Del Rio
SAN ANTONIO
Uvalde
Cuero
Eagle Pass
Victoria
Beeville
Aransas Pass
Corpus Christi
Laredo
Alice
Kingsville
Falfurrias
Raymondville
Edinburg
McAllen
Harlingen
Brownsville
Rio Grande
MEXICO
ALASKA
ARCTIC OCEAN
BEAUFORT SEA
CHUKCHI SEA
BERING SEA
RUSSIA
Barrow
Wainwright
Point Lay
Atqasuk
Prudhoe Bay
Kaktovik
Point Hope
Umiat
North Slope
BROOKS RANGE
Noatak
Kivalina
ARCTIC CIRCLE
Kotzebue
Shishmaref
Shungnak
Kobuk
Kiana
Selawik
Wiseman
Deering
Wales
Teller
Bering Str.
Nome
Allakaket
Hughes
Beaver
Fort Yukon
Circle
Yukon
Koyuk
Nulato
Galena
Tanana
Rampart
Gambell
Savoonga
St. Lawrence Island
Golovin
Unalakleet
Kaltag
Ruby
Fairbanks
Eagle
Lake Minchumina
Nenana
Big Delta
St. Michael
Alakanuk
Kotlik
Tanacross
Cantwell
Northway
McGrath
ALASKA RANGE
Mt. McKinley (Denali) 20320
Mountain Village
Anvik
Hooper Bay
Holy Cross
Flat
Farewell
Gulkana
Tununak
Aniak
Red Devil
Skwentna
Palmer
Mekoryuk
Bethel
Nyac
Anchorage
Valdez
Kashegelok
Whittier
Cordova
Nunivak Island
Quinhagak
Kenai
Seward
Cape Yakataga
Goodnews Bay
Newhalen
Homer
Yakutat
Togiak
Iliamna Lake
Seldovia
Dillingham
Naknek
King Salmon
GULF OF ALASKA
Egegik
Kodiak
Pilot Point
Karluk
Kodiak Island
Chignik
Cold Bay
Sand Point
CANADA U.S.
NORTHWEST TERRITORIES
YUKON
BRITISH COLUMBIA
Skagway
Haines
Juneau
Gustavus
Hoonah
Petersburg
Sitka
Wrangell
Ketchikan
Hydaburg
PACIFIC OCEAN
ALASKA
0 100 200 300 km
0 50 100 150 statute mi

Albers Conic Equal-Area Projection
SCALE 1:10,824,000
1 CENTIMETER = 108 KILOMETERS; 1 INCH = 171 MILES
PRINCIPAL HAWAIIAN ISLANDS
ATLANTIC OCEAN
GULF OF MEXICO

P A C I F I C   O C E A N
C A N
Str. of Georgia
Str. of Juan de Fuca
Cape Flattery
Mt. Olympus 7980
Puget Sd.
Mt. Baker 10778
Cape Disappointment
Mt. Rainier 14411
Mt. St. Helens 8366
Mt. Adams 12307
Columbia
Mt. Hood 11239
Willamette
John Day
C A S C A D E   R A N G E
C O A S T   R A N G E S
Columbia Plateau
Okanogan
Columbia
Pend Oreille L.
Bitterroot Range
Illinois Pk. 7690
Snake
Blue Mountains
Wallowa Mts.
Buffalo Hump 8924
Salmon
Clearwater Mts.
Flathead Lake
Continental Divide
R O C K Y   M O U N T A I N S
Bear Paw Mts.
Milk
Missouri
Fort Peck Lake
Musselshell
Yellowstone
G R E A T   P L A I N S
Souris
Lake Sakakawea
Sheyenne
Red River of the North
L. Ashtabula
Little Missouri
Badlands
Heart
White Butte 3506
Cape Blanco
Harney Basin
Great Sandy Desert
Salmon River Mountains
10340 Twin Peaks
Borah Pk. 12662
Granite Pk. 12799
Absaroka Range
Bighorn
Bighorn Mts.
Cloud Pk. 13165
Tongue
Powder
Grand
Moreau
Lake Oahe
Geographical Center of the 50 United States
Yellowstone L.
Jackson L.
Grand Teton 13770
Snake River Plain
Wind River Ra.
Belle Fourche
Black Hills
Harney Pk. 7242
Cheyenne
L. Sharpe
James
Goose L.
Mt. Shasta 14162
Klamath Mountains
Steens Mt. 9733
Warner Mts.
Snake
American Falls Res.
Shoshone Falls
Gannett Pk. 13804
White
Cape Mendocino
Eagle Pk. 9892
Black Rock Desert
Granite Pk. 9732
Sherman Pk. 9682
Bear River Ra.
Great Divide Basin
Lake Francis Case
Niobrara
Missouri
Lassen Peak 10457
Sacramento
Sacramento Valley
Great Salt Lake
Wasatch Ra.
Great Salt Lake Desert
Ruby Dome 11387
Humboldt
Pyramid L.
Laramie Mts.
Laramie Pk. 10272
Sand Hills
Elkhorn
Point Arena
Donner Pass 7088
S I E R R A   N E V A D A
L. Tahoe
Carson Sink
Ruby Mts.
G R E A T   B A S I N
Flaming Gorge Reservoir
Kings Pk. 13528
Uinta Mts.
Utah Lake
N. Platte
Medicine Bow Mts.
Front Range
N. Platte
Panorama Pt. 5423
S. Platte
Loup
Platte
Point Reyes
Farallon Is.
San Francisco Bay
Shoshone Mts.
Toiyabe Ra.
Monitor Ra.
Schell Cr. Ra.
Mt. Moriah 12050
Wheeler Pk. 13063
Sevier Lake
Roan Cliffs
Longs Peak 14255
Republican
Monterey Bay
Mono L.
Diablo Range
San Joaquin
San Joaquin Valley
Boundary Peak 13140
Troy Pk. 11298
Colorado
Green
Mt. Elbert 14433
Geographical Center of the 48 Contiguous United States
Solomon
Point Sur
Santa Lucia Ra.
Mt. Whitney 14494 (4418 m)
Death Valley
-282 (-86 m)
Bald Mt. 9380
Uncompahgre Plateau
Uncompahgre Pk. 14309
Pikes Peak 14110
Mt. Sunflower 4039
Smoky Hills 1654
Smokey Hill
Arkansas
Point Buchon
Mojave Desert
Spring Mts.
Lake Mead
Mount Trumbull 8029
Kaibab Plateau
Lake Powell
San Juan Mts.
Blanca Pk. 14345
Rio Grande
Sangre de Cristo Mts.
Arkansas
1459
Flint
Point Conception
Santa Barbara Chan.
San Miguel
Santa Rosa
Santa Cruz
Channel Islands
San Nicolas
Santa Catalina
San Clemente
Gulf of Santa Catalina
Grand Canyon
C O L O R A D O   P L A T E A U
Matthews Pk. 9512
Chuska Mts.
Painted Desert
Black Mts.
Mt. San Antonio 10064
San Francisco Mt. 12633
Wheeler Pk. 13161
Black Mesa 4973
2265 Red Hills
Cimarron
N. Canadian
Keystone L.
Canadian
L. Meredith
Mogollon Rim
Continental Divide
Palomar Mt. 6140
-232
Salton Sea
Imperial Valley
Colorado
Sonoran Desert
Gila
Salt
Baldy Peak 11403
Black Range
Elephant Butte Res.
Caballo Res.
Gila
San Andres Mts.
Sierra Blanca Pk. 11973
Sacramento Mts.
Guadalupe Mts.
Guadalupe Pk. 8749
Llano Estacado
Cap Rock Escarpment
Washita
2479 Wichita Mts.
Red
L. Texoma
Brazos
Red Bluff Lake
Colorado
Rio Grande
Pecos
Edwards Plateau 2487
Amistad Reservoir
Guadalupe
Matagorda Bay
San Antonio
Nueces
Rio Grande
Corpus Christi Bay
Baffin Bay
Falcon Reservoir
Padre Island
M E X I C O
C
CHUKCHI SEA
BEAUFORT SEA
Point Barrow
Dease Inlet
Smith Bay
Harrison Bay
Prudhoe Bay
Camden Bay
Demarcation Point
Icy Cape
Teshekpuk Lake
North Slope
Mt. Isto 9060
British Mts.
Cape Lisburne
Point Hope
Tingmerkpuk Mt. 3787
BROOKS RANGE
Davidson Mts.
De Long Mountains
Colville
Philip Smith Mts.
Endicott Mts.
Noatak
Baird Mountains
ARCTIC CIRCLE
RUSSIA
Kotzebue Sd.
Kobuk
Bering Str.
Diomede Is.
Porcupine
Selawik Lake
C. Prince of Wales
SEWARD PENINSULA
Koyukuk
Yukon Flats
Ray Mts.
White Mts.
CANADA
U.S.
Norton Bay
Yukon
2207
St. Lawrence Island
Norton Sound
Stuart I.
A L A S K A
Kaiyuh Mts.
Tanana
Yukon Delta
Kuskokwim Mountains
ALASKA RANGE
Yukon
Cape Romanzof
Mt. McKinley (Denali) 20320 (6194 m)
Susitna
Talkeetna Mts.
Copper
Wrangell Mts.
Mt. Blackburn 16390
Kuskokwim
Mt. Gerdine 11258
Nunivak I.
Roberts Mt. 1675
Kilbuck Mts.
Chugach Mountains
St. Elias Mountains
Mt. St. Elias 18008
Kuskokwim Bay
Iliamna Lake
Cook Inlet
KENAI PENINSULA
Prince William Sd.
Montague I.
Yakutat Bay
COAST MOUNTAINS
Cape Newenham
Mt. Fairweather 15300
Kennedy Entrance
Cross Sound
Admiralty Island
Bristol Bay
GULF OF ALASKA
Mt. Katmai 6715
Afognak I.
Chichagof Island
Kupreanof I.
ALASKA
Kruzof I.
Baranof I.
ALEXANDER ARCHIPELAGO
ALASKA PENINSULA
ALEUTIAN RANGE
Shelikof Str.
4470
Kodiak Island
Kuiu I.
Revillagigedo Island
Prince of Wales I.
Dall I.
BERING SEA
Mt. Veniaminof 8225
Trinity Is.
0 100 200 300 km
0 50 100 150 statute mi

Lake Superior
Lake Michigan
Lake Huron
Lake Erie
Lake Ontario
CENTRAL LOWLAND
APPALACHIAN MOUNTAINS
Appalachian Plateau
Allegheny Mountains
Blue Ridge
Piedmont
Cumberland Plateau
Ozark Plateau
Black Belt
COASTAL PLAIN
ATLANTIC OCEAN
GULF OF MAINE
GULF OF MEXICO
Straits of Florida
Florida Keys
CUBA
HAITI
TROPIC OF CANCER
Mt. Katahdin 5268
Mt. Washington 6288
Mt. Mansfield 4393
Mt. Marcy 5344
Adirondack Mts.
Catskill Mts.
Slide Mt. 4180
Mt. Greylock 3491
Mt. Frissell 2380
Jerimoth Hill 812
High Pt. 1803
Mt. Davis 3213
Backbone Mt. 3360
Spruce Knob 4863
Mt. Rogers 5729
Black Mt. 4145
Mt. Mitchell 6684
Clingmans Dome 6643
Great Smoky Mts.
Sassafras Mt. 3560
Brasstown Bald 4784
Cheaha Mt. 2407
Woodall Mt. 806
Taum Sauk Mt. 1772
Boston Mts.
Magazine Mt. 2753
Ouachita Mts. 2660
Driskill Mt. 535
Charles Mound 1235
Campbell Hill 1550
Timms Hill 1951
Mt. Arvon 1979
Eagle Mt. 2301
Hawkeye Point 1670
Source of the Mississippi (Lake Itasca)
Upper Peninsula
Lower Peninsula
Isle Royale
Keweenaw Peninsula
Cape Cod
Cape Ann
Cape Charles
Cape Hatteras
Cape Lookout
Cape Fear
Cape Canaveral
Cape Sable
Cape Romano
Sea Islands
Mississippi River Delta
Lake Okeechobee
The Everglades
Albers Conic Equal-Area Projection
SCALE 1:10,824,000
1 CENTIMETER = 108 KILOMETERS; 1 INCH = 171 MILES
KILOMETERS
STATUTE MILES
elevations in feet
10,000
9,000
8,000
7,000
6,000
5,000
4,000
3,000
2,000
1,000
250
0 (sea level)
PRINCIPAL HAWAIIAN ISLANDS
Longitude West 159° of Greenwich
Longitude West 90° of Greenwich
PACIFIC OCEAN
KAUA'I
NI'IHAU
O'AHU
MOLOKA'I
LĀNA'I
MAUI
Kaho'olawe
HAWAI'I
Kawaikini 5243
Pāni'au 1281
Ka'ula
Ka'ena Point 4019
Kahuku Point
Kamakou 4970
Nānu'alele Point
Upolu Point
Mauna Kea 13796
Mauna Loa 13679
Kilauea 4077
Kalae (South Cape)
0 100 km
0 100 statute mi

Population Change

WASH. OREG. CALIF. NEV. IDAHO MONT. WYO. UTAH ARIZ. COLO. N. MEX. N. DAK. S. DAK. NEBR. KANS. OKLA. TEXAS MINN. IOWA MO. ARK. LA. WIS. ILL. MICH. IND. OHIO KY. TENN. MISS. ALA. GA. FLA. S.C. N.C. VA. W. VA. MD. DEL. D.C. PA. N.J. N.Y. CONN. R.I. MASS. VT. N.H. ME. ALASKA HAWAI'I

miles 0 400 800
0 400 800 kilometers

Alaska: 0 miles 400; 0 km 400

Hawai'i: 0 miles 200; 0 km 200

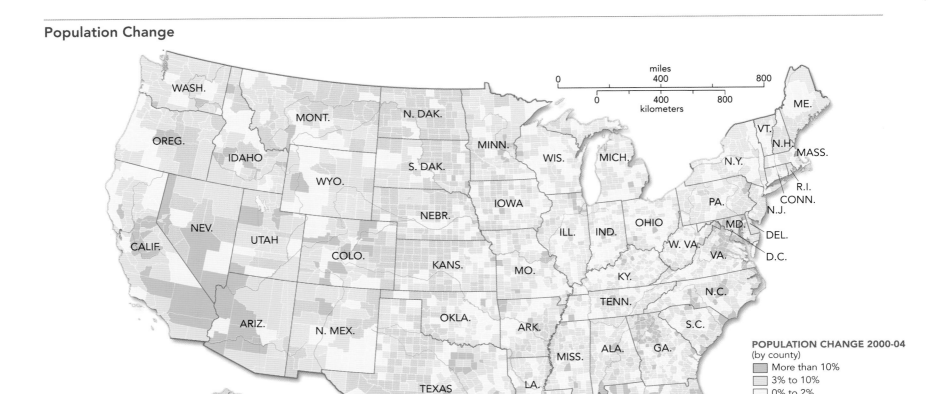

POPULATION CHANGE 2000-04
(by county)
- More than 10%
- 3% to 10%
- 0% to 2%
- -2% to -1%
- More than -2%

Most Prevalent Religious Group

WASH. OREG. CALIF. NEV. IDAHO MONT. WYO. UTAH ARIZ. COLO. N. MEX. N. DAK. S. DAK. NEBR. KANS. OKLA. TEXAS MINN. IOWA MO. ARK. LA. WIS. ILL. MICH. IND. OHIO KY. TENN. MISS. ALA. GA. FLA. S.C. N.C. VA. W. VA. MD. DEL. D.C. PA. N.J. N.Y. CONN. R.I. MASS. VT. N.H. ME. ALASKA HAWAI'I

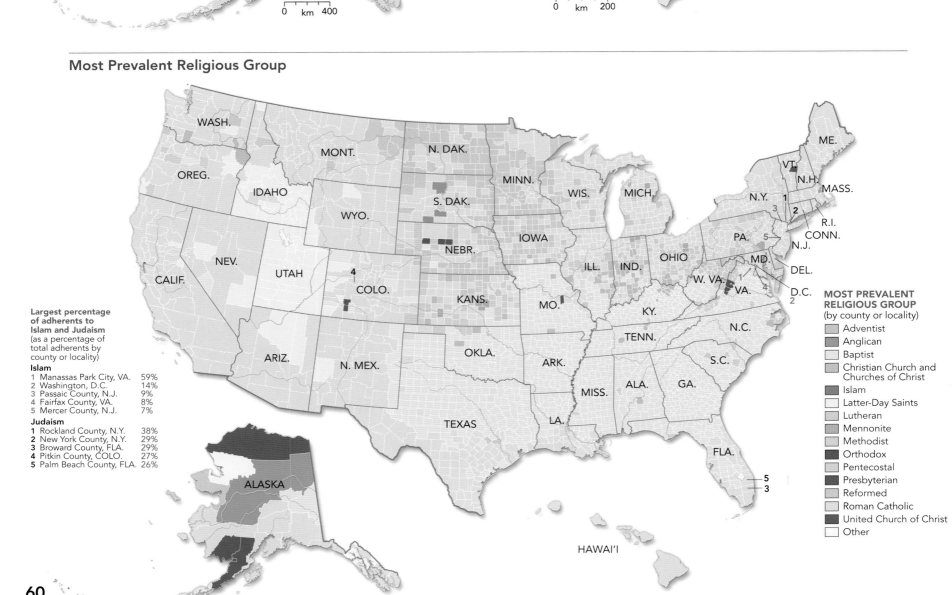

Largest percentage of adherents to Islam and Judaism
(as a percentage of total adherents by county or locality)

Islam
1. Manassas Park City, VA. 59%
2. Washington, D.C. 14%
3. Passaic County, N.J. 9%
4. Fairfax County, VA. 8%
5. Mercer County, N.J. 7%

Judaism
1. Rockland County, N.Y. 38%
2. New York County, N.Y. 29%
3. Broward County, FLA. 29%
4. Pitkin County, COLO. 27%
5. Palm Beach County, FLA. 26%

MOST PREVALENT RELIGIOUS GROUP
(by county or locality)
- Adventist
- Anglican
- Baptist
- Christian Church and Churches of Christ
- Islam
- Latter-Day Saints
- Lutheran
- Mennonite
- Methodist
- Orthodox
- Pentecostal
- Presbyterian
- Reformed
- Roman Catholic
- United Church of Christ
- Other

Risk to Property from Natural Disasters

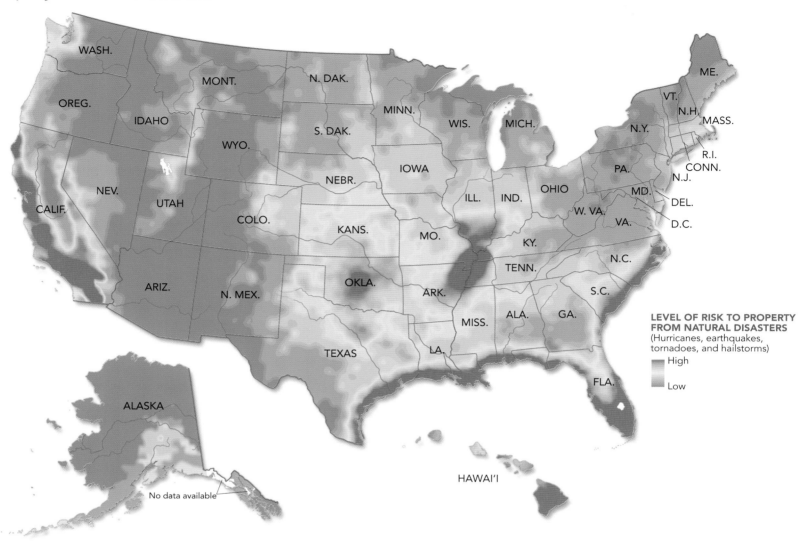

LEVEL OF RISK TO PROPERTY FROM NATURAL DISASTERS
(Hurricanes, earthquakes, tornadoes, and hailstorms)

High

Low

National Parks and Reserves

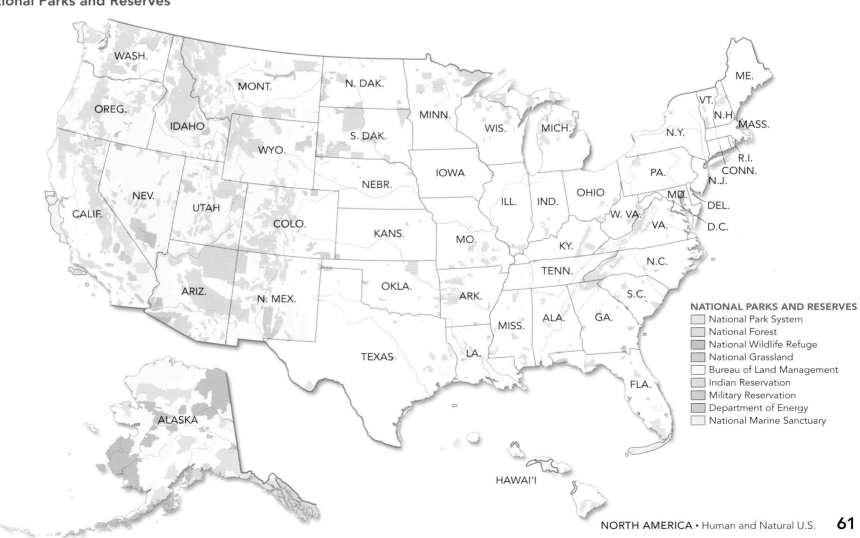

NATIONAL PARKS AND RESERVES

- National Park System
- National Forest
- National Wildlife Refuge
- National Grassland
- Bureau of Land Management
- Indian Reservation
- Military Reservation
- Department of Energy
- National Marine Sanctuary

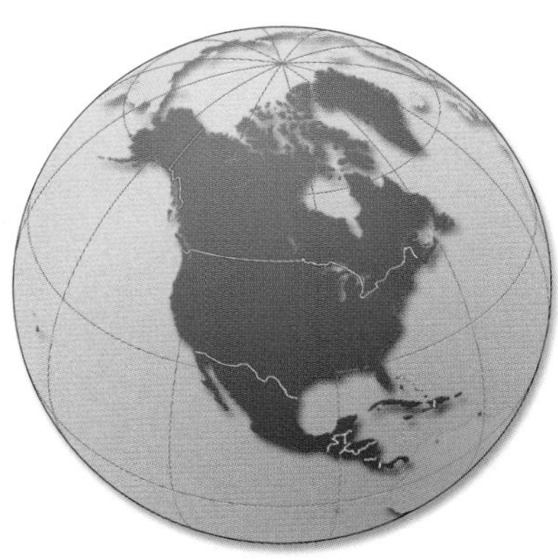

Nations

Antigua and Barbuda
ANTIGUA AND BARBUDA

AREA 442 sq km (171 sq mi)
POPULATION 69,000
CAPITAL St. John's 32,000
RELIGION Anglican, other Protestant, Roman Catholic
LANGUAGE English, local dialects
LITERACY 86%
LIFE EXPECTANCY 71 years
GDP PER CAPITA $10,900
ECONOMY **IND:** tourism, construction, light manufacturing (clothing, alcohol, household appliances) **AGR:** cotton, fruits, vegetables, bananas; livestock **EXP:** petroleum products, manufactures, machinery and transport equipment, food and live animals

Bahamas
COMMONWEALTH OF THE BAHAMAS

AREA 13,939 sq km (5,382 sq mi)
POPULATION 304,000
CAPITAL Nassau 233,000
RELIGION Baptist, Anglican, Roman Catholic, Pentecostal
LANGUAGE English, Creole
LITERACY 96%
LIFE EXPECTANCY 70 years
GDP PER CAPITA $21,300
ECONOMY **IND:** tourism, banking, cement, oil transshipment **AGR:** citrus, vegetables; poultry **EXP:** mineral products and salt, animal products, rum, chemicals

Barbados
BARBADOS

AREA 430 sq km (166 sq mi)
POPULATION 270,000
CAPITAL Bridgetown 142,000
RELIGION Anglican, Pentecostal, Methodist
LANGUAGE English
LITERACY 100%
LIFE EXPECTANCY 72 years
GDP PER CAPITA $18,200
ECONOMY **IND:** tourism, sugar, light manufacturing, component assembly for export **AGR:** sugarcane, vegetables, cotton **EXP:** sugar and molasses, rum, other foods and beverages, chemicals

Belize
BELIZE

AREA 22,965 sq km (8,867 sq mi)
POPULATION 301,000
CAPITAL Belmopan 14,000
RELIGION Roman Catholic, Protestant
LANGUAGE Spanish, Creole, Mayan dialects
LITERACY 94%
LIFE EXPECTANCY 70 years
GDP PER CAPITA $8,400
ECONOMY **IND:** garment production, food processing, tourism, construction **AGR:** bananas, cacao, citrus, sugar; lumber, fish **EXP:** sugar, bananas, citrus, clothing

Canada
CANADA

AREA 9,984,670 sq km (3,855,101 sq mi)
POPULATION 32,582,000
CAPITAL Ottawa 1,156,000
RELIGION Roman Catholic, Protestant
LANGUAGE English, French
LITERACY 99%
LIFE EXPECTANCY 80 years
GDP PER CAPITA $35,200
ECONOMY **IND:** transportation equipment, chemicals, processed and unprocessed minerals, food products **AGR:** wheat, barley, oilseed, tobacco; dairy products; forest products; fish **EXP:** motor vehicles and parts, industrial machinery, aircraft, telecommunications equipment

Costa Rica
REPUBLIC OF COSTA RICA

AREA 51,100 sq km (19,730 sq mi)
POPULATION 4,272,000
CAPITAL San José 1,217,000
RELIGION Roman Catholic, Evangelical
LANGUAGE Spanish, English
LITERACY 96%
LIFE EXPECTANCY 79 years
GDP PER CAPITA $12,000
ECONOMY **IND:** microprocessors, food processing, textiles and clothing, construction materials **AGR:** bananas, pineapples, coffee, melons; beef; timber **EXP:** bananas, pineapples, coffee, melons

Cuba
REPUBLIC OF CUBA

AREA 110,860 sq km (42,803 sq mi)
POPULATION 11,269,000
CAPITAL Havana 2,189,000
RELIGION Roman Catholic, Protestant, Jehovah's Witness, Jewish, Santeria
LANGUAGE Spanish
LITERACY 97%
LIFE EXPECTANCY 77 years
GDP PER CAPITA $3,900
ECONOMY **IND:** sugar, petroleum, tobacco, construction **AGR:** sugar, tobacco, citrus, coffee; livestock **EXP:** sugar, nickel, tobacco, fish

Dominica
COMMONWEALTH OF DOMINICA

AREA 751 sq km (290 sq mi)
POPULATION 69,000
CAPITAL Roseau 14,000
RELIGION Roman Catholic, Protestant
LANGUAGE English, French patois
LITERACY 94%
LIFE EXPECTANCY 74 years
GDP PER CAPITA $3,800
ECONOMY **IND:** soap, coconut oil, tourism, copra **AGR:** bananas, citrus, mangoes, root crops; forest and fishery potential not exploited **EXP:** bananas, soap, bay oil, vegetables

Dominican Republic
DOMINICAN REPUBLIC

AREA 48,442 sq km (18,704 sq mi)
POPULATION 9,017,000
CAPITAL Santo Domingo 2,022,000
RELIGION Roman Catholic
LANGUAGE Spanish
LITERACY 85%
LIFE EXPECTANCY 68 years
GDP PER CAPITA $8,000
ECONOMY **IND:** tourism, sugar processing, ferronickel and gold mining, textiles **AGR:** sugarcane, coffee, cotton, cocoa; cattle **EXP:** ferronickel, sugar, gold, silver

El Salvador
REPUBLIC OF EL SALVADOR

AREA 21,041 sq km (8,124 sq mi)
POPULATION 6,999,000
CAPITAL San Salvador 1,517,000
RELIGION Roman Catholic
LANGUAGE Spanish, Nahua
LITERACY 80%
LIFE EXPECTANCY 70 years
GDP PER CAPITA $4,900
ECONOMY **IND:** food processing, beverages, petroleum, chemicals **AGR:** coffee, sugar, corn, rice; beef; shrimp **EXP:** offshore assembly exports, coffee, sugar, shrimp

Grenada
GRENADA

AREA 344 sq km (133 sq mi)
POPULATION 99,000
CAPITAL St. George's 32,000
RELIGION Roman Catholic, Anglican, other Protestant
LANGUAGE English, French patois
LITERACY 96%
LIFE EXPECTANCY 71 years
GDP PER CAPITA $3,900
ECONOMY **IND:** food and beverages, textiles, light assembly operations, tourism **AGR:** bananas, cocoa, nutmeg, mace **EXP:** bananas, cocoa, nutmeg, fruit and vegetables

Guatemala
REPUBLIC OF GUATEMALA

AREA 108,889 sq km (42,042 sq mi)
POPULATION 13,019,000
CAPITAL Guatemala City 984,000
RELIGION Roman Catholic, Protestant, indigenous Mayan beliefs
LANGUAGE Spanish, Amerindian languages
LITERACY 71%
LIFE EXPECTANCY 67 years
GDP PER CAPITA $4,900
ECONOMY **IND:** sugar, textiles and clothing, furniture, chemicals **AGR:** sugarcane, corn, bananas, coffee; cattle **EXP:** coffee, sugar, petroleum, apparel

Haiti
REPUBLIC OF HAITI

AREA 27,750 sq km (10,714 sq mi)
POPULATION 8,522,000
CAPITAL Port-au-Prince 2,129,000
RELIGION Roman Catholic, Protestant
LANGUAGE French, Creole
LITERACY 53%
LIFE EXPECTANCY 52 years
GDP PER CAPITA $1,800
ECONOMY **IND:** sugar refining, flour milling, textiles, cement **AGR:** coffee, mangoes, sugarcane, rice; wood **EXP:** manufactures, coffee, oils, cocoa

Honduras
REPUBLIC OF HONDURAS

AREA 112,492 sq km (43,433 sq mi)
POPULATION 7,362,000
CAPITAL Tegucigalpa 927,000
RELIGION Roman Catholic
LANGUAGE Spanish, Amerindian dialects
LITERACY 76%
LIFE EXPECTANCY 71 years
GDP PER CAPITA $3,000
ECONOMY **IND:** sugar, coffee, textiles, clothing **AGR:** bananas, coffee, citrus; beef; timber; shrimp **EXP:** coffee, shrimp, bananas, gold

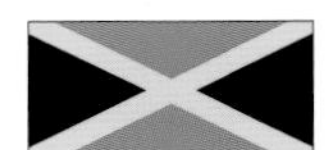

Jamaica
JAMAICA

AREA 10,991 sq km (4,244 sq mi)
POPULATION 2,666,000
CAPITAL Kingston 576,000
RELIGION Protestant
LANGUAGE English, English patois
LITERACY 88%
LIFE EXPECTANCY 71 years
GDP PER CAPITA $4,600
ECONOMY **IND:** tourism, bauxite/alumina, agro processing, light manufactures **AGR:** sugarcane, bananas, coffee, citrus; poultry; crustaceans **EXP:** alumina, bauxite, sugar, bananas

Mexico
UNITED MEXICAN STATES

AREA 1,964,375 sq km (758,449 sq mi)
POPULATION 108,327,000
CAPITAL Mexico City 19,411,000
RELIGION Roman Catholic, Protestant
LANGUAGE Spanish, various Mayan, Nahuatl, other indigenous languages
LITERACY 92%
LIFE EXPECTANCY 75 years
GDP PER CAPITA $10,600
ECONOMY **IND:** food and beverages, tobacco, chemicals, iron and steel **AGR:** corn, wheat, soybeans, rice; beef; wood products **EXP:** manufactured goods, oil and oil products, silver, fruits

Nicaragua
REPUBLIC OF NICARAGUA

AREA 130,000 sq km (50,193 sq mi)
POPULATION 5,600,000
CAPITAL Managua 1,165,000
RELIGION Roman Catholic, Evangelical
LANGUAGE Spanish
LITERACY 68%
LIFE EXPECTANCY 69 years
GDP PER CAPITA $3,000
ECONOMY **IND:** food processing, chemicals, machinery and metal products, textiles **AGR:** coffee, bananas, sugarcane, cotton; beef, shrimp **EXP:** coffee, beef, shrimp and lobster, tobacco

Panama
REPUBLIC OF PANAMA

AREA 75,517 sq km (29,157 sq mi)
POPULATION 3,284,000
CAPITAL Panama City 1,216,000
RELIGION Roman Catholic, Protestant
LANGUAGE Spanish, English
LITERACY 93%
LIFE EXPECTANCY 75 years
GDP PER CAPITA $7,900
ECONOMY **IND:** construction, brewing, cement and other construction materials, sugar milling **AGR:** bananas, rice, corn, coffee; livestock; shrimp **EXP:** bananas, shrimp, sugar, coffee

St. Kitts and Nevis
FEDERATION OF SAINT KITTS AND NEVIS

AREA 269 sq km (104 sq mi)
POPULATION 47,000
CAPITAL Basseterre 13,000
RELIGION Anglican, other Protestant, Roman Catholic
LANGUAGE English
LITERACY 98%
LIFE EXPECTANCY 70 years
GDP PER CAPITA $8,200
ECONOMY **IND:** tourism, cotton, salt, copra **AGR:** sugarcane, rice, yams, vegetables; fish **EXP:** machinery, food, electronics, beverages

St. Lucia

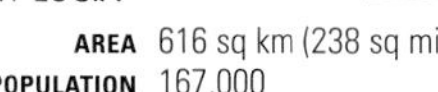

SAINT LUCIA

AREA 616 sq km (238 sq mi)
POPULATION 167,000
CAPITAL Castries 13,000
RELIGION Roman Catholic, Seventh-Day Adventist, Pentecostal
LANGUAGE English, French patois
LITERACY 90%
LIFE EXPECTANCY 74 years
GDP PER CAPITA $4,800
ECONOMY **IND:** clothing, assembly of electronic components, beverages, corrugated cardboard boxes **AGR:** bananas, coconuts, vegetables, citrus **EXP:** bananas, clothing, cocoa, vegetables

St. Vincent and the Grenadines

SAINT VINCENT AND THE GRENADINES

AREA 389 sq km (150 sq mi)
POPULATION 111,000
CAPITAL Kingstown 26,000
RELIGION Anglican, Methodist, Roman Catholic
LANGUAGE English, French patois
LITERACY 96%
LIFE EXPECTANCY 71 years
GDP PER CAPITA $3,600
ECONOMY **IND:** food processing, cement, furniture, clothing **AGR:** bananas, coconuts, sweet potatoes, spices; cattle; fish **EXP:** bananas, eddoes and dasheen (taro), arrowroot starch, tennis racquets

Trinidad and Tobago

REPUBLIC OF TRINIDAD AND TOBAGO

AREA 5,128 sq km (1,980 sq mi)
POPULATION 1,307,000
CAPITAL Port-of-Spain 52,000
RELIGION Roman Catholic, Hindu, Anglican, Baptist, Pentecostal, Muslim
LANGUAGE English, Hindustani, French, Spanish, Chinese
LITERACY 99%
LIFE EXPECTANCY 70 years
GDP PER CAPITA $19,700
ECONOMY **IND:** petroleum, chemicals, tourism, food processing **AGR:** cocoa, rice, citrus, coffee; poultry **EXP:** petroleum and petroleum products, chemicals, steel products, fertilizer

United States

UNITED STATES OF AMERICA

AREA 9,826,630 sq km (3,794,083 sq mi)
POPULATION 299,112,000
CAPITAL Washington, D.C. 4,238,000
RELIGION Protestant, Roman Catholic
LANGUAGE English, Spanish
LITERACY 99%
LIFE EXPECTANCY 78 years
GDP PER CAPITA $43,500
ECONOMY **IND:** petroleum, steel, motor vehicles, aerospace **AGR:** wheat, corn, other grains, fruits; beef; forest products; fish **EXP:** capital goods, industrial supplies, consumer goods, agricultural products

Dependencies

Anguilla (U.K.)

ANGUILLA

AREA 96 sq km (37 sq mi)
POPULATION 13,000
CAPITAL The Valley 1,000
RELIGION Anglican, Methodist, other Protestant, Roman Catholic
LANGUAGE English
LITERACY 95%
LIFE EXPECTANCY 79 years
GDP PER CAPITA $8,800
ECONOMY **IND:** tourism, boat building, offshore financial services **AGR:** small quantities of tobacco, vegetables; cattle raising **EXP:** lobster, fish, livestock, salt

Aruba (Netherlands)

ARUBA

AREA 193 sq km (75 sq mi)
POPULATION 98,000
CAPITAL Oranjestad 30,000
RELIGION Roman Catholic, Protestant
LANGUAGE Papiamento, Spanish, English, Dutch
LITERACY 97%
LIFE EXPECTANCY 79 years
GDP PER CAPITA $21,800
ECONOMY **IND:** tourism, transshipment facilities, oil refining **AGR:** aloes; livestock; fish **EXP:** live animals and animal products, art and collectibles, machinery and electrical equipment, transport equipment

Bermuda (U.K.)

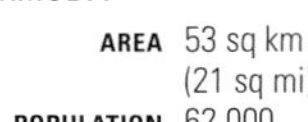

BERMUDA

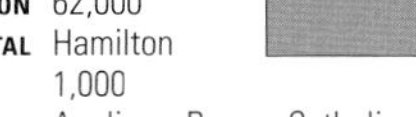

AREA 53 sq km (21 sq mi)
POPULATION 62,000
CAPITAL Hamilton 1,000
RELIGION Anglican, Roman Catholic, African Methodist Episcopal
LANGUAGE English, Portuguese
LITERACY 98%
LIFE EXPECTANCY 78 years
GDP PER CAPITA $69,900
ECONOMY **IND:** tourism, international business, light manufacturing **AGR:** bananas, vegetables, citrus, flowers; dairy products **EXP:** reexports of pharmaceuticals

British Virgin Islands (U.K.)

BRITISH VIRGIN ISLANDS

AREA 153 sq km (59 sq mi)
POPULATION 22,000
CAPITAL Road Town 13,000
RELIGION Protestant, Roman Catholic
LANGUAGE English
LITERACY 98%
LIFE EXPECTANCY 74 years
GDP PER CAPITA $38,500
ECONOMY **IND:** tourism, light industry, construction, rum **AGR:** fruits, vegetables; livestock; fish **EXP:** rum, fresh fish, fruits, animals

Cayman Islands (U.K.)

CAYMAN ISLANDS

AREA 262 sq km (101 sq mi)
POPULATION 45,000
CAPITAL George Town 26,000
RELIGION United Church, Anglican, Baptist, Church of God
LANGUAGE English
LITERACY 98%
LIFE EXPECTANCY 79 years
GDP PER CAPITA $43,800
ECONOMY **IND:** tourism, banking, insurance and finance, construction **AGR:** vegetables, fruit; livestock; turtle farming **EXP:** turtle products, manufactured consumer goods

Greenland (Denmark)

GREENLAND

AREA 2,166,086 sq km (836,086 sq mi)
POPULATION 57,000
CAPITAL Nuuk (Godthåb) 15,000
RELIGION Evangelical Lutheran
LANGUAGE Greenlandic, Danish, English
LITERACY 100%
LIFE EXPECTANCY 67 years
GDP PER CAPITA $20,000
ECONOMY **IND:** fish processing (shrimp, halibut), mining, handicrafts, hides and skins **AGR:** forage crops, garden and greenhouse vegetables; sheep; fish **EXP:** prawns, fish and fish products

Guadeloupe (France)

OVERSEAS DEPARTMENT OF FRANCE

AREA 1,705 sq km (658 sq mi)
POPULATION 461,000
CAPITAL Basse-Terre 11,000
RELIGION Roman Catholic
LANGUAGE French
LITERACY 90%
LIFE EXPECTANCY 78 years
GDP PER CAPITA $7,900
ECONOMY **IND:** construction, cement, rum, sugar **AGR:** bananas, sugarcane, tropical fruits and vegetables; cattle **EXP:** bananas, sugar, rum

Martinique (France)

OVERSEAS DEPARTMENT OF FRANCE

AREA 1,100 sq km (425 sq mi)
POPULATION 398,000
CAPITAL Fort-de-France 91,000
RELIGION Roman Catholic, Protestant
LANGUAGE French, Creole patois
LITERACY 98%
LIFE EXPECTANCY 79 years
GDP PER CAPITA $14,400
ECONOMY **IND:** construction, rum, cement, oil refining **AGR:** pineapples, avocados, bananas, flowers **EXP:** refined petroleum products, bananas, rum, pineapples

Montserrat (U.K.)

MONTSERRAT

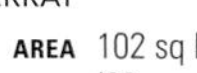

AREA 102 sq km (39 sq mi)
POPULATION 5,000
CAPITAL Brades (administrative) 1,000; Plymouth (abandoned) 0
RELIGION Anglican, Methodist, Roman Catholic, other Protestant
LANGUAGE English
LITERACY 97%
LIFE EXPECTANCY NA
GDP PER CAPITA $3,400
ECONOMY **IND:** tourism, rum, textiles, electronic appliances **AGR:** cabbages, carrots, cucumbers, tomatoes; livestock products **EXP:** electronic components, plastic bags, apparel, hot peppers

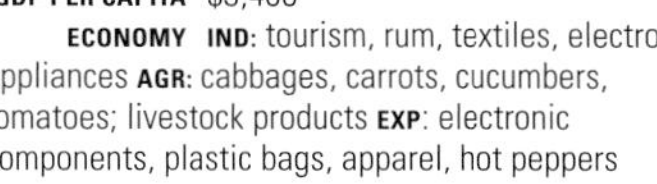

Puerto Rico (U.S.)

COMMONWEALTH OF PUERTO RICO

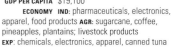

AREA 9,086 sq km (3,508 sq mi)
POPULATION 3,929,000
CAPITAL San Juan 2,605,000
RELIGION Roman Catholic, Protestant
LANGUAGE Spanish, English
LITERACY 94%
LIFE EXPECTANCY 77 years
GDP PER CAPITA $19,100
ECONOMY **IND:** pharmaceuticals, electronics, apparel, food products **AGR:** sugarcane, coffee, pineapples, plantains; livestock products **EXP:** chemicals, electronics, apparel, canned tuna

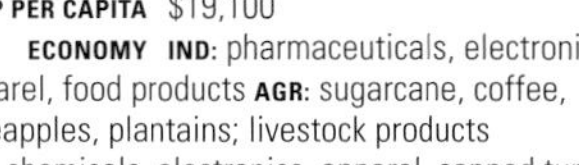

St.-Pierre and Miquelon (France)

TERRITORIAL COLLECTIVITY OF SAINT PIERRE AND MIQUELON

AREA 242 sq km (93 sq mi)
POPULATION 7,000
CAPITAL St.-Pierre 5,000
RELIGION Roman Catholic
LANGUAGE French
LITERACY 99%
LIFE EXPECTANCY NA
GDP PER CAPITA $7,000
ECONOMY **IND:** fish processing and supply base for fishing fleets, tourism **AGR:** vegetables; poultry, cattle; fish **EXP:** fish and fish products, soybeans, animal feed, mollusks and crustaceans

Dependencies, continued

Turks and Caicos Islands
(U.K.)

SOVEREIGN

LOCAL

TURKS AND CAICOS ISLANDS

AREA 430 sq km (166 sq mi)
POPULATION 21,000
CAPITAL Cockburn Town (on Grand Turk island) 4,000
RELIGION Baptist, Anglican, Methodist, Church of God
LANGUAGE English
LITERACY 98%
LIFE EXPECTANCY 74 years
GDP PER CAPITA $11,500
ECONOMY **IND:** tourism, offshore financial services **AGR:** corn, beans, cassava, citrus fruits; fish **EXP:** lobster, dried and fresh conch, conch shells

Virgin Islands
(U.S.)

SOVEREIGN

LOCAL

UNITED STATES VIRGIN ISLANDS

AREA 386 sq km (149 sq mi)
POPULATION 109,000
CAPITAL Charlotte Amalie 52,000
RELIGION Baptist, Roman Catholic, Episcopalian
LANGUAGE English, Spanish or Spanish Creole, French or French Creole
LITERACY 90-95%
LIFE EXPECTANCY 79 years
GDP PER CAPITA $14,500
ECONOMY **IND:** tourism, petroleum refining, watch assembly, rum distilling **AGR:** fruit, vegetables, sorghum; Senepol cattle **EXP:** refined petroleum products

United States' State Flags

Alabama
POPULATION 4,599,000
CAPITAL Montgomery

Alaska
POPULATION 670,000
CAPITAL Juneau

Arizona
POPULATION 6,166,000
CAPITAL Phoenix

Arkansas
POPULATION 2,811,000
CAPITAL Little Rock

California
POPULATION 36,458,000
CAPITAL Sacramento

Colorado
POPULATION 4,753,000
CAPITAL Denver

Connecticut
POPULATION 3,505,000
CAPITAL Hartford

Delaware
POPULATION 853,000
CAPITAL Dover

Florida
POPULATION 18,090,000
CAPITAL Tallahassee

Georgia
POPULATION 9,364,000
CAPITAL Atlanta

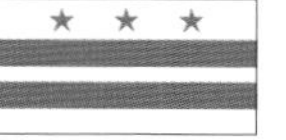

District of Columbia
POPULATION 582,000
United States capital

Hawai'i
POPULATION 1,285,000
CAPITAL Honolulu

Idaho
POPULATION 1,466,000
CAPITAL Boise

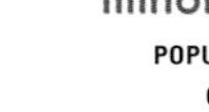

Illinois
POPULATION 12,832,000
CAPITAL Springfield

Indiana
POPULATION 6,314,000
CAPITAL Indianapolis

Iowa
POPULATION 2,982,000
CAPITAL Des Moines

Kansas
POPULATION 2,764,000
CAPITAL Topeka

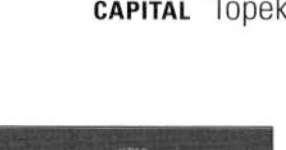

Kentucky
POPULATION 4,206,000
CAPITAL Frankfort

Louisiana
POPULATION 4,288,000
CAPITAL Baton Rouge

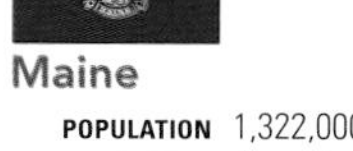

Maine
POPULATION 1,322,000
CAPITAL Augusta

Maryland
POPULATION 5,616,000
CAPITAL Annapolis

Massachusetts
POPULATION 6,437,000
CAPITAL Boston

Michigan
POPULATION 10,096,000
CAPITAL Lansing

Minnesota
POPULATION 5,167,000
CAPITAL St. Paul

Mississippi
POPULATION 2,911,000
CAPITAL Jackson

Missouri
POPULATION 5,843,000
CAPITAL Jefferson City

Montana
POPULATION 945,000
CAPITAL Helena

Nebraska
POPULATION 1,768,000
CAPITAL Lincoln

Nevada
POPULATION 2,496,000
CAPITAL Carson City

New Hampshire
POPULATION 1,315,000
CAPITAL Concord

New Jersey
POPULATION 8,725,000
CAPITAL Trenton

New Mexico
POPULATION 1,955,000
CAPITAL Santa Fe

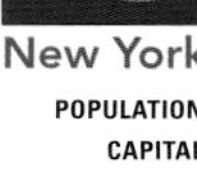

New York
POPULATION 19,306,000
CAPITAL Albany

North Carolina
POPULATION 8,857,000
CAPITAL Raleigh

North Dakota
POPULATION 636,000
CAPITAL Bismarck

Ohio
POPULATION 11,478,000
CAPITAL Columbus

Oklahoma
POPULATION 3,579,000
CAPITAL Oklahoma City

Oregon
POPULATION 3,701,000
CAPITAL Salem

Pennsylvania
POPULATION 12,441,000
CAPITAL Harrisburg

Rhode Island
POPULATION 1,068,000
CAPITAL Providence

South Carolina
POPULATION 4,321,000
CAPITAL Columbia

South Dakota
POPULATION 782,000
CAPITAL Pierre

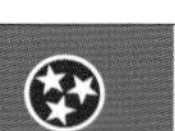
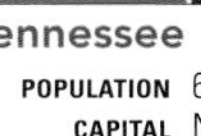

Tennessee
POPULATION 6,039,000
CAPITAL Nashville

Texas
POPULATION 23,508,000
CAPITAL Austin

Utah
POPULATION 2,550,000
CAPITAL Salt Lake City

Vermont
POPULATION 624,000
CAPITAL Montpelier

Virginia
POPULATION 7,643,000
CAPITAL Richmond

Washington
POPULATION 6,396,000
CAPITAL Olympia

West Virginia
POPULATION 1,818,000
CAPITAL Charleston

Wisconsin
POPULATION 5,557,000
CAPITAL Madison

Wyoming
POPULATION 515,000
CAPITAL Cheyenne

Dates of National Independence

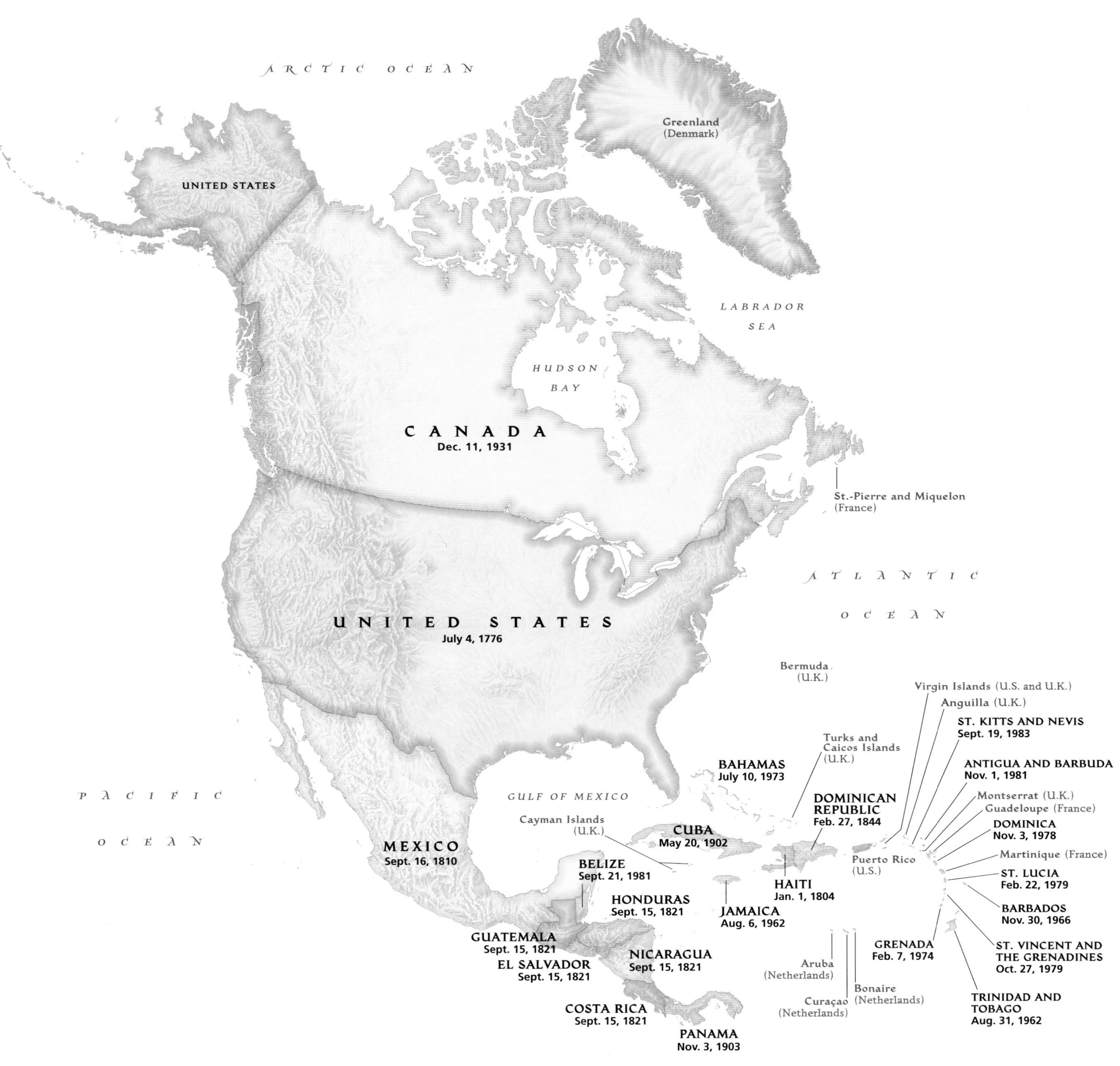

NOTE: For some countries, the date given may not represent "independence" in the strict sense—but rather some significant nationhood event: the traditional founding date; a fundamental change in the form of government; or perhaps the date of unification, secession, federation, confederation, or state succession.

Land Cover
Water
Evergreen needleleaf forest
Evergreen broadleaf forest
Deciduous broadleaf forest
Mixed forest
Closed shrubland
Open shrubland
Woody savanna
Savanna
Grassland
Permanent wetland
Cropland
Urban and built-up
Cropland/natural vegetation mosaic
Snow and ice
Barren or sparsely vegetated

South America

CONTINENT OF EXTREMES, South America extends from the Isthmus of Panama, in the Northern Hemisphere, to a ragged tail less than 700 miles from Antarctica. There the Andes, a continuous continental rampart that forms the world's second highest range, finally dives undersea to continue as a submarine ridge. Occupying nearly half the continent, the world's largest and biologically richest rain forest spans the Equator, drained by the Amazon River, second longest river but largest by volume anywhere.

These formidable natural barriers shaped lopsided patterns of settlement in South America, the fourth largest continent. As early as 1531, when Spaniard Francisco Pizarro began his conquest of the Inca Empire, Iberians were pouring into coastal settlements that now hold most of the continent's burgeoning population. Meanwhile, Portuguese planters imported millions of African slaves to work vast sugar estates on Brazil's littoral. There and elsewhere, wealth and power coalesced in family oligarchies and in the Roman Catholic Church, building a system that 19th-century liberal revolutions failed to dismantle.

But eventual independence did not necessarily bring regional unity: Boundary wars dragged on into the 20th century before yielding the present-day borders of 12 nations. French Guiana remains an overseas department ruled from Paris; the Falkland Islands are a dependent territory of the United Kingdom. Natural riches still dominate economies, in the form of processed agricultural goods and minerals, as manufacturing matures. Privatization of nationalized industries in the 1990s followed free-market policies instituted by military regimes in the '70s and '80s, sometimes adding tumult to nations troubled by debt and inflation. By the end of the century however, democracy had flowered across the continent, spurring an era of relative prosperity.

A rich blend of Iberian, African, and Amerindian traditions, South America has one of the world's most lively and distinctive cultures. Although the majority of people can still trace their ancestors back to Spain or Portugal, waves of immigration have transformed South America into an ethnic smorgasbord. This blend has produced a vibrant modern culture with influence far beyond the bounds of its South American cradle.

The vast majority of South Americans live in cities rather than the rain forest or mountains. A massive rural exodus since the 1950s has transformed South America into the second most urbanized continent (after Australia), a region that now boasts three of the world's 15 largest cities—São Paulo, Buenos Aires, and Rio de Janeiro. Ninety percent of the people live within 200 miles (320 km) of the coast, leaving huge expanses of the interior virtually unpopulated. Despite protests from indigenous tribes and environmental groups, South American governments have tried to spur growth by opening up the Amazon region to economic exploitation, thereby wreaking ecological havoc. The Amazon could very well be the key to the region's economic future—not by the decimation of the world's richest forest, but by the sustainable management and commercial development of its largely untapped biodiversity into medical, chemical, and nutritional products.

Longitude West 55° of Greenwich
EQUATOR
TROPIC OF CAPRICORN
COLOMBIA
VENEZUELA
GUYANA
SURINAME
FRENCH GUIANA
France
Boundary claimed by Suriname
ECUADOR
PERU
BRAZIL
BOLIVIA
PARAGUAY
TRINIDAD AND TOBAGO
PANAMA
Panamá
PANAMA CANAL
Golfo de Panamá
Golfo de Venezuela
Golfo de Guayaquil
I. de San Andrés
Colombia
Isla de Malpelo
Colombia
Arquipélago de Fernando de Noronha
Brazil
Atol das Rocas
Brazil
Ilha de Marajó
Lago Titicaca
Represa da Balbina
Represa de Sobradinho
Orinoco
Negro
Branco
Amazonas (Amazon)
Solimões (Amazonas)
Marañón
Madeira
Purus
Tapajós
Teles Pires (São Manuel)
Xingu
Araguaia
Tocantins
São Francisco
Paraguay
Paranaíba
BOGOTÁ
CARACAS
QUITO
LIMA
LA PAZ (administrative)
Sucre (constitutional)
BRASÍLIA
Asunción
Georgetown
Paramaribo
Cayenne
Port-of-Spain
BARRANQUILLA
CARTAGENA
MARACAIBO
MEDELLÍN
CALI
VALENCIA
GUAYAQUIL
TRUJILLO
COCHABAMBA
Santa Cruz
MANAUS
BELÉM
FORTALEZA
RECIFE
SALVADOR (Bahia)
BELO HORIZONTE
RIO DE JANEIRO
SÃO PAULO
CURITIBA
GOIÂNIA
NOVA IGUAÇU
Duque de Caxias
Niterói
Natal
João Pessoa
Maceió
Aracaju
Teresina
São Luís
Santarém
Macapá
Porto Velho
Rio Branco
Iquitos
Barquisimeto
Ciudad Guayana
Ciudad Bolívar
Maturín
Cumaná
Barcelona
Santa Marta
Cúcuta
Bucaramanga
Ibagué
Pereira
Manizales
Popayán
Pasto
Cuenca
Chiclayo
Piura
Arequipa
Cusco
Huancayo
Oruro
Potosí
Tarija
Campo Grande
Cuiabá
Londrina
Santos
Uberlândia
Ribeirão Preto
Juiz de Fora
Vitória
Feira de Santana
Campina Grande
Imperatriz
Marabá
Santa Maria
Boa Vista

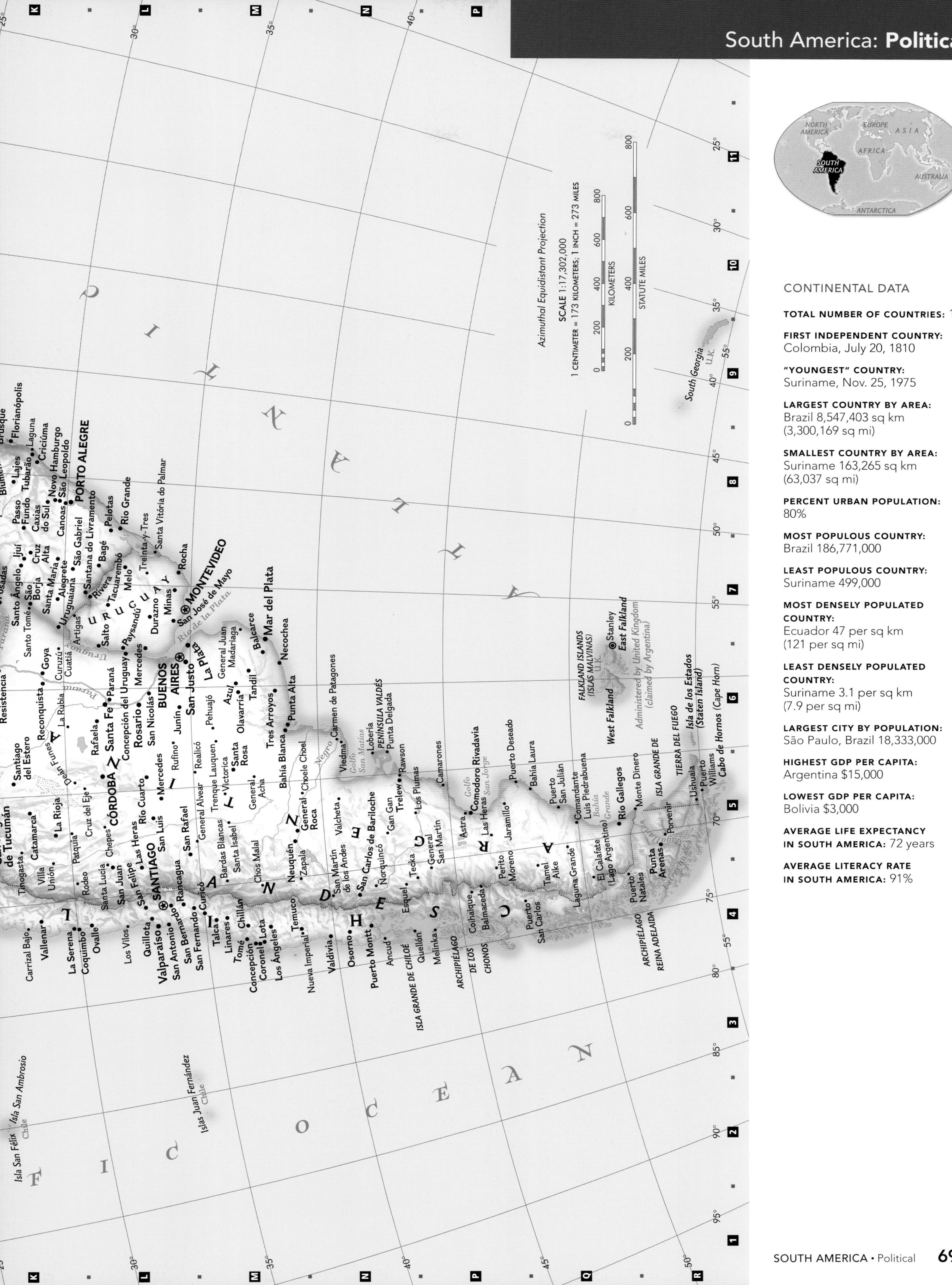

CONTINENTAL DATA

TOTAL NUMBER OF COUNTRIES: 12

FIRST INDEPENDENT COUNTRY:
Colombia, July 20, 1810

"YOUNGEST" COUNTRY:
Suriname, Nov. 25, 1975

LARGEST COUNTRY BY AREA:
Brazil 8,547,403 sq km
(3,300,169 sq mi)

SMALLEST COUNTRY BY AREA:
Suriname 163,265 sq km
(63,037 sq mi)

PERCENT URBAN POPULATION:
80%

MOST POPULOUS COUNTRY:
Brazil 186,771,000

LEAST POPULOUS COUNTRY:
Suriname 499,000

MOST DENSELY POPULATED COUNTRY:
Ecuador 47 per sq km
(121 per sq mi)

LEAST DENSELY POPULATED COUNTRY:
Suriname 3.1 per sq km
(7.9 per sq mi)

LARGEST CITY BY POPULATION:
São Paulo, Brazil 18,333,000

HIGHEST GDP PER CAPITA:
Argentina $15,000

LOWEST GDP PER CAPITA:
Bolivia $3,000

AVERAGE LIFE EXPECTANCY IN SOUTH AMERICA: 72 years

AVERAGE LITERACY RATE IN SOUTH AMERICA: 91%

Longitude West 55° of Greenwich
CARIBBEAN SEA
LESSER ANTILLES
Guajira Peninsula
Gulf of Venezuela
Paraguaná Pen.
Margarita I.
Paria Pen.
Tobago
Trinidad
Tortuga I.
Serra Nevada de Santa Marta
5775
Lake Maracaibo
L. Valencia
Coast Range
2660
Maracaibo Basin
Gulf of Morrosquillo
Gulf of Urabá
PANAMA CANAL
Isthmus of Panama
Gulf of Panama
Magdalena
Cordillera de Mérida
5007
Apure
Orinoco
Orinoco River Delta
Shell Beach
LLANOS
Angel Falls
Total drop 979 meters
World's highest waterfall
Pakaraima Mts.
Mt. Roraima
2772
GUIANA HIGHLANDS
Sierra Pacaraima
Essequibo
Maroni
Devil's Island
Cape Orange
Wilhelmina Mts.
Kanuku Mts.
854
Serra de Tumucumaque
Maracá Island
Mouths of the Amazon
Serranía de Baudó
4080
Cauca
5493
Cordillera Central
Cordillera Oriental
Tomo
Guaviare
Malpelo Island
Buenaventura Bay
Source of the Orinoco
Pico da Neblina
3014
Ajajú
Negro
Branco
Balbina Reservoir
Paru
Galera Point
Gurupá I.
Marajó Island
Marajó Bay
Cape Gurupi
EQUATOR
AMAZON
Chimborazo
6310
Amazon (Solimões)
Napo
Amazon
Tapajós
Xingu
Tocantins
Serra do Tiracambu
São Marcos Bay
Pt. Jericoacoara
Santa Elena Peninsula
Gulf of Guayaquil
Pongo de Manseriche
Juruá
Purus
Madeira
Parnaíba
Sa. da Ibiapaba
725
Fernando de Noronha
Atol das Rocas
Cape São Roque
Marañón
Selvas
Caatinga
Araguaia
Aguja Point
Sechura Desert
Lobos Islands
BASIN
Ucayali
LA MONTAÑA
Cordillera Oriental
Cordillera Central
Teles Pires
Sa. do Uruçuí
Sobradinho Reservoir
Borborema Plateau
1123
São Francisco
Sertão
Nevado Huascarán
6768
Beni
Jiparaná
Juruena
Serra do Tombador
Serra Formosa
BRAZILIAN
Manguinho Point
Serra dos Parecis
640
670
Sa. do Roncador
Espigão Mestre
Guaporé
Mamoré
ANDES
OCCIDENTAL
Chincha Is.
Apurímac
Source of the Amazon
Lake Titicaca
3810
Illampu
6362
Yungas
Securé
Serra Dourada
1349
Campos
Todos os Santos Bay
Illimani
6462
Cord. Oriental
Cordillera Central
Altiplano
5453
Grande
Bañados del Izozog
Pantanal
HIGHLANDS
Serra do Espinhaço
2040
Baleia Point
Madrid Point
Atacama Desert
Salar de Uyuni
Chaco Boreal
Paraguay
Serra de Maracaju
558
Paraná
Paranaíba
Pico de la Bandeira
2890
Source of the Paraná
Serra da Mantiqueira
Cape São Tomé
Cape Frio
Angamos Point
Pilcomayo
Sete Quedas Falls
Iguazú Falls
Serra do Mar
Puna de Atacama
Cerro Galan
6600
TROPIC OF CAPRICORN
PACIFIC
OCEAN

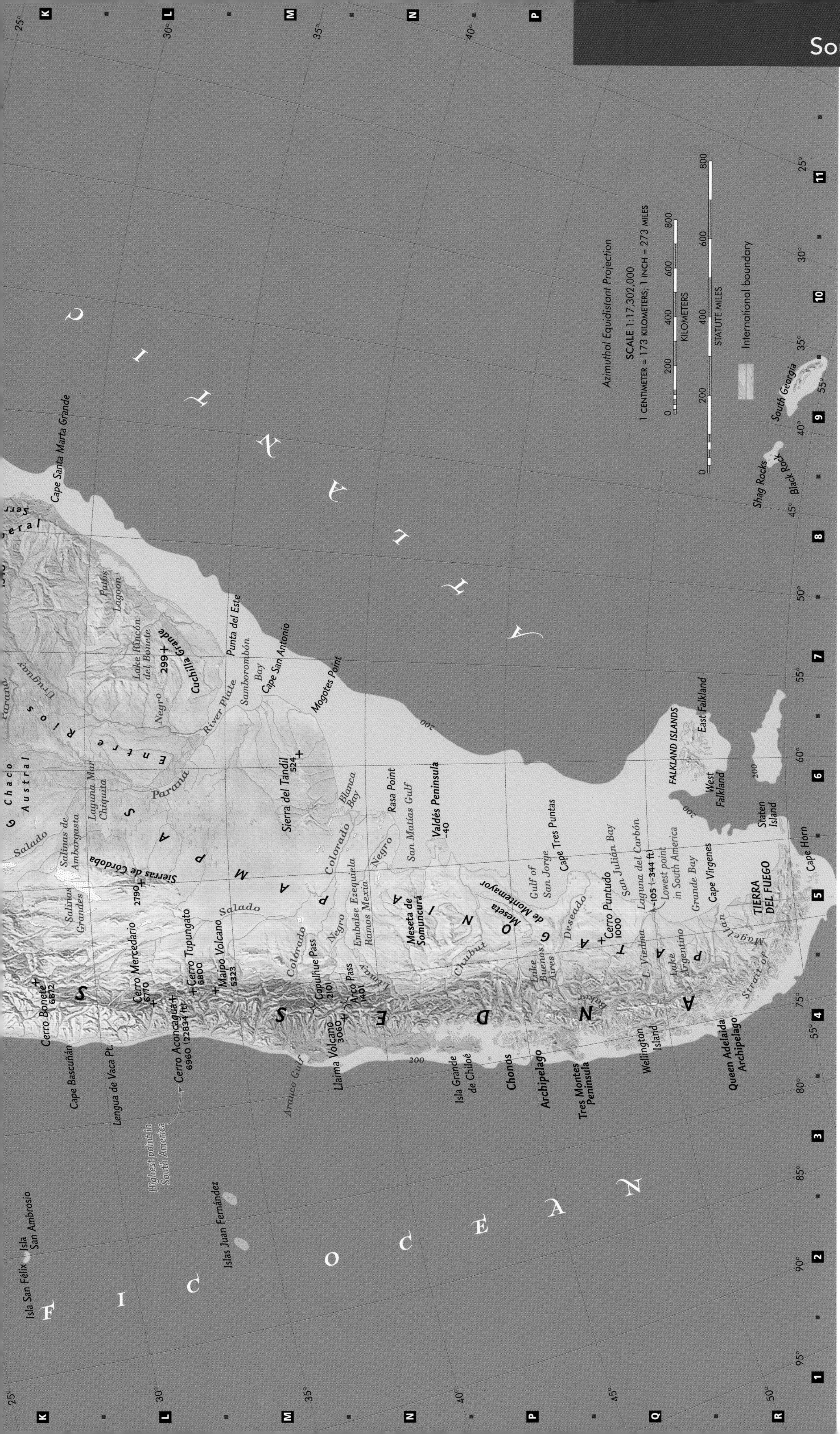

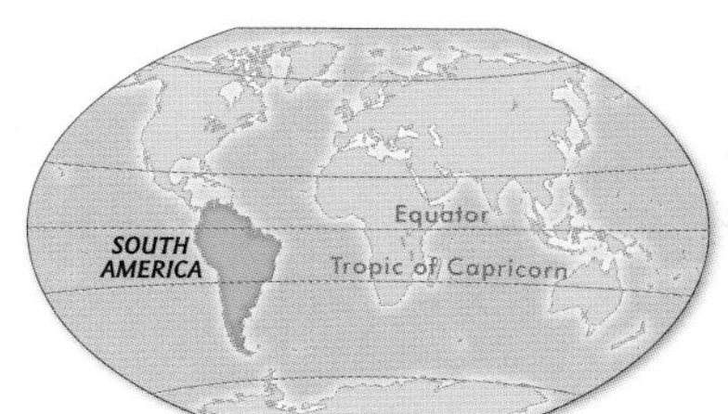

CONTINENTAL DATA

AREA:
17,819,000 sq km
(6,880,000 sq mi)

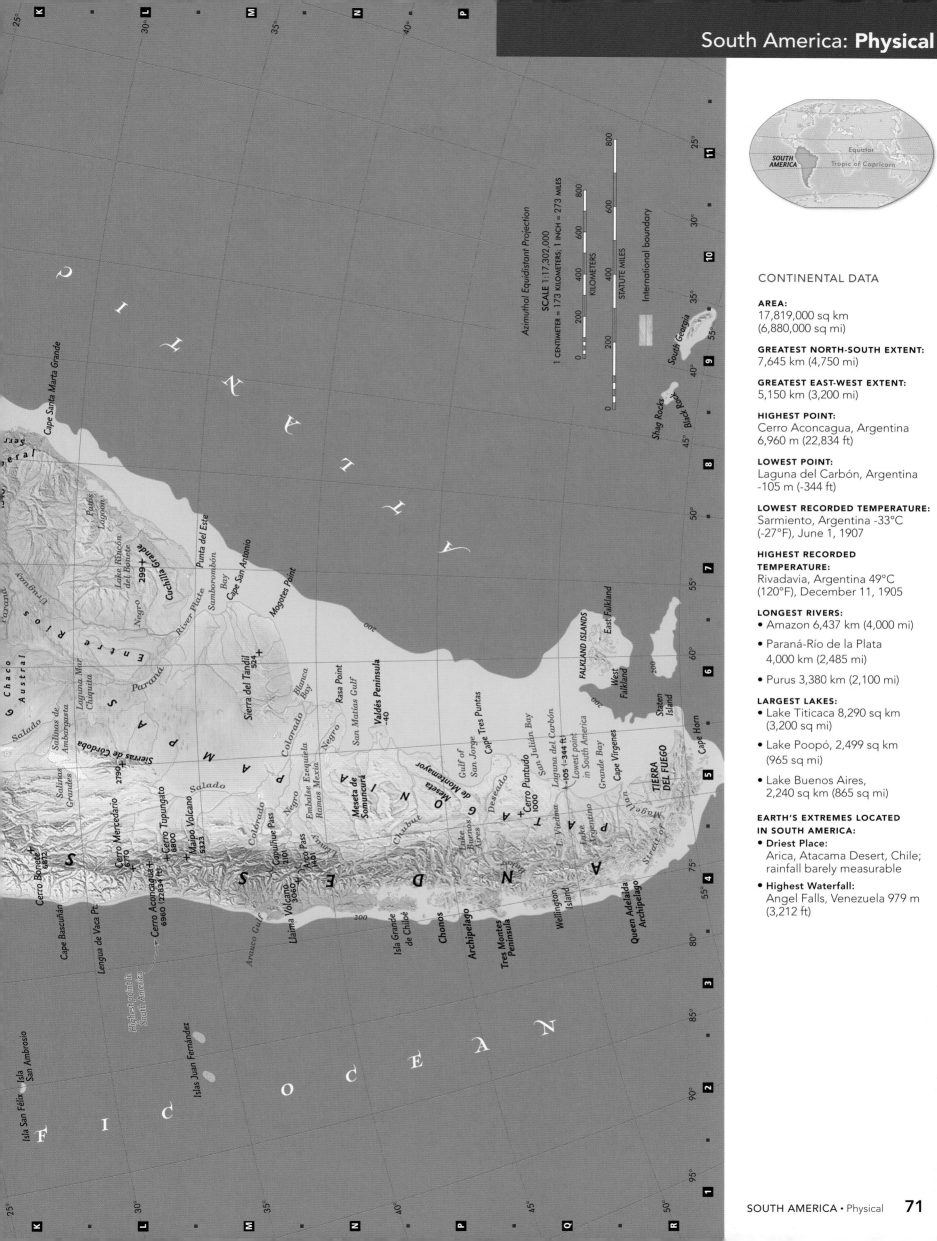

GREATEST NORTH-SOUTH EXTENT:
7,645 km (4,750 mi)

GREATEST EAST-WEST EXTENT:
5,150 km (3,200 mi)

HIGHEST POINT:
Cerro Aconcagua, Argentina
6,960 m (22,834 ft)

LOWEST POINT:
Laguna del Carbón, Argentina
-105 m (-344 ft)

LOWEST RECORDED TEMPERATURE:
Sarmiento, Argentina -33°C
(-27°F), June 1, 1907

HIGHEST RECORDED TEMPERATURE:
Rivadavia, Argentina 49°C
(120°F), December 11, 1905

LONGEST RIVERS:
- Amazon 6,437 km (4,000 mi)
- Paraná-Río de la Plata 4,000 km (2,485 mi)
- Purus 3,380 km (2,100 mi)

LARGEST LAKES:
- Lake Titicaca 8,290 sq km (3,200 sq mi)
- Lake Poopó, 2,499 sq km (965 sq mi)
- Lake Buenos Aires, 2,240 sq km (865 sq mi)

EARTH'S EXTREMES LOCATED IN SOUTH AMERICA:
- **Driest Place:** Arica, Atacama Desert, Chile; rainfall barely measurable
- **Highest Waterfall:** Angel Falls, Venezuela 979 m (3,212 ft)

Population Density
VENEZUELA
GUYANA
SURINAME
French Guiana (FRANCE)
COLOMBIA
St. Peter and St. Paul Rocks (BRAZIL)
Arquipélago Fernando de Noronha
ECUADOR
Galápagos Islands (ECUADOR)
Atol das Rocas (BRAZIL)
PERU
BRAZIL
BOLIVIA
Is. Martin Vaz
I. de Trindade (BRAZIL)
CHILE
PARAGUAY
I. San Félix
Isla San Ambrosio (CHILE)
URUGUAY
POPULATION DENSITY
People per square km
People per square mi
More than 195 | More than 500
60 - 195 | 150 - 500
10 - 59 | 25 - 149
1 - 9 | 1 - 24
Less than 1 | Less than 1
Archipiélago Juan Fernández (CHILE)
ARGENTINA
Falkland Islands (U.K.)
Is. Diego Ramírez (CHILE)
Energy Consumption
VENEZUELA
GUYANA
SURINAME
French Guiana (FRANCE)
COLOMBIA
ECUADOR
Galápagos Islands (ECUADOR)
BRAZIL
PERU
BOLIVIA
PER CAPITA ENERGY CONSUMPTION
(in million Btu)
More than 300
201 - 300
101 - 200
31 - 100
Less than 30
Major energy deposit
Coal
Natural gas
Oil
Oil pipeline
CHILE
PARAGUAY
ARGENTINA
URUGUAY
Falkland Islands (U.K.)
Dominant Economy
VENEZUELA
GUYANA
SURINAME
French Guiana (FRANCE)
COLOMBIA
ECUADOR
Galápagos Islands (ECUADOR)
PERU
BRAZIL
BOLIVIA
PARAGUAY
CHILE
URUGUAY
ARGENTINA
DOMINANT ECONOMY
(per GDP sector)
Service
Service - Industrial
Service - Industrial - Agricultural
No data available
Falkland Islands (U.K.)
SERVICE 100%
PERU
SURINAME
VENEZUELA
GUYANA
AGRICULTURAL 100%
INDUSTRIAL 100%
SOUTH AMERICA'S ECONOMY
per Gross Domestic Product (GDP) sector

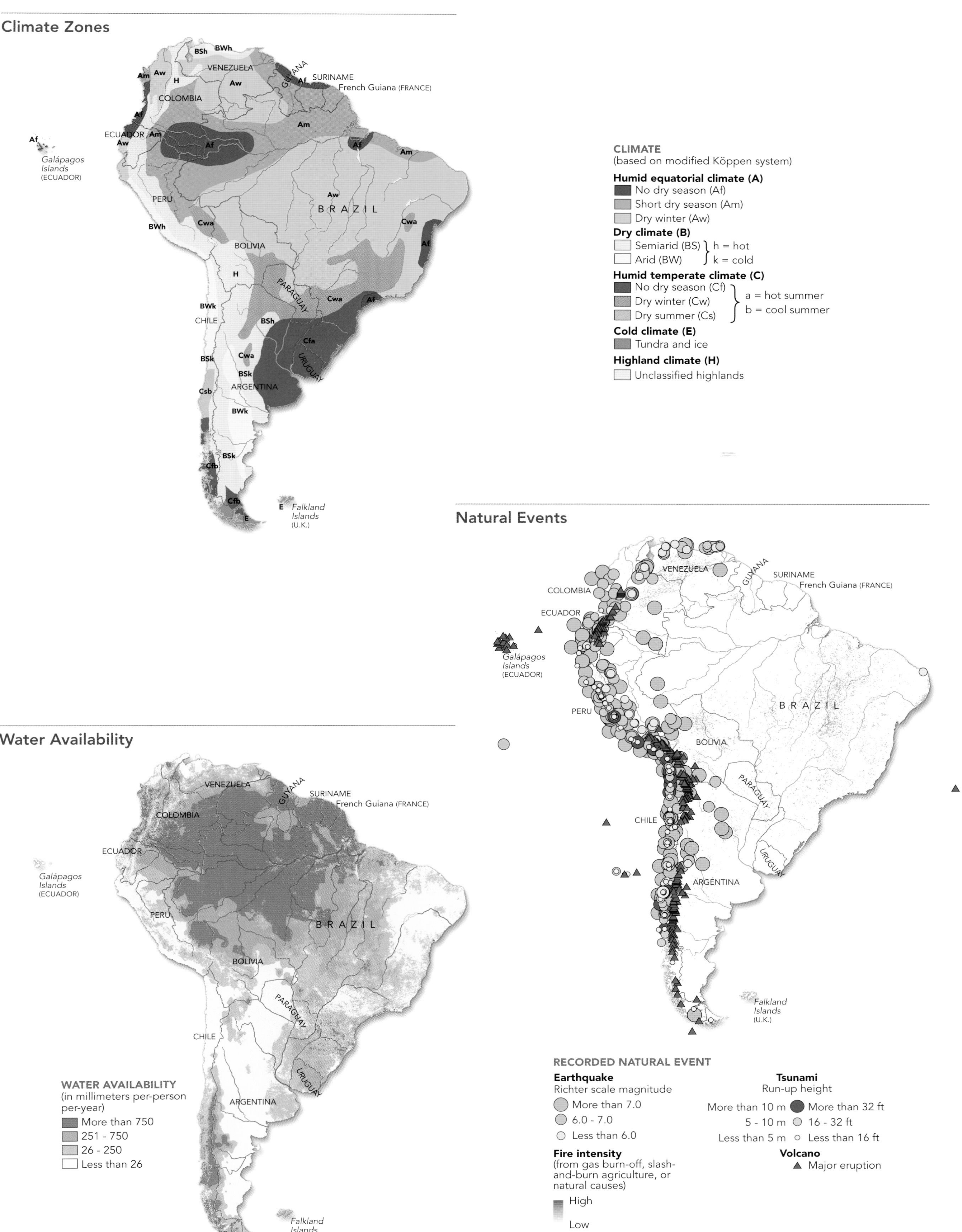

Climate Zones
BSh
BWh
VENEZUELA
Am
Aw
H
Aw
GUYANA
Af
SURINAME
French Guiana (FRANCE)
COLOMBIA
Af
Af
Galápagos
Islands
(ECUADOR)
ECUADOR
Am
Aw
Af
Am
Af
Am
PERU
Aw
BRAZIL
BWh
Cwa
Cwa
Af
BOLIVIA
H
PARAGUAY
Cwa
Af
BWk
CHILE
BSh
Cfa
BSk
Cwa
URUGUAY
BSk
ARGENTINA
Csb
BWk
BSk
Cfb
Cfb
E
E
Falkland
Islands
(U.K.)
CLIMATE
(based on modified Köppen system)
Humid equatorial climate (A)
No dry season (Af)
Short dry season (Am)
Dry winter (Aw)
Dry climate (B)
Semiarid (BS)
Arid (BW)
h = hot
k = cold
Humid temperate climate (C)
No dry season (Cf)
Dry winter (Cw)
Dry summer (Cs)
a = hot summer
b = cool summer
Cold climate (E)
Tundra and ice
Highland climate (H)
Unclassified highlands
Natural Events
VENEZUELA
GUYANA
SURINAME
French Guiana (FRANCE)
COLOMBIA
ECUADOR
Galápagos
Islands
(ECUADOR)
BRAZIL
PERU
BOLIVIA
PARAGUAY
CHILE
URUGUAY
ARGENTINA
Falkland
Islands
(U.K.)
RECORDED NATURAL EVENT
Earthquake
Richter scale magnitude
More than 7.0
6.0 - 7.0
Less than 6.0
Tsunami
Run-up height
More than 10 m
More than 32 ft
5 - 10 m
16 - 32 ft
Less than 5 m
Less than 16 ft
Fire intensity
(from gas burn-off, slash-and-burn agriculture, or natural causes)
High
Low
Volcano
Major eruption
Water Availability
VENEZUELA
GUYANA
SURINAME
French Guiana (FRANCE)
COLOMBIA
ECUADOR
Galápagos
Islands
(ECUADOR)
PERU
BRAZIL
BOLIVIA
PARAGUAY
CHILE
URUGUAY
ARGENTINA
Falkland
Islands
(U.K.)
WATER AVAILABILITY
(in millimeters per-person per-year)
More than 750
251 - 750
26 - 250
Less than 26

Nations

Argentina

ARGENTINE REPUBLIC

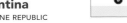

AREA 2,780,400 sq km (1,073,518 sq mi)
POPULATION 38,971,000
CAPITAL Buenos Aires 12,550,000
RELIGION Roman Catholic
LANGUAGE Spanish, English, Italian, German, French
LITERACY 97%
LIFE EXPECTANCY 74 years
GDP PER CAPITA $15,000
ECONOMY **IND:** food processing, motor vehicles, consumer durables, textiles **AGR:** sunflower seeds, lemons, soybeans, grapes; livestock **EXP:** edible oils, fuels and energy, cereals, feed

Bolivia
REPUBLIC OF BOLIVIA

AREA 1,098,581 sq km (424,164 sq mi)
POPULATION 9,116,000
CAPITAL La Paz (administrative) 1,527,000; Sucre (legal) 227,000
RELIGION Roman Catholic
LANGUAGE Spanish, Quechua, Aymara
LITERACY 87%
LIFE EXPECTANCY 64 years
GDP PER CAPITA $3,000
ECONOMY **IND:** mining, smelting, petroleum, food and beverages **AGR:** soybeans, coffee, coca, cotton; timber **EXP:** natural gas, soybeans and soy products, crude petroleum, zinc ore

Brazil
FEDERATIVE REPUBLIC OF BRAZIL

AREA 8,547,403 sq km (3,300,169 sq mi)
POPULATION 186,771,000
CAPITAL Brasília 3,341,000
RELIGION Roman Catholic, Protestant
LANGUAGE Portuguese
LITERACY 86%
LIFE EXPECTANCY 72 years
GDP PER CAPITA $8,600
ECONOMY **IND:** textiles, shoes, chemicals, cement **AGR:** coffee, soybeans, wheat, rice; beef **EXP:** transport equipment, iron ore, soybeans, footwear

Chile
REPUBLIC OF CHILE

AREA 756,096 sq km (291,930 sq mi)
POPULATION 16,433,000
CAPITAL Santiago 5,683,000
RELIGION Roman Catholic, Protestant
LANGUAGE Spanish
LITERACY 96%
LIFE EXPECTANCY 78 years
GDP PER CAPITA $12,700
ECONOMY **IND:** copper, other minerals, foodstuffs, fish processing **AGR:** grapes, apples, pears, onions; beef; timber; fish **EXP:** copper, fruit, fish products, paper and pulp

Colombia

REPUBLIC OF COLOMBIA

AREA 1,141,748 sq km (440,831 sq mi)
POPULATION 46,772,000
CAPITAL Bogotá 7,747,000
RELIGION Roman Catholic
LANGUAGE Spanish
LITERACY 93%
LIFE EXPECTANCY 72 years
GDP PER CAPITA $8,400
ECONOMY **IND:** textiles, food processing, oil, clothing and footwear **AGR:** coffee, cut flowers, bananas, rice; forest products; shrimp **EXP:** petroleum, coffee, coal, nickel

Ecuador
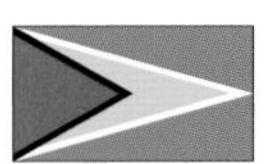
REPUBLIC OF ECUADOR

AREA 283,560 sq km (109,483 sq mi)
POPULATION 13,261,000
CAPITAL Quito 1,514,000
RELIGION Roman Catholic
LANGUAGE Spanish, Quechua, other Amerindian languages
LITERACY 93%
LIFE EXPECTANCY 74 years
GDP PER CAPITA $4,500
ECONOMY **IND:** petroleum, food processing, textiles, wood products **AGR:** bananas, coffee, cocoa, rice; cattle; balsa wood; fish **EXP:** petroleum, bananas, cut flowers, shrimp

Guyana

CO-OPERATIVE REPUBLIC OF GUYANA

AREA 214,969 sq km (83,000 sq mi)
POPULATION 749,000
CAPITAL Georgetown 134,000
RELIGION Christian, Hindu, Muslim
LANGUAGE English, Amerindian dialects, Creole, Hindustani, Urdu
LITERACY 99%
LIFE EXPECTANCY 63 years
GDP PER CAPITA $4,700
ECONOMY **IND:** bauxite, sugar, rice milling, timber **AGR:** sugarcane, rice, wheat, vegetable oils; beef; fish **EXP:** sugar, gold, bauxite, alumina

Paraguay

REPUBLIC OF PARAGUAY

AREA 406,752 sq km (157,048 sq mi)
POPULATION 6,301,000
CAPITAL Asunción 1,858,000
RELIGION Roman Catholic, Protestant
LANGUAGE Spanish, Guarani
LITERACY 94%
LIFE EXPECTANCY 71 years
GDP PER CAPITA $4,700
ECONOMY **IND:** sugar, cement, textiles, beverages **AGR:** cotton, sugarcane, soybeans, corn; beef; timber **EXP:** soybeans, feed, cotton, meat

Peru
REPUBLIC OF PERU

AREA 1,285,216 sq km (496,224 sq mi)
POPULATION 28,380,000
CAPITAL Lima 7,186,000
RELIGION Roman Catholic
LANGUAGE Spanish, Quechua, Aymara, Amazonian languages
LITERACY 88%
LIFE EXPECTANCY 70 years
GDP PER CAPITA $6,400
ECONOMY **IND:** mining and refining of minerals and metals, steel, metal fabrication, petroleum extraction and refining **AGR:** asparagus, coffee, cotton, sugarcane; poultry; fish **EXP:** copper, gold, zinc, crude petroleum and petroleum products

Suriname

REPUBLIC OF SURINAME

AREA 163,265 sq km (63,037 sq mi)
POPULATION 499,000
CAPITAL Paramaribo 268,000
RELIGION Hindu, Protestant, Roman Catholic, Muslim, indigenous beliefs
LANGUAGE Dutch, English, Sranang Tongo, Hindustani, Javanese
LITERACY 88%
LIFE EXPECTANCY 69 years
GDP PER CAPITA $7,100
ECONOMY **IND:** bauxite and gold mining, alumina production, oil, lumbering **AGR:** paddy rice, bananas, palm kernels, coconuts; beef; forest products; shrimp **EXP:** alumina, crude oil, lumber, shrimp and fish

Uruguay

ORIENTAL REPUBLIC OF URUGUAY

AREA 176,215 sq km (68,037 sq mi)
POPULATION 3,314,000
CAPITAL Montevideo 1,264,000
RELIGION Roman Catholic
LANGUAGE Spanish, Portunol, Brazilero
LITERACY 98%
LIFE EXPECTANCY 75 years
GDP PER CAPITA $10,700
ECONOMY **IND:** food processing, electrical machinery, transportation equipment, petroleum products **AGR:** rice, wheat, corn, barley; livestock; fish **EXP:** meat, rice, leather products, wool

Venezuela

BOLIVARIAN REPUBLIC OF VENEZUELA

AREA 912,050 sq km (352,144 sq mi)
POPULATION 27,031,000
CAPITAL Caracas 2,913,000
RELIGION Roman Catholic
LANGUAGE Spanish, numerous indigenous dialects
LITERACY 93%
LIFE EXPECTANCY 73 years
GDP PER CAPITA $6,900
ECONOMY **IND:** petroleum, construction materials, food processing, textiles **AGR:** corn, sorghum, sugarcane, rice; beef; fish **EXP:** petroleum, bauxite and aluminum, steel, chemicals

Dependencies

Falkland Islands
(U.K.)

SOVEREIGN

FALKLAND ISLANDS

LOCAL

AREA 12,173 sq km (4,700 sq mi)
POPULATION 3,000
CAPITAL Stanley 2,000
RELIGION Protestant, Roman Catholic
LANGUAGE English
LITERACY NA
LIFE EXPECTANCY NA
GDP PER CAPITA $25,000
ECONOMY **IND:** fish and wool processing, tourism **AGR:** fodder and vegetable crops; sheep; fish **EXP:** wool, hides, meat, fish

French Guiana
(France)

OVERSEAS DEPARTMENT OF FRANCE

AREA 86,504 sq km (33,400 sq mi)
POPULATION 199,000
CAPITAL Cayenne 59,000
RELIGION Roman Catholic
LANGUAGE French
LITERACY 83%
LIFE EXPECTANCY 76 years
GDP PER CAPITA $8,300
ECONOMY **IND:** construction, shrimp processing, forestry products, rum **AGR:** corn, rice, manioc (tapioca), sugar; cattle **EXP:** shrimp, timber, gold, rum

Dates of National Independence

NOTE: For some countries, the date given may not represent "independence" in the strict sense—but rather some significant nationhood event: the traditional founding date; a fundamental change in the form of government; or perhaps the date of unification, secession, federation, confederation, or state succession.

Land Cover
Water
Evergreen needleleaf forest
Deciduous broadleaf forest
Mixed forest
Closed shrubland
Open shrubland
Woody savanna
Savanna
Grassland
Permanent wetland
Cropland
Urban and built-up
Cropland/natural vegetation mosaic
Snow and ice
Barren or sparsely vegetated

Europe

EUROPE APPEARS FROM SPACE as a cluster of peninsulas and islands thrusting westward from Asia into the Atlantic Ocean. The smallest continent except Australia, Europe nonetheless has a population density second only to Asia's. Colliding tectonic plates and retreating Ice Age glaciers continue to shape Europe's fertile plains and rugged mountains, and the North Atlantic's Gulf Stream tempers the continent's climate. Europe's highly irregular coastline mea-sures more than one and a half times the length of the Equator, leaving only 14 out of 45 counties landlocked.

Europe has been inhabited for some 40,000 years. During the last millennium Europeans explored the planet and established far-flung empires, leaving their imprint on every corner of the Earth. Europe led the world in science and invention, and launched the industrial revolution. Great periods of creativity in the arts have occurred at various times all over the continent and shape its collective culture. By the end of the 19th century Europe dominated world commerce, spreading European ideas, languages, legal systems, and political patterns around the globe. But the Europeans who explored, colonized, and knitted the world's regions together knew themselves only as Portuguese, Spanish, Dutch, British, French, German, Russian. After centuries of rivalry and war, the two devastating world wars launched from its soil in the 20th century ended Europe's world dominance. By the 1960s nearly all its colonies had gained independence.

European countries divided into two blocs, playing out the new superpowers' Cold War—the west allied to North America and the east bound to the Soviet Union, with Germany split between them. From small beginnings in the 1950s, Western Europe began to unify. Germany's unification and the Soviet Union's unexpected breakup in the early 1990s sped the movement. Led by former enemies France and Germany, 25 countries of Western Europe now form the European Union (EU), with common European citizenship. Several Eastern European countries clamor to join. In 1999, 12 of the EU members adopted a common currency, the euro, creating a single economic market, one of the largest in the world. Political union will come harder. A countercurrent of nationalism and ethnic identity has splintered the Balkan Peninsula, and the future of Russia is impossible to predict.

Next to Asia, Europe has the world's densest population. Scores of distinct ethnic groups, speaking some 40 languages, inhabit more than 40 countries, which vary in size from European Russia to tiny Luxembourg, each with its own history and traditions. Yet Europe has a more uniform culture than any other continent. Its population is overwhelmingly of one race, Caucasian, despite the recent arrival of immigrants from Africa and Asia. Most of its languages fall into three groups with Indo-European roots: Germanic, Romance, or Slavic. One religion, Christianity, predominates in various forms, and social structures nearly every-where are based on economic classes. However, immigrant groups established as legitimate and illegal workers, refugees, and asylum seekers cling to their own habits, religions, and languages. Every European society is becoming more multicultural, with political as well as cultural consequences.

Azimuthal Equidistant Projection
SCALE 1:13,664,000
1 CENTIMETER = 137 KILOMETERS; 1 INCH = 215 MILES
0 100 200 300 400 500
KILOMETERS
0 100 200 300 400 500
STATUTE MILES
Small country
ARCTIC CIRCLE
Meridian of Greenwich (London)
NORWEGIAN SEA
NORTH SEA
ATLANTIC OCEAN
BAY OF BISCAY
CELTIC SEA
IRISH SEA
ENGLISH CHANNEL
BALEARIC SEA
TYRRHENIAN SEA
IONIAN SEA
MEDITERRANEAN SEA
ADRIATIC SEA
ALBORAN SEA
SEA OF CRETE
BALTIC SEA
GULF OF BOTHNIA
GULF OF FINLAND
Gulf of Riga
BARENTS
ICELAND
Ísafjördur
Akureyri
Keflavík
Reykjavík
Surtsey
Vestmannaeyjar
Neskaupstadur
Höfn
FAROE ISLANDS (FØROYAR) Denmark
Tórshavn
SHETLAND ISLANDS
Mainland
Lerwick
ORKNEY ISLANDS
Kirkwall
Rockall U.K.
Isle of Lewis
Outer Hebrides
Stornoway
Thurso
Island of Skye
Inverness
Aberdeen
SCOTLAND
Perth
Dundee
Greenock
Glasgow
Edinburgh
Londonderry
NORTHERN IRELAND
Sligo
Dundalk
Belfast
Baile Átha Cliath (Dublin)
Galway
IRELAND
Limerick
Tralee
Waterford
Cork
Newcastle
Sunderland
UNITED KINGDOM
Leeds
Liverpool
Manchester
Sheffield
ENGLAND
WALES
Swansea
Cardiff
BIRMINGHAM
Bristol
LONDON
Plymouth
Southampton
Isles of Scilly
Channel Islands U.K.
NETHERLANDS
Groningen
Amsterdam
Rotterdam
Antwerpen
Bruxelles (Brussels)
BELGIUM
Lille
Charleroi
LUXEMBOURG
Luxembourg
FRANCE
Cherbourg-Octeville
Le Havre
Amiens
Caen
Brest
Rennes
Rouen
PARIS
Reims
Lorient
Alençon
Le Mans
Angers
Nantes
Tours
Orléans
Troyes
Nancy
Strasbourg
Mulhouse
Dijon
Besançon
La Rochelle
Poitiers
Limoges
Clermont-Ferrand
MASSIF CENTRAL
Lyon
Saint-Étienne
Bordeaux
Grenoble
Agen
Montauban
Toulouse
Pau
Valence
Montpellier
Nîmes
Aix-en-Provence
Marseille
Toulon
Nice
MONACO
Perpignan
PYRENEES
ANDORRA
Andorra
CORSE (CORSICA) France
Bastia
Ajaccio
SPAIN
A Coruña
Santiago de Compostela
Gijón
Oviedo
Santander
Lugo
Vigo
Ourense
León
Bilbao
Donostia-San Sebastián
Bayonne
Vitoria-Gasteiz
Burgos
Pamplona
Valladolid
Salamanca
Segovia
Zaragoza
Lleida
Tarragona
BARCELONA
MADRID
Toledo
Cáceres
Mérida
Badajoz
Ciudad Real
Castelló de la Plana
Valencia
Albacete
Linares
Córdoba
Jaén
Murcia
Alicante
Cartagena
Lucena
Sevilla
Huelva
Cádiz
Jerez
Granada
Málaga
Almería
Algeciras
GIBRALTAR U.K.
Strait of Gibraltar
Ceuta Sp.
Alborán Spain
Melilla Sp.
Menorca
Mallorca
Palma de Mallorca
Ibiza
BALEARIC ISLANDS Spain
PORTUGAL
Porto
Braga
Coimbra
Santarém
(Lisbon) Lisboa
Setúbal
Faro
Duero
Tajo
Ebro
Guadiana
Garonne
Loire
Seine
Rhône
NORWAY
Tromsø
Harstad
Narvik
Lofoten
Vesterålen
Svolvær
Bodø
Mo i Rana
Mosjøen
Namsos
Steinkjer
Trondheim
Kristiansund
Molde
Ålesund
Florø
Bergen
Sognefjorden
Lillehammer
Gjøvik
Hamar
Hønefoss
Oslo
Drammen
Haugesund
Stavanger
Skien
Egersund
Kristiansand
Mandal
Fredrikstad
Arendal
Røros
Glåma
SWEDEN
Kiruna
Gällivare
Boden
Luleå
Arvidsjaur
Piteå
Skellefteå
Storuman
Gäddede
Umeå
Örnsköldsvik
Östersund
Kramfors
Sundsvall
Bollnäs
Falun
Borlänge
Gävle
Uppsala
Västerås
Karlstad
Örebro
Stockholm
Vänern
Vättern
Norrköping
Linköping
Trollhättan
Jönköping
Göteborg
Borås
Visby
GOTLAND
Växjö
Halmstad
Kalmar
ÖLAND
Karlskrona
Helsingborg
Malmö
ÅLAND
DENMARK
JUTLAND
Frederikshavn
Ålborg
Randers
Århus
Esbjerg
Odense
København (Copenhagen)
FINLAND
LAPLAND
Inari
Ivalo
Rovaniemi
Kemijärvi
Kemi
Oulu
Raahe
Kajaani
Kokkola
Jakobstad
Vaasa
Seinäjoki
Jyväskylä
Kuopio
Joensuu
Nurmes
Savonlinna
Mikkeli
Pori
Tampere
Lappeenranta
Imatra
Rauma
Hämeenlinna
Turku
Lahti
Kotka
Helsinki
Sortavala
Ladozhskoye Ozero
Kandalakshskiy Zaliv
Sørøya
Hammerfest
Berlevåg
Vadsø
Lakselv
Alta
Kirkenes
Nikel'
Murmansk
Polyarny
Monchegorsk
Apatity
Kandalaksha
Umba
SANKT-PETERBURG (St. Petersburg)
ESTONIA
Tallinn
Narva
Slantsy
Luga
Pärnu
Tartu
Lake Peipus
Velikiye
Novgorod
Pskov
LATVIA
Ventspils
Valmiera
Riga
Liepāja
Jelgava
Rēzekne
Daugavpils
Velikiye Luki
LITHUANIA
Klaipėda
Šiauliai
Panevėžys
Kaunas
Vilnius
Polatsk
Vitsyebsk
Navapolatsk
Orsha
Mahilyo
MINSK
BELARUS
Lida
Hrodna
Neman
Babruysk
Salihorsk
Baranavichy
Pinsk
Mazyr
Brest
Kaliningrad
Russia
EAST PRUSSIA
GERMANY
Kiel
Lübeck
Rostock
Bremerhaven
Oldenburg
HAMBURG
Elbe
Bremen
Hannover
Braunschweig
BERLIN
Magdeburg
Bielefeld
Essen
Dortmund
Köln
Bonn
Erfurt
Leipzig
Dresden
Chemnitz
Zwickau
Wiesbaden
Frankfurt
Darmstadt
Würzburg
Karlsruhe
Mannheim
Nürnberg
Stuttgart
Augsburg
Freiburg
MÜNCHEN (Munich)
Donau
Rhein
Oder
POLAND
Słupsk
Koszalin
Gdańsk
Olsztyn
Szczecin
Bydgoszcz
Toruń
Białystok
Poznań
Wisła
Łódź
WARSZAWA (Warsaw)
Wrocław
Radom
Lublin
Częstochowa
Kielce
Wałbrzych
Katowice
Kraków
Rzeszów
CZECH REP.
PRAHA (Prague)
Plzeň
Ostrava
Olomouc
České Budějovice
Brno
SLOVAKIA
Bratislava
Košice
AUSTRIA
WIEN (Vienna)
Linz
Salzburg
Innsbruck
Graz
SWITZERLAND
Basel
Zürich
Bern
Lausanne
Genève
LIECH.
SLOVENIA
Ljubljana
Maribor
HUNGARY
Győr
BUDAPEST
Miskolc
Nyíregyháza
Debrecen
Szeged
CARPATHIAN MOUNTAINS
UKRAINE
Kovel'
Korosten'
Zhytomyr
Luts'k
Rivne
Berdychiv
Khmel'nyts'kyy
L'viv
Przemyśl
Ternopil'
Ivano-Frankivs'k
Vinnytsya
Chernivtsi
MOLDOVA
Bălţi
Chişinău
ROMANIA
Baia Mare
Satu Mare
Oradea
Cluj-Napoca
Târgu Mureş
Bacău
Arad
Timişoara
Sibiu
Braşov
Galaţi
Buzău
Ploieşti
BUCUREŞTI (Bucharest)
Craiova
Slatina
Dunărea (Danube)
ITALY
Bergamo
Trento
Bolzano
MILANO (Milan)
Brescia
Verona
Padova
Venezia (Venice)
Trieste
Torino
Genova (Genoa)
Modena
Ferrara
Bologna
Rimini
Riviera
La Spezia
Pisa
Firenze
SAN MARINO
Perugia
Ancona
Terni
Teramo
Pescara
Civitavecchia
VATICAN CITY
ROMA (Rome)
APENNINES
Foggia
Benevento
NAPOLI (NAPLES)
Salerno
Potenza
Bari
Brindisi
Taranto
Castrovillari
Cosenza
Catanzaro
Reggio di Calabria
Messina
Palermo
Marsala
SICILY
Catania
Ragusa
Siracusa
Pantelleria Italy
Isole Pelagie Italy
MALTA
Valletta
SARDEGNA (SARDINIA) Italy
Sassari
Olbia
Nuoro
Oristano
Iglesias
Carbonia
Cagliari
Elba
CROATIA
Zagreb
Osijek
Zadar
Split
Dubrovnik
BOSNIA & HERZEGOVINA
Banja Luka
Tuzla
Sarajevo
Mostar
SERBIA
Subotica
Novi Sad
BEOGRAD (Belgrade)
Novi Pazar
Niš
Priština
Prizren
MONTENEGRO
Podgorica
Shkodër
ALBANIA
Tiranë (Tirana)
Elbasan
Vlorë
Korçë
MACEDONIA
Skopje
Bitola
BULGARIA
Ruse
Varna
Pleven
Vratsa
Gabrovo
Burgas
SOFIYA (Sofia)
Stara Zagora
Plovdiv
Khaskovo
Edirne
Zaječar
Xánthi
Kavála
Tekirdağ
Thessaloníki
GREECE
Lecce
Ioánina
Lárissa
Vólos
Kérkira (Corfu)
Lefkáda
Kefaloniá
Zákinthos
Pátra
PELOPONNISOS
Pireás
Athína (Athens)
Kalamáta
Évia
Kikládes
Dodekánisa
Híos
Lésvos
İZMIR
Thira
Haniá (Canea)
Iráklio
KRÍTI (CRETE)
AEGEAN SEA
Dardanelles
MOROCCO
RABAT
ALGERIA
ALGER (Algiers)
TUNISIA
TUNIS
LIBYA
TARĀBULUS (Tripoli)
AFRICA
Longitude West 5° of Greenwich
Longitude East 5° of Greenwich

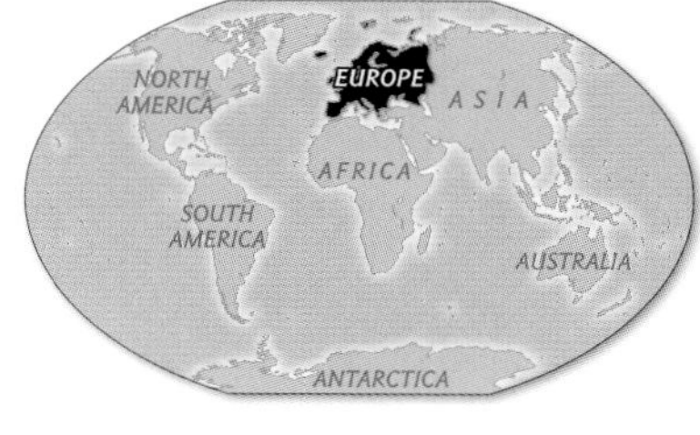

CONTINENTAL DATA

TOTAL NUMBER OF COUNTRIES: 45

FIRST INDEPENDENT COUNTRY:
San Marino, September 3, 301

"YOUNGEST" COUNTRY:
Montenegro, June 3, 2006

LARGEST COUNTRY BY AREA:
Russia 17,075,400 sq km (6,592,850 sq mi)

SMALLEST COUNTRY BY AREA:
Vatican City 0.4 sq km (0.2 sq mi)

PERCENT URBAN POPULATION:
75%

MOST POPULOUS COUNTRY:
Russia 142,336,000

LEAST POPULOUS COUNTRY:
Vatican City 800

MOST DENSELY POPULATED COUNTRY:
Monaco 16,923 per sq km (44,000 per sq mi)

LEAST DENSELY POPULATED COUNTRY:
Iceland 2.9 per sq km (7.6 per sq mi)

LARGEST CITY BY POPULATION:
Moscow, Russia 10,654,000

HIGHEST GDP PER CAPITA:
Luxembourg $68,800

LOWEST GDP PER CAPITA:
Moldova $2,000

AVERAGE LIFE EXPECTANCY IN EUROPE: 75 years

AVERAGE LITERACY RATE IN EUROPE: 99%

A commonly accepted division between Asia and Europe—here marked with a green line—is formed by the Ural Mountains, Ural River, Caspian Sea, Caucasus Mountains, and the Black Sea with its outlets, the Bosporus and Dardanelles.

A commonly accepted division between Asia and Europe–here marked by a green line–is formed by the Ural Mountains, Ural River, Caspian Sea, Caucasus Mountains, and the Black Sea with its outlets, the Bosporus and Dardanelles.
Azimuthal Equidistant Projection
SCALE 1:13,664,000
1 CENTIMETER = 137 KILOMETERS; 1 INCH = 215 MILES
KILOMETERS
STATUTE MILES
International boundary
ICELAND
Hekla
Hvannadalshnúkur
Surtsey
Vestmannaeyjar
Reykjanes
Rifstangi
NORWEGIAN SEA
ARCTIC CIRCLE
ATLANTIC OCEAN
Faroe Islands
Shetland Islands
Orkney Islands
Outer Hebrides
Inner Hebrides
Moray Firth
Ben Nevis
Grampian Mts.
BRITISH ISLES
GREAT BRITAIN
Firth of Forth
Southern Uplands
IRELAND
IRISH SEA
Isle of Man
The Pennines
Snowdon
Cambrian Mts.
Carrantuohill
Thames
CELTIC SEA
Land's End
English Channel
Channel Islands
Point St.-Mathieu
Armorican Massif
PARIS BASIN
NORTH SEA
Frisian Islands
JUTLAND
FYN
ZEALAND
Kattegat
Skagerrak
SCANDINAVIA
Galdhøpiggen
Sognefjorden
Hardangerfjorden
Lofoten
Vesterålen
Kebnekaise
Finnmark Plateau
North Cape
GULF OF BOTHNIA
Åland Is.
GULF OF FINLAND
Gotland
Öland
Hiiumaa
Saaremaa
Gulf of Riga
BALTIC SEA
Gulf of Gdańsk
Lake Region
Suomen Ridge
Salpaus Ridge
BALTIC PLAINS
NORTHERN EUROPEAN PLAIN
MITTELLAND CANAL
Harz
Ardennes
Ore Mts.
Sudeten
Bohemian Forest
Black Forest
Vosges
Source of the Danube
Lake Constance
Sources of the Rhine
Jura Mts.
Mont Blanc
Matterhorn
ALPS
Grossglockner
CARPATHIAN MOUNTAINS
Gerlach
Volyn-Podolian Upland
Pripyats'
Pinsk Marshes
Great Hungarian Plain
Bakony
Transylvania
Transylvanian Alps
Iron Gate
Puy de Sancy
MASSIF CENTRAL
Cévennes
AQUITAINE BASIN
BAY OF BISCAY
Cape Finisterre
Cantabrian Mountains
PYRENEES
Pico de Aneto
IBERIAN PENINSULA
Iberian Mountains
MESETA
Sierra Morena
Baetic Mountains
Mulhacén
Cape St. Vincent
Strait of Gibraltar
ALBORAN SEA
Er Rif
ATLAS MOUNTAINS
SAHARA
AFRICA
Gulf of Lions
BALEARIC SEA
BALEARIC ISLANDS
Minorca
Majorca
Iviza
LIGURIAN SEA
Riviera
Piedmont
CORSICA
SARDINIA
APENNINES
Corno Grande
Vesuvius
TYRRHENIAN SEA
Gulf of Venice
ADRIATIC SEA
DINARIC ALPS
Dalmatia
Durmitor
Calabria
SICILY
Etna
MALTESE ISLANDS
Malta
MEDITERRANEAN
IONIAN SEA
IONIAN ISLANDS
Strait of Otranto
BALKAN PENINSULA
Balkan Mountains
Rhodope Mts.
Ludogori
Olympus
Pindus Mts.
Thessaly
Northern Sporades
Euboea
Parnassus
PELOPONNESUS
Cyclades
Dodecanese
AEGEAN SEA
SEA OF CRETE
CRETE
Dardanelles
Gulf of Sidra
Longitude West 5° of Greenwich
Longitude East 5° of Greenwich

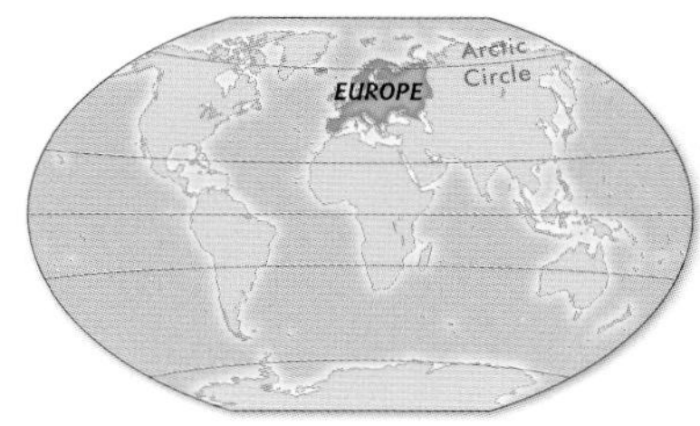

CONTINENTAL DATA

AREA: 9,947,000 sq km (3,841,000 sq mi)

GREATEST NORTH-SOUTH EXTENT: 4,800 km (2,980 mi)

GREATEST EAST-WEST EXTENT: 6,400 km (3,980 mi)

HIGHEST POINT: El'brus, Russia 5,642 m (18,510 ft)

LOWEST POINT: Caspian Sea -28 m (-92 ft)

LOWEST RECORDED TEMPERATURE: Ust'Shchugor, Russia -55°C (-67°F), Date unknown

HIGHEST RECORDED TEMPERATURE: Seville, Spain 50°C (122°F), August 4, 1881

LONGEST RIVERS:
- Volga 3,685 km (2,290 mi)
- Danube 2,848 km (1,770 mi)
- Dnieper 2,285 km (1,420 mi)

LARGEST LAKES:
- Caspian Sea 371,000 sq km (143,200 sq mi)
- Lake Ladoga 17,872 sq km (6,900 sq mi)
- Lake Onega 9,842 sq km (3,800 sq mi)

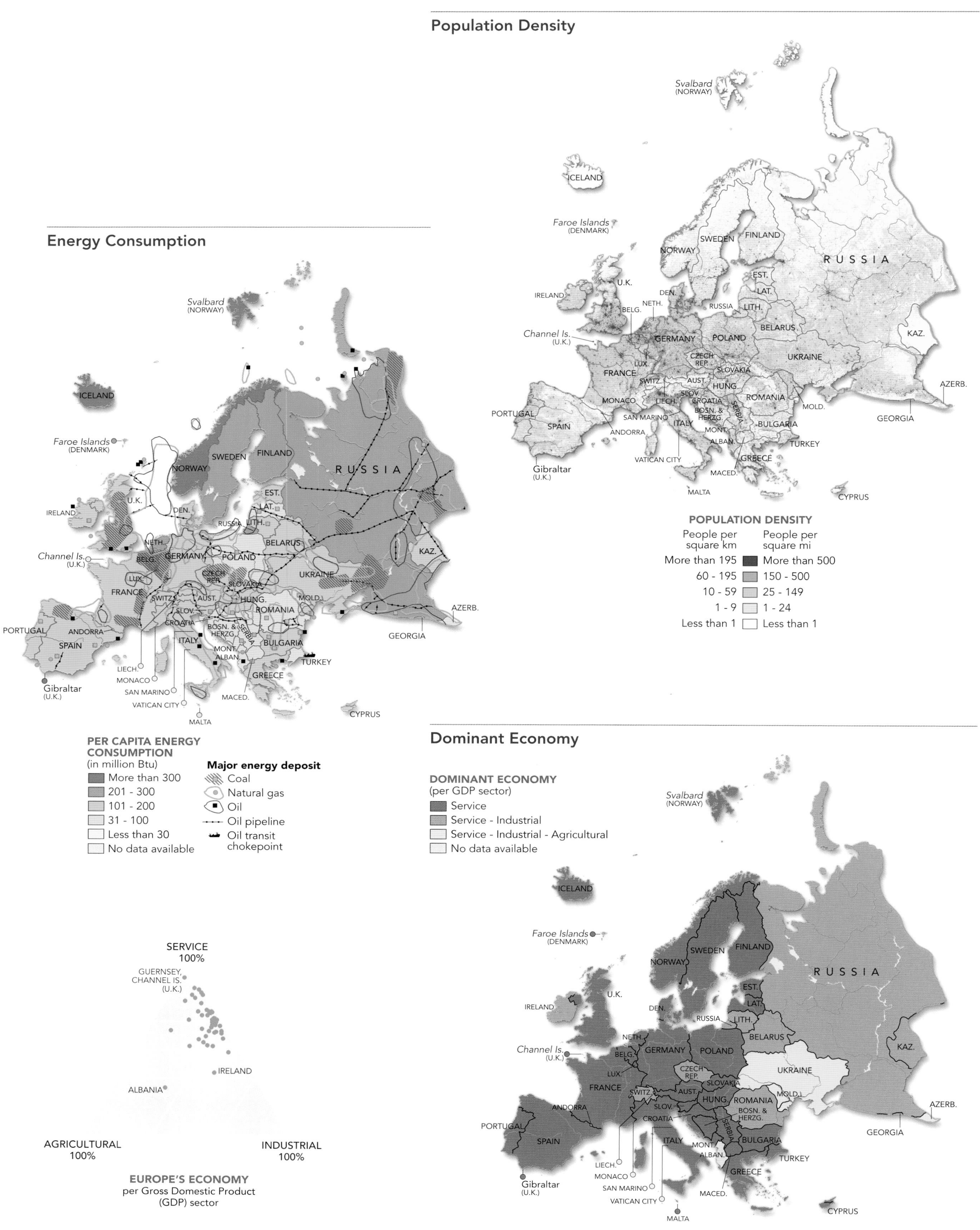

Population Density
Svalbard (NORWAY)
ICELAND
Faroe Islands (DENMARK)
NORWAY
SWEDEN
FINLAND
RUSSIA
EST.
LAT.
LITH.
RUSSIA
DEN.
U.K.
IRELAND
NETH.
BELG.
Channel Is. (U.K.)
GERMANY
POLAND
BELARUS
UKRAINE
KAZ.
CZECH REP.
SLOVAKIA
LUX.
FRANCE
SWITZ.
AUST.
HUNG.
ROMANIA
MOLD.
AZERB.
GEORGIA
MONACO
LIECH.
SLOV.
CROATIA
BOSN. & HERZG.
SERBIA
PORTUGAL
SPAIN
SAN MARINO
ANDORRA
ITALY
MONT.
ALBAN.
BULGARIA
TURKEY
VATICAN CITY
GREECE
Gibraltar (U.K.)
MACED.
MALTA
CYPRUS
POPULATION DENSITY
People per square km
People per square mi
More than 195 More than 500
60 - 195 150 - 500
10 - 59 25 - 149
1 - 9 1 - 24
Less than 1 Less than 1
Energy Consumption
Svalbard (NORWAY)
ICELAND
Faroe Islands (DENMARK)
NORWAY
SWEDEN
FINLAND
RUSSIA
U.K.
IRELAND
DEN.
EST.
LAT.
RUSSIA
LITH.
NETH.
BELARUS
Channel Is. (U.K.)
BELG.
GERMANY
POLAND
KAZ.
CZECH REP.
UKRAINE
LUX.
SLOVAKIA
FRANCE
SWITZ.
AUST.
HUNG.
MOLD.
SLOV.
ROMANIA
AZERB.
CROATIA
PORTUGAL
ANDORRA
BOSN. & HERZG.
SERBIA
GEORGIA
SPAIN
ITALY
BULGARIA
MONT.
ALBAN.
TURKEY
LIECH.
MONACO
GREECE
Gibraltar (U.K.)
SAN MARINO
MACED.
VATICAN CITY
CYPRUS
MALTA
PER CAPITA ENERGY CONSUMPTION
(in million Btu)
More than 300
201 - 300
101 - 200
31 - 100
Less than 30
No data available
Major energy deposit
Coal
Natural gas
Oil
Oil pipeline
Oil transit chokepoint
Dominant Economy
DOMINANT ECONOMY
(per GDP sector)
Service
Service - Industrial
Service - Industrial - Agricultural
No data available
Svalbard (NORWAY)
ICELAND
Faroe Islands (DENMARK)
SWEDEN
FINLAND
NORWAY
RUSSIA
U.K.
EST.
LAT.
IRELAND
DEN.
RUSSIA
LITH.
NETH.
BELARUS
Channel Is. (U.K.)
BELG.
GERMANY
POLAND
KAZ.
CZECH REP.
UKRAINE
LUX.
FRANCE
SLOVAKIA
SWITZ.
AUST.
MOLD.
HUNG.
ROMANIA
SLOV.
BOSN. & HERZG.
AZERB.
ANDORRA
CROATIA
PORTUGAL
SERBIA
GEORGIA
SPAIN
ITALY
MONT.
BULGARIA
ALBAN.
TURKEY
LIECH.
GREECE
MONACO
Gibraltar (U.K.)
SAN MARINO
MACED.
VATICAN CITY
CYPRUS
MALTA
SERVICE 100%
GUERNSEY, CHANNEL IS. (U.K.)
IRELAND
ALBANIA
AGRICULTURAL 100%
INDUSTRIAL 100%
EUROPE'S ECONOMY
per Gross Domestic Product (GDP) sector

Climate Zones

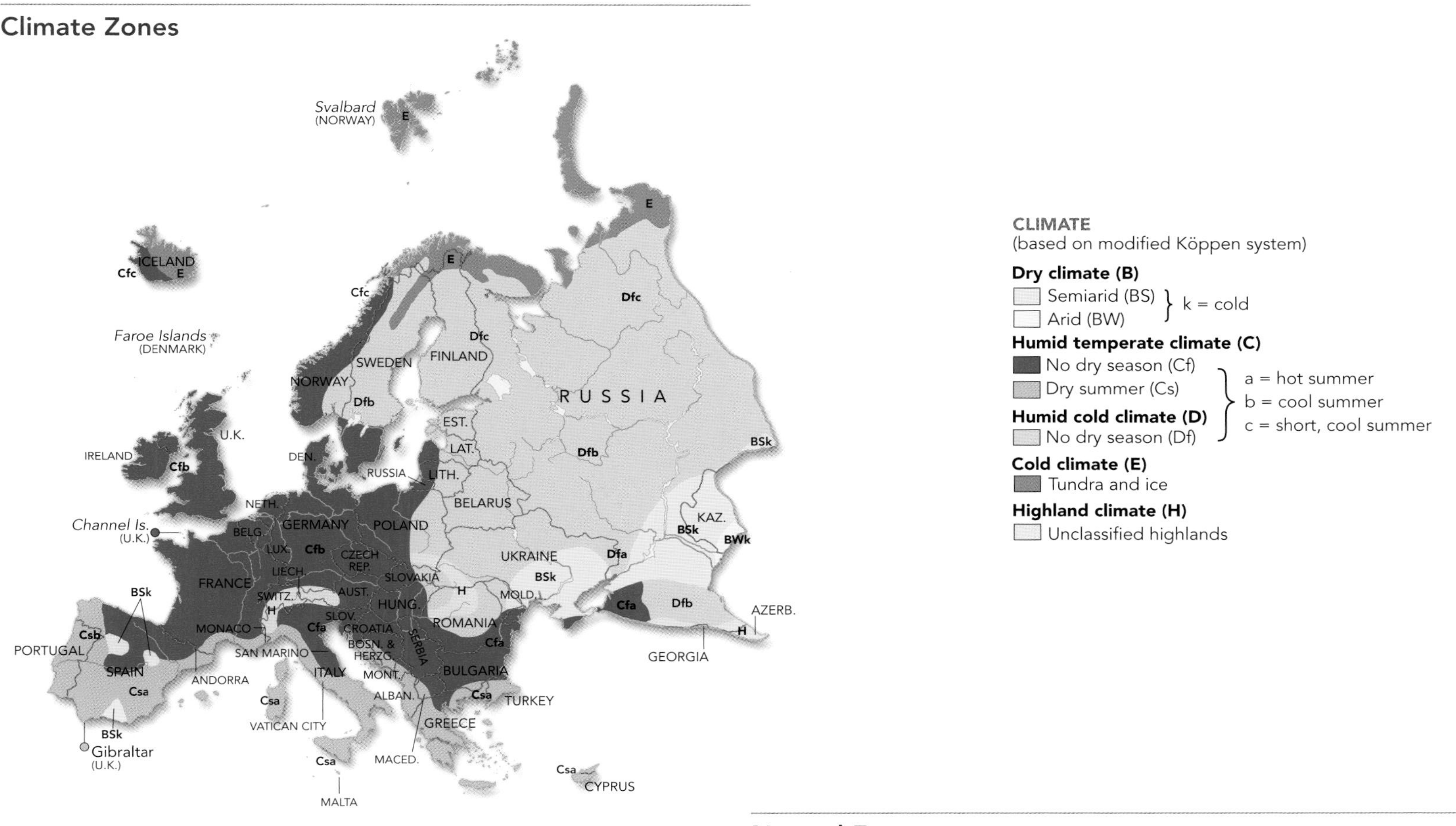

Natural Events

RECORDED NATURAL EVENT

Earthquake
Richter scale magnitude
- More than 7.0
- 6.0 - 7.0
- Less than 6.0

Fire intensity
(from gas burn-off, slash-and-burn agriculture, or natural causes)
High
Low

Tsunami
Run-up height
- More than 10 m — More than 32 ft
- 5 - 10 m — 16 - 32 ft
- Less than 5 m — Less than 16 ft

Volcano
▲ Major eruption

Water Availability

WATER AVAILABILITY
(in millimeters per-person per-year)
- More than 750
- 251 - 750
- 26 - 250
- Less than 26
- No data available

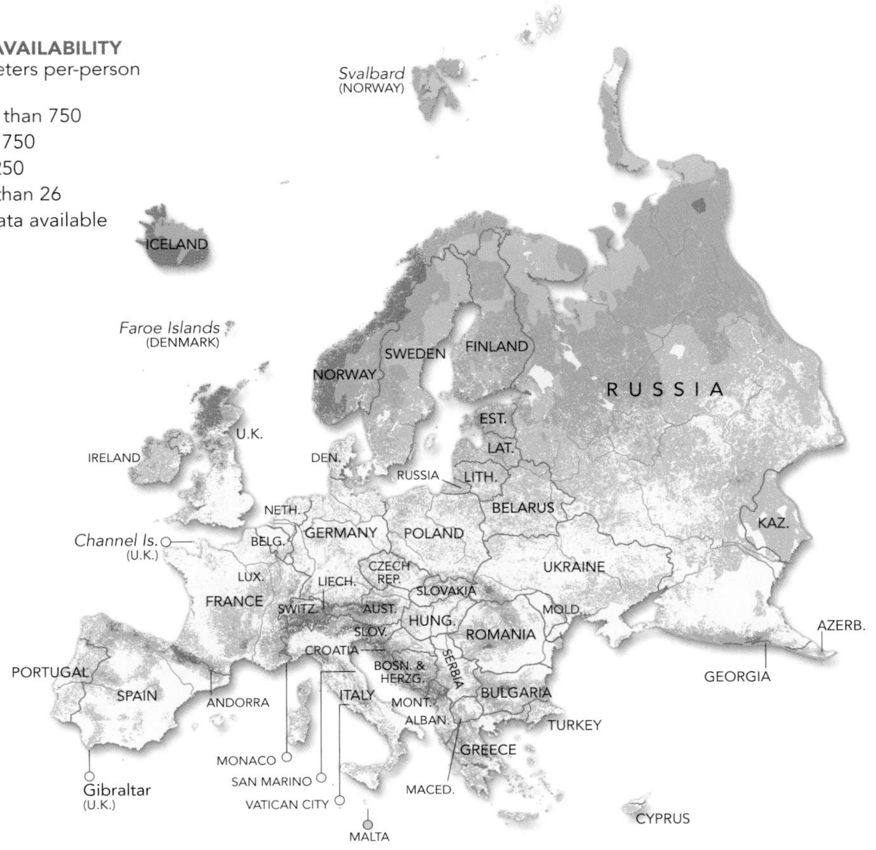

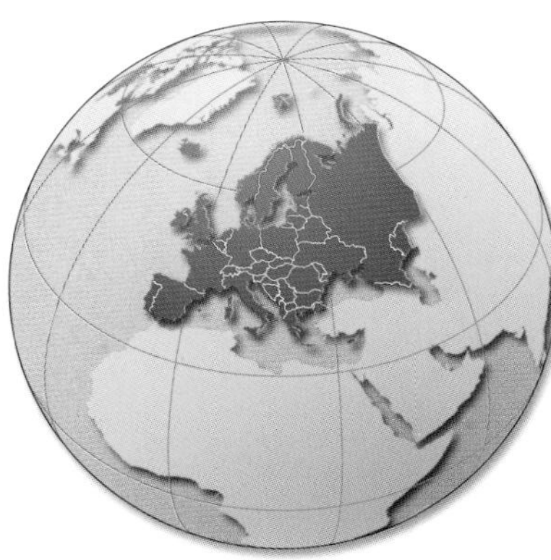

Nations

Albania
REPUBLIC OF ALBANIA

AREA 28,748 sq km (11,100 sq mi)
POPULATION 3,150,000
CAPITAL Tirana 388,000
RELIGION Muslim, Albanian Orthodox, Roman Catholic
LANGUAGE Albanian, Greek, Vlach, Romani, Slavic dialects
LITERACY 87%
LIFE EXPECTANCY 75 years
GDP PER CAPITA $5,600
ECONOMY **IND:** food processing, textiles and clothing, lumber, oil **AGR:** wheat, corn, potatoes, vegetables; meat **EXP:** textiles and footwear, asphalt, metals and metallic ores, crude oil

Andorra
PRINCIPALITY OF ANDORRA

AREA 468 sq km (181 sq mi)
POPULATION 87,000
CAPITAL Andorra la Vella 22,000
RELIGION Roman Catholic
LANGUAGE Catalan, French, Castilian, Portuguese
LITERACY 100%
LIFE EXPECTANCY NA
GDP PER CAPITA $38,800
ECONOMY **IND:** tourism (particularly skiing), cattle raising, timber, banking **AGR:** rye, wheat, barley, oats; sheep **EXP:** tobacco products, furniture

Austria
REPUBLIC OF AUSTRIA

AREA 83,858 sq km (32,378 sq mi)
POPULATION 8,289,000
CAPITAL Vienna 2,260,000
RELIGION Roman Catholic, Protestant
LANGUAGE German
LITERACY 98%
LIFE EXPECTANCY 79 years
GDP PER CAPITA $35,500
ECONOMY **IND:** construction, machinery, vehicles and parts, food **AGR:** grains, potatoes, sugar beets, wine; dairy products; lumber **EXP:** machinery and equipment, motor vehicles and parts, paper and paperboard, metal goods

Belarus
REPUBLIC OF BELARUS

AREA 207,595 sq km (80,153 sq mi)
POPULATION 9,727,000
CAPITAL Minsk 1,778,000
RELIGION Eastern Orthodox, Roman Catholic, Protestant, Jewish, Muslim
LANGUAGE Belarusian, Russian
LITERACY 100%
LIFE EXPECTANCY 69 years
GDP PER CAPITA $7,800
ECONOMY **IND:** metal-cutting machine tools, tractors, trucks, earthmovers **AGR:** grain, potatoes, vegetables, sugar beets; beef **EXP:** machinery and equipment, mineral products, chemicals, metals

Belgium
KINGDOM OF BELGIUM

AREA 30,528 sq km (11,787 sq mi)
POPULATION 10,529,000
CAPITAL Brussels 1,012,000
RELIGION Roman Catholic, Protestant
LANGUAGE Dutch, French
LITERACY 99%
LIFE EXPECTANCY 79 years
GDP PER CAPITA $31,800
ECONOMY **IND:** engineering and metal products, motor vehicle assembly, transportation equipment, scientific instruments **AGR:** sugar beets, fresh vegetables, fruits, grain; beef **EXP:** machinery and equipment, chemicals, diamonds, metals and metal products

Bosnia and Herzegovina
BOSNIA AND HERZEGOVINA

AREA 51,129 sq km (19,741 sq mi)
POPULATION 3,862,000
CAPITAL Sarajevo 380,000
RELIGION Muslim, Orthodox, Roman Catholic
LANGUAGE Bosnian, Croatian, Serbian
LITERACY 95%
LIFE EXPECTANCY 74 years
GDP PER CAPITA $5,500
ECONOMY **IND:** steel, coal, iron ore, lead **AGR:** wheat, corn, fruits, vegetables; livestock **EXP:** metals, clothing, wood products

Bulgaria
REPUBLIC OF BULGARIA

AREA 110,994 sq km (42,855 sq mi)
POPULATION 7,698,000
CAPITAL Sofia 1,093,000
RELIGION Bulgarian Orthodox, Muslim
LANGUAGE Bulgarian, Turkish
LITERACY 99%
LIFE EXPECTANCY 72 years
GDP PER CAPITA $10,400
ECONOMY **IND:** electricity, gas, food and beverages, machinery and equipment **AGR:** vegetables, fruits, tobacco, wine; livestock **EXP:** clothing, footwear, iron and steel, machinery and equipment

Croatia
REPUBLIC OF CROATIA

AREA 56,542 sq km (21,831 sq mi)
POPULATION 4,449,000
CAPITAL Zagreb 689,000
RELIGION Roman Catholic
LANGUAGE Croatian
LITERACY 99%
LIFE EXPECTANCY 75 years
GDP PER CAPITA $13,200
ECONOMY **IND:** chemicals and plastics, machine tools, fabricated metal, electronics **AGR:** wheat, corn, sugar beets, sunflower seed; livestock **EXP:** transport equipment, textiles, chemicals, foodstuffs

Cyprus
REPUBLIC OF CYPRUS

AREA 9,251 sq km (3,572 sq mi)
POPULATION 1,035,000
CAPITAL Nicosia 211,000
RELIGION Greek Orthodox, Muslim
LANGUAGE Greek, Turkish, English
LITERACY 98%
LIFE EXPECTANCY 78 years
GDP PER CAPITA $22,700
ECONOMY **IND:** tourism, food and beverage processing, cement and gypsum production, ship repair **AGR:** citrus, vegetables, barley, grapes; poultry **EXP:** citrus, potatoes, pharmaceuticals, cement

Czech Republic
CZECH REPUBLIC

AREA 78,866 sq km (30,450 sq mi)
POPULATION 10,266,000
CAPITAL Prague 1,171,000
RELIGION Roman Catholic
LANGUAGE Czech
LITERACY 99%
LIFE EXPECTANCY 76 years
GDP PER CAPITA $21,600
ECONOMY **IND:** metallurgy, machinery and equipment, motor vehicles, glass **AGR:** wheat, potatoes, sugar beets, hops; pigs **EXP:** machinery and transport equipment, chemicals, raw materials and fuel

Denmark
KINGDOM OF DENMARK

AREA 43,098 sq km (16,640 sq mi)
POPULATION 5,436,000
CAPITAL Copenhagen 1,088,000
RELIGION Evangelical Lutheran
LANGUAGE Danish, Faroese, Greenlandic
LITERACY 99%
LIFE EXPECTANCY 78 years
GDP PER CAPITA $37,000
ECONOMY **IND:** iron, steel, nonferrous metals, chemicals **AGR:** barley, wheat, potatoes, sugar beets; pork; fish **EXP:** machinery and instruments, meat and meat products, dairy products, fish

Estonia
REPUBLIC OF ESTONIA

AREA 45,227 sq km (17,462 sq mi)
POPULATION 1,342,000
CAPITAL Tallinn 392,000
RELIGION Evangelical Lutheran, Orthodox
LANGUAGE Estonian, Russian
LITERACY 100%
LIFE EXPECTANCY 72 years
GDP PER CAPITA $19,600
ECONOMY **IND:** engineering, electronics, wood and wood products, textiles **AGR:** potatoes, vegetables; livestock and dairy products; fish **EXP:** machinery and equipment, wood and paper, textiles, food products

Finland
REPUBLIC OF FINLAND

AREA 338,145 sq km (130,558 sq mi)
POPULATION 5,265,000
CAPITAL Helsinki 1,091,000
RELIGION Lutheran National Church
LANGUAGE Finnish, Swedish
LITERACY 100%
LIFE EXPECTANCY 79 years
GDP PER CAPITA $32,800
ECONOMY **IND:** metals and metal products, electronics, machinery and scientific instruments, shipbuilding **AGR:** barley, wheat, sugar beets, potatoes; dairy cattle; fish **EXP:** machinery and equipment, chemicals, metals, timber

France
FRENCH REPUBLIC

AREA 543,965 sq km (210,026 sq mi)
POPULATION 61,217,000
CAPITAL Paris 9,820,000
RELIGION Roman Catholic, Muslim
LANGUAGE French
LITERACY 99%
LIFE EXPECTANCY 80 years
GDP PER CAPITA $30,100
ECONOMY **IND:** machinery, chemicals, automobiles, metallurgy **AGR:** wheat, cereals, sugar beets, potatoes; beef; fish **EXP:** machinery and transportation equipment, aircraft, plastics, chemicals

Germany

FEDERAL REPUBLIC OF GERMANY

AREA 357,022 sq km (137,847 sq mi)
POPULATION 82,387,000
CAPITAL Berlin 3,389,000
RELIGION Protestant, Roman Catholic
LANGUAGE German
LITERACY 99%
LIFE EXPECTANCY 79 years
GDP PER CAPITA $31,400
ECONOMY **IND:** iron, steel, coal, cement **AGR:** potatoes, wheat, barley, sugar beets; cattle **EXP:** machinery, vehicles, chemicals, metals and manufactures

Greece
HELLENIC REPUBLIC

AREA 131,957 sq km (50,949 sq mi)
POPULATION 11,128,000
CAPITAL Athens 3,230,000
RELIGION Greek Orthodox
LANGUAGE Greek
LITERACY 98%
LIFE EXPECTANCY 79 years
GDP PER CAPITA $23,500
ECONOMY **IND:** tourism, food and tobacco processing, textiles, chemicals **AGR:** wheat, corn, barley, sugar beets; beef **EXP:** food and beverages, manufactured goods, petroleum products, chemicals

Hungary
REPUBLIC OF HUNGARY

AREA 93,030 sq km (35,919 sq mi)
POPULATION 10,067,000
CAPITAL Budapest 1,693,000
RELIGION Roman Catholic, Calvinist
LANGUAGE Hungarian
LITERACY 99%
LIFE EXPECTANCY 73 years
GDP PER CAPITA $17,300
ECONOMY **IND:** mining, metallurgy, construction materials, processed foods **AGR:** wheat, corn, sunflower seed, potatoes; pigs **EXP:** machinery and equipment, other manufactures, food products, raw materials

Iceland
REPUBLIC OF ICELAND

AREA 103,000 sq km (39,769 sq mi)
POPULATION 303,000
CAPITAL Reykjavík 185,000
RELIGION Lutheran Church of Iceland
LANGUAGE Icelandic, English, Nordic languages, German
LITERACY 99%
LIFE EXPECTANCY 81 years
GDP PER CAPITA $38,100
ECONOMY **IND:** fish processing, aluminum smelting, ferrosilicon production, geothermal power **AGR:** potatoes, green vegetables; mutton; fish **EXP:** fish and fish products, aluminum, animal products, ferrosilicon

Ireland
IRELAND

AREA 70,273 sq km (27,133 sq mi)
POPULATION 4,234,000
CAPITAL Dublin 1,037,000
RELIGION Roman Catholic
LANGUAGE Irish (Gaelic), English
LITERACY 99%
LIFE EXPECTANCY 78 years
GDP PER CAPITA $43,600
ECONOMY **IND:** mining processing (steel, lead, zinc), food products, brewing, textiles **AGR:** turnips, barley, potatoes, sugar beets; beef **EXP:** machinery and equipment, computers, chemicals, pharmaceuticals

Italy

ITALIAN REPUBLIC

AREA 301,333 sq km (116,345 sq mi)
POPULATION 58,990,000
CAPITAL Rome 3,348,000
RELIGION Roman Catholic
LANGUAGE Italian, German, French, Slovene
LITERACY 99%
LIFE EXPECTANCY 80 years
GDP PER CAPITA $29,700
ECONOMY **IND:** tourism, machinery, iron and steel, chemicals **AGR:** fruits, vegetables, grapes, potatoes; beef; fish **EXP:** engineering products, textiles and clothing, production machinery, motor vehicles

Latvia

REPUBLIC OF LATVIA

AREA 64,589 sq km (24,938 sq mi)
POPULATION 2,287,000
CAPITAL Riga 729,000
RELIGION Lutheran, Roman Catholic, Russian Orthodox
LANGUAGE Latvian, Russian
LITERACY 100%
LIFE EXPECTANCY 73 years
GDP PER CAPITA $15,400
ECONOMY **IND:** buses, vans, street- and railroad cars, synthetic fibers **AGR:** grain, sugar beets, potatoes, vegetables; beef; fish **EXP:** wood and wood products, machinery and equipment, metals, textiles

Liechtenstein

PRINCIPALITY OF LIECHTENSTEIN

AREA 160 sq km (62 sq mi)
POPULATION 35,000
CAPITAL Vaduz 5,000
RELIGION Roman Catholic, Protestant
LANGUAGE German, Alemannic dialect
LITERACY 100%
LIFE EXPECTANCY 80 years
GDP PER CAPITA $25,000
ECONOMY **IND:** electronics, metal manufacturing, dental products, ceramics **AGR:** wheat, barley, corn, potatoes; livestock **EXP:** small machinery, audio/video connectors, motor vehicle parts, dental products

Lithuania

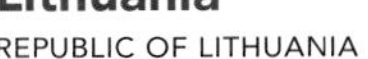

REPUBLIC OF LITHUANIA

AREA 65,300 sq km (25,212 sq mi)
POPULATION 3,392,000
CAPITAL Vilnius 553,000
RELIGION Roman Catholic
LANGUAGE Lithuanian, Russian, Polish
LITERACY 100%
LIFE EXPECTANCY 72 years
GDP PER CAPITA $15,100
ECONOMY **IND:** metal-cutting machine tools, electric motors, television sets, refrigerators and freezers **AGR:** grain, potatoes, sugar beets, flax; beef; fish **EXP:** mineral products, textiles and clothing, machinery and equipment, chemicals

Luxembourg

GRAND DUCHY OF LUXEMBOURG

AREA 2,586 sq km (998 sq mi)
POPULATION 460,000
CAPITAL Luxembourg 77,000
RELIGION Roman Catholic
LANGUAGE Luxembourgish, German, French
LITERACY 100%
LIFE EXPECTANCY 78 years
GDP PER CAPITA $68,800
ECONOMY **IND:** banking, iron and steel, information technology, telecommunications **AGR:** wine, grapes, barley, oats; dairy products **EXP:** machinery, steel products, chemicals, rubber products

Macedonia

REPUBLIC OF MACEDONIA

AREA 25,713 sq km (9,928 sq mi)
POPULATION 2,042,000
CAPITAL Skopje 475,000
RELIGION Macedonian Orthodox, Muslim
LANGUAGE Macedonian, Albanian
LITERACY 96%
LIFE EXPECTANCY 73 years
GDP PER CAPITA $8,200
ECONOMY **IND:** food processing, beverages, textiles, chemicals **AGR:** grapes, wine, tobacco, vegetables; milk **EXP:** food, beverages, tobacco, textiles

Malta

REPUBLIC OF MALTA

AREA 316 sq km (122 sq mi)
POPULATION 405,000
CAPITAL Valletta 210,000
RELIGION Roman Catholic
LANGUAGE Maltese, English
LITERACY 93%
LIFE EXPECTANCY 79 years
GDP PER CAPITA $20,300
ECONOMY **IND:** tourism, electronics, ship building and repair, construction **AGR:** potatoes, cauliflower, grapes, wheat; pork **EXP:** machinery and transport equipment, manufactures

Moldova

REPUBLIC OF MOLDOVA

AREA 33,800 sq km (13,050 sq mi)
POPULATION 3,980,000
CAPITAL Chisinau 598,000
RELIGION Eastern Orthodox
LANGUAGE Moldovan, Russian, Gagauz
LITERACY 99%
LIFE EXPECTANCY 69 years
GDP PER CAPITA $2,000
ECONOMY **IND:** sugar, vegetable oil, food processing, agricultural machinery **AGR:** vegetables, fruits, wine, grain; beef **EXP:** foodstuffs, textiles, machinery

Monaco

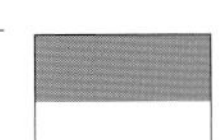

PRINCIPALITY OF MONACO

AREA 2 sq km (1 sq mi)
POPULATION 33,000
CAPITAL Monaco 33,000
RELIGION Roman Catholic
LANGUAGE French, English, Italian, Monegasque
LITERACY 99%
LIFE EXPECTANCY NA
GDP PER CAPITA $30,000
ECONOMY **IND:** tourism, construction, small-scale industrial and consumer products **AGR:** NA **EXP:** NA

Montenegro

REPUBLIC OF MONTENEGRO

AREA 14,026 sq km (5,415 sq mi)
POPULATION 625,000
CAPITAL Podgorica 163,000
RELIGION Orthodox, Muslim, Roman Catholic
LANGUAGE Serbian (Ijekavian dialect), Bosnian, Albanian, Croatian
LITERACY NA
LIFE EXPECTANCY NA
GDP PER CAPITA $3,800
ECONOMY **IND:** steelmaking, aluminum, agricultural processing, consumer goods **AGR:** grains, tobacco, potatoes, citrus fruits; sheepherding; fishing **EXP:** NA

Netherlands

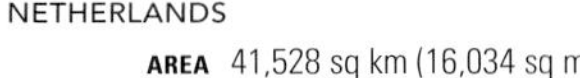

KINGDOM OF THE NETHERLANDS

AREA 41,528 sq km (16,034 sq mi)
POPULATION 16,355,000
CAPITAL Amsterdam 1,147,000
RELIGION Roman Catholic, Dutch Reformed, Calvinist, Muslim
LANGUAGE Dutch, Frisian
LITERACY 99%
LIFE EXPECTANCY 79 years
GDP PER CAPITA $31,700
ECONOMY **IND:** agro-industries, metal and engineering products, electrical machinery and equipment, chemicals **AGR:** grains, potatoes, sugar beets, fruits; livestock **EXP:** machinery and equipment, chemicals, fuels, foodstuffs

Norway

KINGDOM OF NORWAY

AREA 323,758 sq km (125,004 sq mi)
POPULATION 4,657,000
CAPITAL Oslo 802,000
RELIGION Church of Norway (Lutheran)
LANGUAGE Norwegian
LITERACY 100%
LIFE EXPECTANCY 80 years
GDP PER CAPITA $47,800
ECONOMY **IND:** petroleum and gas, food processing, shipbuilding, pulp and paper products **AGR:** barley, wheat, potatoes; pork; fish **EXP:** petroleum and petroleum products, machinery and equipment, metals, chemicals

Poland

REPUBLIC OF POLAND

AREA 312,685 sq km (120,728 sq mi)
POPULATION 38,149,000
CAPITAL Warsaw 1,680,000
RELIGION Roman Catholic
LANGUAGE Polish
LITERACY 100%
LIFE EXPECTANCY 75 years
GDP PER CAPITA $14,100
ECONOMY **IND:** machine building, iron and steel, coal mining, chemicals **AGR:** potatoes, fruits, vegetables, wheat; poultry **EXP:** machinery and transport equipment, other manufactured goods, food and live animals

Portugal

PORTUGUESE REPUBLIC

AREA 92,345 sq km (35,655 sq mi)
POPULATION 10,612,000
CAPITAL Lisbon 2,761,000
RELIGION Roman Catholic
LANGUAGE Portuguese, Mirandese
LITERACY 93%
LIFE EXPECTANCY 78 years
GDP PER CAPITA $19,100
ECONOMY **IND:** textiles and footwear, wood pulp, paper, and cork, metals and metalworking, oil refining **AGR:** grain, potatoes, tomatoes, olives; sheep; fish **EXP:** clothing and footwear, machinery, chemicals, cork and paper products

Romania

ROMANIA

AREA 238,391 sq km (92,043 sq mi)
POPULATION 21,575,000
CAPITAL Bucharest 1,934,000
RELIGION Eastern Orthodox, Protestant
LANGUAGE Romanian, Hungarian
LITERACY 98%
LIFE EXPECTANCY 71 years
GDP PER CAPITA $8,800
ECONOMY **IND:** textiles and footwear, light machinery and auto assembly, mining, timber **AGR:** wheat, corn, barley, sugar beets; eggs **EXP:** textiles and footwear, metals and metal products, machinery and equipment, minerals and fuels

Russia

RUSSIAN FEDERATION

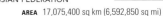

AREA 17,075,400 sq km (6,592,850 sq mi)
POPULATION 142,336,000
CAPITAL Moscow 10,654,000
RELIGION Russian Orthodox, Muslim
LANGUAGE Russian, many minority languages
LITERACY 100%
LIFE EXPECTANCY 65 years
GDP PER CAPITA $12,100
ECONOMY **IND:** mining industries (coal, oil, gas), machine building, defense industries, road and rail transportation equipment **AGR:** grain, sugar beets, sunflower seed, vegetables; beef **EXP:** petroleum and petroleum products, natural gas, wood and wood products, metals

San Marino

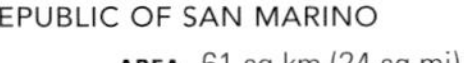

REPUBLIC OF SAN MARINO

AREA 61 sq km (24 sq mi)
POPULATION 31,000
CAPITAL San Marino 4,000
RELIGION Roman Catholic
LANGUAGE Italian
LITERACY 96%
LIFE EXPECTANCY 81 years
GDP PER CAPITA $34,100
ECONOMY **IND:** tourism, banking, textiles, electronics **AGR:** wheat, grapes, corn, olives; cattle **EXP:** building stone, lime, wood, chestnuts

Serbia

REPUBLIC OF SERBIA

AREA 102,173 sq km (39,450 sq mi)
POPULATION 9,458,000
CAPITAL Belgrade 1,106,000
RELIGION Serbian Orthodox, Roman Catholic
LANGUAGE Serbian
LITERACY 96%
LIFE EXPECTANCY 72 years
GDP PER CAPITA $4,400
ECONOMY **IND:** sugar, agricultural machinery, electrical and communication equipment, paper and pulp **AGR:** wheat, maize, sugar beets, sunflowers; beef **EXP:** manufactured goods, food, live animals, machinery and transport equipment

Slovakia

SLOVAK REPUBLIC

AREA 49,035 sq km (18,932 sq mi)
POPULATION 5,392,000
CAPITAL Bratislava 424,000
RELIGION Roman Catholic, Protestant
LANGUAGE Slovak, Hungarian
LITERACY 100%
LIFE EXPECTANCY 74 years
GDP PER CAPITA $17,700
ECONOMY **IND:** metal and metal products, food and beverages, electricity, gas **AGR:** grains, potatoes, sugar beets, hops; pigs; forest products **EXP:** vehicles, machinery and electrical equipment, base metals, chemicals and minerals

Slovenia

REPUBLIC OF SLOVENIA

AREA 20,273 sq km (7,827 sq mi)
POPULATION 2,003,000
CAPITAL Ljubljana 263,000
RELIGION Roman Catholic
LANGUAGE Slovene
LITERACY 100%
LIFE EXPECTANCY 77 years
GDP PER CAPITA $23,400
ECONOMY **IND:** ferrous metallurgy and aluminum products, lead and zinc smelting, electronics, trucks **AGR:** potatoes, hops, wheat, sugar beets; cattle **EXP:** manufactured goods, machinery and transport equipment, chemicals, food

Spain
KINGDOM OF SPAIN

AREA 505,988 sq km (195,363 sq mi)
POPULATION 45,511,000
CAPITAL Madrid 5,608,000
RELIGION Roman Catholic
LANGUAGE Castilian Spanish, Catalan, Galician
LITERACY 98%
LIFE EXPECTANCY 81 years
GDP PER CAPITA $27,000
ECONOMY **IND:** textiles and apparel, food and beverages, metals and metal manufactures, chemicals **AGR:** grain, vegetables, olives, wine grapes; beef; fish **EXP:** machinery, motor vehicles, foodstuffs, pharmaceuticals

Sweden
KINGDOM OF SWEDEN

AREA 449,964 sq km (173,732 sq mi)
POPULATION 9,080,000
CAPITAL Stockholm 1,708,000
RELIGION Lutheran
LANGUAGE Swedish
LITERACY 99%
LIFE EXPECTANCY 81 years
GDP PER CAPITA $31,600
ECONOMY **IND:** iron and steel, precision equipment, wood pulp and paper products, processed foods **AGR:** barley, wheat, sugar beets; meat **EXP:** machinery, motor vehicles, paper products, pulp and wood

Switzerland
SWISS CONFEDERATION

AREA 41,284 sq km (15,940 sq mi)
POPULATION 7,484,000
CAPITAL Bern 357,000
RELIGION Roman Catholic, Protestant
LANGUAGE German, French, Italian, Romansh
LITERACY 99%
LIFE EXPECTANCY 81 years
GDP PER CAPITA $33,600
ECONOMY **IND:** machinery, chemicals, watches, textiles **AGR:** grains, fruits, vegetables; meat **EXP:** machinery, chemicals, metals, watches

Ukraine
UKRAINE

AREA 603,700 sq km (233,090 sq mi)
POPULATION 46,755,000
CAPITAL Kiev 2,672,000
RELIGION Ukrainian Orthodox, Orthodox, Ukrainian Greek Catholic
LANGUAGE Ukrainian, Russian
LITERACY 100%
LIFE EXPECTANCY 68 years
GDP PER CAPITA $7,600
ECONOMY **IND:** coal, electric power, ferrous and nonferrous metals, machinery and transport equipment **AGR:** grain, sugar beets, sunflower seed, vegetables; beef **EXP:** ferrous and nonferrous metals, fuel and petroleum products, chemicals, machinery and transport equipment

United Kingdom

UNITED KINGDOM OF GREAT BRITAIN AND NORTHERN IRELAND

AREA 242,910 sq km (93,788 sq mi)
POPULATION 60,473,000
CAPITAL London 8,505,000
RELIGION Anglican, Roman Catholic, Presbyterian, Methodist
LANGUAGE English, Welsh, Scottish form of Gaelic
LITERACY 99%
LIFE EXPECTANCY 78 years
GDP PER CAPITA $31,400
ECONOMY **IND:** machine tools, electric power equipment, automation equipment, railroad equipment **AGR:** cereals, oilseed, potatoes, vegetables; cattle; fish **EXP:** manufactured goods, fuels, chemicals, food

Vatican City
THE HOLY SEE (STATE OF THE VATICAN CITY)

AREA 0.4 sq km (0.2 sq mi)
POPULATION 800
CAPITAL Vatican City 800
RELIGION Roman Catholic
LANGUAGE Italian, Latin, French
LITERACY 100%
LIFE EXPECTANCY NA
GDP PER CAPITA NA
ECONOMY **IND:** printing, production of coins, medals, and postage stamps, a small amount of mosaics and staff uniforms, worldwide banking and financial activities **AGR:** NA **EXP:** NA

Dependencies

Faroe Islands (Denmark)
SOVEREIGN

LOCAL

FAROE ISLANDS

AREA 1,399 sq km (540 sq mi)
POPULATION 50,000
CAPITAL Tórshavn 18,000
RELIGION Evangelical Lutheran
LANGUAGE Faroese, Danish
LITERACY NA
LIFE EXPECTANCY 79 years
GDP PER CAPITA $31,000
ECONOMY **IND:** fishing, fish processing, small ship repair and refurbishment, handicrafts **AGR:** milk, potatoes, vegetables; sheep; salmon **EXP:** fish and fish products, stamps, ships

Gibraltar (U.K.)
SOVEREIGN

LOCAL

GIBRALTAR

AREA 7 sq km (3 sq mi)
POPULATION 29,000
CAPITAL Gibraltar 28,000
RELIGION Roman Catholic, Church of England
LANGUAGE English, Spanish, Italian, Portuguese
LITERACY above 80%
LIFE EXPECTANCY 81 years
GDP PER CAPITA $27,900
ECONOMY **IND:** tourism, banking and finance, ship repairing, tobacco **AGR:** NA **EXP:** petroleum, manufactured goods

Europe-Asia Boundary

A commonly accepted division between Asia and Europe—marked with a red line on the map above—is formed by the Ural Mountains, Ural River, Caspian Sea, Caucasus Mountains, and the Black Sea with its outlets, the Bosporus and Dardanelles. From north to south, the Europe-Asia boundary divides the nations of Russia, Kazakhstan, Azerbaijan, Georgia, and Turkey, placing territory of each country in both continents.

Russia is grouped in Europe's "Flags & Facts" section of this atlas because its capital, Moscow, is well within the European part of what is the world's largest country. The nations of Kazakhstan, Azerbaijan, Georgia, and Turkey are covered in the Asia section.

Cyprus marks the southeastern extent of Europe because of its cultural and historic ties to Europe, which include joining the European Union in 2004.

Dates of National Independence

NOTE: For some countries, the date given may not represent "independence" in the strict sense—but rather some significant nationhood event: the traditional founding date; a fundamental change in the form of government; or perhaps the date of unification, secession, federation, confederation, or state succession.

Land Cover
Water
Evergreen needleleaf forest
Evergreen broadleaf forest
Deciduous needleleaf forest
Deciduous broadleaf forest
Mixed forest
Closed shrubland
Open shrubland
Woody savanna
Savanna
Grassland
Permanent wetland
Cropland
Urban and built-up
Cropland/natural vegetation mosaic
Snow and ice
Barren or sparsely vegetated

Asia

THE CONTINENT OF ASIA, occupying four-fifths of the giant Eurasian landmass, stretches across ten time zones from the Pacific Ocean in the east to the Ural Mountains and Black Sea in the west. It is the largest of the continents, with dazzling geographic diversity and 30 percent of the Earth's land surface. Asia includes numerous island nations, such as Japan, the Philippines, Indonesia, and Sri Lanka, as well as many of the world's major islands: Borneo, Sumatra, Honshu, Celebes, Java, and half of New Guinea. Siberia, the huge Asian section of Russia, reaches deep inside the Arctic Circle and fills the continent's northern quarter. To its south lie the large countries of Kazakhstan, Mongolia, and China. Within its 46 countries, Asia holds 60 percent of humanity, yet deserts, mountains, jungles, and inhospitable zones render much of the continent empty or underpopulated.

Great river systems allowed the growth of the world's first civilizations in the Middle East, the Indian subcontinent, and North China. Numerous cultural forces, each linked to these broad geographical areas, have formed and influenced Asia's rich civilizations and hundreds of ethnic groups. The two oldest are the cultural milieus of India and China. India's culture still reverberates throughout countries as varied as Sri Lanka, Pakistan, Nepal, Burma, Cambodia, and Indonesia. The world religions of Hinduism and Buddhism originated in India and spread as traders, scholars, and priests sought distant footholds. China's ancient civilization has profoundly influenced the development of all of East Asia, much of Southeast Asia, and parts of Central Asia. Most influential of all Chinese institutions were the Chinese written language, a complex script with thousands of characters, and Confucianism, an ethical worldview that affected philosophy, politics, and relations within society. Islam, a third great influence in Asia, proved formidable in its energy and creative genius. Arabs from the 7th century onwards, spurred on by faith, moved rapidly into Southwest Asia. Their religion and culture, particularly Arabic writing, spread through Iran and Afghanistan to the Indian subcontinent.

Today nearly all of Asia's people continue to live beside rivers or along coastal zones. Dense concentrations of population fill Japan, China's eastern half, Java, parts of Southeast Asia, and much of the Indian subcontinent. China and India, acting as demographic, political, and cultural counterweights, hold nearly half of Asia's population. India, with a billion people, expects to surpass China as the world's most populous nation by 2050. As China seeks to take center stage, flexing economic muscle and pushing steadily into the oil-rich South China Sea, many Asian neighbors grow concerned. The development of nuclear weapons by India and Pakistan complicate international relations. Economic recovery after the financial turmoil of the late 1990s preoccupies many countries, while others yearn to escape dire poverty. Religious, ethnic, and territorial conflicts continue to beset the continent, from the Middle East to Korea, from Cambodia to Uzbekistan. Asians also face the threats of overpopulation, resource depletion, pollution, and the growth of megacities. Yet if vibrant Asia meets the challenges of rebuilding and reconciliation, overcoming age-old habits of rivalry, corruption, and cronyism, it may yet fulfill the promise to claim the first hundred years of the new millennium as Asia's century.

ATLANTIC OCEAN
ARCTIC
GREENLAND
Denmark
North Pole
GREENLAND SEA
NORWEGIAN SEA
ICELAND
ARCTIC CIRCLE
Meridian of Greenwich (London)
IRELAND
Baile Átha Cliath (Dublin)
UNITED KINGDOM
LONDON
Amsterdam
NETHERLANDS
NORTH SEA
DENMARK
København (Copenhagen)
Lisboa (Lisbon)
PORTUGAL
SPAIN
MADRID
FRANCE
PARIS
BELGIUM
Bruxelles (Brussels)
LUXEMBOURG
SWITZERLAND
Bern
GERMANY
BERLIN
PRAHA (Prague)
CZECH REP.
AUSTRIA
WIEN (Vienna)
SLOVENIA
Ljubljana
CROATIA
Zagreb
BOSNIA & HERZEGOVINA
Sarajevo
MONTENEGRO
Podgorica
SERBIA
BEOGRAD (Belgrade)
ALBANIA
Tiranë
MACEDONIA
Skopje
GREECE
Athína (Athens)
ROMA (Rome)
ITALY
MALTA
MEDITERRANEAN SEA
HUNGARY
BUDAPEST
SLOVAKIA
Bratislava
ROMANIA
BUCUREŞTI (Bucharest)
BULGARIA
SOFIYA (Sofia)
MOLDOVA
Chişinău
POLAND
WARSZAWA (Warsaw)
Kaliningrad
Russia
LITHUANIA
Vilnius
LATVIA
Rīga
ESTONIA
Tallinn
BALTIC SEA
BELARUS
MINSK
UKRAINE
KYIV (Kiev)
CRIMEA
BLACK SEA
NORWAY
Oslo
SWEDEN
Stockholm
FINLAND
Helsinki
Gulf of Bothnia
LAPLAND
SVALBARD
Norway
Spitsbergen
Nordaustlandet
Edgeøya
BARENTS SEA
FRANZ JOSEF LAND (Zemlya Frantsa Iosifa)
Russia
Novaya Zemlya
KARA SEA
SEVERNAYA ZEMLYA (North Land)
Ostrov Komsomolets
O. Oktyabr'skoy Revolyutsii
Ostrov Bol'shevik
Poluostrov Taymyr
Dickson
Novorybnoye
Khatanga
Yeniseyskiy Zaliv
Dudinka
Noril'sk
Yessey
Igarka
Chirinda
Tura
Murmansk
Kandalaksha
Segezha
Petrozavodsk
BELOYE MORE (WHITE SEA)
Severodvinsk
Arkhangel'sk
Mezen'
Nar'yan Mar
Vorkuta
Pechora
SANKT-PETERBURG (St. Petersburg)
Vologda
Tver'
MOSKVA (Moscow)
Yaroslavl'
Smolensk
Bryansk
Tula
Kursk
Orel
Ryazan'
Voronezh
Tambov
Penza
Saratov
Volgograd
NIZHNIY NOVGOROD
KAZAN'
Kirov
Perm'
Izhevsk
Ul'yanovsk
SAMARA
Ufa
Oral
Orenburg
Orsk
Magnitogorsk
Aqtöbe
Ukhta
Syktyvkar
URAL MOUNTAINS
RUSSIA
SIBERIA
Salekhard
Nadym
Novyy Urengoy
Khanty Mansiysk
Nizhnevartovsk
Surgut
Serov
Nizhniy Tagil
Tavda
Tobol'sk
Tyumen'
YEKATERINBURG
CHELYABINSK
Qostanay
Petropavlovsk
Kökshetaū
Ekibastuz
Astana
Pavlodar
Semey
Rubtsovsk
Öskemen
Qaraghandy
NOVOSIBIRSK
OMSK
Tomsk
Kemerovo
Prokop'yevsk
Novokuznetsk
Barnaul
Biysk
Kolpashevo
Yeniseysk
Achinsk
Krasnoyarsk
Kansk
Bratsk
Tulun
Abakan
Kyzyl
Ust' Ilimsk
Severo Yeniseyskiy
ROSTOV NA DONU
Krasnodar
Stavropol'
Sochi
Vladikavkaz
Groznyy
Astrakhan'
Atyraū
Fort Shevchenko
Aqtaū
CASPIAN SEA
KAZAKHSTAN
Oktyabr'sk
Aral
Aral Sea
Qazaly
Syr Darya
Qyzylorda
Balqash Köli
Balqash
Ayaköz
Zaysan Köli
Taldyqorghan
Shymkent
Taraz
ALMATY
Saryözek
UZBEKISTAN
Nukus
Daşoguz
TOSHKENT (Tashkent)
Farg'ona
Namangan
Bukhara
Samarqand
TURKMENISTAN
Türkmenbaşy
Türkmenabat
Aşgabat
Mary
KYRGYZSTAN
Bishkek
TAJIKISTAN
Dushanbe
Termiz
Mazar-e Sharif
Kondoz
AFGHANISTAN
Herat
Kabol (Kabul)
Kandahar
Farah
KHORĀSĀN
Mashhad
Bojnūrd
Sabzevār
TURKEY
İSTANBUL
Bosporus
BURSA
Eskişehir
ANKARA
İZMİR
Konya
Samsun
Kayseri
Trabzon
Adana
İskenderun
Diyarbakır
CYPRUS
Lefkosia (Nicosia)
GEORGIA
T'BILISI
ARMENIA
YEREVAN
AZERBAIJAN
BAKI (Baku)
Tabrīz
Ardabīl
Rasht
Qazvīn
Bābol
TEHRĀN
Qom
Hamadān
Kermānshāh
Sanandaj
Arāk
IRAN
EŞFAHĀN
Yazd
Kermān
Shīrāz
Bandar-e Būshehr
Ahvāz
Ābādān
Bīrjand
Zāhedān
Zābol
Bam
Jahrom
Bandar-e 'Abbās
BALUCHISTAN
SYRIA
HALAB (Aleppo)
DIMASHQ (Damascus)
LEBANON
BEYROUTH (Beirut)
ISRAEL
Jerusalem
GAZA STRIP
WEST BANK
JORDAN
'AMMĀN
IRAQ
MESOPOTAMIA
Al Mawşil
Karkūk
BAGHDĀD
Karbalā'
An Najaf
An Nāşirīyah
Al Başrah
KUWAIT
Al Kuwayt
Tabūk
Dawmat al Jandal
Ḩā'il
Buraydah
AL ḨIJĀZ
Al Madīnah (Medina)
Yanbu' al Baḩr
JEDDAH
Makkah (Mecca)
Aţ Ţā'if
SAUDI ARABIA
AR RIYĀD (Riyadh)
Al Hufūf
Ad Dammām
Al Manāmah (Manama)
BAHRAIN
Ad Dawḩah (Doha)
QATAR
PERSIAN GULF
Dubayy (Dubai)
Abū Z̧aby (Abu Dhabi)
UNITED ARAB EMIRATES
Nizwá
Masqaţ (Muscat)
Şūr
OMAN
Jazīrat Maşīrah
Şalālah
Gulf of Oman
Khamīs Mushayţ
Qal'at Bīshah
'ASĪR
Jīzān
AR RUB' AL KHĀLĪ (Empty Quarter)
Şa'dah
Şan'ā'
YEMEN
Ta'izz
'Adan
Saywūn
Al Mukallā
Ash Shiḩr
GULF OF ADEN
Suquţrá (Socotra)
Yemen
RED SEA
SUEZ CANAL
Nile
EL QĀHIRA (Cairo)
EGYPT
LIBYA
ṬARĀBULUS (Tripoli)
TUNISIA
TUNIS
ALGERIA
ALGER (Algiers)
MOROCCO
TROPIC OF CANCER
SUDAN
Khartoum
ERITREA
Asmara
DJIBOUTI
Djibouti
ETHIOPIA
ĀDĪS ĀBEBA (Addis Ababa)
SOMALILAND
Hargeysa
SOMALIA
MUQDISHO (Mogadishu)
UGANDA
KENYA
Lake Victoria
NAIROBI
EQUATOR
TANZANIA
Dodoma
DAR ES SALAAM
MOZAMBIQUE
COMOROS
Moroni
MADAGASCAR
SEYCHELLES
Victoria
Mahé I.
INDIAN OCEAN
ARABIAN SEA
Lakshadweep
India
Maldive Islands
Maale (Male)
MALDIVES
British Indian Ocean Territory
Chagos Archipelago (Oil Islands)
Diego Garcia
Turkey, Cyprus, Syria, Lebanon, Israel, Jordan, Egypt, Iraq, Iran, and the countries of the Arabian Peninsula form the heart of the Middle East region.
PAKISTAN
Islamabad
Peshawar
Rawalpindi
LAHORE
Faisalabad
Multan
Quetta
Bahawalpur
Khanpur
Sukkur
Turbat
KARACHI
Hyderabad
Indus
KASHMIR
Gilgit
Srinagar
Boundary claimed by India
Amritsar
Jalandhar
LUDHIANA
DELHI
New Delhi
MEERUT
AGRA
JAIPUR
Jodhpur
Udaipur
AHMADABAD
Rajkot
VADODARA
SURAT
NASIK
MUMBAI (Bombay)
KALYAN
PUNE
Kolhapur
Sholapur
Gwalior
Kota
KANPUR
LUCKNOW
Allahabad
Varanasi
PATNA
INDIA
BHOPAL
INDORE
Jabalpur
Amravati
NAGPUR
Ranchi
JAMSHEDPUR
KOLKATA (Calcutta)
HYDERABAD
VISHAKHAPATNAM
VIJAYAWADA
Guntur
Hubli
Nellore
BANGALORE
Mysore
Salem
CHENNAI (Madras)
Puducherry
KOZHIKODE
COIMBATORE
Tiruchchirappalli
MADURAI
COCHIN
Thiruvananthapuram (Trivandrum)
Jaffna
SRI LANKA
Colombo
Galle
BAY OF BENGAL
Ganga (Ganges)
NEPAL
Kathmandu
HIMALAYA
BHUTAN
Thimphu
Shiliguri
Guwahati
Dibrugarh
Imphal
Rajshahi
Khulna
DHAKA
BANGLADESH
CHITTAGONG
MYANMAR (BURMA)
Mandalay
Monywa
Sittwe
Nay Pyi Taw (administrative)
Hinthada
YANGON (Rangoon) (legislative)
Andaman Islands
India
Nicobar Islands
India
Banda Aceh
Simeulue
CHINA
TIBET
Plateau of Tibet
Lhasa
Xigazê
Gyangzê
KUNLUN SHAN
ALTUN SHAN
Taklimakan Shamo
Kashi
Aksu
Kuqa
Korla
SINKIANG
TIAN SHAN
Yining
Shihezi
ÜRÜMQI
Turpan
Hami
Jiayuguan
Anxi
Yumen
Lenghu
Da Qaidam
Golmud
Dulan
Shache
Hotan
Qiemo
Tacheng
Altay
ALTAY MTS.
Hovd
Uliastay
Ulaangom
Longitude East 90° of Greenwich

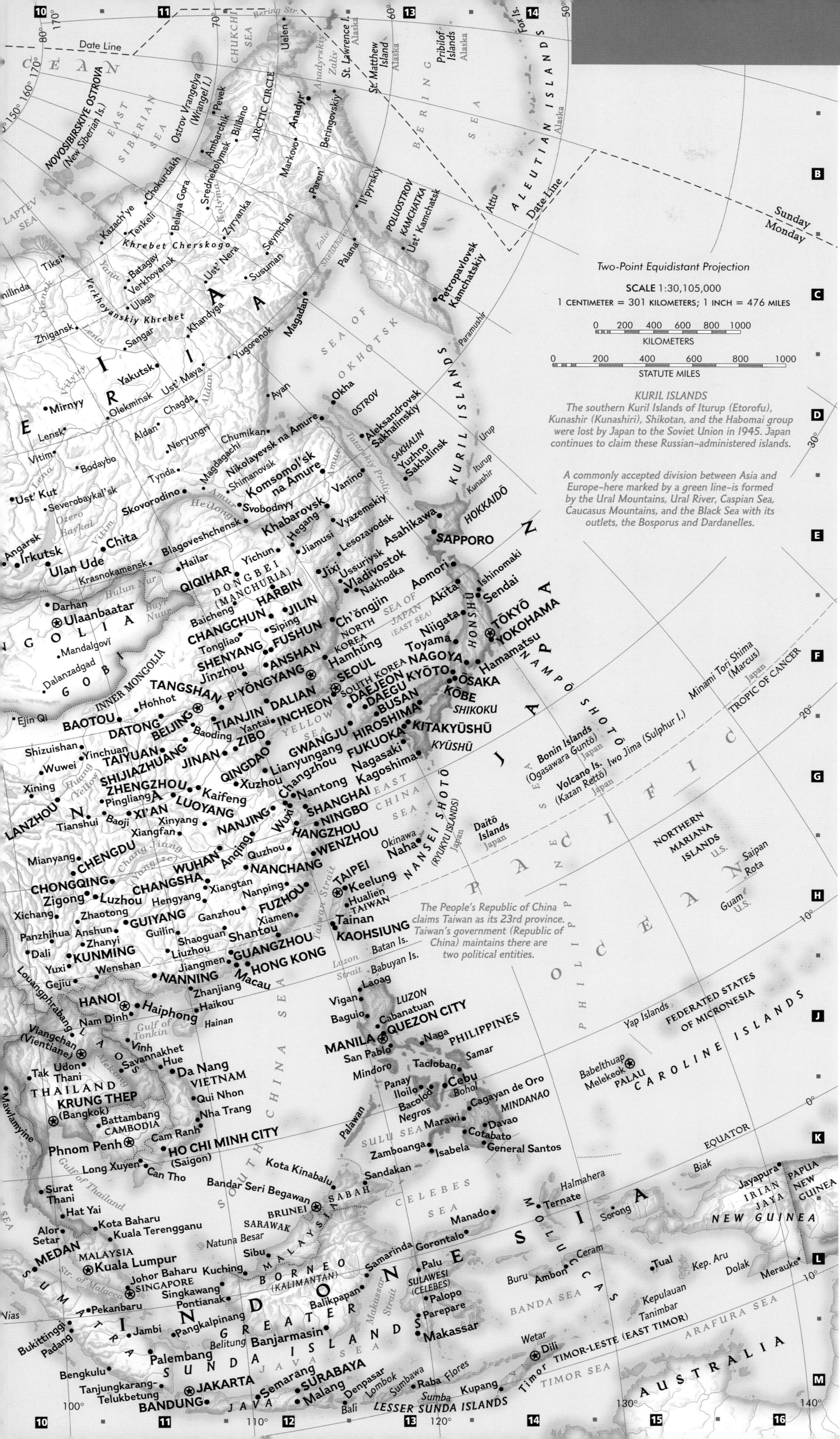

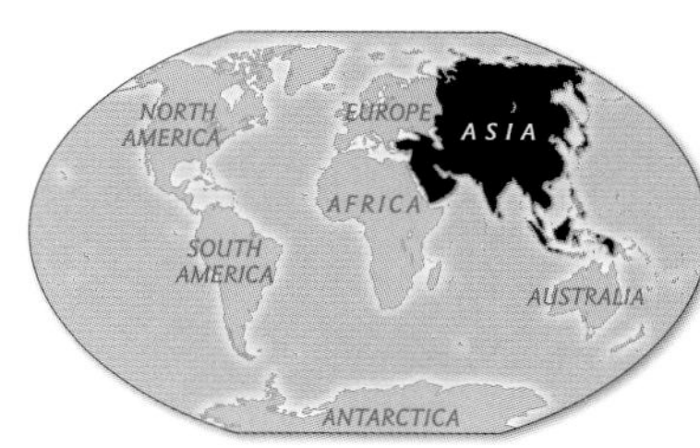

Two-Point Equidistant Projection
SCALE 1:30,105,000
1 CENTIMETER = 301 KILOMETERS; 1 INCH = 476 MILES
0 200 400 600 800 1000
KILOMETERS
0 200 400 600 800 1000
STATUTE MILES
KURIL ISLANDS
The southern Kuril Islands of Iturup (Etorofu), Kunashir (Kunashiri), Shikotan, and the Habomai group were lost by Japan to the Soviet Union in 1945. Japan continues to claim these Russian-administered islands.
A commonly accepted division between Asia and Europe–here marked by a green line–is formed by the Ural Mountains, Ural River, Caspian Sea, Caucasus Mountains, and the Black Sea with its outlets, the Bosporus and Dardanelles.
The People's Republic of China claims Taiwan as its 23rd province. Taiwan's government (Republic of China) maintains there are two political entities.
Sunday
Monday
Date Line
TROPIC OF CANCER
EQUATOR
JAPAN
TŌKYŌ
YOKOHAMA
SAPPORO
BEIJING
SEOUL
P'YŎNGYANG
MANILA
QUEZON CITY
HONG KONG
HANOI
KRUNG THEP (Bangkok)
Phnom Penh
HO CHI MINH CITY (Saigon)
Kuala Lumpur
SINGAPORE
JAKARTA
TAIPEI
Ulaanbaatar
PACIFIC OCEAN
SEA OF OKHOTSK
SOUTH CHINA SEA
INDONESIA
AUSTRALIA

NORTH AMERICA
EUROPE
ASIA
AFRICA
SOUTH AMERICA
AUSTRALIA
ANTARCTICA

CONTINENTAL DATA

TOTAL NUMBER OF COUNTRIES: 46

FIRST INDEPENDENT COUNTRY:
Japan 660 B.C.

"YOUNGEST" COUNTRY:
Timor-Leste, May 20, 2002

LARGEST COUNTRY BY AREA:
*China 9,596,960 sq km (3,705,405 sq mi)

SMALLEST COUNTRY BY AREA:
Maldives 298 sq km (115 sq mi)

PERCENT URBAN POPULATION:
38%

MOST POPULOUS COUNTRY:
China 1,341,715,000

LEAST POPULOUS COUNTRY:
Maldives 298,000

MOST DENSELY POPULATED COUNTRY:
Singapore 6,765 per sq km (17,510 per sq mi)

LEAST DENSELY POPULATED COUNTRY:
Mongolia 1.6 per sq km (4.3 per sq mi)

LARGEST CITY BY POPULATION:
Tokyo, Japan 35,197,000

HIGHEST GDP PER CAPITA:
United Arab Emirates $49,700

LOWEST GDP PER CAPITA:
Timor-Leste $800

AVERAGE LIFE EXPECTANCY IN ASIA: 68 years

AVERAGE LITERACY RATE IN ASIA: 79%

*The world's largest country, Russia, straddles both Asia and Europe. China, which is entirely within Asia, is considered the continent's largest country.

ATLANTIC OCEAN
ARCTIC
GREENLAND
North Pole
GREENLAND SEA
NORWEGIAN SEA
BRITISH ISLES
Ireland
Great Britain
Meridian of Greenwich (London)
NORTH SEA
ARCTIC CIRCLE
SVALBARD
FRANZ JOSEF LAND
Komsomolets I.
NORTH LAND
October Revolution I.
Bol'shevik I.
BARENTS SEA
IBERIAN PENINSULA
SCANDINAVIA
Gulf of Bothnia
BALTIC SEA
NOVAYA ZEMLYA
KARA SEA
Taymyr Peninsula
Lake Taymyr
ATLAS MOUNTAINS
ALPS
NORTHERN EUROPEAN PLAIN
Kola Peninsula
White Sea
Yamal Peninsula
Gulf of Ob
Gyda Pen.
Yenisey Gulf
North Siberian
MEDITERRANEAN SEA
EUROPE
Lake Ladoga
Lake Onega
Volga
Narodnaya 1895
URAL MOUNTAINS
Ob
Taz
Yenisey
CENTRAL SIBERIAN PLATEAU
869
BALKAN PENINSULA
WEST SIBERIAN PLAIN
Kama
Irtysh
Vasyugan'ye
Angara
AEGEAN SEA
Dardanelles
Bosporus
BLACK SEA
Crimea
Don
Volga
Ural
Tobol
Ishim Steppe
Bratsk Reservoir
ANATOLIA (ASIA MINOR)
Taurus Mts.
3916
Cyprus
CAUCASUS MOUNTAINS
El'brus 5642
Caspian Depression
THE STEPPES
Lake Tengiz
Kazakh Uplands
Eastern Sayan
Western Sayan Mountains
AFRICA
TROPIC OF CANCER
Levant Coast
3088
Mt. Ararat 5137
Lake Urmia
CASPIAN SEA
Aral Sea
Ustyurt Plateau
Belukha 4506
Source of the Yenisey-Angara
ALTAY MOUNTAINS
Black Irtysh
Source of the Ob-Irtysh
SUEZ CANAL
Nile
SINAI
Dead Sea
-416 (-1365 ft) World's lowest point
Euphrates
Tigris
Syrian Desert
Mesopotamia
Kura
-28
Turan Lowland
Qizilqum
Syr Darya
Amu Darya
Lake Balkhash
Betpaqdala
Ili
Dzungarian Basin
5445
Bogda Shan
-154
Turpan Depression
SAHARA
Gulf of Aqaba
Hejaz
Hawr al Hammar
Elburz Mts.
5671
Kopet Mts.
Garagum
Victory Peak 7439
TIAN SHAN
Tarim
Lop Nur
Bei Shan
An Nafūd
ARABIAN PENINSULA
Ad Dahnā'
Zagros Mountains
4548
Dasht-e Lūt
7495
TARIM BASIN
Taklimakan Desert
7690
Hindu Kush
5143
Karakoram Ra.
Muztag 7282
Altun Shan
Qaidam Basin
KUNLUN MOUNTAINS
K2 (Godwin Austen) 8611
KASHMIR
PLATEAU OF TIBET
6300
RED SEA
Tihāmah
2386
Tuwayq Mountains
Hasa Plain
PERSIAN GULF
Helmand
Indus
Source of the Yangtze
Nganglong Range
Tanggula Range
Gangdise Ra.
7059
Nyainqêntanglha Shan
Sutlej
Rub al Khali
GULF OF OMAN
2980
Ra's al Hadd
Great Indian Desert
HIMALAYA
World's highest point
Mt. Everest 8850 (29035 ft)
Ganges Plain
Ganges
Brahmaputra
ETHIOPIAN HIGHLANDS
3760
Hadhramaut
1730
Gulf of Masira
Gulf of Kutch
Vindhya Range
Narmada
1350
Chota Nagpur Plateau
Mt. Victoria 3053
GULF OF ADEN
Gulf of Khambhat
DECCAN PLATEAU
Western Ghats
Eastern Ghats
1589
Krishna
Irrawaddy
Somali Peninsula
Socotra
ARABIAN SEA
Coromandel Coast
BAY OF BENGAL
Lakshadweep
LACCADIVE SEA
Malabar Coast
2695
Andaman Islands
Nicobar Islands
EQUATOR
Cape Comorin
2524
Sri Lanka
Maldive Islands
INDIAN OCEAN
Seychelles
Comoro Is.
Madagascar
Chagos Archipelago
Longitude East 90° of Greenwich

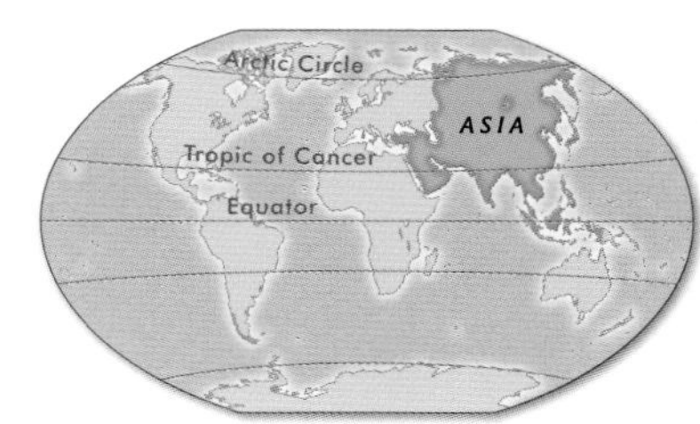

Two-Point Equidistant Projection

SCALE 1:30,105,000
1 CENTIMETER = 301 KILOMETERS; 1 INCH = 476 MILES

0 200 400 600 800 1000
KILOMETERS

0 200 400 600 800 1000
STATUTE MILES

International boundary

Disputed or undefined boundary

A commonly accepted division between Asia and Europe–here marked by a green line–is formed by the Ural Mountains, Ural River, Caspian Sea, Caucasus Mountains, and the Black Sea with its outlets, the Bosporus and Dardanelles.

CONTINENTAL DATA

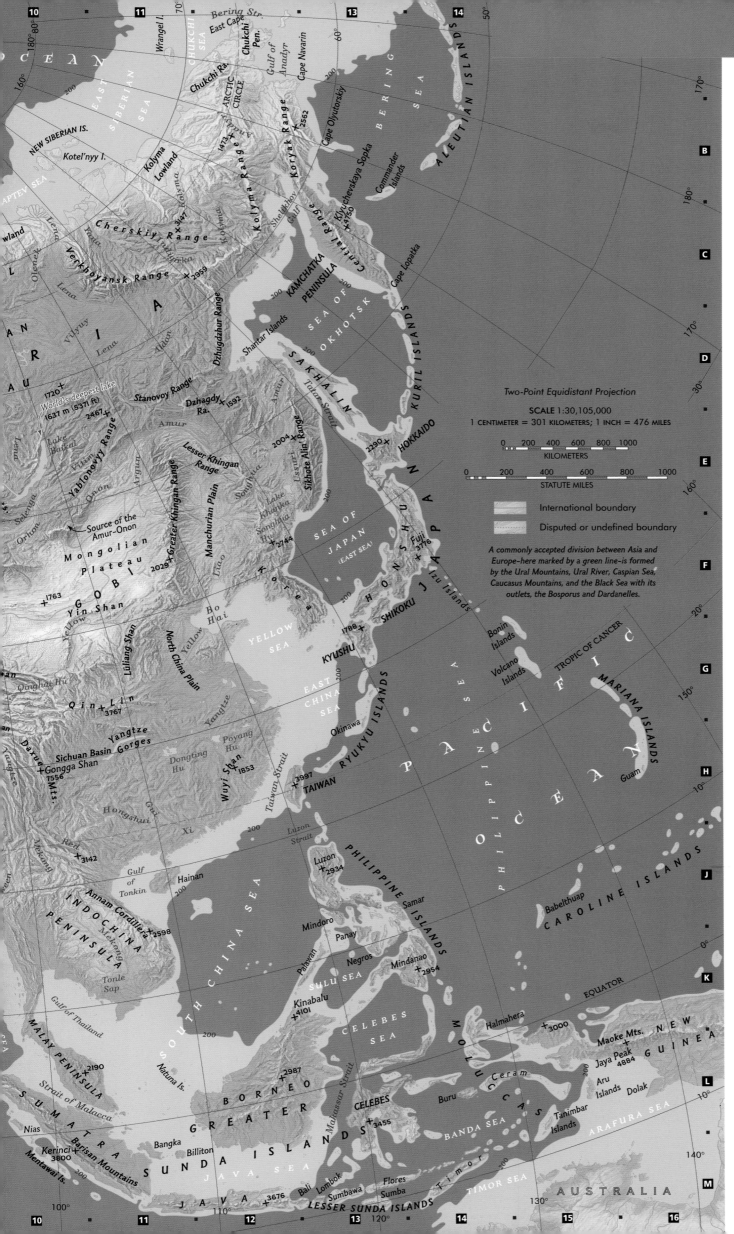

AREA:
44,570,000 sq km
(17,208,000 sq mi)

GREATEST NORTH-SOUTH EXTENT:
8,690 km (5,400 mi)

GREATEST EAST-WEST EXTENT:
9,700 km (6,030 mi)

HIGHEST POINT:
Mount Everest, China-Nepal
8,850 m (29,035 ft)

LOWEST POINT:
Dead Sea, Israel-Jordan
-416 m (-1,365 ft)

LOWEST RECORDED TEMPERATURE:
- Oymyakon, Russia -68°C (-90°F), February 6, 1933
- Verkhoyansk, Russia -68°C (-90°F), February 7, 1892

HIGHEST RECORDED TEMPERATURE:
Tirat Zevi, Israel 54°C (129°F), June 21, 1942

LONGEST RIVERS:
- Chang Jiang (Yangtze) 6,380 km (3,964 mi)
- Yenisey-Angara 5,536 km (3,440 mi)
- Huang (Yellow) 5,464 km (3,395 mi)

LARGEST LAKES:
- Caspian Sea 371,000 sq km (143,200 sq mi)
- Lake Baikal 31,500 sq km (12,200 sq mi)
- Aral Sea 25,508 sq km (9,849 sq mi)

EARTH'S EXTREMES LOCATED IN ASIA:
- **Wettest Place:** Mawsynram, India; annual average rainfall 1,187 cm (467 in)
- **Largest Cave Chamber:** Sarawak Cave, Gunung Mulu National Park, Malaysia; 16 hectares and 79 m high (40 acres, 260 ft)

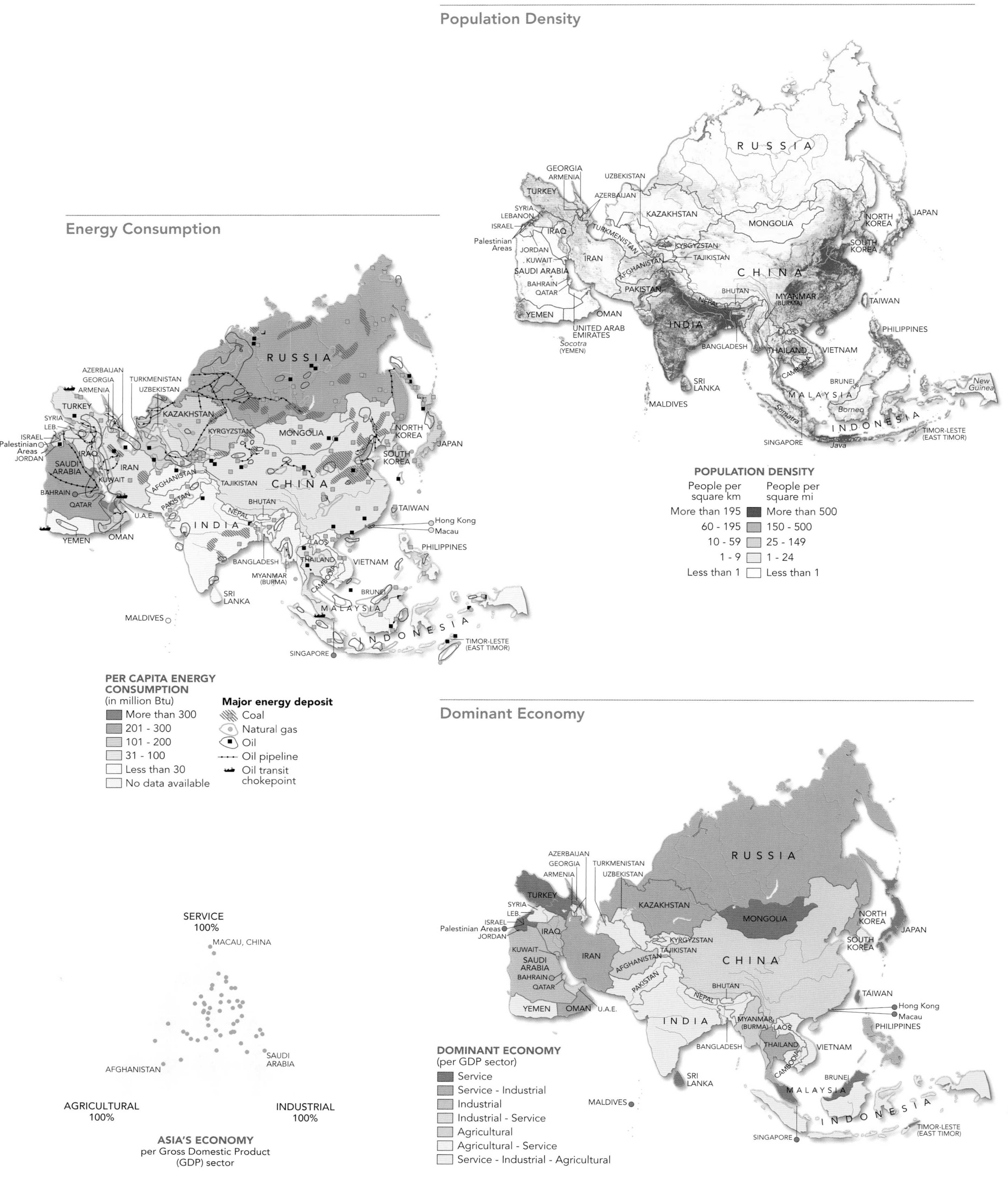
Population Density
RUSSIA
GEORGIA
ARMENIA
UZBEKISTAN
AZERBAIJAN
TURKEY
SYRIA
LEBANON
ISRAEL
Palestinian Areas
JORDAN
KUWAIT
SAUDI ARABIA
BAHRAIN
QATAR
YEMEN
IRAQ
IRAN
TURKMENISTAN
KAZAKHSTAN
MONGOLIA
KYRGYZSTAN
TAJIKISTAN
AFGHANISTAN
PAKISTAN
CHINA
NORTH KOREA
SOUTH KOREA
JAPAN
OMAN
UNITED ARAB EMIRATES
Socotra (YEMEN)
NEPAL
BHUTAN
MYANMAR (BURMA)
TAIWAN
INDIA
LAOS
PHILIPPINES
BANGLADESH
THAILAND
VIETNAM
CAMBODIA
SRI LANKA
BRUNEI
MALAYSIA
MALDIVES
Borneo
Sumatra
INDONESIA
New Guinea
TIMOR-LESTE (EAST TIMOR)
SINGAPORE
Java
POPULATION DENSITY
People per square km
People per square mi
More than 195 | More than 500
60 - 195 | 150 - 500
10 - 59 | 25 - 149
1 - 9 | 1 - 24
Less than 1 | Less than 1
Energy Consumption
RUSSIA
AZERBAIJAN
GEORGIA
ARMENIA
TURKMENISTAN
UZBEKISTAN
TURKEY
SYRIA
LEB.
ISRAEL
Palestinian Areas
JORDAN
KAZAKHSTAN
KYRGYZSTAN
MONGOLIA
NORTH KOREA
SOUTH KOREA
JAPAN
IRAQ
SAUDI ARABIA
IRAN
KUWAIT
BAHRAIN
QATAR
AFGHANISTAN
TAJIKISTAN
CHINA
PAKISTAN
U.A.E.
BHUTAN
NEPAL
TAIWAN
Hong Kong
Macau
YEMEN
OMAN
INDIA
LAOS
PHILIPPINES
BANGLADESH
THAILAND
VIETNAM
MYANMAR (BURMA)
CAMBODIA
SRI LANKA
BRUNEI
MALAYSIA
MALDIVES
INDONESIA
TIMOR-LESTE (EAST TIMOR)
SINGAPORE
PER CAPITA ENERGY CONSUMPTION
(in million Btu)
More than 300
201 - 300
101 - 200
31 - 100
Less than 30
No data available
Major energy deposit
Coal
Natural gas
Oil
Oil pipeline
Oil transit chokepoint
Dominant Economy
RUSSIA
AZERBAIJAN
GEORGIA
ARMENIA
TURKMENISTAN
UZBEKISTAN
TURKEY
KAZAKHSTAN
SYRIA
LEB.
ISRAEL
Palestinian Areas
JORDAN
IRAQ
MONGOLIA
NORTH KOREA
SOUTH KOREA
JAPAN
KUWAIT
SAUDI ARABIA
BAHRAIN
QATAR
IRAN
KYRGYZSTAN
TAJIKISTAN
AFGHANISTAN
CHINA
PAKISTAN
BHUTAN
NEPAL
TAIWAN
Hong Kong
Macau
YEMEN
OMAN
U.A.E.
INDIA
MYANMAR (BURMA)
LAOS
PHILIPPINES
BANGLADESH
THAILAND
VIETNAM
CAMBODIA
SRI LANKA
BRUNEI
MALAYSIA
MALDIVES
INDONESIA
SINGAPORE
TIMOR-LESTE (EAST TIMOR)
DOMINANT ECONOMY
(per GDP sector)
Service
Service - Industrial
Industrial
Industrial - Service
Agricultural
Agricultural - Service
Service - Industrial - Agricultural
SERVICE 100%
MACAU, CHINA
AFGHANISTAN
SAUDI ARABIA
AGRICULTURAL 100%
INDUSTRIAL 100%
ASIA'S ECONOMY
per Gross Domestic Product (GDP) sector

Climate Zones

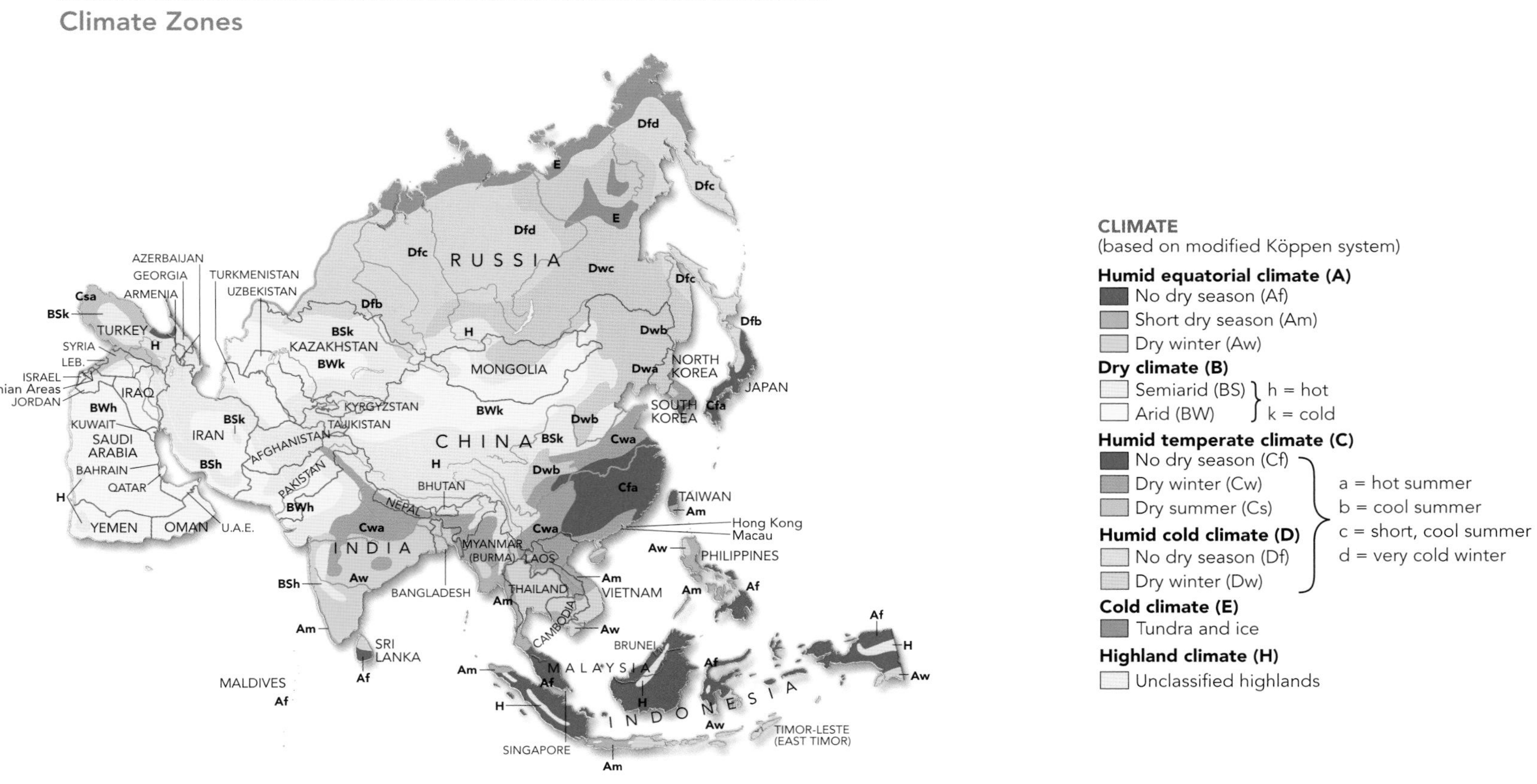

Natural Events

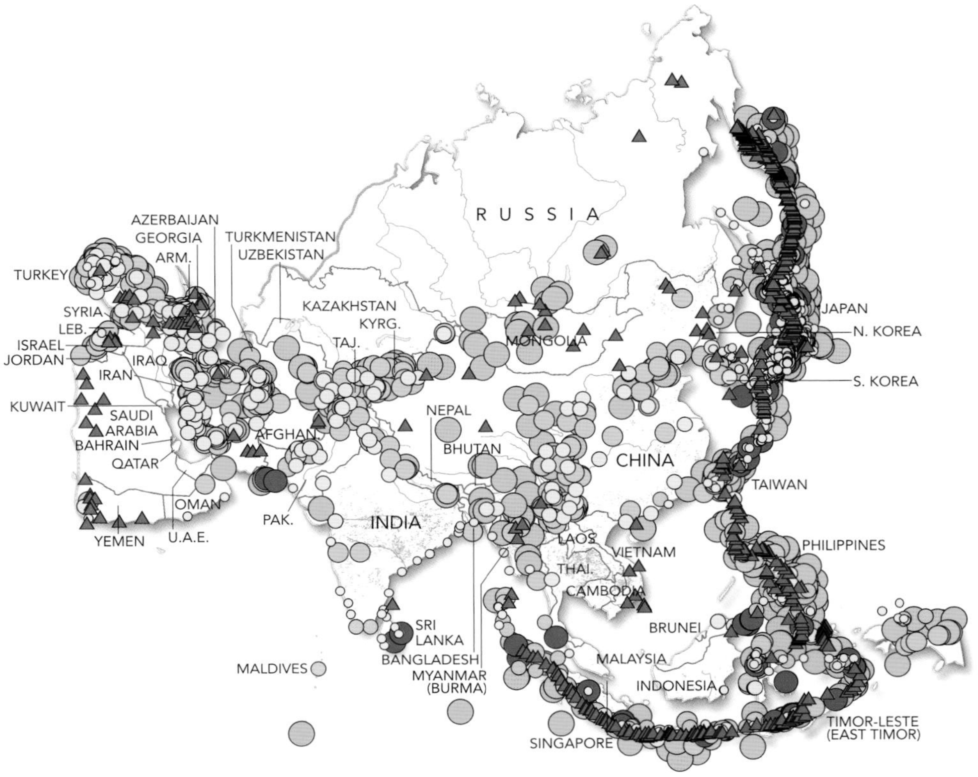

RECORDED NATURAL EVENT

Earthquake
Richter scale magnitude
- More than 7.0
- 6.0 - 7.0
- Less than 6.0

Fire intensity
(from gas burn-off, slash-and-burn agriculture, or natural causes)
High
Low

Tsunami
Run-up height
- More than 10 m / More than 32 ft
- 5 - 10 m / 16 - 32 ft
- Less than 5 m / Less than 16 ft

Volcano
- Major eruption

Water Availability

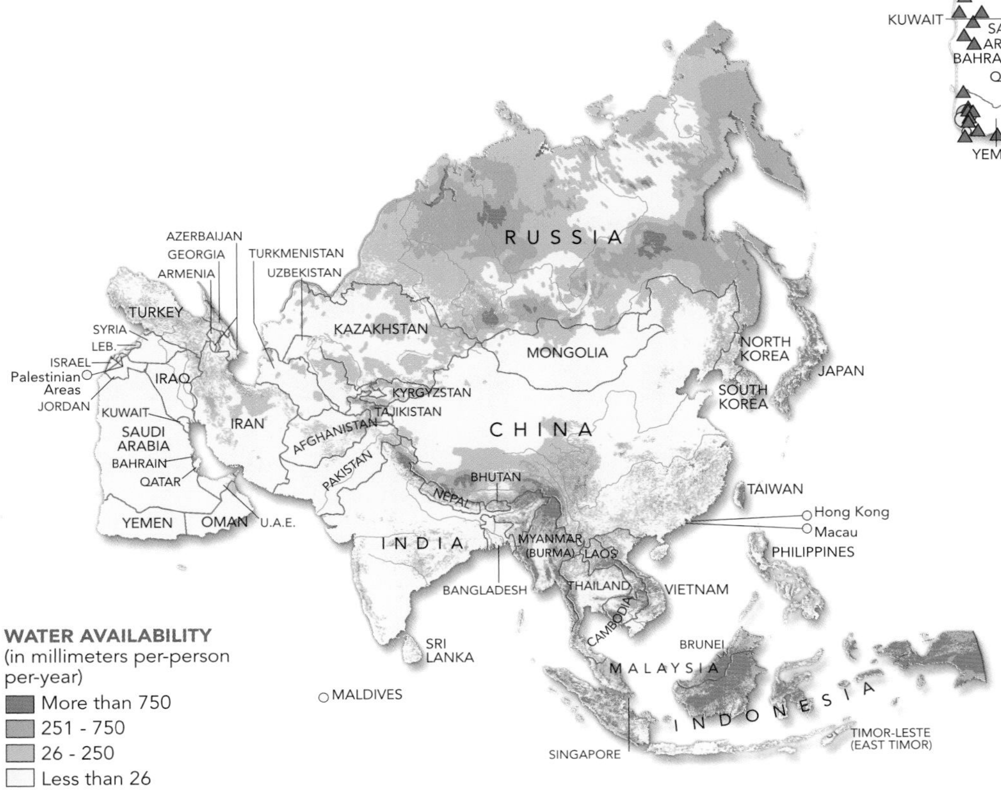

WATER AVAILABILITY
(in millimeters per-person per-year)
- More than 750
- 251 - 750
- 26 - 250
- Less than 26

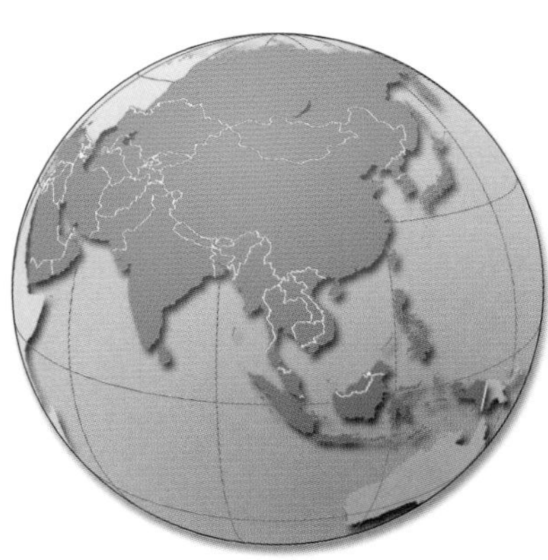

Nations

Afghanistan
ISLAMIC REPUBLIC OF AFGHANISTAN

AREA 652,090 sq km (251,773 sq mi)
POPULATION 31,057,000
CAPITAL Kabul 2,994,000
RELIGION Sunni Muslim, Shi'a Muslim
LANGUAGE Afghan Persian or Dari, Pashtu, Turkic languages
LITERACY 36%
LIFE EXPECTANCY 42 years
GDP PER CAPITA $800
ECONOMY **IND:** small-scale production of textiles, soap, furniture, shoes **AGR:** opium, wheat, fruits, nuts; wool **EXP:** opium, fruits and nuts, handwoven carpets, wool

Armenia
REPUBLIC OF ARMENIA

AREA 29,743 sq km (11,484 sq mi)
POPULATION 3,011,000
CAPITAL Yerevan 1,103,000
RELIGION Armenian Apostolic
LANGUAGE Armenian
LITERACY 99%
LIFE EXPECTANCY 71 years
GDP PER CAPITA $5,400
ECONOMY **IND:** diamond-processing, metal-cutting machine tools, forging-pressing machines, electric motors **AGR:** fruit (especially grapes), vegetables; livestock **EXP:** diamonds, mineral products, foodstuffs, energy

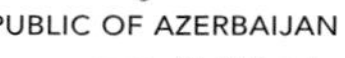

Azerbaijan
REPUBLIC OF AZERBAIJAN

AREA 86,600 sq km (33,436 sq mi)
POPULATION 8,481,000
CAPITAL Baku 1,856,000
RELIGION Muslim
LANGUAGE Azerbaijani (Azeri)
LITERACY 99%
LIFE EXPECTANCY 72 years
GDP PER CAPITA $7,300
ECONOMY **IND:** petroleum and natural gas products, oilfield equipment, steel, iron ore, cement **AGR:** cotton, grain, rice, grapes; cattle **EXP:** oil and gas, machinery, cotton, foodstuffs

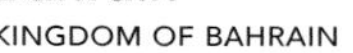

Bahrain
KINGDOM OF BAHRAIN

AREA 717 sq km (277 sq mi)
POPULATION 744,000
CAPITAL Manama 162,000
RELIGION Muslim, Christian
LANGUAGE Arabic, English, Farsi, Urdu
LITERACY 89%
LIFE EXPECTANCY 74 years
GDP PER CAPITA $25,300
ECONOMY **IND:** petroleum processing and refining, aluminum smelting, iron pelletization, fertilizers **AGR:** fruit, vegetables; poultry; shrimp **EXP:** petroleum and petroleum products, aluminum, textiles

Bangladesh
PEOPLE'S REPUBLIC OF BANGLADESH

AREA 147,570 sq km (56,977 sq mi)
POPULATION 146,598,000
CAPITAL Dhaka 12,430,000
RELIGION Muslim, Hindu
LANGUAGE Bangla (also known as Bengali), English
LITERACY 43%
LIFE EXPECTANCY 61 years
GDP PER CAPITA $2,200
ECONOMY **IND:** cotton textiles, jute, garments, tea processing **AGR:** rice, jute, tea, wheat; beef **EXP:** garments, jute and jute goods, leather, frozen fish and seafood

Bhutan
KINGDOM OF BHUTAN

AREA 46,500 sq km (17,954 sq mi)
POPULATION 881,000
CAPITAL Thimphu 85,000
RELIGION Lamaistic Buddhist, Hindu
LANGUAGE Dzongkha, Tibetan dialects, Nepalese dialects
LITERACY 47%
LIFE EXPECTANCY 63 years
GDP PER CAPITA $1,400
ECONOMY **IND:** cement, wood products, processed fruits, alcoholic beverages **AGR:** rice, corn, root crops, citrus; dairy products **EXP:** electricity (to India), cardamom, gypsum, timber

Brunei
NEGARA BRUNEI DARUSSALAM

AREA 5,765 sq km (2,226 sq mi)
POPULATION 365,000
CAPITAL Bandar Seri Begawan 64,000
RELIGION Muslim, Buddhist, Christian, indigenous beliefs
LANGUAGE Malay, English, Chinese
LITERACY 94%
LIFE EXPECTANCY 75 years
GDP PER CAPITA $25,600
ECONOMY **IND:** petroleum, petroleum refining, liquefied natural gas, construction **AGR:** rice, vegetables, fruits; chickens **EXP:** crude oil, natural gas, refined products, clothing

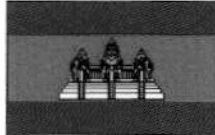

Cambodia
KINGDOM OF CAMBODIA

AREA 181,035 sq km (69,898 sq mi)
POPULATION 14,081,000
CAPITAL Phnom Penh 1,364,000
RELIGION Theravada Buddhist
LANGUAGE Khmer
LITERACY 74%
LIFE EXPECTANCY 60 years
GDP PER CAPITA $2,600
ECONOMY **IND:** tourism, garments, rice milling, fishing **AGR:** rice, rubber, corn, vegetables **EXP:** clothing, timber, rubber, rice

China
PEOPLE'S REPUBLIC OF CHINA

AREA 9,596,960 sq km (3,705,405 sq mi)
POPULATION 1,341,715,000
CAPITAL Beijing 10,717,000
RELIGION Daoist, Buddhist
LANGUAGE Chinese (Mandarin), Cantonese, other local languages
LITERACY 91%
LIFE EXPECTANCY 72 years
GDP PER CAPITA $7,600
ECONOMY **IND:** mining and ore processing (iron, steel, aluminum), coal, machine building, armaments **AGR:** rice, wheat, potatoes, corn; pork; fish **EXP:** machinery and equipment, plastics, optical and medical equipment, iron and steel

Georgia
REPUBLIC OF GEORGIA

AREA 69,700 sq km (26,911 sq mi)
POPULATION 4,434,000
CAPITAL T'bilisi 1,047,000
RELIGION Orthodox Christian, Muslim
LANGUAGE Georgian, Russian, Armenian, Azeri
LITERACY 100%
LIFE EXPECTANCY 72 years
GDP PER CAPITA $3,800
ECONOMY **IND:** steel, aircraft, machine tools, electrical appliances **AGR:** citrus, grapes, tea, hazelnuts; livestock **EXP:** scrap metal, machinery, chemicals, fuel reexports

India
REPUBLIC OF INDIA

AREA 3,287,270 sq km (1,269,221 sq mi)
POPULATION 1,121,788,000
CAPITAL New Delhi 15,048,000
RELIGION Hindu, Muslim
LANGUAGE Hindi, English, 21 other official languages
LITERACY 60%
LIFE EXPECTANCY 63 years
GDP PER CAPITA $3,700
ECONOMY **IND:** textiles, chemicals, food processing, steel **AGR:** rice, wheat, oilseed, cotton; cattle; fish **EXP:** textile goods, gems and jewelry, engineering goods, chemicals

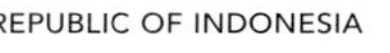

Indonesia
REPUBLIC OF INDONESIA

AREA 1,922,570 sq km (742,308 sq mi)
POPULATION 225,465,000
CAPITAL Jakarta 13,215,000
RELIGION Muslim, Christian
LANGUAGE Bahasa Indonesia, English, Dutch, Javanese
LITERACY 88%
LIFE EXPECTANCY 69 years
GDP PER CAPITA $3,800
ECONOMY **IND:** petroleum and natural gas, textiles, apparel, footwear **AGR:** rice, cassava (tapioca), peanuts, rubber; poultry **EXP:** oil and gas, electrical appliances, plywood, textiles

Iran
ISLAMIC REPUBLIC OF IRAN

AREA 1,648,000 sq km (636,296 sq mi)
POPULATION 70,324,000
CAPITAL Tehran 7,314,000
RELIGION Shi'a Muslim, Sunni Muslim
LANGUAGE Persian, Turkic, Kurdish
LITERACY 79%
LIFE EXPECTANCY 70 years
GDP PER CAPITA $8,900
ECONOMY **IND:** petroleum, petrochemicals, fertilizers, caustic soda **AGR:** wheat, rice, other grains, sugar beets; dairy products; caviar **EXP:** petroleum, chemical and petrochemical products, fruits and nuts, carpets

Iraq
REPUBLIC OF IRAQ

AREA 437,072 sq km (168,754 sq mi)
POPULATION 29,551,000
CAPITAL Baghdad 5,904,000
RELIGION Shi'a Muslim, Sunni Muslim
LANGUAGE Arabic, Kurdish, Assyrian, Armenian
LITERACY 40%
LIFE EXPECTANCY 59 years
GDP PER CAPITA $2,900
ECONOMY **IND:** petroleum, chemicals, textiles, leather **AGR:** wheat, barley, rice, vegetables; cattle **EXP:** crude oil, crude materials excluding fuels, food, live animals

Israel
STATE OF ISRAEL

AREA 22,145 sq km (8,550 sq mi)
POPULATION 7,236,000
CAPITAL Jerusalem 711,000
RELIGION Jewish, Muslim
LANGUAGE Hebrew, Arabic, English
LITERACY 95%
LIFE EXPECTANCY 80 years
GDP PER CAPITA $26,200
ECONOMY **IND:** high-technology projects (aviation, communications), wood and paper products, potash and phosphates, food **AGR:** citrus, vegetables, cotton; beef **EXP:** machinery and equipment, software, cut diamonds, agricultural products

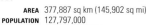

Japan
JAPAN

AREA 377,887 sq km (145,902 sq mi)
POPULATION 127,797,000
CAPITAL Tokyo 35,197,000
RELIGION Shinto, Buddhist
LANGUAGE Japanese
LITERACY 99%
LIFE EXPECTANCY 82 years
GDP PER CAPITA $33,100
ECONOMY **IND:** motor vehicles, electronic equipment, machine tools, steel and nonferrous metals **AGR:** rice, sugar beets, vegetables, fruit; pork; fish **EXP:** transport equipment, motor vehicles, semiconductors, electrical machinery

Jordan
HASHEMITE KINGDOM OF JORDAN

AREA 89,342 sq km (34,495 sq mi)
POPULATION 5,636,000
CAPITAL Amman 1,292,000
RELIGION Sunni Muslim, Christian
LANGUAGE Arabic, English
LITERACY 91%
LIFE EXPECTANCY 72 years
GDP PER CAPITA $4,900
ECONOMY **IND:** clothing, phosphate mining, fertilizers, pharmaceuticals **AGR:** citrus, tomatoes, cucumbers, olives; sheep **EXP:** clothing, pharmaceuticals, potash, phosphates

Kazakhstan
REPUBLIC OF KAZAKHSTAN

AREA 2,717,300 sq km (1,049,155 sq mi)
POPULATION 15,292,000
CAPITAL Astana 331,000
RELIGION Muslim, Russian Orthodox
LANGUAGE Kazakh (Qazaq), Russian
LITERACY 98%
LIFE EXPECTANCY 66 years
GDP PER CAPITA $9,100
ECONOMY **IND:** oil, coal, iron ore, manganese **AGR:** grain (mostly spring wheat), cotton; livestock **EXP:** oil and oil products, ferrous metals, chemicals, machinery

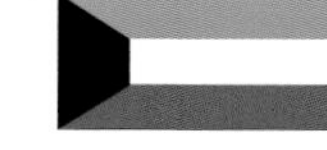

Kuwait
STATE OF KUWAIT

AREA 17,818 sq km (6,880 sq mi)
POPULATION 2,660,000
CAPITAL Kuwait 1,810,000
RELIGION Sunni Muslim, Shi'a Muslim, Christian, Hindu, Parsi
LANGUAGE Arabic, English
LITERACY 84%
LIFE EXPECTANCY 78 years
GDP PER CAPITA $21,600
ECONOMY **IND:** petroleum, petrochemicals, cement, shipbuilding and repair **AGR:** practically no crops; fish **EXP:** oil and refined products, fertilizers

Kyrgyzstan
KYRGYZ REPUBLIC

AREA 199,900 sq km (77,182 sq mi)
POPULATION 5,162,000
CAPITAL Bishkek 798,000
RELIGION Muslim, Russian Orthodox
LANGUAGE Kyrgyz, Uzbek, Russian
LITERACY 99%
LIFE EXPECTANCY 68 years
GDP PER CAPITA $2,000
ECONOMY **IND:** small machinery, textiles, food processing, cement **AGR:** tobacco, cotton, potatoes, vegetables; sheep **EXP:** cotton, wool, meat, tobacco

Laos
LAO PEOPLE'S DEMOCRATIC REPUBLIC

AREA 236,800 sq km (91,429 sq mi)
POPULATION 6,058,000
CAPITAL Vientiane 702,000
RELIGION Buddhist, animist
LANGUAGE Lao, French, English, various ethnic languages
LITERACY 66%
LIFE EXPECTANCY 54 years
GDP PER CAPITA $2,100
ECONOMY **IND:** copper, tin, and gypsum mining, timber, electric power, agricultural processing **AGR:** sweet potatoes, vegetables, corn, coffee; water buffalo **EXP:** garments, wood products, coffee, electricity

Lebanon
LEBANESE REPUBLIC

AREA 10,452 sq km (4,036 sq mi)
POPULATION 3,865,000
CAPITAL Beirut 1,777,000
RELIGION Muslim, Christian
LANGUAGE Arabic, French, English, Armenian
LITERACY 87%
LIFE EXPECTANCY 72 years
GDP PER CAPITA $5,500
ECONOMY **IND:** banking, tourism, food processing, jewelry **AGR:** citrus, grapes, tomatoes, apples; sheep **EXP:** authentic jewelry, inorganic chemicals, miscellaneous consumer goods, fruit

Malaysia
MALAYSIA

AREA 329,847 sq km (127,355 sq mi)
POPULATION 26,894,000
CAPITAL Kuala Lumpur 1,405,000
RELIGION Muslim, Buddhist, Christian, Hindu
LANGUAGE Bahasa Melayu, English, Chinese dialects, Tamil, Telugu
LITERACY 89%
LIFE EXPECTANCY 74 years
GDP PER CAPITA $12,700
ECONOMY **IND:** rubber and palm oil processing and manufacturing, light manufacturing, logging, petroleum production **AGR:** rubber, palm oil, subsistence crops, rice; timber **EXP:** electronic equipment, petroleum and liquefied natural gas, wood and wood products, palm oil

Maldives
REPUBLIC OF MALDIVES

AREA 298 sq km (115 sq mi)
POPULATION 298,000
CAPITAL Male 89,000
RELIGION Sunni Muslim
LANGUAGE Maldivian Dhivehi, English
LITERACY 97%
LIFE EXPECTANCY 70 years
GDP PER CAPITA $3,900
ECONOMY **IND:** tourism, fish processing, shipping, boat building **AGR:** coconuts, corn, sweet potatoes; fish **EXP:** fish

Mongolia
MONGOLIA

AREA 1,564,116 sq km (603,909 sq mi)
POPULATION 2,578,000
CAPITAL Ulaanbaatar 863,000
RELIGION Lamaistic Buddhist
LANGUAGE Khalkha Mongol, Turkic, Russian
LITERACY 98%
LIFE EXPECTANCY 66 years
GDP PER CAPITA $2,000
ECONOMY **IND:** construction and construction materials, mining (coal, copper), oil, food and beverages **AGR:** wheat, barley, vegetables, forage crops; sheep **EXP:** copper, apparel, livestock, animal products

Myanmar (Burma)
UNION OF MYANMAR

AREA 676,552 sq km (261,218 sq mi)
POPULATION 51,009,000
CAPITAL Nay Pyi Taw (administrative) NA; Yangon (Rangoon) (legislative) 4,107,000
RELIGION Buddhist
LANGUAGE Burmese, minority ethnic languages
LITERACY 85%
LIFE EXPECTANCY 60 years
GDP PER CAPITA $1,800
ECONOMY **IND:** agricultural processing, wood and wood products, copper, tin **AGR:** rice, pulses, beans, sesame; hardwood; fish and fish products **EXP:** gas, wood products, pulses, beans

Nepal
KINGDOM OF NEPAL

AREA 147,181 sq km (56,827 sq mi)
POPULATION 25,959,000
CAPITAL Kathmandu 815,000
RELIGION Hindu, Buddhist
LANGUAGE Nepali, Maithali, Bhojpuri, Tharu, Tamang
LITERACY 49%
LIFE EXPECTANCY 62 years
GDP PER CAPITA $1,500
ECONOMY **IND:** tourism, carpet, textiles; small rice, jute, sugar, and oilseed mills **AGR:** rice, corn, wheat, sugarcane; milk **EXP:** carpet, clothing, leather goods, jute goods

North Korea
DEMOCRATIC PEOPLE'S REPUBLIC OF KOREA

AREA 120,538 sq km (46,540 sq mi)
POPULATION 23,113,000
CAPITAL Pyongyang 3,351,000
RELIGION Buddhist, Confucianist
LANGUAGE Korean
LITERACY 99%
LIFE EXPECTANCY 71 years
GDP PER CAPITA $1,800
ECONOMY **IND:** military products, machine building, electric power, chemicals **AGR:** rice, corn, potatoes, soybeans; cattle **EXP:** minerals, metallurgical products, manufactures (including armaments), textiles

Oman
SULTANATE OF OMAN

AREA 309,500 sq km (119,500 sq mi)
POPULATION 2,573,000
CAPITAL Muscat 565,000
RELIGION Ibadhi Muslim, Sunni Muslim, Shi'a Muslim, Hindu
LANGUAGE Arabic, English, Baluchi, Urdu, Indian dialects
LITERACY 76%
LIFE EXPECTANCY 74 years
GDP PER CAPITA $14,100
ECONOMY **IND:** crude oil production and refining, natural and liquefied natural gas (LNG) production, construction, cement **AGR:** dates, limes, bananas, alfalfa; camels; fish **EXP:** petroleum, reexports, fish, metals

Pakistan
ISLAMIC REPUBLIC OF PAKISTAN

AREA 796,095 sq km (307,374 sq mi)
POPULATION 165,804,000
CAPITAL Islamabad 736,000
RELIGION Sunni Muslim, Shi'a Muslim
LANGUAGE Punjabi, Sindhi, Siraiki, Pashtu, Urdu, English
LITERACY 49%
LIFE EXPECTANCY 62 years
GDP PER CAPITA $2,600
ECONOMY **IND:** textiles and apparel, food processing, pharmaceuticals, construction materials **AGR:** cotton, wheat, rice, sugarcane; milk **EXP:** textiles (garments, bed linen, cotton cloth, yarn), rice, leather goods, sports goods

Philippines
REPUBLIC OF THE PHILIPPINES

AREA 300,000 sq km (115,831 sq mi)
POPULATION 86,264,000
CAPITAL Manila 10,686,000
RELIGION Roman Catholic, Muslim
LANGUAGE Filipino (based on Tagalog), English, eight major dialects
LITERACY 93%
LIFE EXPECTANCY 70 years
GDP PER CAPITA $5,000
ECONOMY **IND:** electronics assembly, garments, footwear, pharmaceuticals **AGR:** sugarcane, coconuts, rice, corn; pork; fish **EXP:** semiconductors and electronic products, transport equipment, garments, copper products

Qatar
STATE OF QATAR

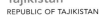

AREA 11,521 sq km (4,448 sq mi)
POPULATION 832,000
CAPITAL Doha 357,000
RELIGION Muslim, Christian
LANGUAGE Arabic, English
LITERACY 89%
LIFE EXPECTANCY 73 years
GDP PER CAPITA $29,400
ECONOMY **IND:** crude oil production and refining, ammonia, fertilizers, petrochemicals **AGR:** fruits, vegetables; poultry; fish **EXP:** liquefied natural gas (LNG), petroleum products, fertilizers, steel

Saudi Arabia
KINGDOM OF SAUDI ARABIA

AREA 1,960,582 sq km (756,985 sq mi)
POPULATION 24,118,000
CAPITAL Riyadh 4,193,000
RELIGION Muslim
LANGUAGE Arabic
LITERACY 79%
LIFE EXPECTANCY 72 years
GDP PER CAPITA $13,800
ECONOMY **IND:** crude oil production, petroleum refining, basic petrochemicals, ammonia **AGR:** wheat, barley, tomatoes, melons; mutton **EXP:** petroleum and petroleum products

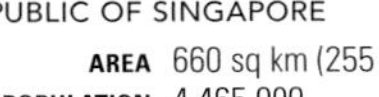

Singapore
REPUBLIC OF SINGAPORE

AREA 660 sq km (255 sq mi)
POPULATION 4,465,000
CAPITAL Singapore 4,326,000
RELIGION Buddhist, Muslim, Christian, Taoist
LANGUAGE Mandarin, English, Malay, Hokkien, Cantonese
LITERACY 93%
LIFE EXPECTANCY 80 years
GDP PER CAPITA $30,900
ECONOMY **IND:** electronics, chemicals, financial services, oil drilling equipment **AGR:** rubber, copra, fruit, orchids; poultry; fish **EXP:** machinery and equipment (including electronics), consumer goods, chemicals, mineral fuels

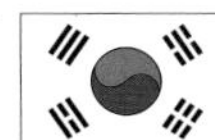

South Korea
REPUBLIC OF KOREA

AREA 99,250 sq km (38,321 sq mi)
POPULATION 48,497,000
CAPITAL Seoul 9,645,000
RELIGION Christian, Buddhist
LANGUAGE Korean, English widely taught
LITERACY 98%
LIFE EXPECTANCY 77 years
GDP PER CAPITA $24,200
ECONOMY **IND:** electronics, telecommunications, automobile production, chemicals **AGR:** rice, root crops, barley, vegetables; cattle; fish **EXP:** semiconductors, wireless telecommunications equipment, motor vehicles, computers

Sri Lanka
DEMOCRATIC SOCIALIST REPUBLIC OF SRI LANKA

AREA 65,525 sq km (25,299 sq mi)
POPULATION 19,859,000
CAPITAL Colombo 652,000
RELIGION Buddhist, Muslim, Hindu, Christian
LANGUAGE Sinhala, Tamil
LITERACY 92%
LIFE EXPECTANCY 74 years
GDP PER CAPITA $4,600
ECONOMY **IND:** rubber processing, tea, coconuts, tobacco **AGR:** rice, sugarcane, grains, pulses; milk; fish **EXP:** textiles and apparel, tea and spices, diamonds, emeralds

Syria
SYRIAN ARAB REPUBLIC

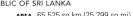

AREA 185,180 sq km (71,498 sq mi)
POPULATION 19,498,000
CAPITAL Damascus 2,272,000
RELIGION Sunni, other Muslim (including Alawite, Druze), Christian
LANGUAGE Arabic, Kurdish, Armenian, Aramaic, Circassian
LITERACY 77%
LIFE EXPECTANCY 73 years
GDP PER CAPITA $4,000
ECONOMY **IND:** petroleum, textiles, food processing, beverages **AGR:** wheat, barley, cotton, lentils; beef **EXP:** crude oil, petroleum products, fruits and vegetables, cotton fiber

Tajikistan
REPUBLIC OF TAJIKISTAN

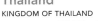

AREA 143,100 sq km (55,251 sq mi)
POPULATION 6,997,000
CAPITAL Dushanbe 549,000
RELIGION Sunni Muslim, Shi'a Muslim
LANGUAGE Tajik, Russian
LITERACY 99%
LIFE EXPECTANCY 64 years
GDP PER CAPITA $1,300
ECONOMY **IND:** aluminum, zinc, lead, chemicals and fertilizers **AGR:** cotton, grain, fruits, grapes; cattle **EXP:** aluminum, electricity, cotton, fruits

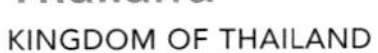

Thailand
KINGDOM OF THAILAND

AREA 513,115 sq km (198,115 sq mi)
POPULATION 65,233,000
CAPITAL Bangkok 6,593,000
RELIGION Buddhist
LANGUAGE Thai, English, ethnic and regional dialects
LITERACY 93%
LIFE EXPECTANCY 71 years
GDP PER CAPITA $9,100
ECONOMY **IND:** tourism, textiles and garments, agricultural processing, beverages **AGR:** rice, cassava (tapioca), rubber, corn **EXP:** textiles and footwear, fishery products, rice, rubber

Timor-Leste (East Timor)

DEMOCRATIC REPUBLIC OF TIMOR-LESTE

AREA 14,609 sq km (5,640 sq mi)
POPULATION 977,000
CAPITAL Dili 156,000
RELIGION Roman Catholic
LANGUAGE Tetum, Portuguese, Indonesian, English
LITERACY 59%
LIFE EXPECTANCY 56 years
GDP PER CAPITA $800
ECONOMY **IND:** printing, soap manufacturing, handicrafts, woven cloth **AGR:** coffee, rice, corn, cassava **EXP:** coffee, sandalwood, marble; potential for oil and vanilla

Turkey

REPUBLIC OF TURKEY

AREA 779,452 sq km (300,948 sq mi)
POPULATION 73,665,000
CAPITAL Ankara 3,573,000
RELIGION Muslim
LANGUAGE Turkish, Kurdish, Dimli, Azeri, Kabardian
LITERACY 87%
LIFE EXPECTANCY 71 years
GDP PER CAPITA $8,900
ECONOMY **IND:** textiles, food processing, automobiles, electronics **AGR:** tobacco, cotton, grain, olives; livestock **EXP:** apparel, foodstuffs, textiles, metal manufactures

Turkmenistan

TURKMENISTAN

AREA 488,100 sq km (188,456 sq mi)
POPULATION 5,324,000
CAPITAL Ashgabat 711,000
RELIGION Muslim, Eastern Orthodox
LANGUAGE Turkmen, Russian, Uzbek
LITERACY 99%
LIFE EXPECTANCY 62 years
GDP PER CAPITA $8,900
ECONOMY **IND:** natural gas, oil, petroleum products, textiles **AGR:** cotton, grain; livestock **EXP:** gas, crude oil, petrochemicals, cotton fiber

United Arab Emirates

UNITED ARAB EMIRATES

AREA 77,700 sq km (30,000 sq mi)
POPULATION 4,937,000
CAPITAL Abu Dhabi 597,000
RELIGION Muslim
LANGUAGE Arabic, Persian, English, Hindi, Urdu
LITERACY 78%
LIFE EXPECTANCY 77 years
GDP PER CAPITA $49,700
ECONOMY **IND:** petroleum and petrochemicals, fishing, aluminum, cement **AGR:** dates, vegetables, watermelons; poultry; fish **EXP:** crude oil, natural gas, reexports, dried fish

Uzbekistan

REPUBLIC OF UZBEKISTAN

AREA 447,400 sq km (172,742 sq mi)
POPULATION 26,180,000
CAPITAL Tashkent 2,181,000
RELIGION Muslim, Eastern Orthodox
LANGUAGE Uzbek, Russian
LITERACY 99%
LIFE EXPECTANCY 67 years
GDP PER CAPITA $2,000
ECONOMY **IND:** textiles, food processing, machine building, metallurgy **AGR:** cotton, vegetables, fruits, grain; livestock **EXP:** cotton, gold, energy products, mineral fertilizers

Vietnam

SOCIALIST REPUBLIC OF VIETNAM

AREA 331,114 sq km (127,844 sq mi)
POPULATION 84,176,000
CAPITAL Hanoi 4,161,000
RELIGION Buddhist, Catholic
LANGUAGE Vietnamese, English, French, Chinese, Khmer
LITERACY 90%
LIFE EXPECTANCY 72 years
GDP PER CAPITA $3,100
ECONOMY **IND:** food processing, garments, shoes, machine-building **AGR:** paddy rice, coffee, rubber, cotton; poultry; fish **EXP:** crude oil, marine products, rice, coffee

Yemen

REPUBLIC OF YEMEN

AREA 536,869 sq km (207,286 sq mi)
POPULATION 21,639,000
CAPITAL Sanaa 1,801,000
RELIGION Muslim
LANGUAGE Arabic
LITERACY 50%
LIFE EXPECTANCY 60 years
GDP PER CAPITA $900
ECONOMY **IND:** crude oil production, petroleum refining, cotton textiles, leather goods **AGR:** grain, fruits, vegetables, pulses; dairy products; fish **EXP:** crude oil, coffee, dried and salted fish

Area of Special Status

Taiwan

TAIWAN

AREA 35,980 sq km (13,892 sq mi)
POPULATION 22,811,000
CAPITAL Taipei 2,616,000
RELIGION Buddhist, Taoist
LANGUAGE Mandarian Chinese, Taiwanese (Min)
LITERACY 96%
LIFE EXPECTANCY 76 years
GDP PER CAPITA $29,000
ECONOMY **IND:** electronics, petroleum refining, armaments, chemicals **AGR:** rice, corn, vegetables, fruit; pigs; fish **EXP:** computer products, electrical equipment, metals, textiles

Dates of National Independence

NOTE: For some countries, the date given may not represent "independence" in the strict sense—but rather some significant nationhood event: the traditional founding date; a fundamental change in the form of government; or perhaps the date of unification, secession, federation, confederation, or state succession.

Land Cover
Water
Evergreen needleleaf forest
Evergreen broadleaf forest
Deciduous broadleaf forest
Mixed forest
Closed shrubland
Open shrubland
Woody savanna
Savanna
Grassland
Permanent wetland
Cropland
Urban and built-up
Cropland/natural vegetation mosaic
Snow and ice
Barren or sparsely vegetated

Africa

ELEMENTAL AND UNCONQUERABLE, Africa remains something of a paradox among continents. Birthplace of humankind and of the great early civilizations of Egypt and Kush, also called Nubia, the continent has since thwarted human efforts to exploit many of its resources. The forbidding sweep of the Sahara, largest desert in the world, holds the northern third of Africa in thrall, while the bordering Sahel sands alternately advance and recede in unpredictable, drought-invoking rhythms. In contrast to the long, life-giving thread of the Nile, the lake district in the east, and the Congo drainage in central Africa, few major waterways provide irrigation and commercial navigation to large, arid segments of the continent.

Africa's unforgettable form, bulging to the west, lies surrounded by oceans and seas. The East African Rift System is the continent's most dramatic geologic feature. This great rent actually begins in the Red Sea, then cuts southward to form the stunning landscape of lakes, volcanoes, and deep valleys that finally ends near the mouth of the Zambezi River. Caused by the Earth's crust pulling apart, the rift may one day separate East Africa from the rest of the continent.

Most of Africa is made up of savannah—high, rolling, grassy plains. These savannahs have been home since earliest times to people often called Bantu, a reference to both social groupings and their languages. Other distinct physical types exist around the continent as well: BaMbuti (Pygmies), San (Bushmen), Nilo-Saharans, and Hamito-Semitics (Berbers and Cushites). Africa's astonishing 1,600 spoken languages—more than any other continent—reflect the great diversity of ethnic and social groups.

Africa ranks among the richest regions in the world in natural resources; it contains vast reserves of fossil fuels, precious metals, ores, and gems, including almost all of the world's chromium, much uranium, copper, enormous underground gold reserves, and diamonds. Yet Africa accounts for a mere one percent of world economic output. South Africa's economy alone nearly equals that of all other sub-Saharan countries. Many obstacles complicate the way forward. African countries experience great gaps in wealth between city and country, and many face growing slums around megacities such as Lagos and Cairo. Nearly 40 other African cities have populations over a million. Lack of clean water and the spread of diseases—malaria, tuberculosis, cholera, and AIDS—undermine people's health. Nearly 24 million Africans are now infected with HIV/AIDS, which killed 1.9 million Africans in 2005. AIDS has shortened life expectancy to 47 years in parts of Africa, destroyed families, and erased decades of social progress and economic activity by killing people in their prime working years. In addition, war and huge concentrations of refugees displaced by fighting, persecution, and famine deter any chance of growth and stability.

Africa's undeveloped natural beauty—along with its wealth of animal life, despite a vast dimunition in their numbers due to poaching and habitat loss—has engendered a booming tourist industry. Names such as "Serengeti Plain," "Kalahari Desert," "Okavango Delta," and "Victoria Falls" still evoke images of an Africa unspoiled, unconquerable, and, throughout the Earth, unsurpassed.

Longitude West 20° of Greenwich
AZORES (AÇORES)
Portugal
MADEIRA ISLANDS
Portugal
CANARY ISLANDS (ISLAS CANARIAS)
Spain
Santa Cruz
Las Palmas
PORTUGAL
Lisboa (Lisbon)
SPAIN
MADRID
ANDORRA
GIBRALTAR U.K.
Strait of Gibraltar
FRANCE
PARIS
U.K.
LONDON
Bruxelles (Brussels)
BELGIUM
LUX.
GERMANY
SWITZERLAND
Bern
ITALY
ROMA (Rome)
AUSTRIA
WIEN (Vienna)
PRAHA (Prague)
CZECH REP.
POLAND
SLOVAKIA
Bratislava
BUDAPEST
HUNGARY
SLOVENIA
Ljubljana
CROATIA
Zagreb
BOSNIA & HERZEGOVINA
Sarajevo
SERBIA
BEOGRAD (Belgrade)
MONTENEGRO
Podgorica
(Tirana) Tiranë
ALBANIA
MACEDONIA
Skopje
GREECE
Athína (Athens)
BULGARIA
SOFIYA (Sofia)
ROMANIA
BUCUREŞTI (Bucharest)
MOLDOVA
Chişinău
UKRAINE
KYIV (Kiev)
RUSSIA
KAZAKHSTAN
UZBEKISTAN
TURKMENISTAN
Aşgabat
CASPIAN SEA
BLACK SEA
GEORGIA
T'BILISI
ARMENIA
YEREVAN
AZERBAIJAN
BAKI (Baku)
TURKEY
ANKARA
CYPRUS
Lefkosia (Nicosia)
SYRIA
LEBANON
(Beirut) BEYROUTH
DIMASHQ (Damascus)
ISRAEL
Jerusalem
JORDAN
'AMMĀN
IRAQ
BAGHDĀD
IRAN
TEHRĀN
KUWAIT
Al Kuwayt (Kuwait)
PERSIAN GULF
BAHRAIN
Al Manāmah (Manama)
QATAR
Ad Dawḩah (Doha)
U.A.E.
SAUDI ARABIA
AR RIYĀD (Riyadh)
TROPIC OF CANCER
MEDITERRANEAN SEA
MALTA
RED SEA
MOROCCO
RABAT
CASABLANCA
Marrakech
Fès (Fez)
Tanger (Tangier)
WESTERN SAHARA
Morocco
Laayoune
ALGERIA
ALGER (Algiers)
Oran
Constantine
TUNISIA
TUNIS
LIBYA
ṬARĀBULUS (Tripoli)
Banghāzī (Benghazi)
TRIPOLITANIA
CYRENAICA
FEZZAN
EGYPT
EL QÂHIRA (Cairo)
EL ISKANDARÎYA (Alexandria)
EL GÎZA
Bûr Sa'îd (Port Said)
El Suweis (Suez)
Asyût
Aswân
Nile
SAHARA
MAURITANIA
Nouakchott
Nouadhibou
MALI
BAMAKO
Tombouctou (Timbuktu)
Niger
NIGER
Niamey
Agadez
AOZOU STRIP
CHAD
N'Djamena
Lake Chad
Boundary claimed by Sudan
Treaty boundary
SUDAN
KHARTOUM
OMDURMAN (Umm Durmān)
Khartoum North
Bûr Sūdān (Port Sudan)
DARFUR
White Nile
Blue Nile
ERITREA
Asmara
YEMEN
Şan'ā' (Sanaa)
GULF OF ADEN
DJIBOUTI
Djibouti
ETHIOPIA
ĀDĪS ĀBEBA (Addis Ababa)
SOMALILAND
Hargeysa
PUNTLAND
SOMALIA
MUQDISHO (Mogadishu) (historic; no central government since 1991)
Boundary undemarcated and in dispute
KENYA
UGANDA
KAMPALA
SENEGAL
DAKAR
GAMBIA
Banjul
GUINEA-BISSAU
Bissau
GUINEA
CONAKRY
SIERRA LEONE
Freetown
LIBERIA
Monrovia
CÔTE D'IVOIRE (IVORY COAST)
Yamoussoukro (legislative)
ABIDJAN (administrative)
BURKINA FASO
OUAGADOUGOU
GHANA
ACCRA
TOGO
Lomé
BENIN
Porto-Novo
Cotonou
NIGERIA
Abuja
LAGOS
IBADAN
KANO
CAMEROON
YAOUNDÉ
DOUALA
EQUATORIAL GUINEA
Malabo
Bioko
RÍO MUNI
SAO TOME & PRINCIPE
Príncipe
CENTRAL AFRICAN REPUBLIC
Bangui
Congo
Kisangani
GULF OF GUINEA
EQUATOR
TROPIC OF CANCER

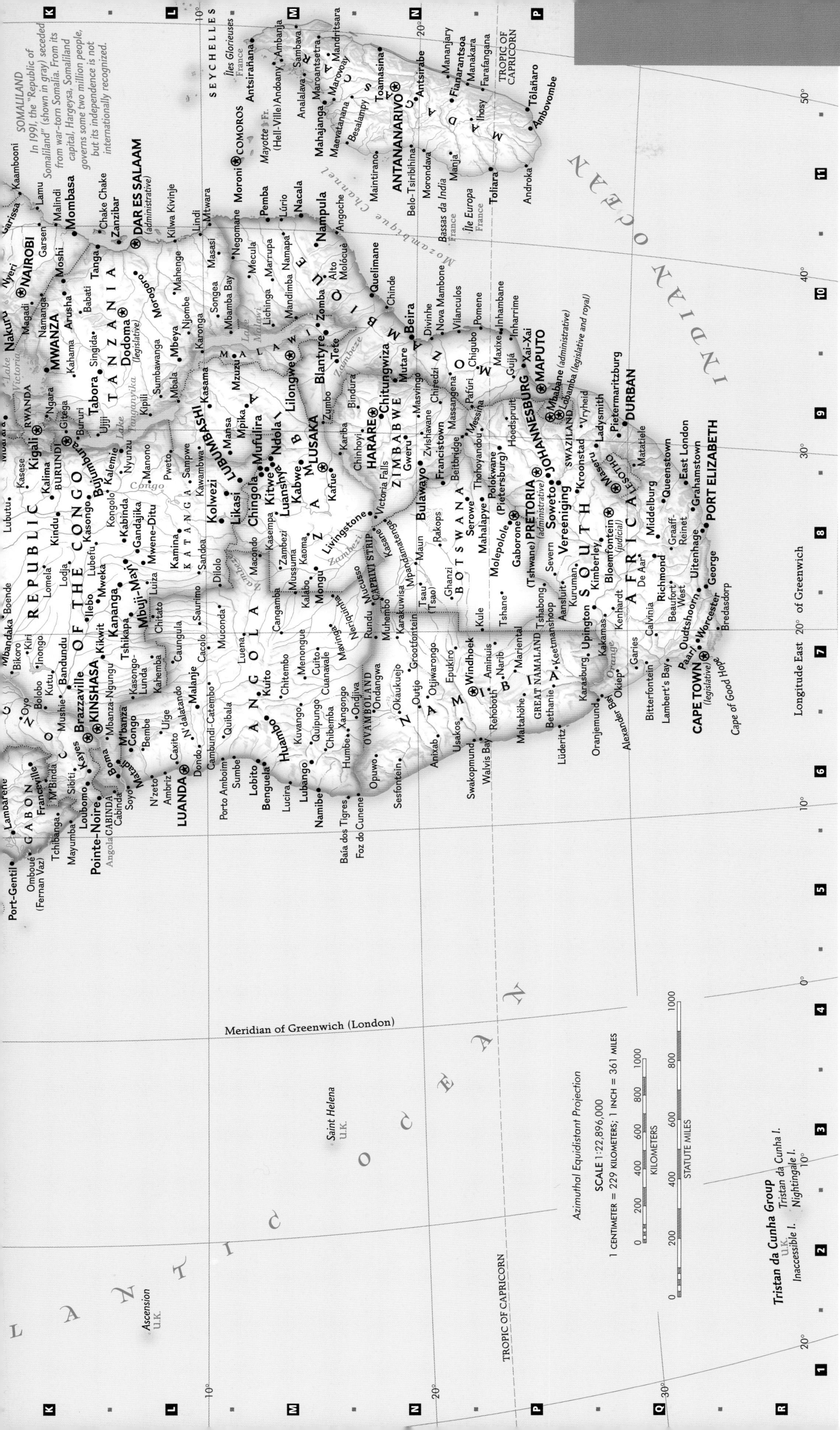

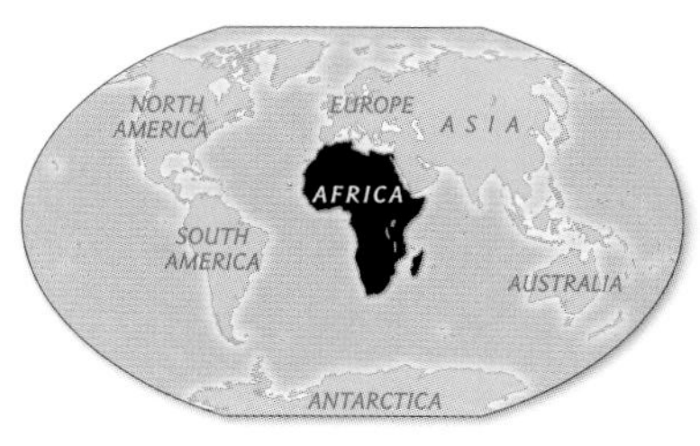

CONTINENTAL DATA

TOTAL NUMBER OF COUNTRIES: 53

FIRST INDEPENDENT COUNTRY:
Ethiopia, over 2,000 years old

"YOUNGEST" COUNTRY:
Eritrea, May 24, 1993

LARGEST COUNTRY IN AREA:
Sudan 2,505,813 sq km
(967,500 sq mi)

SMALLEST COUNTRY IN AREA:
Seychelles 455 sq km
(176 sq mi)

PERCENT URBAN POPULATION:
37%

MOST POPULOUS COUNTRY:
Nigeria 134,500,000

LEAST POPULOUS COUNTRY:
Seychelles 80,000

MOST DENSELY POPULATED COUNTRY:
Mauritius 615 per sq km
(1,591 per sq mi)

LEAST DENSELY POPULATED COUNTRY:
Namibia 2.5 per sq km
(6.4 per sq mi)

LARGEST CITY BY POPULATION:
Cairo, Egypt 11,128,000

HIGHEST GDP PER CAPITA:
Equatorial Guinea $50,200

LOWEST GDP PER CAPITA:
Comoros, Malawi, Somalia $600

AVERAGE LIFE EXPECTANCY IN AFRICA: 52 years

AVERAGE LITERACY RATE IN AFRICA: 63%

Longitude West 20° of Greenwich
Longitude East 20° of Greenwich
E U R O P E
A S I A
IBERIAN PENINSULA
BALKAN PENINSULA
ANATOLIA (ASIA MINOR)
BLACK SEA
CASPIAN SEA
MEDITERRANEAN SEA
AZORES
Corsica
Sardinia
Balearic Is.
Sicily
Peloponnesus
Crete
Rhodes
Cyprus
Cape Blanc
G. of Tunis
G. of Hamamet
G. of Gabes
Jerba I.
Strait of Gibraltar
Madeira
MADEIRA ISLANDS
C. Beddouza
Salvage Islands
Cape Rhir
CANARY ISLANDS
La Palma
Tenerife
Gomera
Ferro
Gran Canaria
Lanzarote
Fuerteventura
C. Boujdour
Er Rif 2456
Tell Atlas
2308
2326
ATLAS MOUNTAINS
High Atlas
Saharan Atlas
Jebel Toubkal 4165
Oued Drâa
Hamada du Drâa
Chott Melrhir
Shott el Jerid
Great Western Dunes
Great Eastern Dunes
Tademaït Plateau
Sebkha Mekerrhane
Sebkha Azzel Matti
Hamada de Tinrhert
Şaḩrā' Awbārī
Tassili-n-Ajjer
Gefara
Jabal Nafūsah
Cape Misurata
Gulf of Sidra
Jabal al Akhḑar
Ras al Hilāl
G. of Bomba
G. of Salûm
Arabs Gulf
Nile River Delta
Libyan Plateau 264
-133 Qattara Depression
Sand Sea of Calanscio
Sarīr Calanscio
Jabal as Sawdā'
Al Harūjal Aswad
1200
Şaḩrā' Marzūq
Rebiana Sand Sea
Kufra Oasis
Libyan Desert
Western Desert
Abu Ballâs 467
Gilf Kebîr Plateau
Toshka Lakes
Lake Nasser
Gebel Siri 420
Lake Nubia
Nubian Desert
Jebel 'Uweinat 1893
SUEZ CANAL
SINAI
G. of Suez
Mt. Sinai 2285
Gulf of Aqaba
Râs Muḩammad
Eastern Desert
Nile
RED SEA
Râs Banâs
Cape Elba (Ras Hadarba)
Suakin Archipelago
Ras Kasar
Dahlak Archipelago
Jebel Sabidana 1907
ARABIAN PENINSULA
PERSIAN GULF
TROPIC OF CANCER
Zednes 460
'Erg Iguidi
'Erg Chech
Tanezrouft
Mount Tahat 3003
Ahaggar Mts.
Djado Plateau
Pic Touside 3315
Tibesti Mountains
Emi Koussi 3415
C. Blanc
C. Timiris
Akchâr
El Djouf
S A H A R A
1000
Adrar des Iforas
Tassili Oua-n-Ahaggar
Tarazit Massif
Ténéré
Aïr Massif
Mt. Bagzane 2022
Trarza
Tagant
El Mreyyé
Lake Faguibine
Niger
Inland Niger Delta
Lake Débo
Bodele Depression
Ennedi
1310
Jabel Abyad Plateau
C. Verde
Sénégal
Gambia
Falémé
Bafing
Bani
Fouta Djallon
1116
Bissagos Is.
Loma Mts. 1948
Source of the Niger
765
S A H E L
White Volta
Black Volta
Komoé
Manga
Lake Chad
Yobe
Hadejia
Gana
Kainji Res.
Guéra Massif 1613
Marra Mts. 3088
Jebel Teljo 1954
Jebel ed Dair 1412
Nuba Mts. 1325
Atbara
Blue Nile
El Gezira
White Nile
Ras Dejen 4533
Lake Tana
ETHIOPIAN HIGHLANDS
Danakil Desert
Lake Assal -156 (-512 ft)
Lowest point in Africa
Bab al Mandab
G. of Tadjoura
GULF OF ADEN
Cape Gwardafuy
2408
SOMALI PENINSULA
Ogadēn
Haud
Shebele
Jubba
Benadir
Jos Plateau 1781
Nimba Mts.
UPPER GUINEA
Lake Volta
Cavalla
Grain Coast
Ivory Coast
Gold Coast
Slave Coast
Bight of Benin
Cape Palmas
GULF OF GUINEA
Niger Delta
Bioko
Príncipe
São Tomé
Benue
Cameroon Mt. 4100
Sanaga
1213
Mbang Mts.
Karre Mts.
Logone
Chari
Dar Rounga
1400
Chaîne des Bongos
Tondou Massif
Bahr el Arab
Sudd
Mountain Nile
Gurage 3719
Mendebo Mts.
Batu 4307
Lake Abaya
Lake Chew Bahir
Dawa
Chalbi Desert
Lake Turkana (L. Rudolf)
GREAT RIFT VALLEY
Lorian Swamp
Mt. Elgon 4321
KENYA
Lake Albert
Albert Nile
Ruwenzori 5109
Ntem
Ngoko
Lobaya
Ubangi
Kotto
Bomu
Uele
Itimbiri
Aruwimi
Congo
Lulonga
Boyoma Falls
C O N G O
EQUATOR
200

Africa: **Physical**

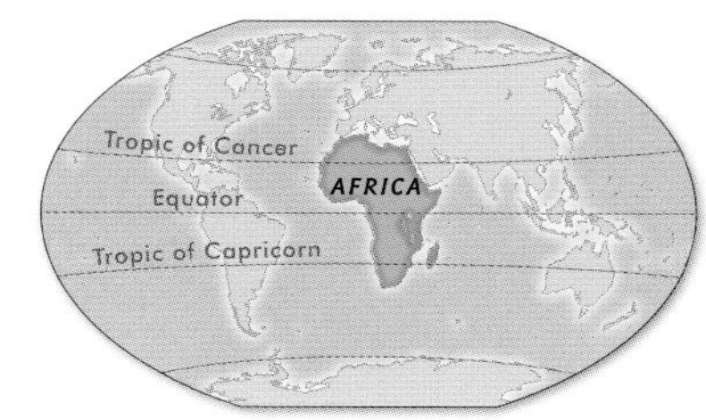

CONTINENTAL DATA

AREA:
30,065,000 sq km
(11,608,000 sq mi)

GREATEST NORTH-SOUTH EXTENT:
8,047 km (5,000 mi)

GREATEST EAST-WEST EXTENT:
7,564 km (4,700 mi)

HIGHEST POINT:
Kilimanjaro, Tanzania
5,895 m (19,340 ft)

LOWEST POINT:
Lake Assal, Djibouti
-156 m (-512 ft)

LOWEST RECORDED TEMPERATURE:
Ifrane, Morocco -24°C (-11°F),
February 11, 1935

HIGHEST RECORDED TEMPERATURE:
Al Aziziyah, Libya 58°C (136.4°F)
September 13, 1922

LONGEST RIVERS:
- Nile 6,825 km (4,241 mi)
- Congo 4,370 km (2,715 mi)
- Niger 4,170 km (2,591 mi)

LARGEST LAKES:
- Lake Victoria 69,500 sq km (26,800 sq mi)
- Lake Tanganyika 32,600 sq km (12,600 sq mi)
- Lake Malawi 28,900 sq km (11,200 sq mi)

EARTH'S EXTREMES LOCATED IN AFRICA:
- **Largest Desert on Earth:** Sahara 9,000,000 sq km (3,475,000 sq mi)
- **Hottest Place on Earth:** Dalol, Danakil Desert, Ethiopia; annual average temperature 34°C (93°F)

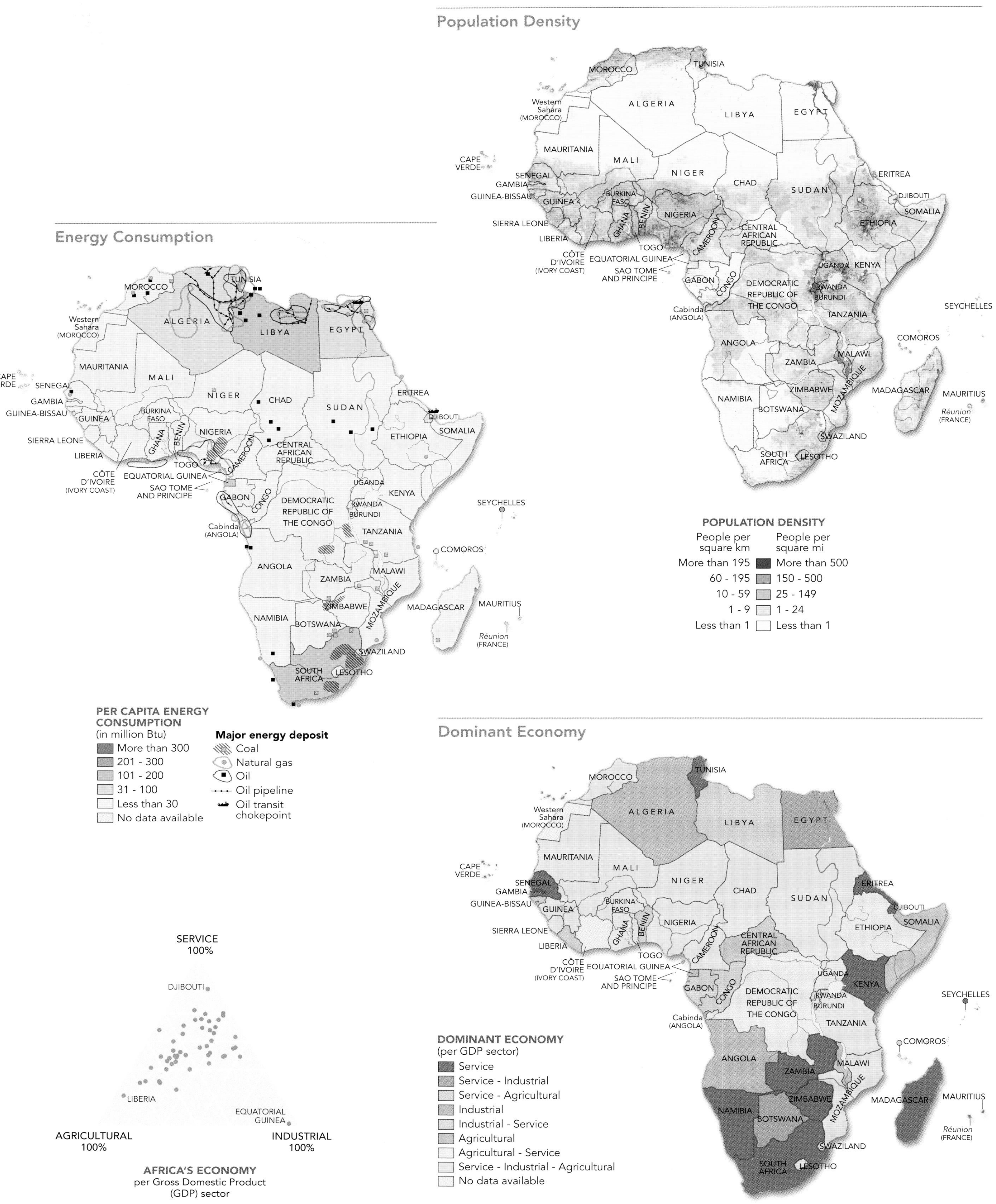
Population Density
POPULATION DENSITY
People per square km
People per square mi
More than 195
More than 500
60 - 195
150 - 500
10 - 59
25 - 149
1 - 9
1 - 24
Less than 1
Less than 1
Energy Consumption
PER CAPITA ENERGY CONSUMPTION
(in million Btu)
More than 300
201 - 300
101 - 200
31 - 100
Less than 30
No data available
Major energy deposit
Coal
Natural gas
Oil
Oil pipeline
Oil transit chokepoint
Dominant Economy
DOMINANT ECONOMY
(per GDP sector)
Service
Service - Industrial
Service - Agricultural
Industrial
Industrial - Service
Agricultural
Agricultural - Service
Service - Industrial - Agricultural
No data available
SERVICE 100%
DJIBOUTI
LIBERIA
EQUATORIAL GUINEA
AGRICULTURAL 100%
INDUSTRIAL 100%
AFRICA'S ECONOMY
per Gross Domestic Product (GDP) sector

Climate Zones

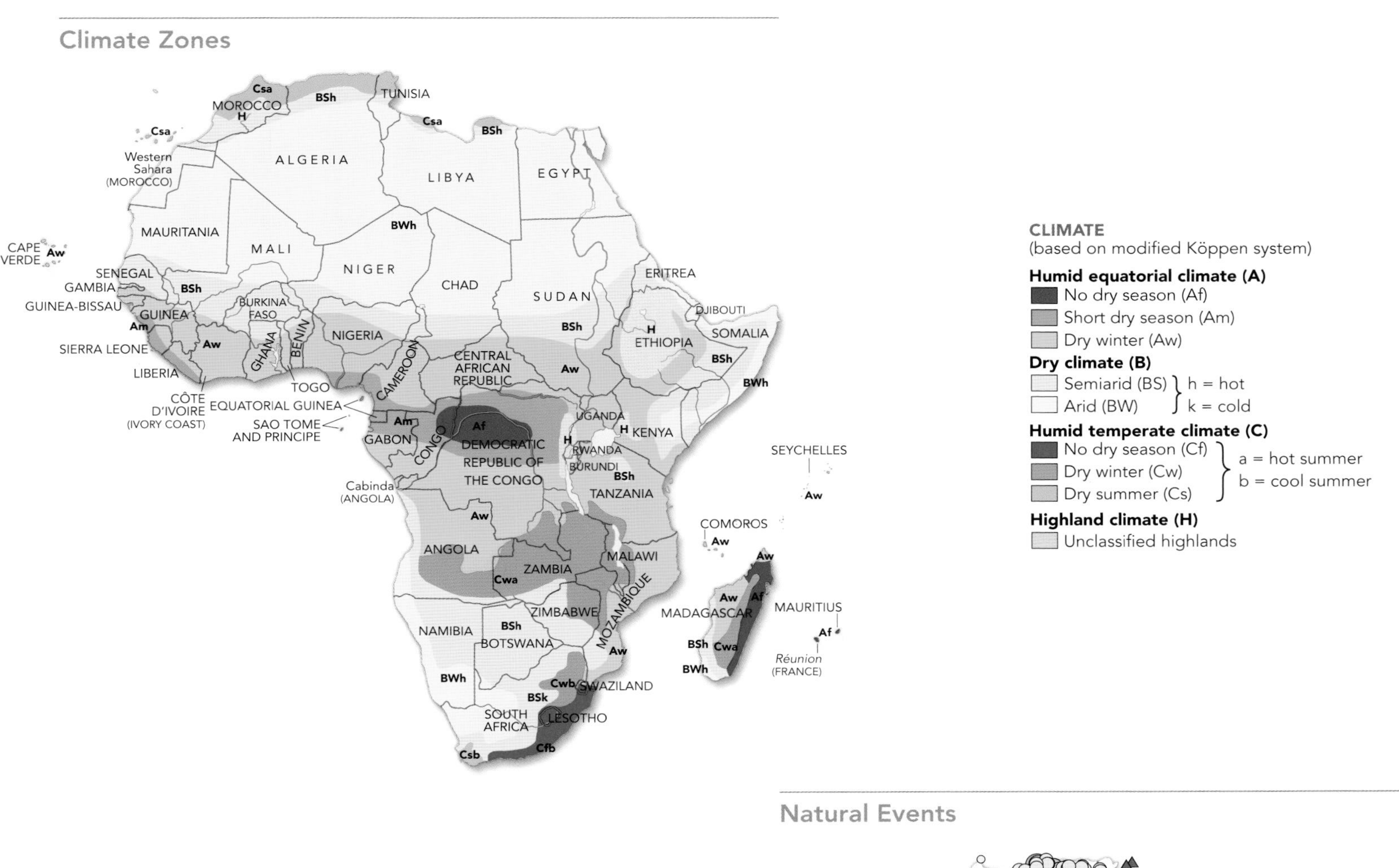

Natural Events

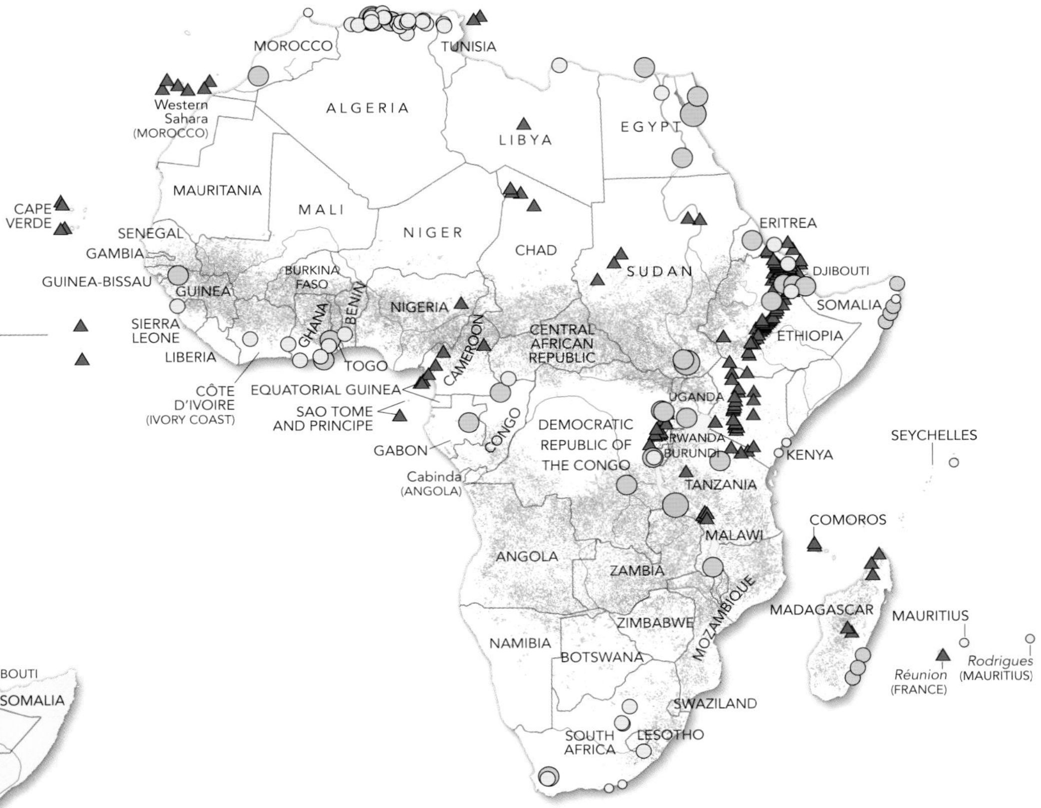

RECORDED NATURAL EVENT

Earthquake
Richter scale magnitude
- More than 7.0
- 6.0 - 7.0
- Less than 6.0

Tsunami
Run-up height
- 5 - 10 m / 16 - 32 ft
- Less than 5 m / Less than 16 ft

Fire intensity
(from gas burn-off, slash-and-burn agriculture, or natural causes)
High
Low

Volcano
- Major eruption

Water Availability

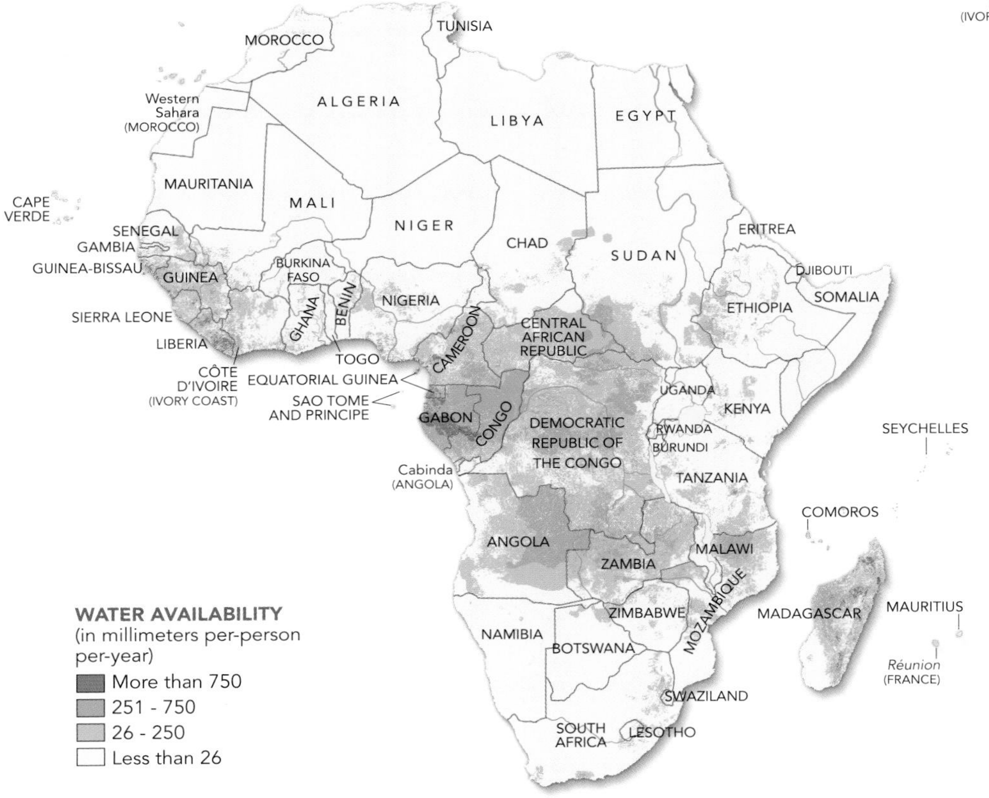

WATER AVAILABILITY
(in millimeters per-person per-year)
- More than 750
- 251 - 750
- 26 - 250
- Less than 26

Nations

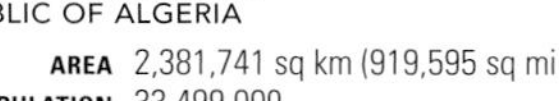

Algeria
PEOPLE'S DEMOCRATIC REPUBLIC OF ALGERIA

AREA 2,381,741 sq km (919,595 sq mi)
POPULATION 33,499,000
CAPITAL Algiers 3,200,000
RELIGION Sunni Muslim
LANGUAGE Arabic, French, Berber dialects
LITERACY 70%
LIFE EXPECTANCY 75 years
GDP PER CAPITA $7,700
ECONOMY **IND:** petroleum, natural gas, light industries, mining **AGR:** wheat, barley, oats, grapes; sheep **EXP:** petroleum, natural gas, petroleum products

Angola
REPUBLIC OF ANGOLA

AREA 1,246,700 sq km (481,354 sq mi)
POPULATION 15,828,000
CAPITAL Luanda 2,766,000
RELIGION indigenous beliefs, Roman Catholic, Protestant
LANGUAGE Portuguese, Bantu and other African languages
LITERACY 67%
LIFE EXPECTANCY 41 years
GDP PER CAPITA $4,300
ECONOMY **IND:** petroleum, diamonds, iron ore, phosphates **AGR:** bananas, sugarcane, coffee, sisal; livestock; forest products; fish **EXP:** crude oil, diamonds, refined petroleum products, gas

Benin
REPUBLIC OF BENIN

AREA 112,622 sq km (43,484 sq mi)
POPULATION 8,703,000
CAPITAL Porto-Novo (constitutional) 242,000; Cotonou (seat of government) 719,000

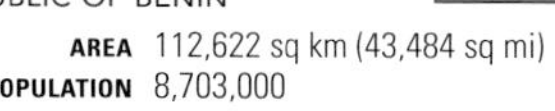

RELIGION Christian, Muslim, Vodoun
LANGUAGE French, Fon, Yoruba, tribal languages
LITERACY 34%
LIFE EXPECTANCY 54 years
GDP PER CAPITA $1,100
ECONOMY **IND:** textiles, food processing, construction materials, cement **AGR:** cotton, corn, cassava (tapioca), yams; livestock **EXP:** cotton, cashews, shea butter, textiles

Botswana
REPUBLIC OF BOTSWANA

AREA 581,730 sq km (224,607 sq mi)
POPULATION 1,760,000
CAPITAL Gaborone 210,000
RELIGION Christian, Badimo
LANGUAGE Setswana, Kalanga
LITERACY 80%
LIFE EXPECTANCY 34 years
GDP PER CAPITA $11,400
ECONOMY **IND:** diamonds, copper, nickel, salt **AGR:** livestock, sorghum, maize, millet **EXP:** diamonds, copper, nickel, soda ash

Burkina Faso
BURKINA FASO

AREA 274,200 sq km (105,869 sq mi)
POPULATION 13,634,000
CAPITAL Ouagadougou 926,000
RELIGION Muslim, indigenous beliefs, Christian
LANGUAGE French, native African languages
LITERACY 27%
LIFE EXPECTANCY 48 years
GDP PER CAPITA $1,300
ECONOMY **IND:** cotton lint, beverages, agricultural processing, soap **AGR:** cotton, peanuts, shea nuts, sesame; livestock **EXP:** cotton, livestock, gold

Burundi
REPUBLIC OF BURUNDI

AREA 27,834 sq km (10,747 sq mi)
POPULATION 7,834,000
CAPITAL Bujumbura 447,000
RELIGION Roman Catholic, indigenous beliefs, Muslim, Protestant
LANGUAGE Kirundi, French, Swahili
LITERACY 52%
LIFE EXPECTANCY 45 years
GDP PER CAPITA $700
ECONOMY **IND:** light consumer goods, assembly of imported components, public works construction, food processing **AGR:** coffee, cotton, tea, corn; beef **EXP:** coffee, tea, sugar, cotton

Cameroon
REPUBLIC OF CAMEROON

AREA 475,442 sq km (183,569 sq mi)
POPULATION 17,341,000
CAPITAL Yaoundé 1,485,000
RELIGION indigenous beliefs, Christian, Muslim
LANGUAGE 24 major African language groups, English, French
LITERACY 79%
LIFE EXPECTANCY 51 years
GDP PER CAPITA $2,400
ECONOMY **IND:** petroleum production and refining, aluminum production, food processing, light consumer goods **AGR:** coffee, cocoa, cotton, rubber; livestock; timber **EXP:** crude oil and petroleum products, lumber, cocoa beans, aluminum

Cape Verde
REPUBLIC OF CAPE VERDE

AREA 4,036 sq km (1,558 sq mi)
POPULATION 485,000
CAPITAL Praia 117,000
RELIGION Roman Catholic, Protestant
LANGUAGE Portuguese, Crioulo
LITERACY 77%
LIFE EXPECTANCY 71 years
GDP PER CAPITA $6,000
ECONOMY **IND:** food and beverages, fish processing, shoes and garments, salt mining **AGR:** bananas, corn, beans, sweet potatoes; fish **EXP:** fuel, shoes, garments, fish

Central African Republic
CENTRAL AFRICAN REPUBLIC

AREA 622,984 sq km (240,535 sq mi)
POPULATION 4,303,000
CAPITAL Bangui 541,000
RELIGION indigenous beliefs, Protestant, Roman Catholic, Muslim
LANGUAGE French, Sangho, tribal languages
LITERACY 51%
LIFE EXPECTANCY 44 years
GDP PER CAPITA $1,100
ECONOMY **IND:** gold and diamond mining, logging, brewing, textiles **AGR:** cotton, coffee, tobacco, manioc (tapioca); timber **EXP:** diamonds, timber, cotton, coffee

Chad
REPUBLIC OF CHAD

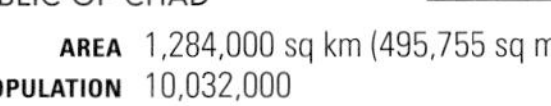

AREA 1,284,000 sq km (495,755 sq mi)
POPULATION 10,032,000
CAPITAL N'Djamena 888,000
RELIGION Muslim, Christian, animist
LANGUAGE French, Arabic, Sara, over 120 different languages and dialects
LITERACY 48%
LIFE EXPECTANCY 44 years
GDP PER CAPITA $1,500
ECONOMY **IND:** oil, cotton textiles, meatpacking, beer brewing **AGR:** cotton, sorghum, millet, peanuts; cattle **EXP:** cotton, cattle, gum arabic, oil

Comoros
UNION OF THE COMOROS

AREA 1,862 sq km (719 sq mi)
POPULATION 691,000
CAPITAL Moroni 44,000
RELIGION Sunni Muslim
LANGUAGE Arabic, French, Shikomoro
LITERACY 57%
LIFE EXPECTANCY 64 years
GDP PER CAPITA $600
ECONOMY **IND:** fishing, tourism, perfume distillation **AGR:** vanilla, cloves, perfume essence, copra **EXP:** vanilla, ylang-ylang (perfume essence), cloves, copra

Congo
REPUBLIC OF THE CONGO

AREA 342,000 sq km (132,047 sq mi)
POPULATION 3,702,000
CAPITAL Brazzaville 1,173,000
RELIGION Christian, animist
LANGUAGE French, Lingala, Monokutuba, local languages
LITERACY 84%
LIFE EXPECTANCY 51 years
GDP PER CAPITA $1,300
ECONOMY **IND:** petroleum extraction, cement, lumber, brewing **AGR:** cassava (tapioca), sugar, rice, corn; forest products **EXP:** petroleum, lumber, plywood, sugar

Côte d'Ivoire (Ivory Coast)
REPUBLIC OF CÔTE D'IVOIRE

AREA 322,462 sq km (124,503 sq mi)
POPULATION 19,658,000
CAPITAL Abidjan (administrative) 3,577,000; Yamoussoukro (legislative) 490,000
RELIGION Muslim, indigenous beliefs, Christian
LANGUAGE French, Dioula, other native dialects
LITERACY 51%
LIFE EXPECTANCY 51 years
GDP PER CAPITA $1,600
ECONOMY **IND:** foodstuffs, beverages, wood products, oil refining **AGR:** coffee, cocoa beans, bananas, palm kernels; timber **EXP:** cocoa, coffee, timber, petroleum

Democratic Republic of the Congo
DEMOCRATIC REPUBLIC OF THE CONGO

AREA 2,344,885 sq km (905,365 sq mi)
POPULATION 62,661,000
CAPITAL Kinshasa 6,049,000
RELIGION Roman Catholic, Protestant, Kimbanguist, Muslim
LANGUAGE French, Lingala, Kingwana, Kikongo, Tshiluba
LITERACY 66%
LIFE EXPECTANCY 50 years
GDP PER CAPITA $700
ECONOMY **IND:** mining (diamonds, copper, zinc), mineral processing, consumer products, cement **AGR:** coffee, sugar, palm oil, rubber; wood products **EXP:** diamonds, copper, crude oil, coffee

Djibouti
REPUBLIC OF DJIBOUTI

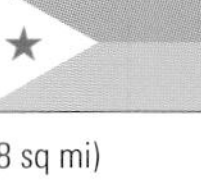

AREA 23,200 sq km (8,958 sq mi)
POPULATION 807,000
CAPITAL Djibouti 555,000
RELIGION Muslim, Christian
LANGUAGE French, Arabic, Somali, Afar
LITERACY 68%
LIFE EXPECTANCY 53 years
GDP PER CAPITA $1,000
ECONOMY **IND:** construction, agricultural processing **AGR:** fruits, vegetables; goats, sheep **EXP:** reexports, hides and skins, coffee (in transit)

Egypt
ARAB REPUBLIC OF EGYPT

AREA 1,002,000 sq km (386,874 sq mi)
POPULATION 75,437,000
CAPITAL Cairo 11,128,000
RELIGION Muslim, Coptic Christian
LANGUAGE Arabic, English, French
LITERACY 58%
LIFE EXPECTANCY 70 years
GDP PER CAPITA $4,200
ECONOMY **IND:** textiles, food processing, tourism, chemicals **AGR:** cotton, rice, corn, wheat; cattle **EXP:** crude oil and petroleum products, cotton, textiles, metal products

Equatorial Guinea
REPUBLIC OF EQUATORIAL GUINEA

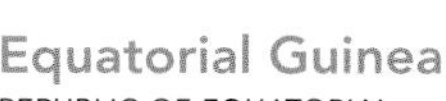

AREA 28,051 sq km (10,831 sq mi)
POPULATION 504,000
CAPITAL Malabo 96,000
RELIGION Roman Catholic, pagan practices
LANGUAGE Spanish, French, Fang, Bubi
LITERACY 86%
LIFE EXPECTANCY 44 years
GDP PER CAPITA $50,200
ECONOMY **IND:** petroleum, fishing, sawmilling, natural gas **AGR:** coffee, cocoa, rice, yams; livestock; timber **EXP:** petroleum, methanol, timber, cocoa

Eritrea
STATE OF ERITREA

AREA 121,144 sq km (46,774 sq mi)
POPULATION 4,560,000
CAPITAL Asmara 551,000
RELIGION Muslim, Coptic Christian, Roman Catholic, Protestant
LANGUAGE Afar, Arabic, Tigre, Kunama, Tigrinya, other Cushitic languages
LITERACY 59%
LIFE EXPECTANCY 55 years
GDP PER CAPITA $1,000
ECONOMY **IND:** food processing, beverages, clothing and textiles, light manufacturing **AGR:** sorghum, lentils, vegetables, corn; livestock; fish **EXP:** livestock, sorghum, textiles, food

Ethiopia
FEDERAL DEMOCRATIC REPUBLIC OF ETHIOPIA

AREA 1,133,380 sq km (437,600 sq mi)
POPULATION 74,778,000
CAPITAL Addis Ababa 2,893,000
RELIGION Christian, Muslim
LANGUAGE Amharic, Oromigna, Tigrinya, Guaragigna, Somali
LITERACY 43%
LIFE EXPECTANCY 49 years
GDP PER CAPITA $1,000
ECONOMY **IND:** food processing, beverages, textiles, leather **AGR:** cereals, pulses, coffee, oilseed; hides; fish **EXP:** coffee, qat, gold, leather products

Gabon
GABONESE REPUBLIC

AREA 267,667 sq km (103,347 sq mi)
POPULATION 1,406,000
CAPITAL Libreville 556,000
RELIGION Christian, animist
LANGUAGE French, Fang, Myene, Nzebi, Bapounou/Eschira
LITERACY 63%
LIFE EXPECTANCY 54 years
GDP PER CAPITA $7,200
ECONOMY **IND:** petroleum extraction and refining, manganese and gold mining, chemicals, ship repair **AGR:** cocoa, coffee, sugar, palm oil; okoume (a tropical softwood); fish **EXP:** crude oil, timber, manganese, uranium

Gambia
REPUBLIC OF THE GAMBIA

AREA 11,295 sq km (4,361 sq mi)
POPULATION 1,476,000
CAPITAL Banjul 381,000
RELIGION Muslim, Christian
LANGUAGE English, Mandinka, Wolof, Fula
LITERACY 40%
LIFE EXPECTANCY 53 years
GDP PER CAPITA $2,000
ECONOMY **IND:** peanut, fish, and hide processing, tourism, beverages, agricultural machinery assembly **AGR:** rice, millet, sorghum, peanuts; cattle **EXP:** peanut products, fish, cotton lint, palm kernels

Ghana
REPUBLIC OF GHANA

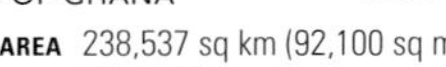

AREA 238,537 sq km (92,100 sq mi)
POPULATION 22,575,000
CAPITAL Accra 1,981,000
RELIGION Christian, Muslim, traditional beliefs
LANGUAGE Asante, Ewe, Fante, other native languages
LITERACY 75%
LIFE EXPECTANCY 57 years
GDP PER CAPITA $2,600
ECONOMY **IND:** mining, lumbering, light manufacturing, aluminum smelting **AGR:** cocoa, rice, coffee, cassava (tapioca); timber **EXP:** gold, cocoa, timber, tuna

Guinea
REPUBLIC OF GUINEA

AREA 245,857 sq km (94,926 sq mi)
POPULATION 9,803,000
CAPITAL Conakry 1,425,000
RELIGION Muslim, Christian, indigenous beliefs
LANGUAGE French, ethnic languages
LITERACY 36%
LIFE EXPECTANCY 54 years
GDP PER CAPITA $2,000
ECONOMY **IND:** bauxite, gold, diamonds, alumina refining **AGR:** rice, coffee, pineapples, palm kernels; cattle; timber **EXP:** bauxite, alumina, gold, diamonds

Guinea-Bissau
REPUBLIC OF GUINEA-BISSAU

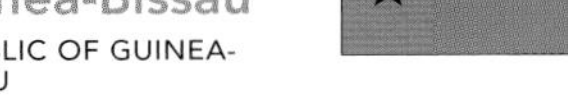

AREA 36,125 sq km (13,948 sq mi)
POPULATION 1,356,000
CAPITAL Bissau 367,000
RELIGION indigenous beliefs, Muslim, Christian
LANGUAGE Portuguese, Crioulo, African languages
LITERACY 42%
LIFE EXPECTANCY 45 years
GDP PER CAPITA $900
ECONOMY **IND:** agricultural products processing, beer, soft drinks **AGR:** rice, corn, beans, cassava (tapioca); timber; fish **EXP:** cashew nuts, shrimp, peanuts, palm kernels

Kenya
REPUBLIC OF KENYA

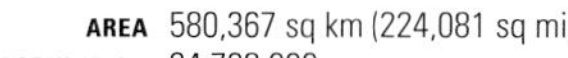

AREA 580,367 sq km (224,081 sq mi)
POPULATION 34,708,000
CAPITAL Nairobi 2,773,000
RELIGION Protestant, Roman Catholic, indigenous beliefs, Muslim
LANGUAGE English, Kiswahili, many indigenous languages
LITERACY 85%
LIFE EXPECTANCY 48 years
GDP PER CAPITA $1,200
ECONOMY **IND:** small-scale consumer goods (plastic, furniture), agricultural products, horticulture, oil refining **AGR:** tea, coffee, corn, wheat; dairy products **EXP:** tea, horticultural products, coffee, petroleum products

Lesotho
KINGDOM OF LESOTHO

AREA 30,355 sq km (11,720 sq mi)
POPULATION 1,801,000
CAPITAL Maseru 172,000
RELIGION Christian, indigenous beliefs
LANGUAGE Sesotho, English, Zulu, Xhosa
LITERACY 85%
LIFE EXPECTANCY 36 years
GDP PER CAPITA $2,600
ECONOMY **IND:** food, beverages, textiles, apparel assembly **AGR:** corn, wheat, pulses, sorghum; livestock **EXP:** clothing, footwear, road vehicles, wool and mohair

Liberia
REPUBLIC OF LIBERIA

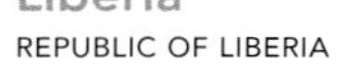

AREA 111,370 sq km (43,000 sq mi)
POPULATION 3,356,000
CAPITAL Monrovia 936,000
RELIGION indigenous beliefs, Christian, Muslim
LANGUAGE English, some 20 ethnic group languages
LITERACY 58%
LIFE EXPECTANCY 43 years
GDP PER CAPITA $1,000
ECONOMY **IND:** rubber processing, palm oil processing, timber, diamonds **AGR:** rubber, coffee, cocoa, rice; sheep; timber **EXP:** rubber, timber, iron, diamonds

Libya
GREAT SOCIALIST PEOPLE'S LIBYAN ARAB JAMAHIRIYA

AREA 1,759,540 sq km (679,362 sq mi)
POPULATION 5,901,000
CAPITAL Tripoli 2,098,000
RELIGION Sunni Muslim
LANGUAGE Arabic, Italian, English
LITERACY 83%
LIFE EXPECTANCY 76 years
GDP PER CAPITA $12,700
ECONOMY **IND:** petroleum, iron and steel, food processing, textiles **AGR:** wheat, barley, olives, dates; cattle **EXP:** crude oil, refined petroleum products, natural gas, chemicals

Madagascar
REPUBLIC OF MADAGASCAR

AREA 587,041 sq km (226,658 sq mi)
POPULATION 17,774,000
CAPITAL Antananarivo 1,585,000
RELIGION indigenous beliefs, Christian, Muslim
LANGUAGE French, Malagasy
LITERACY 69%
LIFE EXPECTANCY 55 years
GDP PER CAPITA $900
ECONOMY **IND:** meat processing, seafood, soap, breweries **AGR:** coffee, vanilla, sugarcane, cloves; livestock products **EXP:** coffee, vanilla, shellfish, sugar

Malawi
REPUBLIC OF MALAWI

AREA 118,484 sq km (45,747 sq mi)
POPULATION 12,758,000
CAPITAL Lilongwe 676,000
RELIGION Christian, Muslim
LANGUAGE Chichewa, Chinyanja, Chiyao, Chitumbuka
LITERACY 63%
LIFE EXPECTANCY 45 years
GDP PER CAPITA $600
ECONOMY **IND:** tobacco, tea, sugar, sawmill products **AGR:** tobacco, sugarcane, cotton, tea; cattle **EXP:** tobacco, tea, sugar, cotton

Mali
REPUBLIC OF MALI

AREA 1,240,192 sq km (478,841 sq mi)
POPULATION 13,918,000
CAPITAL Bamako 1,368,000
RELIGION Muslim, indigenous beliefs
LANGUAGE French, Bambara, numerous African languages
LITERACY 46%
LIFE EXPECTANCY 49 years
GDP PER CAPITA $1,200
ECONOMY **IND:** food processing, construction, phosphate and gold mining **AGR:** cotton, millet, rice, corn; cattle **EXP:** cotton, gold, livestock

Mauritania
ISLAMIC REPUBLIC OF MAURITANIA

AREA 1,030,700 sq km (397,955 sq mi)
POPULATION 3,158,000
CAPITAL Nouakchott 637,000
RELIGION Muslim
LANGUAGE Arabic, Pulaar, Soninke, French, Hassaniya, Wolof
LITERACY 42%
LIFE EXPECTANCY 54 years
GDP PER CAPITA $2,600
ECONOMY **IND:** fish processing, mining of iron ore and gypsum **AGR:** dates, millet, sorghum, rice; cattle **EXP:** iron ore, fish and fish products, gold

Mauritius
REPUBLIC OF MAURITIUS

AREA 2,040 sq km (788 sq mi)
POPULATION 1,254,000
CAPITAL Port Louis 146,000
RELIGION Hindu, Roman Catholic, Muslim, other Christian
LANGUAGE Creole, Bhojpuri
LITERACY 86%
LIFE EXPECTANCY 72 years
GDP PER CAPITA $13,500
ECONOMY **IND:** food processing (largely sugar milling), textiles, clothing, mining **AGR:** sugarcane, tea, corn, potatoes; cattle; fish **EXP:** clothing and textiles, sugar, cut flowers, molasses

Morocco
KINGDOM OF MOROCCO

AREA 710,850 sq km (274,461 sq mi)
POPULATION 31,725,000
CAPITAL Rabat 1,647,000
RELIGION Muslim
LANGUAGE Arabic, Berber dialects, French
LITERACY 52%
LIFE EXPECTANCY 70 years
GDP PER CAPITA $4,400
ECONOMY **IND:** phosphate rock mining and processing, food processing, leather goods, textiles **AGR:** barley, wheat, citrus, wine; livestock **EXP:** clothing, fish, inorganic chemicals, transistors

Mozambique
REPUBLIC OF MOZAMBIQUE

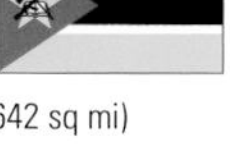

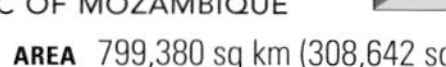

AREA 799,380 sq km (308,642 sq mi)
POPULATION 19,889,000
CAPITAL Maputo 1,320,000
RELIGION Catholic, Muslim, Zionist Christian
LANGUAGE Emakhuwa, Xichangana, Portuguese, Elomwe, Cisena, Echuwabo
LITERACY 48%
LIFE EXPECTANCY 42 years
GDP PER CAPITA $1,500
ECONOMY **IND:** food, beverages, chemicals (fertilizer, soap, paints), aluminum **AGR:** cotton, cashew nuts, sugarcane, tea; beef **EXP:** aluminum, prawns, cashews, cotton

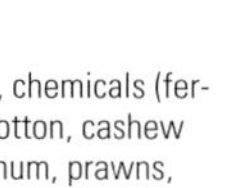

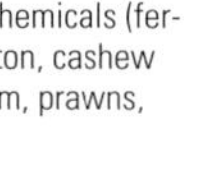

Namibia
REPUBLIC OF NAMIBIA

AREA 824,292 sq km (318,261 sq mi)
POPULATION 2,052,000
CAPITAL Windhoek 289,000
RELIGION Lutheran, other Christian, indigenous beliefs
LANGUAGE Afrikaans, German, English
LITERACY 84%
LIFE EXPECTANCY 47 years
GDP PER CAPITA $7,400
ECONOMY **IND:** meatpacking, fish processing, dairy products, mining (diamonds, lead, zinc) **AGR:** millet, sorghum, peanuts, grapes; livestock; fish **EXP:** diamonds, copper, gold, zinc

Niger
REPUBLIC OF NIGER

AREA 1,267,000 sq km (489,191 sq mi)
POPULATION 14,426,000
CAPITAL Niamey 850,000
RELIGION Muslim, indigenous beliefs, Christian
LANGUAGE French, Hausa, Djerma
LITERACY 18%
LIFE EXPECTANCY 44 years
GDP PER CAPITA $1,000
ECONOMY **IND:** uranium mining, cement, brick, soap **AGR:** cowpeas, cotton, peanuts, millet; cattle **EXP:** uranium ore, livestock, cowpeas, onions

Nigeria
FEDERAL REPUBLIC OF NIGERIA

AREA 923,768 sq km (356,669 sq mi)
POPULATION 134,500,000
CAPITAL Abuja 612,000
RELIGION Muslim, Christian, indigenous beliefs
LANGUAGE English, Hausa, Yoruba, Igbo (Ibo), Fulani
LITERACY 68%
LIFE EXPECTANCY 44 years
GDP PER CAPITA $1,400
ECONOMY **IND:** crude oil, coal, tin, columbite **AGR:** cocoa, peanuts, palm oil, corn; cattle; timber; fish **EXP:** petroleum and petroleum products, cocoa, rubber

Rwanda
REPUBLIC OF RWANDA

AREA 26,338 sq km (10,169 sq mi)
POPULATION 9,052,000
CAPITAL Kigali 779,000
RELIGION Roman Catholic, Protestant, Adventist
LANGUAGE Kinyarwanda, French, English, Kiswahili
LITERACY 70%
LIFE EXPECTANCY 47 years
GDP PER CAPITA $1,600
ECONOMY **IND:** cement, agricultural products, small-scale beverages, soap **AGR:** coffee, tea, pyrethrum, bananas; livestock **EXP:** coffee, tea, hides, tin ore

Sao Tome and Principe

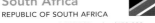

DEMOCRATIC REPUBLIC OF SAO TOME AND PRINCIPE

AREA 1,001 sq km (386 sq mi)
POPULATION 152,000
CAPITAL São Tomé 57,000
RELIGION Roman Catholic
LANGUAGE Portuguese
LITERACY 79%
LIFE EXPECTANCY 63 years
GDP PER CAPITA $1,200
ECONOMY **IND:** light construction, textiles, soap, beer **AGR:** cocoa, coconuts, palm kernels, copra; poultry; fish **EXP:** cocoa, copra, coffee, palm oil

Senegal

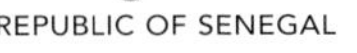

REPUBLIC OF SENEGAL

AREA 196,722 sq km (75,955 sq mi)
POPULATION 11,936,000
CAPITAL Dakar 2,159,000
RELIGION Muslim, Christian
LANGUAGE French, Wolof, Pulaar, Jola, Mandinka
LITERACY 40%
LIFE EXPECTANCY 56 years
GDP PER CAPITA $1,800
ECONOMY **IND:** agricultural and fish processing, phosphate mining, fertilizer production, petroleum refining **AGR:** peanuts, millet, corn, sorghum; cattle; fish **EXP:** fish, groundnuts (peanuts), petroleum products, phosphates

Seychelles

REPUBLIC OF SEYCHELLES

AREA 455 sq km (176 sq mi)
POPULATION 80,000
CAPITAL Victoria 25,000
RELIGION Roman Catholic, Anglican
LANGUAGE Creole
LITERACY 92%
LIFE EXPECTANCY 71 years
GDP PER CAPITA $7,800
ECONOMY **IND:** fishing, tourism, processing of coconuts and vanilla, coir (coconut fiber) rope **AGR:** coconuts, cinnamon, vanilla, sweet potatoes; poultry; tuna **EXP:** canned tuna, frozen fish, cinnamon bark, copra

Sierra Leone

REPUBLIC OF SIERRA LEONE

AREA 71,740 sq km (27,699 sq mi)
POPULATION 5,679,000
CAPITAL Freetown 799,000
RELIGION Muslim, indigenous beliefs, Christian
LANGUAGE English, Mende, Temne, Krio
LITERACY 30%
LIFE EXPECTANCY 41 years
GDP PER CAPITA $900
ECONOMY **IND:** diamond mining, small-scale manufacturing, petroleum refining, small ship repair **AGR:** rice, coffee, cocoa, palm kernels; poultry; fish **EXP:** diamonds, rutile, cocoa, coffee

Somalia

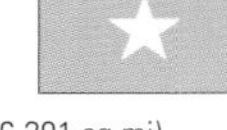

SOMALIA

AREA 637,657 sq km (246,201 sq mi)
POPULATION 8,863,000
CAPITAL Mogadishu 1,320,000
RELIGION Sunni Muslim
LANGUAGE Somali, Arabic, Italian, English
LITERACY 38%
LIFE EXPECTANCY 48 years
GDP PER CAPITA $600
ECONOMY **IND:** sugar refining, textiles, wireless communication **AGR:** bananas, sorghum, corn, coconuts; cattle; fish **EXP:** livestock, bananas, hides, fish

South Africa

REPUBLIC OF SOUTH AFRICA

AREA 1,219,090 sq km (470,693 sq mi)
POPULATION 47,322,000
CAPITAL Pretoria (administrative) 1,271,000; Bloemfontein (judicial) 400,000; Cape Town (legislative) 3,083,000
RELIGION Zion Christian, Pentecostal, Catholic, Methodist, Dutch Reformed
LANGUAGE IsiZulu, IsiXhosa, Afrikaans, Sepedi, English, Setswana, Sesotho
LITERACY 86%
LIFE EXPECTANCY 47 years
GDP PER CAPITA $13,000
ECONOMY **IND:** mining (platinum, gold, chromium), automobile assembly, metalworking, machinery **AGR:** corn, wheat, sugarcane, fruits; beef **EXP:** gold, diamonds, platinum, other metals and minerals

Sudan

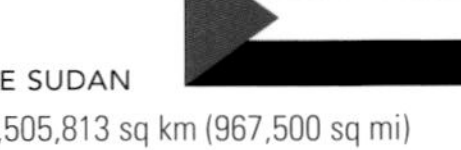

REPUBLIC OF THE SUDAN

AREA 2,505,813 sq km (967,500 sq mi)
POPULATION 41,236,000
CAPITAL Khartoum 4,518,000
RELIGION Sunni Muslim, indigenous beliefs, Christian
LANGUAGE Arabic, Nubian, Ta Bedawie, many diverse dialects
LITERACY 61%
LIFE EXPECTANCY 58 years
GDP PER CAPITA $2,300
ECONOMY **IND:** oil, cotton ginning, textiles, cement **AGR:** cotton, groundnuts (peanuts), sorghum, millet; sheep **EXP:** oil and petroleum products, cotton, sesame, livestock

Swaziland

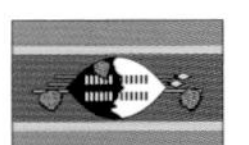

KINGDOM OF SWAZILAND

AREA 17,363 sq km (6,704 sq mi)
POPULATION 1,136,000
CAPITAL Mbabane (administrative) 73,000; Lobamba (legislative and royal) 5,000
RELIGION Zionist, Roman Catholic, Muslim
LANGUAGE English, siSwati
LITERACY 82%
LIFE EXPECTANCY 34 years
GDP PER CAPITA $5,500
ECONOMY **IND:** coal, wood pulp, sugar, soft drink concentrates **AGR:** sugarcane, cotton, corn, tobacco; cattle **EXP:** soft drink concentrates, sugar, wood pulp, cotton yarn

Tanzania

UNITED REPUBLIC OF TANZANIA

AREA 945,087 sq km (364,900 sq mi)
POPULATION 37,858,000
CAPITAL Dar es Salaam (administrative) 2,916,000; Dodoma (legislative) 168,000
RELIGION Muslim, indigenous beliefs, Christian
LANGUAGE Swahili, English, Arabic, local languages
LITERACY 78%
LIFE EXPECTANCY 45 years
GDP PER CAPITA $800
ECONOMY **IND:** agricultural processing (sugar, beer), diamond, gold and iron mining, salt **AGR:** coffee, sisal, tea, cotton; cattle **EXP:** gold, coffee, cashew nuts, manufactures

Togo

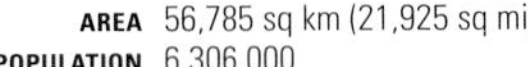

TOGOLESE REPUBLIC

AREA 56,785 sq km (21,925 sq mi)
POPULATION 6,306,000
CAPITAL Lomé 1,337,000
RELIGION indigenous beliefs, Christian, Muslim
LANGUAGE French, Ewe, Mina, Kabye, Dagomba
LITERACY 61%
LIFE EXPECTANCY 55 years
GDP PER CAPITA $1,700
ECONOMY **IND:** phosphate mining, agricultural processing, cement, handicrafts **AGR:** coffee, cocoa, cotton, yams; livestock; fish **EXP:** reexports, cotton, phosphates, coffee

Tunisia

TUNISIAN REPUBLIC

AREA 163,610 sq km (63,170 sq mi)
POPULATION 10,120,000
CAPITAL Tunis 734,000
RELIGION Muslim
LANGUAGE Arabic, French
LITERACY 74%
LIFE EXPECTANCY 73 years
GDP PER CAPITA $8,600
ECONOMY **IND:** petroleum, mining (phosphate, iron ore), tourism, textiles **AGR:** olives, olive oil, grain, tomatoes; beef **EXP:** clothing, semi-finished goods and textiles, agricultural products, mechanical goods

Uganda

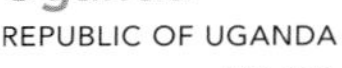

REPUBLIC OF UGANDA

AREA 241,139 sq km (93,104 sq mi)
POPULATION 27,651,000
CAPITAL Kampala 1,319,000
RELIGION Roman Catholic, Protestant, Muslim
LANGUAGE English, Ganda, many local languages
LITERACY 70%
LIFE EXPECTANCY 47 years
GDP PER CAPITA $1,800
ECONOMY **IND:** sugar, brewing, tobacco, cotton textiles **AGR:** coffee, tea, cotton, tobacco; beef **EXP:** coffee, fish and fish products, tea, cotton

Zambia

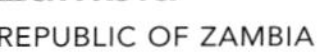

REPUBLIC OF ZAMBIA

AREA 752,614 sq km (290,586 sq mi)
POPULATION 11,861,000
CAPITAL Lusaka 1,260,000
RELIGION Christian, Muslim, Hindu
LANGUAGE English, indigenous languages
LITERACY 81%
LIFE EXPECTANCY 37 years
GDP PER CAPITA $1,000
ECONOMY **IND:** copper mining and processing, construction, foodstuffs, beverages **AGR:** corn, sorghum, rice, peanuts; cattle **EXP:** copper, cobalt, electricity, tobacco

Zimbabwe

REPUBLIC OF ZIMBABWE

AREA 390,757 sq km (150,872 sq mi)
POPULATION 13,085,000
CAPITAL Harare 1,515,000
RELIGION Syncretic (part Christian, part indigenous beliefs), Christian, indigenous beliefs
LANGUAGE English, Shona, Sindebele
LITERACY 91%
LIFE EXPECTANCY 37 years
GDP PER CAPITA $2,000
ECONOMY **IND:** mining (coal, gold, platinum), steel, wood products, cement **AGR:** corn, cotton, tobacco, wheat; sheep **EXP:** cotton, tobacco, gold, ferroalloys

Dependencies

Mayotte (France)

TERRITORIAL COLLECTIVITY OF MAYOTTE

AREA 374 sq km (144 sq mi)
POPULATION 188,000
CAPITAL Mamoudzou 61,000
RELIGION Muslim
LANGUAGE Mahorian (a Swahili dialect), French
LITERACY NA
LIFE EXPECTANCY 76 years
GDP PER CAPITA $4,900
ECONOMY **IND:** newly created lobster and shrimp industry, construction **AGR:** vanilla, ylang-ylang (perfume essence), coffee, copra **EXP:** ylang-ylang, vanilla, copra, coconuts

Réunion (France)

OVERSEAS DEPARTMENT OF FRANCE

AREA 2,507 sq km (968 sq mi)
POPULATION 793,000
CAPITAL St.-Denis 137,000
RELIGION Roman Catholic, Hindu, Muslim, Buddhist
LANGUAGE French, Creole
LITERACY 89%
LIFE EXPECTANCY 77 years
GDP PER CAPITA $6,200
ECONOMY **IND:** sugar, rum, cigarettes, handicraft items **AGR:** sugarcane, vanilla, tobacco, tropical fruits **EXP:** sugar, rum and molasses, perfume essences, lobster

St. Helena (U.K.)

SOVEREIGN

LOCAL

SAINT HELENA

AREA 411 sq km (159 sq mi)
POPULATION 6,000
CAPITAL Jamestown 1,000
RELIGION Anglican, Baptist, Seventh-Day Adventist, Roman Catholic
LANGUAGE English
LITERACY 97%
LIFE EXPECTANCY 77 years
GDP PER CAPITA $2,500
ECONOMY **IND:** construction, crafts (furniture, lacework, woodwork), fishing, philatelic sales **AGR:** coffee, corn, potatoes, vegetables; livestock; timber; fish **EXP:** fish (frozen, canned, salt-dried skipjack, tuna), coffee, handicrafts

Dates of National Independence

NOTE: For some countries, the date given may not represent "independence" in the strict sense—but rather some significant nationhood event: the traditional founding date; a fundamental change in the form of government; or perhaps the date of unification, secession, federation, confederation, or state succession.

Australia and Oceania

AUSTRALIA IS A CONTINENT OF EXTREMES—smallest and flattest, it's also the only continent-nation, with a landmass equal to that of the lower 48 states of the U.S. Yet its population is less than any other continent except Antarctica. And more than 80 percent of its people inhabit only the one percent of the continent that stretches along the southeast and south coasts. The sun-scorched outback that swells across the Australian interior has daunted virtually all comers, except the Aborigines. Traditionally hunter-gatherers, the Aborigines for eons—long before the arrival of Europeans—considered it home, both spiritually and physically.

The continent itself has been on a kind of planetary walkabout since it broke away from the supercontinent of Gondwana about 65 million years ago. Isolated, dry, and scorched by erosion, Australia developed its own unique species. Kangaroos, koalas, and duck-billed platypuses are well-known examples, but it also boasts rare plants, including 600 species of eucalyptus. The land surface has been stable enough to preserve some of the world's oldest rocks and mineral deposits, while the two islands of its neighboring nation New Zealand are younger and tell of a more violent geology that raised high volcanic mountains above deep fjords. Both nations share a past as British colonies, but each has in recent decades transformed itself from a ranching-based society into a fully industrialized and service-oriented economy.

Sitting at the southwestern edge of Oceania, Australia, with its growing ties to Asia and the Pacific Rim, is the economic powerhouse in this region. By contrast the islands of Oceania—more than 10,000 of them sprawling across the vast stretches of the central and South Pacific—are in various states of nationhood or dependency, prosperity or poverty, and often ignored, if not outright exploited. Their diverse populations and cultures are testament to the seafaring peoples who began settling these islands several thousand years ago, again long before the explorations and exploitations of Europeans in the 16th through 19th centuries.

Geographers today divide Oceania into three major ethnographic regions. The largest, Polynesia, or "many islands," comprises an immense oceanic triangle, with apexes at Hawai'i in the north, Easter Island in the east, and New Zealand in the southwest. The second Oceanic region, Melanesia, derives it name from "black islands"—either a reference to its dark lush landscapes or what European explorers described as the dark skin of most of its inhabitants. North and east of Australia, Melanesia encompasses such groups as the Bismarck Archipelago, the Solomon Islands, the Santa Cruz Islands, Vanuatu, the Fiji Islands and New Caledonia. North of Melanesia, Micronesia contains a widely scattered group of small islands and coral atolls, as well as the world's deepest ocean point—the 35,827-foot-deep (10,920 m) Challenger Deep—located in the southern Mariana Trench off the southwest coast of Guam. Micronesia stretches across more than 3,000 miles of the western Pacific with volcanic peaks that reach 2,500 feet. Palau, Nauru, the Caroline, Mariana, Marshall, and Gilbert Islands all form this third subdivision of Oceania.

Land Cover

- Water
- Evergreen needleleaf forest
- Evergreen broadleaf forest
- Deciduous broadleaf forest
- Mixed forest
- Closed shrubland
- Open shrubland
- Woody savanna
- Savanna
- Grassland
- Permanent wetland
- Cropland
- Urban and built-up
- Cropland/natural vegetation mosaic
- Snow and ice
- Barren or sparsely vegetated

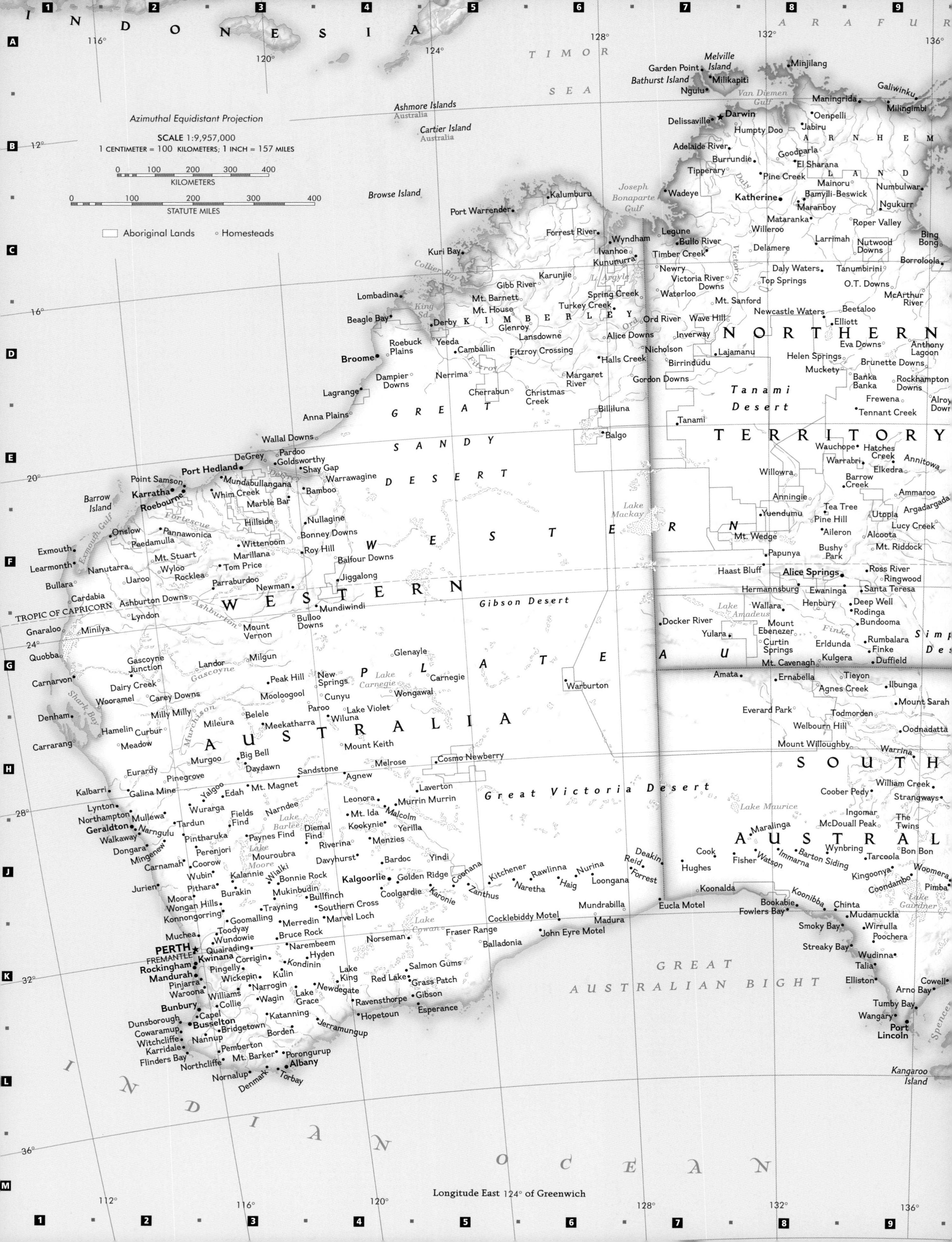

INDONESIA
ARAFURA
TIMOR SEA
Azimuthal Equidistant Projection
SCALE 1:9,957,000
1 CENTIMETER = 100 KILOMETERS; 1 INCH = 157 MILES
0 100 200 300 400
KILOMETERS
0 100 200 300 400
STATUTE MILES
Aboriginal Lands
Homesteads
Ashmore Islands
Australia
Cartier Island
Australia
Browse Island
Melville Island
Garden Point
Bathurst Island
Milikapiti
Nguiu
Minjilang
Van Diemen Gulf
Galiwinku
Maningrida
Milingimbi
Oenpelli
Delissaville
Darwin
Humpty Doo
Jabiru
ARNHEM LAND
Adelaide River
Goodparla
Burrundie
El Sharana
Tipperary
Daly
Pine Creek
Mainoru
Numbulwar
Wadeye
Katherine
Bamyili-Beswick
Maranboy
Ngukurr
Joseph Bonaparte Gulf
Kalumburu
Port Warrender
Mataranka
Roper Valley
Willeroo
Larrimah
Forrest River
Wyndham
Legune
Bullo River
Nutwood Downs
Bing Bong
Kuri Bay
Ivanhoe
Kununurra
Timber Creek
Delamere
Victoria
Borroloola
Collier Bay
L. Argyle
Newry
Daly Waters
Tanumbirini
Victoria River Downs
Top Springs
O.T. Downs
Karunjie
Gibb River
Lombadina
Mt. Barnett
Spring Creek
Waterloo
Mt. Sanford
McArthur River
King Sd.
Mt. House
Turkey Creek
Newcastle Waters
Beetaloo
Beagle Bay
Derby
KIMBERLEY
Ord
Ord River
Wave Hill
Elliott
Glenroy
Lansdowne
Alice Downs
Inverway
NORTHERN
Eva Downs
Anthony Lagoon
Roebuck Plains
Yeeda
Camballin
Fitzroy Crossing
Nicholson
Lajamanu
Helen Springs
Brunette Downs
Broome
Halls Creek
Birrindudu
Muckety
Fitzroy
Dampier Downs
Nerrima
Margaret River
Gordon Downs
Banka Banka
Rockhampton Downs
Cherrabun
Christmas Creek
Tanami Desert
Lagrange
Frewena
Alroy Downs
GREAT
Billiluna
Tennant Creek
Anna Plains
Tanami
SANDY
TERRITORY
Wallal Downs
Balgo
Wauchope
Hatches Creek
Pardoo
DeGrey
Goldsworthy
Warrabri
Annitowa
Port Hedland
Shay Gap
Elkedra
Point Samson
Warrawagine
DESERT
Willowra
Barrow Creek
Karratha
Mundabullangana
De Grey
Roebourne
Whim Creek
Bamboo
Ammaroo
Barrow Island
Anningie
Argadargada
Marble Bar
Tea Tree
Lake Mackay
Fortescue
Yuendumu
Utopia
Exmouth Gulf
Hillside
Nullagine
Pine Hill
Lucy Creek
Onslow
Pannawonica
Bonney Downs
Mt. Wedge
Aileron
Alcoota
WESTERN
Peedamulla
Wittenoom
Exmouth
Mt. Stuart
Roy Hill
Papunya
Bushy Park
Mt. Riddock
Marillana
Learmonth
Balfour Downs
Nanutarra
Wyloo
Tom Price
Haast Bluff
Alice Springs
Ross River
Rocklea
Jiggalong
Ringwood
Bullara
Uaroo
Parraburdoo
Newman
Hermannsburg
Ewaninga
Santa Teresa
Cardabia
Ashburton Downs
Gibson Desert
Wallara
Deep Well
TROPIC OF CAPRICORN
Lyndon
Mundiwindi
Lake Amadeus
Henbury
Rodinga
Ashburton
Bulloo Downs
Docker River
Bundooma
Gnaraloo
Minilya
Mount Vernon
Mount Ebenezer
Finke
Yulara
Rumbalara
Curtin Springs
Erldunda
Finke
Simpson Desert
Quobba
Glenayle
Gascoyne Junction
Milgun
Mt. Cavenagh
Kulgera
Duffield
Landor
PLATEAU
Gascoyne
Lake Carnegie
Carnegie
Amata
Ernabella
Tieyon
Carnarvon
New Springs
Peak Hill
Agnes Creek
Ilbunga
Dairy Creek
Warburton
Shark Bay
Carey Downs
Mooloogool
Wongawal
Wooramel
Cunyu
Mount Sarah
Everard Park
Murchison
Paroo
Lake Violet
Todmorden
Denham
Milly Milly
Belele
Wiluna
Welbourn Hill
Oodnadatta
Meekatharra
Mileura
AUSTRALIA
Hamelin
Curbur
Meadow
Carrarang
Mount Keith
Mount Willoughby
Warrina
Cosmo Newberry
Big Bell
Murgoo
SOUTH
Melrose
Daydawn
Eurardy
Sandstone
Agnew
Pinegrove
William Creek
Laverton
Yalgoo
Great Victoria Desert
Coober Pedy
Kalbarri
Galina Mine
Edah
Mt. Magnet
Strangways
Lynton
Wurarga
Leonora
Murrin Murrin
Lake Maurice
Ingomar
Northampton
Mullewa
Fields Find
Narndee
Mt. Ida
Malcolm
The Twins
Geraldton
Tardun
Lake Barlee
McDouall Peak
Narngulu
Maralinga
Walkaway
Pintharuka
Paynes Find
Diemal Find
Kookynie
Yerilla
Dongara
Perenjori
Lake Moore
Riverina
Menzies
Mingenew
Mouroubra
Wynbring
Carnamah
Coorow
Davyhurst
Bardoc
Yindi
Deakin
Cook
Barton Siding
Bon Bon
Wialki
Hughes
Fisher
Watson
Immarna
Tarcoola
Reid
Wubin
Kalannie
Bonnie Rock
Kalgoorlie
Golden Ridge
Coonana
Kitchener
Rawlinna
Nurina
Forrest
Woomera
Kingoonya
Jurien
Pithara
Loongana
Haig
Naretha
Pimba
Mukinbudin
Zanthus
Koonalda
Coondambo
Moora
Burakin
Bullfinch
Coolgardie
Karonie
Lake Gairdner
Wongan Hills
Trayning
Southern Cross
Mundrabilla
Eucla Motel
Konnongorring
Goomalling
Merredin
Marvel Loch
Bookabie
Koonibba
Chinta
Lake Cowan
Fowlers Bay
Mudamuckla
Toodyay
Cocklebiddy Motel
Madura
Muchea
Bruce Rock
Fraser Range
Wundowie
John Eyre Motel
Smoky Bay
Wirrulla
PERTH
Quairading
Narembeem
Norseman
Balladonia
Poochera
FREMANTLE
Kwinana
Hyden
Streaky Bay
Corrigin
Kondinin
Wudinna
Rockingham
Pingelly
Lake King
Salmon Gums
GREAT AUSTRALIAN BIGHT
Talia
Mandurah
Kulin
Wickepin
Red Lake
Grass Patch
Elliston
Pinjarra
Narrogin
Cowell
Waroona
Newdegate
Williams
Lake Grace
Arno Bay
Collie
Wagin
Ravensthorpe
Gibson
Bunbury
Esperance
Tumby Bay
Capel
Katanning
Hopetoun
Dunsborough
Busselton
Wangary
Cowaramup
Bridgetown
Jerramungup
Port Lincoln
Witchcliffe
Borden
Spencer Gulf
Nannup
Karridale
Pemberton
Flinders Bay
Mt. Barker
Porongurup
Northcliffe
Albany
Kangaroo Island
Nornalup
Denmark
Torbay
INDIAN
OCEAN
Longitude East 124° of Greenwich
12°
16°
20°
24°
28°
32°
36°
112°
116°
120°
124°
128°
132°
136°
A
B
C
D
E
F
G
H
J
K
L
M
1
2
3
4
5
6
7
8
9

Australia: **Political**

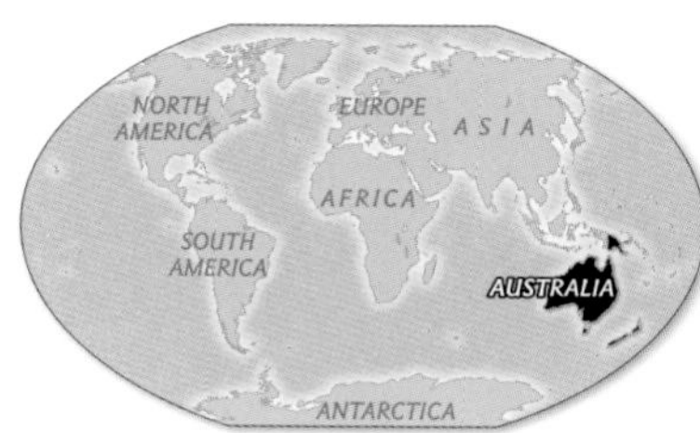

CONTINENTAL DATA

TOTAL NUMBER OF COUNTRIES: 1

DATE OF INDEPENDENCE:
January 1, 1901

AREA OF AUSTRALIA:
7,692,024 sq km
(2,969,906 sq mi)

PERCENT URBAN POPULATION:
73%

POPULATION OF AUSTRALIA:
20,575,000

POPULATION DENSITY:
2.7 per sq km
(6.9 per sq mi)

LARGEST CITY BY POPULATION:
Sydney, Australia 4,331,000

GDP PER CAPITA:
Australia $32,900

AVERAGE LIFE EXPECTANCY IN AUSTRALIA: 81 years

AVERAGE LITERACY RATE IN AUSTRALIA: 93%

Azimuthal Equidistant Projection
SCALE 1:9,957,000
1 CENTIMETER = 100 KILOMETERS; 1 INCH = 157 MILES
KILOMETERS
0 100 200 300 400
STATUTE MILES
0 100 200 300 400
State boundary
Lombok
Sumbawa
LESSER SUNDA ISLANDS
Sumba
SAVU SEA
Sawu
Roti
Timor
TIMOR SEA
Port Essington
Croker I.
Cape Van Diemen
Bathurst I.
Melville Island
Cobourg Pen.
Van Diemen Gulf
Wessel Is.
Cape Wilberforce
Cape Fourcroy
Clarence Str.
Charles Point
Ashmore Islands
Cartier Island
Point Blaze
Murrenja Hill
152
Anson Bay
Cape Ford
Gove Pen.
Cape Bougainville
Cape Talbot
Cape Londonderry
Daly
S. Alligator
Parsons Ra.
Browse Island
Bonaparte Archipelago
Cape Voltaire
Joseph Bonaparte Gulf
Katherine
Limmen Bight
Brunswick Bay
Drysdale
Endeavour Hill
210
Ord
Victoria
Hodgson
Mount Young
65
Buccaneer Archipelago
Collier B.
Cape Leveque
Lake Argyle
Kimberley Plateau
King Sd.
Mount Ord
937
King Leopold Ras.
Barkly
Cape Bertholet
Dampier Land
Fitzroy
Lake Woods
Tarrabool Lake
Roebuck Bay
Cape Latouche Treville
Lake Sylvester
Cape Bossut
Mount Frederick
530
Tanami Desert
Mount Tanami
499
GREAT SANDY DESERT
Eighty Mile Beach
Lewis Range
Southesk Tablelands
Lander
Davenport Ra.
Dampier Archipelago
DeGrey
Lake White
Barrow Island
Lake Waukarlycarly
Percival Lakes
Lake Mackay
Exmouth Gulf
North West Cape
Fortescue
Chichester Ra.
Lake Dora
Lake Auld
Marshall
Hamersley Range
WESTERN
Plenty
Mount Zeil
1531
Macdonnell Ranges
Lake Disappointment
TROPIC OF CAPRICORN
Mt. Meharry
1251
Point Cloates
James Ra.
Lake Neale
Lake Amadeus
Amadeus Depression
Ashburton
Ophthalmia Ra.
Mount Madley
533
Gibson Desert
Lake Macleod
Lyons
Mount Augustus
1106
Lofty Ra.
Petermann Ranges
Finke
Cape Cuvier
Mt. Essendon
906
Collier Range
Mt. Olga
Ayers Rock (Uluru)
Simpson Desert
Geographe Channel
Gascoyne
Lake Burnside
PLATEAU
(Kata Tjuta)
1069
868
Lake Carnegie
Robinson Range
Mount Aloysius
1085
Musgrave Ranges
Cape Inscription
Shark Bay
NORTH WEST BASIN
Lake Gillen
Murchison
Lake Wells
Baker Lake
Mount Sir Thomas
773
LAKE EYRE BASIN
Dirk Hartog I.
Lake Annean
Arckaringa Creek
Lake Throssell
Point Lilian
Nicholson Ra.
Lake Austin
Lake Darlot
Lake Meramangye
Mt. Redcliffe
576
Serpentine Lakes
Stuart Ra.
Lowest point in Australia
-16 (-52 ft)
Rason Lake
Bluff Point
Canning Hill
535
Lake Carey
Great Victoria Desert
Lake Dey Dey
Lake Raeside
Lake Maurice
Geelvink Channel
Houtman Abrolhos
Mongers Lake
Lake Barlee
Lake Minigwal
Lake Ballard
Lake Rebecca
Yarle Lakes
Lake Moore
Lake Goongarrie
Nullarbor Plain
Lake Gairdner
Lake Harris
Lake Yindarlgooda
Island Lagoon
Mt. Grey
404
Walyahmoning Rock
484
Green Head
EUCLA BASIN
Lake Everard
Lake Lefroy
Hampton Tableland
Cape Adieu
Lake Acraman
Darling Range
Lake Cowan
Red Rocks Point
Gawler Ranges
Swan
Lake Johnston
Point Brown
Lake Gilles
Lake Dundas
Point Culver
Eyre Peninsula
Lake Hope
Cape Peron
Mt. Ragged
585
GREAT AUSTRALIAN BIGHT
C. Bouvard
Murray
381
Cape Pasley
Point Whidbey
Geographe Bay
Cape Arid
Spencer
Cape Naturaliste
Bluff Knoll
1096
Archipelago of the Recherche
Cape Carnot
Cape Knob
West Point
Cape Leeuwin
Cape Spencer
Investigator Str.
Point D'Entrecasteaux
King George Sound
Kangaroo I.
West Cape Howe
INDIAN OCEAN
Longitude East 128° of Greenwich
112° 116° 120° 124° 128° 132° 136°
12° 16° 20° 24° 28° 32° 36°
200
1 2 3 4 5 6 7 8 9
A B C D E F G H J K L M

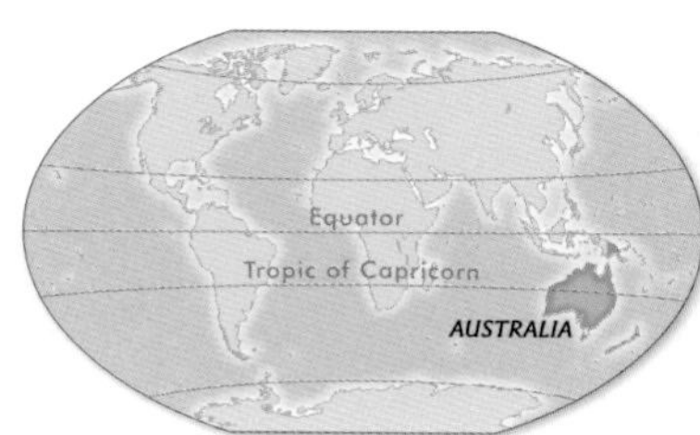

Australia: Physical

NEW GUINEA
Torres Strait
Prince of Wales I.
Cape York
Endeavour Strait
Great Barrier Reef
Cape Arnhem
Duifken Point
Albatross Bay
Cape York Peninsula
Cape Grenville
Temple Bay
Cape Weymouth
Groote Eylandt
GULF OF CARPENTARIA
Cape Keer-weer
Cape Sidmouth
Princess Charlotte Bay
CORAL SEA
Cape Flattery
Cape Bedford
Mornington I.
Mitchell
Cape Tribulation
Cape Kimberley
Wellesley Is.
Gilbert
Atherton Tableland
Bartle Frere 1611
Magdelaine Cays
Herald Cays
Double Point
Tregrosse Islets
Rockingham Bay
Hinchinbrook Island
Tableland
Gregory
Flinders
Cloncurry
Norman
Gregory Range
Herbert
Georgina
Burdekin
Great Barrier Reef
Cumberland Is.
Clarke Range
Repulse Bay
Cloncurry Plateau
Diamantina
Flinders
Landsborough Creek
Lake Galilee
Belyando
Connors Range
Northumberland Islands
Swain Reefs
Capricorn Channel
Cape Manifold
Fitzroy
Mackenzie
Drummond Range
GREAT DIVIDING RANGE
CENTRAL LOWLANDS
GREAT ARTESIAN BASIN
CHANNEL COUNTRY
Thomson
Barcoo
TROPIC OF CAPRICORN
Cato I.
Capricorn Group
Calliope Ra.
Buckland Tableland
Hervey Bay
Sandy Cape
Fraser Island (Great Sandy I.)
Dawson
Lake Yamma Yamma
Sturt Stony Desert
EYRE
Grey Range
Warrego
Double Island Point
Cooper Cr.
Nebine Cr.
Wallam Cr.
Darling Downs
L. Eyre North
Lake Eyre
Lake Gregory
Weir
Moreton Island
Point Lookout
North Stradbroke I.
Lake Blanche
Caryapundy Swamp
Source of the Darling
L. Eyre South
Lake Callabonna
Narran Lake
Barwon
Gwydir
Cape Byron
Lake Torrens
Lake Frome
Peri Lake
Darling
Namoi
New England Range
Woody Head
Solitary Islands
Flinders Ranges
Macquarie
Castlereagh
Bogan
Neckarboo Ra.
Liverpool Ra.
Port Macquarie
TASMAN SEA
Marobee Ra.
Burrendong Res.
Broughton Islands
Gulf
Yorke Pen.
MURRAY RIVER BASIN
Mount Lofty Ranges
Lachlan
Lake Cowal
Gulf St. Vincent
Murray
Murrumbidgee
Riverina
Botany Bay
Lake Alexandrina
Lake Albert
Lake Tyrrell
Edward
Encounter Bay
Lake George
Lake Hindmarsh
Jervis Bay
Lake Eucumbene
Cape Jaffa
Mt. William 1167
Waranga Basin
Source of the Murray
Mount Kosciuszko 2228 (7310 ft)
Highest point in Australia
Lake Eildon
Australian Alps
Snowy
Cape Northumberland
Lake Corangamite
Gippsland
Discovery Bay
Cape Nelson
Lake Wellington
Ninety Mile Beach
Cape Howe
Cape Otway
Port Phillip Bay
Bass Str.
Wilsons Promontory
Wilsons Promontory
Bass Strait
King I.
Flinders I.
FURNEAUX GROUP
Hunter Is.
Cape Barren I.
Great Western Tiers
Mt. Ossa 1617
TASMANIA
Mt. Hobbs 823
L. Gordon
L. Pedder
South West Cape
Same Scale as Main Map
Tasman Pen.
140°
144°
148°
152°
156°
12°
16°
20°
24°
28°
32°
36°
40°
200

Equator
Tropic of Capricorn
AUSTRALIA

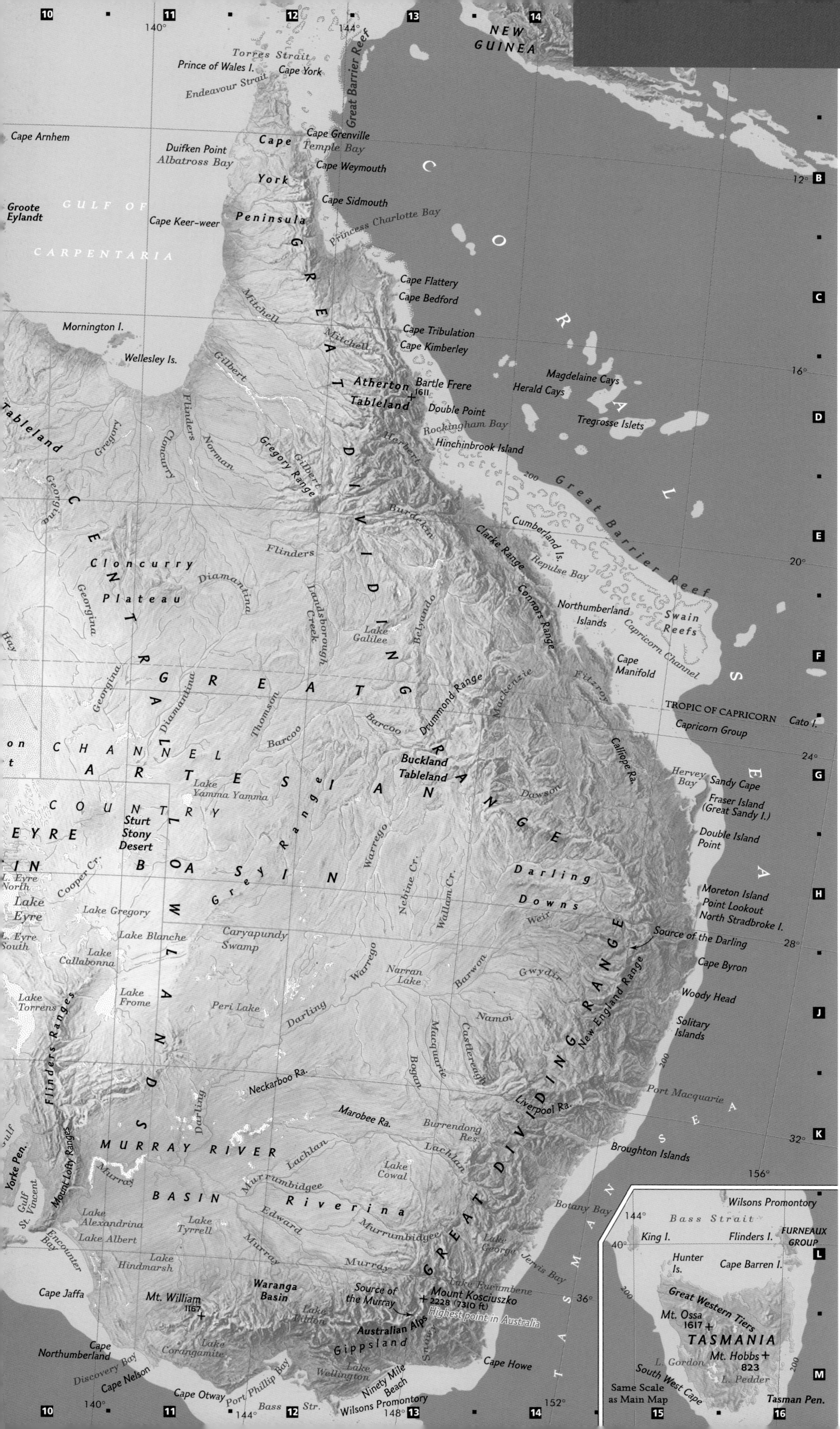

CONTINENTAL DATA

AREA:
7,687,000 sq km
(2,968,000 sq mi)

GREATEST NORTH-SOUTH EXTENT:
3,138 km (1,950 mi)

GREATEST EAST-WEST EXTENT:
3,983 km (2,475 mi)

HIGHEST POINT:
Mount Kosciuszko, New South Wales 2,228 m (7,310 ft)

LOWEST POINT:
Lake Eyre -16 m (-52 ft)

LOWEST RECORDED TEMPERATURE:
Charlotte Pass, New South Wales -23°C (-9.4°F), June 29, 1994

HIGHEST RECORDED TEMPERATURE:
Cloncurry, Queensland 53.3°C (128°F), January 16, 1889

LONGEST RIVERS:
- Murray-Darling 3,718 km (2,310 mi)
- Murrumbidgee 1,575 km (979 mi)
- Lachlan 1,370 km (851 mi)

LARGEST LAKES (AUS.):
- Lake Eyre 9,500 sq km (3,668 sq mi)
- Lake Mackay 3,494 sq km (1,349 sq mi)
- Lake Amadeus 1,032 sq km (398 sq mi)

EARTH'S EXTREMES LOCATED IN AUSTRALIA:
- **Longest Reef:** Great Barrier Reef 2,300 km (1,429 mi)

CHINA
NORTH KOREA
P'YŎNGYANG
SEOUL
SOUTH KOREA
YELLOW SEA
SEA OF JAPAN (EAST SEA)
JAPAN
HONSHŪ
TŌKYŌ
YOKOHAMA
NAGOYA
KŌBE
ŌSAKA
HIROSHIMA
SHIKOKU
KYŪSHŪ
Jeju-Do
Hachijō Jima
Sumisu (Smith)
Izu Shotō
NAMPO SHOTŌ
Yaku Shima
Tanega Shima
EAST CHINA SEA
Amami Ō Shima
Okinawa
Sakishima Shotō
NANSEI SHOTŌ (RYUKYU ISLANDS)
Kita Daitō Jima
Daitō Islands
Japan
Okino Daitō Jima
Sōfu Gan (Lot's Wife)
Bonin Islands (Ogasawara Guntō)
Muko Jima Rettō
Chichi Jima Rettō
Haha Jima Rettō
Kita Iwo Jima
Volcano Islands (Kazan Rettō)
Iwo Jima
Minami Iwo Jima
Minami Tori Shima (Marcus)
TROPIC OF CANCER
NORTH PACIFIC
Monday
Sunday
Date Line
Kure Atoll
Midway Islands
Pearl and Hermes Atoll
Lisianski I.
Laysan I.
Gardner Pinnacles
La Perouse Pinnacle
Necker I.
Nihoa
Ni'ihau
Ka'ula
Kaua'i
O'ahu
Honolulu
Moloka'i
Lāna'i
Maui
Kaho'olawe
Hawai'i
HAWAIIAN ISLANDS
United States
POLYNESIA
Johnston Atoll
U.S.
Batan Is.
Babuyan Is.
LUZON
PHILIPPINES
PHILIPPINE SEA
Samar
Leyte
MINDANAO
Davao
Parece Vela
Farallon de Pajaros
Asuncion
Agrihan
Pagan
Alamagan
Sarigan
Anatahan
Tinian
Saipan
Rota
Guam
NORTHERN MARIANA ISLANDS
Wake Island
Taongi Atoll
MICRONESIA
Ulithi Atoll
Yap Islands
Fais
Gaferut
Woleai Atoll
Ifalik Atoll
Ngulu Atoll
PALAU
Melekeok
Eauripik Atoll
Satawal
Puluwat Atoll
Pulap Atoll
Pulusuk
Namonuito Atoll
Hall Is.
Chuuk (Truk Is.)
Oroluk Atoll
Mortlock Is.
Senyavin Is.
Pohnpei (Ponape)
Palikir
Ngatik Atoll
Enewetak Atoll
Bikini Atoll
Rongelap Atoll
Ujelang Atoll
Kwajalein Atoll
Ailinglapalap Atoll
Ralik Chain
Ratak Chain
Utirik Atoll
Ailuk Atoll
Wotje Atoll
Maloelap Atoll
Majuro
Arno Atoll
Mili Atoll
Jaluit Atoll
Kili I.
MARSHALL ISLANDS
Namorik Atoll
Ebon Atoll
Kosrae (Kusaie)
CAROLINE ISLANDS
FEDERATED STATES OF MICRONESIA
Nukuoro Atoll
Kapingamarangi Atoll
Miangas
Sonsorol Is.
Pulo Anna
Merir
Helen I.
Kepulauan Talaud
Tobi
Celebes Sea
Morotai
Halmahera
SULAWESI (Celebes)
Molucca Sea
Kep. Asia
Waigeo
Kep. Mapia
Biak
Teluk Cenderawasih
EQUATOR
Peleng
Kep. Sula
Buru
Ceram
MOLUCCAS
INDONESIA
Banda Sea
Buton
Kep. Kai
Kep. Aru
Lomblen
Alor
Wetar
Moa
Babar
Timor
Dili
TIMOR-LESTE (EAST TIMOR)
Kep. Tanimbar
Arafura Sea
Timor Sea
Roti
Torres Str.
NEW GUINEA
PAPUA NEW GUINEA
Port Moresby
Admiralty Islands
Manus
Mussau Is.
New Hanover
BISMARCK ARCHIPELAGO
New Ireland
Bismarck Sea
Rabaul
New Britain
Green Islands
Bougainville
Nukumanu Islands
Huon G.
Trobriand Is.
Solomon Sea
Woodlark
D'Entrecasteaux Islands
Choiseul
New Georgia
Santa Isabel
Malaita
Honiara
Guadalcanal
Rennell
San Cristobal
SOLOMON ISLANDS
Louisiade Archipelago
MELANESIA
Abaiang
Butaritari
Marakei
Tarawa (Bairiki)
Abemama
GILBERT ISLANDS
Nonouti
Tabiteuea
Beru
NAURU
Banaba (Ocean I.)
Tamana
Arorae
KIRIBATI
Howland Island
Baker Island
Kanton
Enderbury I.
McKean Island
Birnie I.
Rawaki
Nikumaroro
Orona
Manra
PHOENIX ISLANDS
Palmyra Atoll
Teraina (Washington I.)
Tabuaeran (Fanning I.)
Kiritimati (Christmas I.)
Jarvis Island
Malden Island
Starbuck Island
LINE ISLANDS
Nanumea
Niutao
Nanumanga
Nui
Vaitupu
Nukufetau
Funafuti
Nukulaelae
TUVALU
Niulakita
Atafu
Nukunono
Fakaofu
TOKELAU
(Tongareva) Penrhyn Atoll
Rakahanga Atoll
Pukapuka Atoll (Danger Is.)
Manihiki Atoll
Vostok Island
Nassau
Suwarrow Atoll
COOK ISLANDS
New Zealand
Duff Islands
Nupani
Nendo (Ndeni)
Santa Cruz Islands
Utupua
Vanikolo Is.
Anuta (Cherry I.)
Fataka (Mitre I.)
Tikopia
Torres Islands
Banks Islands
Rotuma
Fiji
France
Îles Wallis
Uvea
Îles de Horne
SAMOA
Savai'i
Apia
Upolu
AMERICAN SAMOA
Pago Pago
Tutuila
Manua Is.
Rose Atoll
SAMOA ISLANDS
Tafahi
Niuatoputapu
Niuafo'ou
Espiritu Santo
Maéwo
Malakula
Port-Vila
Éfaté
Erromango
Tanna
Futuna
Anatom
VANUATU
Vanua Levu
FIJI ISLANDS
Viti Levu
Suva
Taveuni
Lau Group
Kadavu
Vatoa
Ono-i-Lau
Vava'u Group
Ha'apai Group
TONGA ISLANDS
TONGA
Nuku'alofa
Tongatapu Group
'Eua
Ata
Niue
Palmerston Atoll
Aitutaki Atoll
Manuae
Hervey Is.
Mitiaro
Atiu
Mauke
Rarotonga
Mangaia
Motu One
Maupihaa
SOCIETY ISLANDS
Îles Maria
Rimatara
AUSTRAL (TUBUAI)
Willis Islets
CORAL SEA ISLANDS TERRITORY
Australia
Îles Chesterfield
Île Huon
Îles Bélep
Ouvéa
Lifou
Loyalty Is.
Maré
NEW CALEDONIA
Nouméa
France
Île des Pins (Kunié)
Matthew
Hunter
TROPIC OF CAPRICORN
CORAL SEA
Gulf of Carpentaria
Cape York
Cairns
Great Dividing Range
AUSTRALIA
Fraser Island
BRISBANE
Norfolk Island
Phillip Island
Raoul I. (Sunday)
Macauley I.
Curtis I.
Kermadec Islands
N.Z.
L'Esperance Rock
Lord Howe I.
Ball's Pyramid
GREAT AUSTRALIAN BIGHT
SYDNEY
ADELAIDE
Canberra
Kangaroo I.
MELBOURNE
Wilsons Promontory
Bass Strait
King I.
Furneaux Group
TASMANIA
Hobart
South East Cape
TASMAN SEA
Three Kings Islands
Cape Maria van Diemen
North Cape
Great Barrier Island
Auckland
Bay of Plenty
East Cape
NORTH ISLAND
Cape Farewell
Cook Str.
Wellington
SOUTH ISLAND
NEW ZEALAND
Chatham Island
Chatham Is.
Pitt Island
SOUTH PACIFIC
Puysegur Point
Foveaux Strait
Stewart Island/Rakiura
The Snares
Bounty Islands
Antipodes Islands
Auckland Islands
Campbell I.
Macquarie I.
INDIAN OCEAN
Longitude East 140° of Greenwich
130°
140°
150°
160°
170°
180°
170°
160°
40°
30°
20°
10°
10°
20°
30°
40°
50°
A
B
C
D
E
F
G
H
J
K
L
M
1
2
3
4
5
6
7
8
9

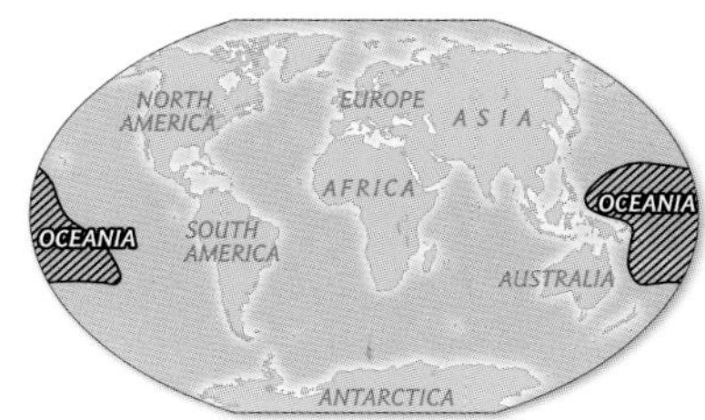

REGIONAL DATA

TOTAL NUMBER OF COUNTRIES: 11

FIRST INDEPENDENT COUNTRY:
Samoa, January 1, 1962

"YOUNGEST" COUNTRY:
Palau, October 1, 1994

LARGEST COUNTRY BY AREA:
Solomon Islands 28,370 sq km (10,954 sq mi)

SMALLEST COUNTRY BY AREA:
Nauru 21 sq km (8 sq mi)

PERCENT URBAN POPULATION:
39%

MOST POPULOUS COUNTRY:
Fiji Islands 842,000

LEAST POPULOUS COUNTRY:
Tuvalu 10,000

MOST DENSELY POPULATED COUNTRY:
Nauru 619 per sq km (1,625 per sq mi)

LEAST DENSELY POPULATED COUNTRY:
Solomon Islands 17 per sq km (43 per sq mi)

LARGEST CITY BY POPULATION:
Suva, Fiji Islands 210,000

HIGHEST GDP PER CAPITA:
Palau $6,717

LOWEST GDP PER CAPITA:
Solomon Islands $600

AVERAGE LIFE EXPECTANCY IN OCEANIA: 67 years

AVERAGE LITERACY RATE IN OCEANIA: 89%

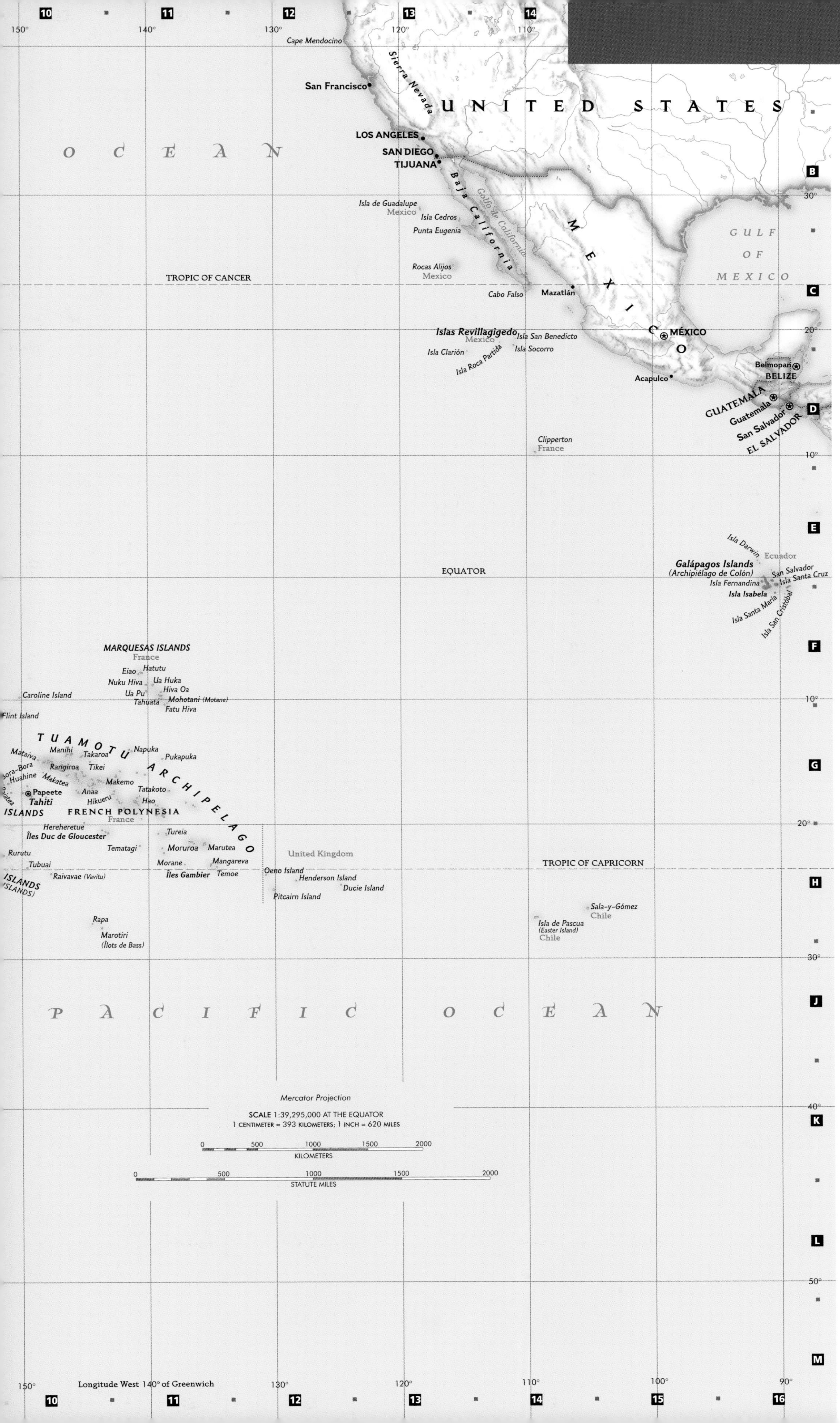

Mercator Projection
SCALE 1:39,295,000 AT THE EQUATOR
1 CENTIMETER = 393 KILOMETERS; 1 INCH = 620 MILES

Longitude West 140° of Greenwich

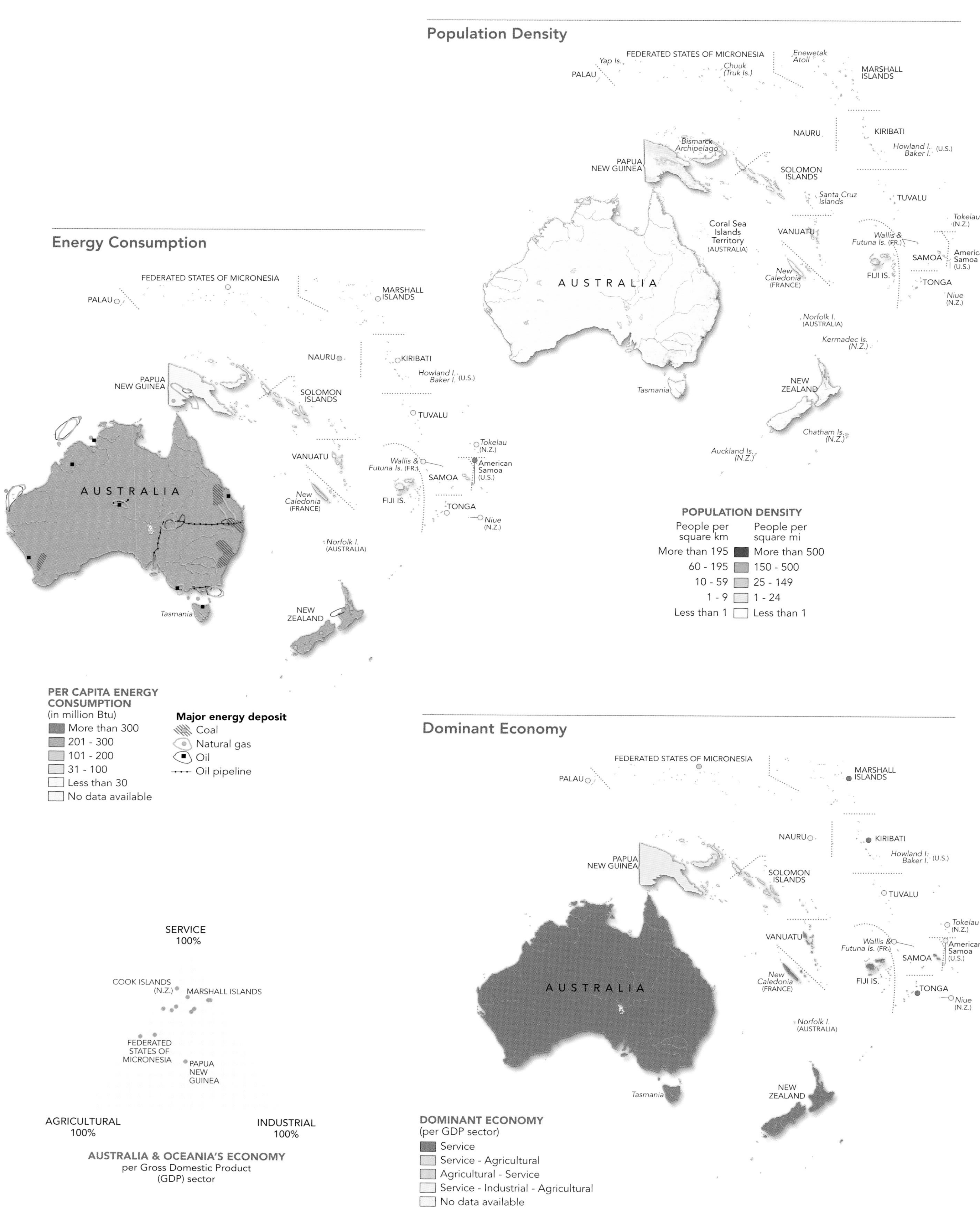

Population Density
FEDERATED STATES OF MICRONESIA
Yap Is.
PALAU
Chuuk (Truk Is.)
Enewetak Atoll
MARSHALL ISLANDS
NAURU
KIRIBATI
Bismarck Archipelago
PAPUA NEW GUINEA
Howland I. Baker I. (U.S.)
SOLOMON ISLANDS
Santa Cruz Islands
TUVALU
Coral Sea Islands Territory (AUSTRALIA)
VANUATU
Tokelau (N.Z.)
Wallis & Futuna Is. (FR.)
SAMOA
American Samoa (U.S.)
AUSTRALIA
New Caledonia (FRANCE)
FIJI IS.
TONGA
Niue (N.Z.)
Norfolk I. (AUSTRALIA)
Kermadec Is. (N.Z.)
Tasmania
NEW ZEALAND
Chatham Is. (N.Z.)
Auckland Is. (N.Z.)
POPULATION DENSITY
People per square km
People per square mi
More than 195 More than 500
60 - 195 150 - 500
10 - 59 25 - 149
1 - 9 1 - 24
Less than 1 Less than 1
Energy Consumption
FEDERATED STATES OF MICRONESIA
PALAU
MARSHALL ISLANDS
NAURU
KIRIBATI
Howland I. Baker I. (U.S.)
PAPUA NEW GUINEA
SOLOMON ISLANDS
TUVALU
VANUATU
Tokelau (N.Z.)
Wallis & Futuna Is. (FR.)
American Samoa (U.S.)
SAMOA
AUSTRALIA
New Caledonia (FRANCE)
FIJI IS.
TONGA
Niue (N.Z.)
Norfolk I. (AUSTRALIA)
Tasmania
NEW ZEALAND
PER CAPITA ENERGY CONSUMPTION (in million Btu)
More than 300
201 - 300
101 - 200
31 - 100
Less than 30
No data available
Major energy deposit
Coal
Natural gas
Oil
Oil pipeline
Dominant Economy
FEDERATED STATES OF MICRONESIA
PALAU
MARSHALL ISLANDS
NAURU
KIRIBATI
Howland I. Baker I. (U.S.)
PAPUA NEW GUINEA
SOLOMON ISLANDS
TUVALU
Tokelau (N.Z.)
VANUATU
Wallis & Futuna Is. (FR.)
American Samoa (U.S.)
SAMOA
New Caledonia (FRANCE)
FIJI IS.
AUSTRALIA
TONGA
Niue (N.Z.)
Norfolk I. (AUSTRALIA)
Tasmania
NEW ZEALAND
DOMINANT ECONOMY (per GDP sector)
Service
Service - Agricultural
Agricultural - Service
Service - Industrial - Agricultural
No data available
SERVICE 100%
COOK ISLANDS (N.Z.)
MARSHALL ISLANDS
FEDERATED STATES OF MICRONESIA
PAPUA NEW GUINEA
AGRICULTURAL 100%
INDUSTRIAL 100%
AUSTRALIA & OCEANIA'S ECONOMY
per Gross Domestic Product (GDP) sector

Climate Zones

CLIMATE
(based on modified Köppen system)

Humid equatorial climate (A)
- No dry season (Af)
- Short dry season (Am)
- Dry winter (Aw)

Dry climate (B)
- Semiarid (BS)
- Arid (BW)

h = hot
k = cold

Humid temperate climate (C)
- No dry season (Cf)
- Dry summer (Cs)

a = hot summer
b = cool summer

Highland climate (H)
- Unclassified highlands

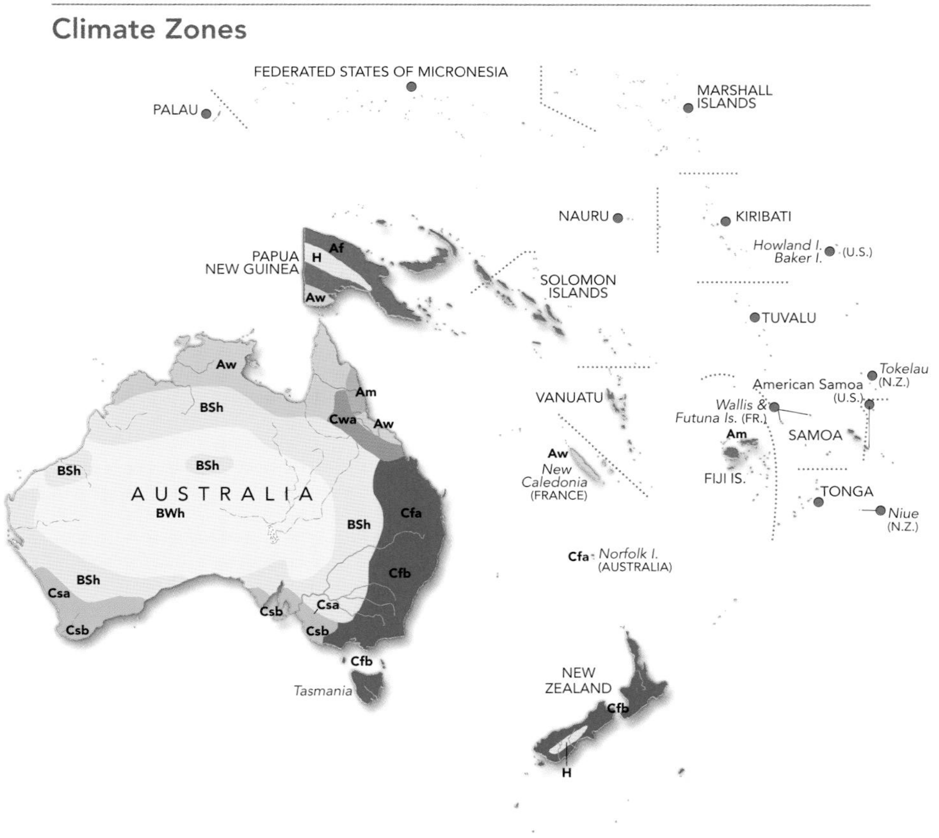

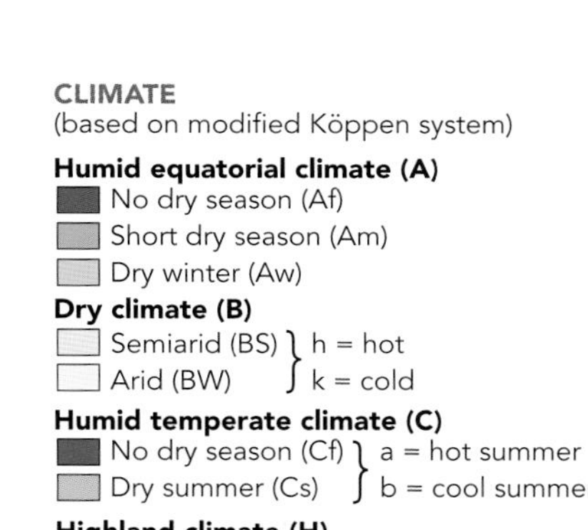

Natural Events

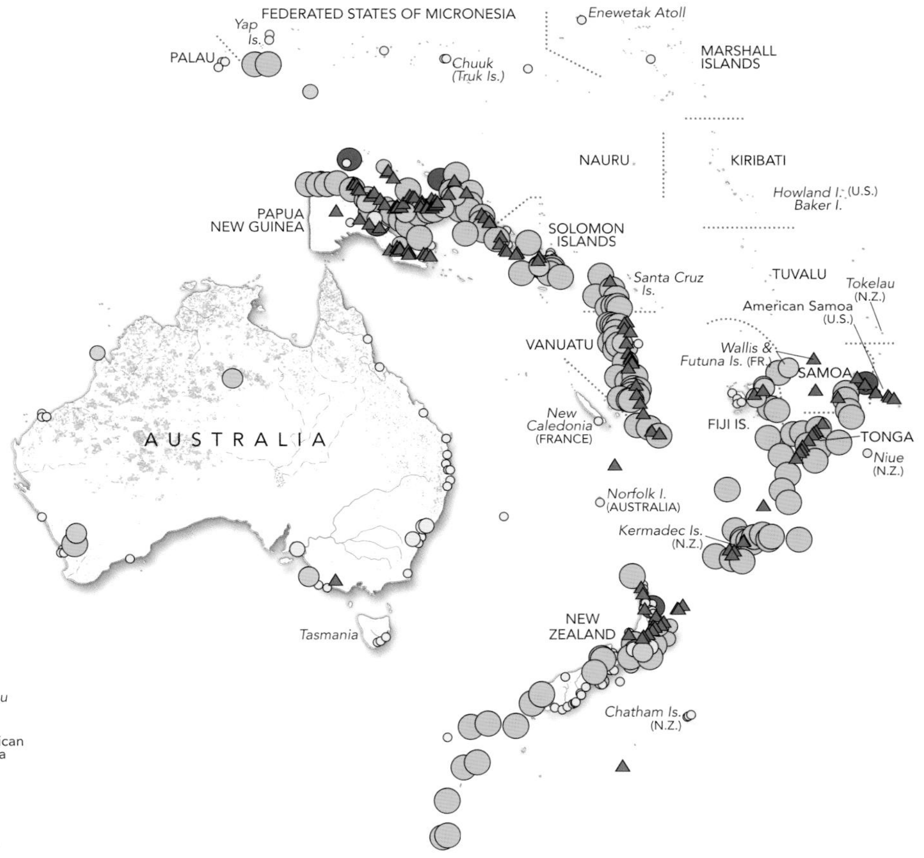

RECORDED NATURAL EVENT

Earthquake
Richter scale magnitude
- More than 7.0
- 6.0 - 7.0
- Less than 6.0

Tsunami
Run-up height
- More than 10 m / More than 32 ft
- 5 - 10 m / 16 - 32 ft
- Less than 5 m / Less than 16 ft

Fire intensity
(from gas burn-off, slash-and-burn agriculture, or natural causes)
High
Low

Volcano
- Major eruption

Water Availability

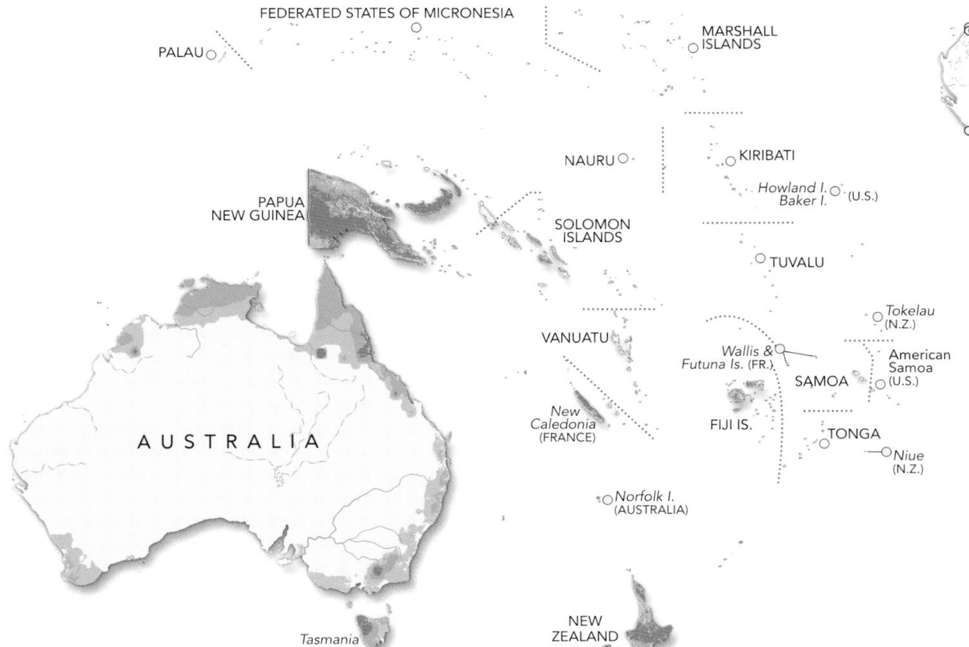

WATER AVAILABILITY
(in millimeters per-person per-year)
- More than 750
- 251 - 750
- 26 - 250
- Less than 26
- No data available

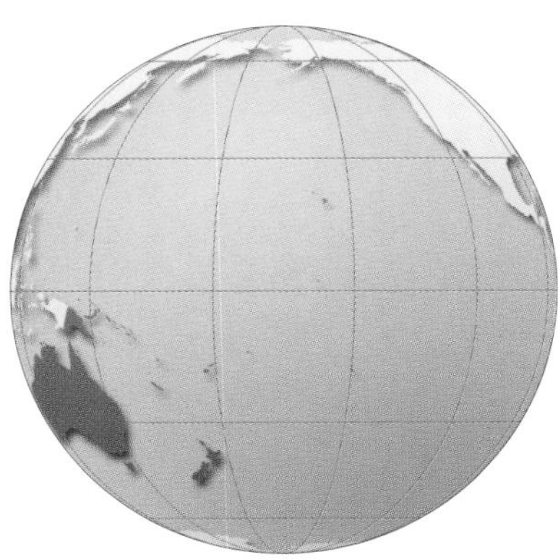

Nations

Australia

COMMONWEALTH OF AUSTRALIA

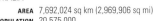

AREA 7,692,024 sq km (2,969,906 sq mi)
POPULATION 20,575,000
CAPITAL Canberra 381,000
RELIGION Roman Catholic, Anglican, other Christian
LANGUAGE English
LITERACY 99%
LIFE EXPECTANCY 81 years
GDP PER CAPITA $32,900
ECONOMY **IND:** mining, industrial and transportation equipment, food processing, chemicals **AGR:** wheat, barley, sugarcane, fruits; cattle **EXP:** coal, gold, meat, wool

Fiji Islands
REPUBLIC OF THE FIJI ISLANDS

AREA 18,376 sq km (7,095 sq mi)
POPULATION 850,000
CAPITAL Suva 219,000
RELIGION Christian, Hindu, Muslim
LANGUAGE English, Fijian, Hindustani
LITERACY 94%
LIFE EXPECTANCY 68 years
GDP PER CAPITA $6,100
ECONOMY **IND:** tourism, sugar, clothing, copra **AGR:** sugarcane, coconuts, cassava (tapioca), rice; cattle; fish **EXP:** sugar, garments, gold, timber

Kiribati
REPUBLIC OF KIRIBATI

AREA 811 sq km (313 sq mi)
POPULATION 94,000
CAPITAL Tarawa 47,000
RELIGION Roman Catholic, Protestant
LANGUAGE I-Kiribati, English
LITERACY NA
LIFE EXPECTANCY 61 years
GDP PER CAPITA $2,700
ECONOMY **IND:** fishing, handicrafts **AGR:** copra, taro, breadfruit, sweet potatoes; fish **EXP:** copra, coconuts, seaweed, fish

Marshall Islands
REPUBLIC OF THE MARSHALL ISLANDS

AREA 181 sq km (70 sq mi)
POPULATION 65,000
CAPITAL Majuro 27,000
RELIGION Protestant, Assembly of God, Roman Catholic
LANGUAGE Marshallese
LITERACY 94%
LIFE EXPECTANCY 70 years
GDP PER CAPITA $2,900
ECONOMY **IND:** copra, tuna processing, tourism, craft items from shell, wood, and pearls **AGR:** coconuts, tomatoes, melons, taro; pigs **EXP:** copra cake, coconut oil, handicrafts, fish

Micronesia
FEDERATED STATES OF MICRONESIA

AREA 702 sq km (271 sq mi)
POPULATION 108,000
CAPITAL Palikir 7,000
RELIGION Roman Catholic, Protestant
LANGUAGE English, Trukese, Pohnpeian, other indigenous languages
LITERACY 89%
LIFE EXPECTANCY 67 years
GDP PER CAPITA $2,300
ECONOMY **IND:** tourism, construction, fish processing, specialized aquaculture **AGR:** black pepper, tropical fruits, vegetables, coconuts; pigs; fish **EXP:** fish, garments, bananas, black pepper

Nauru
REPUBLIC OF NAURU

AREA 21 sq km (8 sq mi)
POPULATION 13,000
CAPITAL Yaren 5,000
RELIGION Protestant, Roman Catholic
LANGUAGE Nauruan, English
LITERACY NA
LIFE EXPECTANCY 62 years
GDP PER CAPITA $5,000
ECONOMY **IND:** phosphate mining, offshore banking, coconut products **AGR:** coconuts **EXP:** phosphates

New Zealand
NEW ZEALAND

AREA 270,534 sq km (104,454 sq mi)
POPULATION 4,140,000
CAPITAL Wellington 346,000
RELIGION Anglican, Roman Catholic, Presbyterian
LANGUAGE English, Maori
LITERACY 99%
LIFE EXPECTANCY 79 years
GDP PER CAPITA $26,000
ECONOMY **IND:** food processing, wood and paper products, textiles, machinery **AGR:** wheat, barley, potatoes, pulses; wool; fish **EXP:** dairy products, meat, wood and wood products, fish

Palau
REPUBLIC OF PALAU

AREA 489 sq km (189 sq mi)
POPULATION 20,000
CAPITAL Melekeok 200
RELIGION Roman Catholic, Protestant, Modekngei, Seventh-Day Adventist
LANGUAGE Palauan, Filipino, English, Chinese
LITERACY 92%
LIFE EXPECTANCY 71 years
GDP PER CAPITA $7,600
ECONOMY **IND:** tourism, craft items (from shell, wood, pearls), construction, garment making **AGR:** coconuts, copra, cassava (tapioca), sweet potatoes; fish **EXP:** shellfish, tuna, copra, garments

Papua New Guinea
INDEPENDENT STATE OF PAPUA NEW GUINEA

AREA 462,840 sq km (178,703 sq mi)
POPULATION 6,001,000
CAPITAL Port Moresby 289,000
RELIGION indigenous beliefs, Roman Catholic, Lutheran, other Protestant
LANGUAGE Melanesian Pidgin, indigenous languages
LITERACY 65%
LIFE EXPECTANCY 55 years
GDP PER CAPITA $2,700
ECONOMY **IND:** copra crushing, palm oil processing, plywood production, wood chip production **AGR:** coffee, cocoa, copra, palm kernels; poultry; shellfish **EXP:** oil, gold, copper ore, logs

Samoa

INDEPENDENT STATE OF SAMOA

AREA 2,831 sq km (1,093 sq mi)
POPULATION 187,000
CAPITAL Apia 41,000
RELIGION Congregationalist, Roman Catholic, Methodist, Latter-Day Saints
LANGUAGE Samoan (Polynesian), English
LITERACY 100%
LIFE EXPECTANCY 73 years
GDP PER CAPITA $2,100
ECONOMY **IND:** food processing, building materials, auto parts **AGR:** coconuts, bananas, taro, yams **EXP:** fish, coconut oil and cream, copra, taro

Solomon Islands
SOLOMON ISLANDS

AREA 28,370 sq km (10,954 sq mi)
POPULATION 485,000
CAPITAL Honiara 61,000
RELIGION Church of Melanesia, Roman Catholic, South Seas Evangelical
LANGUAGE Melanesian pidgin, 120 indigenous languages
LITERACY NA
LIFE EXPECTANCY 62 years
GDP PER CAPITA $600
ECONOMY **IND:** fish (tuna), mining, timber **AGR:** cocoa beans, coconuts, palm kernels, rice; cattle; timber; fish **EXP:** timber, fish, copra, palm oil

Tonga
KINGDOM OF TONGA

AREA 748 sq km (289 sq mi)
POPULATION 103,000
CAPITAL Nuku'alofa 25,000
RELIGION Christian
LANGUAGE Tongan, English
LITERACY 99%
LIFE EXPECTANCY 71 years
GDP PER CAPITA $2,200
ECONOMY **IND:** tourism, fishing **AGR:** squash, coconuts, copra, bananas; fish **EXP:** squash, fish, vanilla beans, root crops

Tuvalu
TUVALU

AREA 26 sq km (10 sq mi)
POPULATION 10,000
CAPITAL Funafuti 5,000
RELIGION Church of Tuvalu (Congregationalist)
LANGUAGE Tuvaluan, English, Samoan, Kiribati
LITERACY NA
LIFE EXPECTANCY 64 years
GDP PER CAPITA $1,600
ECONOMY **IND:** fishing, tourism, copra **AGR:** coconuts; fish **EXP:** copra, fish

Vanuatu

REPUBLIC OF VANUATU

AREA 12,190 sq km (4,707 sq mi)
POPULATION 228,000
CAPITAL Port-Vila 36,000
RELIGION Protestant, Roman Catholic, indigenous beliefs
LANGUAGE local languages, pidgin (Bislama)
LITERACY 74%
LIFE EXPECTANCY 67 years
GDP PER CAPITA $2,900
ECONOMY **IND:** food and fish freezing, wood processing, meat canning **AGR:** copra, coconuts, cocoa, coffee; beef; fish **EXP:** copra, beef, cocoa, timber

Dependencies

American Samoa (U.S.)

SOVEREIGN

TERRITORY OF AMERICAN SAMOA

LOCAL

AREA 199 sq km (77 sq mi)
POPULATION 67,000
CAPITAL Pago Pago 55,000
RELIGION Christian Congregationalist, Roman Catholic, Protestant
LANGUAGE Samoan
LITERACY 97%
LIFE EXPECTANCY 72 years
GDP PER CAPITA $5,800
ECONOMY **IND:** tuna canneries (largely supplied by foreign fishing vessels), handicrafts **AGR:** bananas, coconuts, vegetables, taro; dairy products **EXP:** canned tuna

Cook Islands (New Zealand)
SOVEREIGN

COOK ISLANDS

LOCAL

AREA 240 sq km (93 sq mi)
POPULATION 11,000
CAPITAL Avarua 11,000
RELIGION Cook Islands Christian Church, Roman Catholic, Seventh-Day Adventists
LANGUAGE English, Maori
LITERACY 95%
LIFE EXPECTANCY 70 years
GDP PER CAPITA $9,100
ECONOMY **IND:** fruit processing, tourism, fishing, clothing **AGR:** copra, citrus, pineapples, tomatoes; pigs **EXP:** copra, papayas, fresh and canned citrus fruit, coffee

French Polynesia (France)
SOVEREIGN

OVERSEAS LANDS OF FRENCH POLYNESIA

LOCAL

AREA 4,167 sq km (1,608 sq mi)
POPULATION 259,000
CAPITAL Papeete 130,000
RELIGION Protestant, Roman Catholic
LANGUAGE French, Polynesian
LITERACY 98%
LIFE EXPECTANCY 74 years
GDP PER CAPITA $17,500
ECONOMY **IND:** tourism, pearls, agricultural processing, handicrafts **AGR:** coconuts, vanilla, vegetables, fruits; poultry; fish **EXP:** cultured pearls, coconut products, mother-of-pearl, vanilla

Guam (U.S.)
SOVEREIGN

TERRITORY OF GUAM

LOCAL

AREA 561 sq km (217 sq mi)
POPULATION 171,000
CAPITAL Hagåtña (Agana) 144,000
RELIGION Roman Catholic
LANGUAGE English, Chamorro, Philippine languages
LITERACY 99%
LIFE EXPECTANCY 78 years
GDP PER CAPITA $15,000
ECONOMY **IND:** US military, tourism, construction, transshipment services, concrete products **AGR:** fruits, copra, vegetables; eggs **EXP:** transshipments of refined petroleum products, construction materials, fish, food and beverage products

New Caledonia
(France)

TERRITORY OF NEW CALEDONIA AND DEPENDENCIES

AREA 19,060 sq km (7,359 sq mi)
POPULATION 237,000
CAPITAL Nouméa 149,000
RELIGION Roman Catholic, Protestant
LANGUAGE French, 33 Melanesian-Polynesian dialects
LITERACY 91%
LIFE EXPECTANCY 74 years
GDP PER CAPITA $15,000
ECONOMY **IND:** nickel mining and smelting **AGR:** vegetables; beef, deer; fish **EXP:** ferronickels, nickel ore, fish

Niue
(New Zealand)

SOVEREIGN

LOCAL

NIUE

AREA 263 sq km (102 sq mi)
POPULATION 1,400
CAPITAL Alofi 1,000
RELIGION Ekalesia Niue, Latter-Day Saints, Roman Catholic
LANGUAGE Niuean, English
LITERACY 95%
LIFE EXPECTANCY 70 years
GDP PER CAPITA $5,800
ECONOMY **IND:** tourism, handicrafts, food processing **AGR:** coconuts, passion fruit, honey, limes; pigs **EXP:** canned coconut cream, copra, honey, vanilla

Norfolk Island
(Australia)

SOVEREIGN

LOCAL

TERRITORY OF NORFOLK ISLAND

AREA 35 sq km (14 sq mi)
POPULATION 2,000
CAPITAL Kingston 900
RELIGION Anglican, Roman Catholic, Uniting Church in Australia
LANGUAGE English, Norfolk
LITERACY NA
LIFE EXPECTANCY 78 years
GDP PER CAPITA NA
ECONOMY **IND:** tourism, light industry, ready mixed concrete **AGR:** pine and palm seed, cereals, vegetables, fruit; cattle **EXP:** postage stamps, pine and palm seed, avocados

Northern Mariana Islands (U.S.)

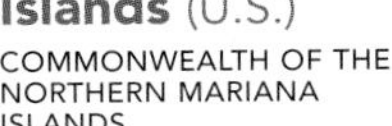

SOVEREIGN

LOCAL

COMMONWEALTH OF THE NORTHERN MARIANA ISLANDS

AREA 477 sq km (184 sq mi)
POPULATION 82,000
CAPITAL Saipan 75,000
RELIGION Christian, traditional beliefs
LANGUAGE Philippine languages, Chinese, Chamorro, English
LITERACY 97%
LIFE EXPECTANCY 75 years
GDP PER CAPITA $12,500
ECONOMY **IND:** tourism, construction, garments, handicrafts **AGR:** coconuts, fruits, vegetables; cattle **EXP:** garments

Pitcairn Islands
(U.K.)

SOVEREIGN

LOCAL

PITCAIRN, HENDERSON, DUCIE, AND OENO ISLANDS

AREA 47 sq km (18 sq mi)
POPULATION 45
CAPITAL Adamstown 45
RELIGION Seventh-Day Adventist
LANGUAGE English, Pitcairnese
LITERACY NA
LIFE EXPECTANCY NA
GDP PER CAPITA NA
ECONOMY **IND:** postage stamps, handicrafts, beekeeping, honey **AGR:** honey, fruits and vegetables; goats; fish **EXP:** fruits, vegetables, curios, stamps

Tokelau
(New Zealand)

SOVEREIGN

LOCAL

TOKELAU

AREA 12 sq km (5 sq mi)
POPULATION 1,800
CAPITAL none
RELIGION Congregational Christian Church, Roman Catholic
LANGUAGE Tokelauan (a Polynesian language), English
LITERACY NA
LIFE EXPECTANCY 69 years
GDP PER CAPITA $1,000
ECONOMY **IND:** copra production, woodworking, plaited craft goods, stamps **AGR:** coconuts, copra, breadfruit, papayas; pigs; fish **EXP:** stamps, copra, handicrafts

Wallis and Futuna Islands (France)

SOVEREIGN

LOCAL

TERRITORY OF THE WALLIS AND FUTUNA ISLANDS

AREA 161 sq km (62 sq mi)
POPULATION 15,000
CAPITAL Matā'utu 1,000
RELIGION Roman Catholic
LANGUAGE Wallisian, Futunian, French
LITERACY 50%
LIFE EXPECTANCY 74 years
GDP PER CAPITA $3,800
ECONOMY **IND:** copra, handicrafts, fishing, lumber **AGR:** breadfruit, yams, taro, bananas; pigs; fish **EXP:** copra, chemicals, construction materials

Uninhabited Dependencies

Baker Island
(U.S.)

BAKER ISLAND

AREA 1.4 sq km (0.5 sq mi)
POPULATION None

Howland Island
(U.S.)

HOWLAND ISLAND

AREA 1.6 sq km (0.6 sq mi)
POPULATION None

Jarvis Island
(U.S.)

JARVIS ISLAND

AREA 4.5 sq km (1.7 sq mi)
POPULATION None

Johnston Atoll
(U.S.)

JOHNSTON ATOLL

AREA 2.8 sq km (1.1 sq mi)
POPULATION None

Kingman Reef
(U.S.)

KINGMAN REEF

AREA 1 sq km (0.4 sq mi)
POPULATION None

Midway Island
(U.S.)

MIDWAY ISLAND

AREA 6.2 sq km (2.4 sq mi)
POPULATION None

Palmyra Atoll
(U.S.)

PALMYRA ATOLL

AREA 11.9 sq km (4.6 sq mi)
POPULATION None

Wake Island
(U.S.)

WAKE ISLAND

AREA 6.5 sq km (2.5 sq mi)
POPULATION None

Dates of National Independence

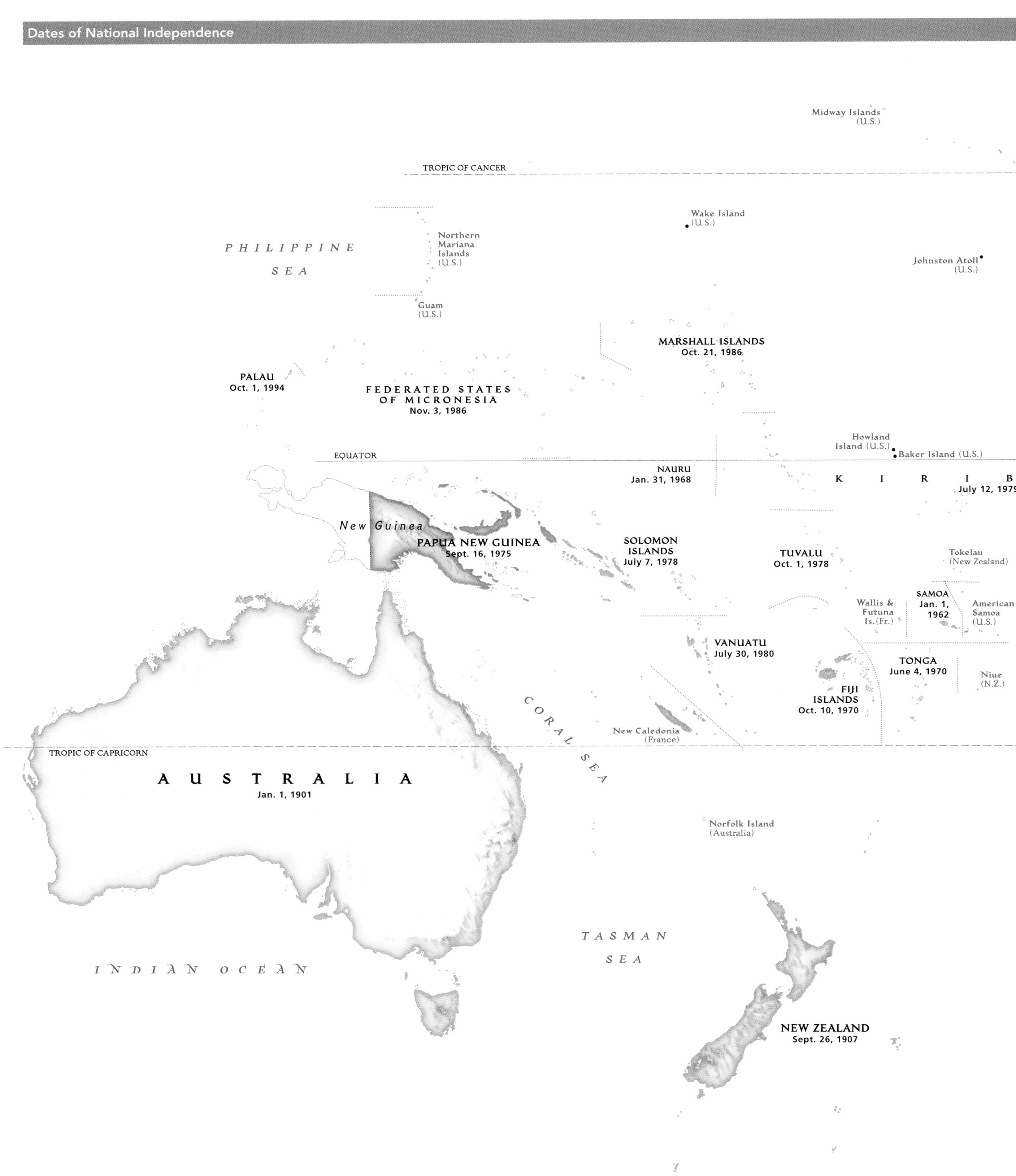

Midway Islands (U.S.)
TROPIC OF CANCER
Wake Island (U.S.)
Northern Mariana Islands (U.S.)
PHILIPPINE SEA
Johnston Atoll (U.S.)
Guam (U.S.)
MARSHALL ISLANDS
Oct. 21, 1986
PALAU
Oct. 1, 1994
FEDERATED STATES OF MICRONESIA
Nov. 3, 1986
EQUATOR
Howland Island (U.S.)
Baker Island (U.S.)
NAURU
Jan. 31, 1968
KIRIB
July 12, 1979
New Guinea
PAPUA NEW GUINEA
Sept. 16, 1975
SOLOMON ISLANDS
July 7, 1978
TUVALU
Oct. 1, 1978
Tokelau (New Zealand)
SAMOA
Jan. 1, 1962
Wallis & Futuna Is. (Fr.)
American Samoa (U.S.)
VANUATU
July 30, 1980
TONGA
June 4, 1970
Niue (N.Z.)
FIJI ISLANDS
Oct. 10, 1970
CORAL SEA
New Caledonia (France)
TROPIC OF CAPRICORN
AUSTRALIA
Jan. 1, 1901
Norfolk Island (Australia)
TASMAN SEA
INDIAN OCEAN
NEW ZEALAND
Sept. 26, 1907

OCEANIA:
Oceania is not a continent, but rather a vast island realm between Asia and the Americas. Definitions vary as to what island groups make up Oceania; however, it usually consists of islands in the central and southern Pacific Ocean. Australia, a continent, is often included as a part of Oceania. Although, the island nations of Japan, the Philippines, and Indonesia are not considered part of Oceania because of their cultural links to Asia. The island of New Guinea, the world's second largest island, is split between Asia and Oceania, with Indonesia administering the western side of the island and the independent country of Papua New Guinea occupying the eastern side. Papua New Guinea is the largest and most populous island country in Oceania, with six million inhabitants speaking some 800 different languages.

Both physical and cultural geography play a role in dividing Oceania into three regions: Melanesia ("black islands"), Micronesia ("small islands"), and Polynesia ("many islands").

European explorers used the term "Melanesia" to describe the dark-skinned inhabitants of the southwestern Pacific islands, south of the Equator, extending from Papua New Guinea to the Fiji Islands. In contrast to Melanesia's large islands, Micronesia consists of small coral and volcanic islands located north of the Equator, starting with Palau and reaching north to the Northern Mariana Islands and east to the Marshall Islands. Polynesia, east of Melanesia and Micronesia, is at the heart of the Pacific, with thousands of islands stretching from New Zealand in the south to the Hawaiian Islands in the north and to Chile's Easter Island in the east.

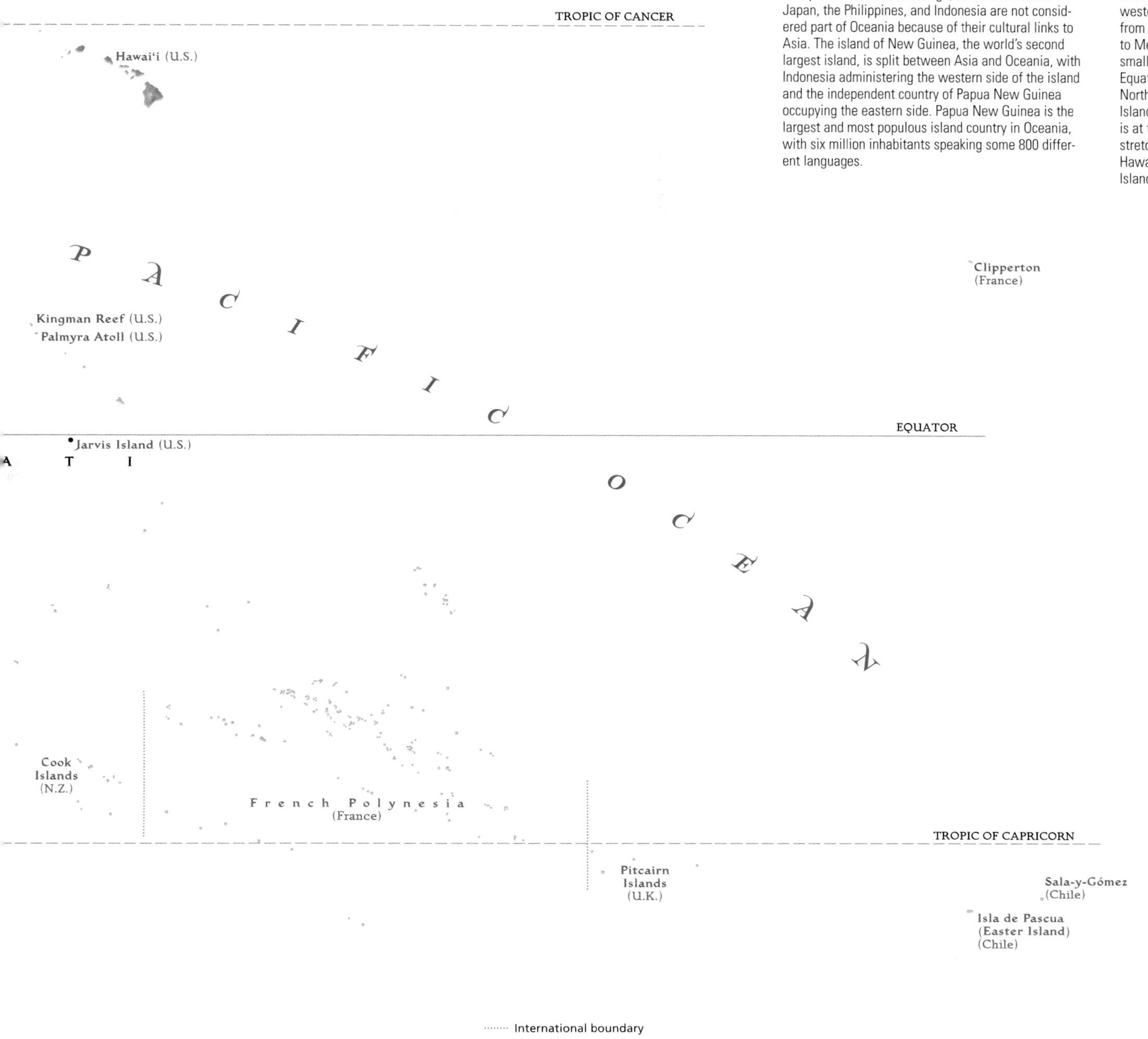

NOTE: For some countries, the date given may not represent "independence" in the strict sense—but rather some significant nationhood event: the traditional founding date; a fundamental change in the form of government; or perhaps the date of unification, secession, federation, confederation, or state succession.

Land Cover

- Water
- Snow and ice
- Barren or sparsely vegetated
- Ice shelf

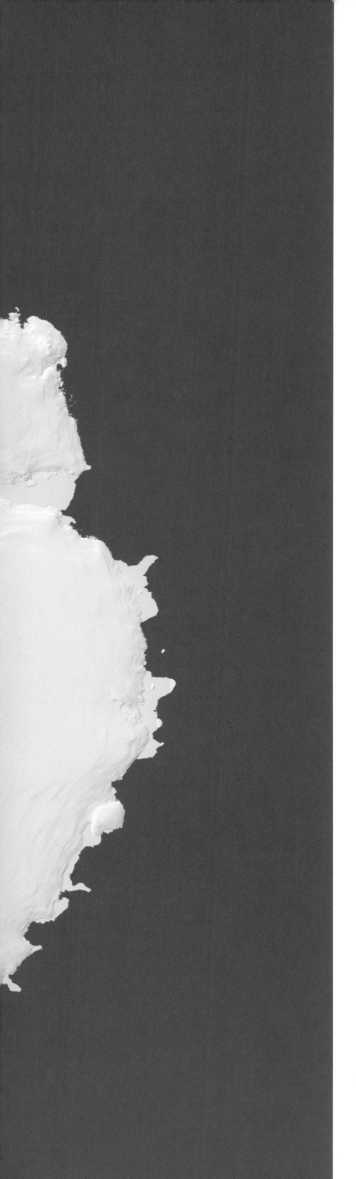

Antarctica

ANTARCTICA, AT THE SOUTHERN extreme of the world, ranks as the coldest, highest, driest, and windiest of Earth's continents. At the South Pole the continent experiences the extremes of day and night, banished from sunlight half the year, bathed in continuous light the other half. As best we know, no indigenous peoples ever lived on this continent. Unlike the Arctic, an ocean surrounded by continents, Antarctica is a continent surrounded by ocean. The only people who live there today, mostly scientists and support staff at research stations, ruefully call Antarctica "the Ice," and with good reason. All but two percent of the continent is covered year-round in ice up to 15,000 feet (4,550 meters) thick.

Not until the early 20th century did men explore the heart of the Antarctic to find an austere beauty and an unmatched hardship. "The crystal showers carpeted the pack ice and the ship," wrote Frank Hurley, "until she looked like a tinseled beauty on a field of diamonds." Wrote Apsley Cherry-Garrard in his book, *The Worst Journey in the World*, "Polar exploration is... the cleanest and most isolated way of having a bad time... [ever] devised." Despite its remoteness, Antarctica has been called the frontier of today's ecological crisis. Temperatures are rising, and a hole in the ozone (caused by atmospheric pollutants) allows harmful ultraviolet radiation to bombard land and sea.

The long tendril of the Antarctic Peninsula reaches to within 700 miles of South America, separated by the tempestuous Drake Passage where furious winds build mountainous waves. This "banana belt" of the Antarctic is not nearly so cold as the polar interior, where a great plateau of ice reaches 10,000 feet (3,050 meters) above sea level and winter temperatures can drop lower than –80°C. In the Antarctic summer (Dec. to March), light fills the region, yet heat is absent. Glaciers flow from the icy plateau, coalescing into massive ice shelves; the largest of these, the Ross Ice Shelf, is the size of France.

Antarctica's ice cap holds some 70 percent of the Earth's fresh water. Yet despite all this ice and water, the Antarctic interior averages only two inches of precipitation a year, making it the largest desert in the world. The little snow that does fall, however, almost never melts. The immensely heavy ice sheet, averaging over a mile (1.6 km) thick compresses the land surface over most of the continent to below sea level. The weight actually deforms the South Pole, creating a slightly pear-shaped Earth.

Beneath the ice exists a continent of valleys, lakes, islands, and mountains, little dreamed of until the compilation of more than 2.5 million ice-thickness measurements revealed startling topography below. Ice and sediment cores provide insight into the world's ancient climate and allow for comparison with conditions today. Studies of the Antarctic ice sheet help predict future sea levels, important news for the three billion people who live in coastal areas. If the ice sheet were to melt, global seas would rise by an estimated 200 feet (61 meters), inundating many oceanic islands and gravely altering the world's coastlines.

Antarctica's animal life has adapted extremely well to the harsh climate. Seasonal feeding and energy storage in fats exemplify this specialization. Well-known animals of the far south include seals, whales, and distinctive birds such as flightless penguins, albatrosses, terns, and petrels.

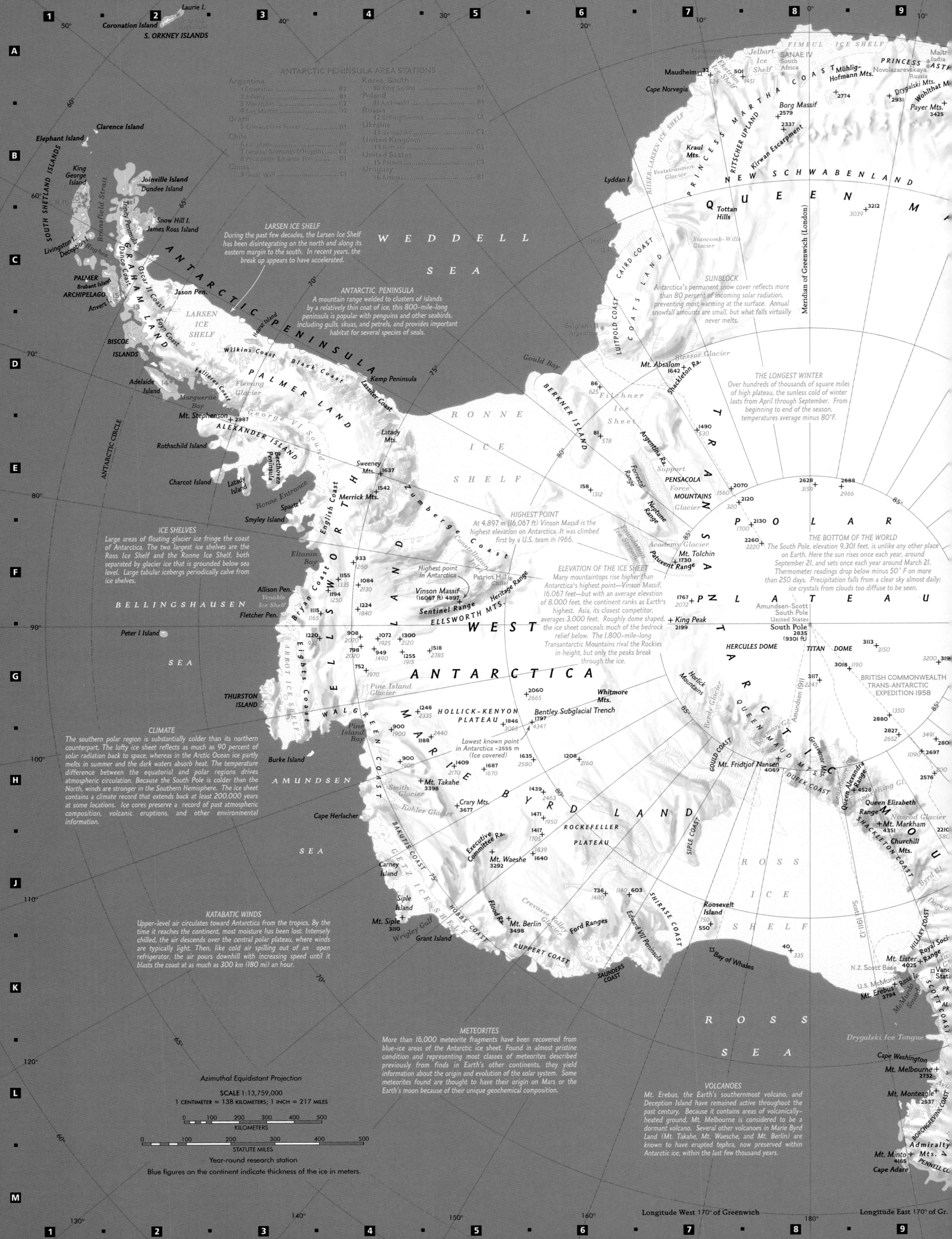
ANTARCTIC PENINSULA AREA STATIONS
Argentina
1 Esperanza B2
2 Jubany B1
3 Marambio C2
4 San Martín D2
Brazil
5 Comandante Ferraz B1
Chile
6 Escudero B1
7 General Bernardo O'Higgins C2
8 Presidente Eduardo Frei B1
China
9 Great Wall C1
Korea, South
10 King Sejong B1
Poland
11 Arctowski B1
Russia
12 Bellingshausen C1
Ukraine
13 Vernadsky C2
United Kingdom
14 Rothera D2
United States
15 Palmer C2
Uruguay
16 Artigas B1
LARSEN ICE SHELF
During the past few decades, the Larsen Ice Shelf has been disintegrating on the north and along its eastern margin to the south. In recent years, the break up appears to have accelerated.
ANTARCTIC PENINSULA
A mountain range welded to clusters of islands by a relatively thin coat of ice, this 800-mile-long peninsula is popular with penguins and other seabirds, including gulls, skuas, and petrels, and provides important habitat for several species of seals.
SUNBLOCK
Antarctica's permanent snow cover reflects more than 80 percent of incoming solar radiation, preventing most warming at the surface. Annual snowfall amounts are small, but what falls virtually never melts.
THE LONGEST WINTER
Over hundreds of thousands of square miles of high plateau, the sunless cold of winter lasts from April through September. From beginning to end of the season, temperatures average minus 80°F.
HIGHEST POINT
At 4,897 m (16,067 ft) Vinson Massif is the highest elevation on Antarctica. It was climbed first by a U.S. team in 1966.
ICE SHELVES
Large areas of floating glacier ice fringe the coast of Antarctica. The two largest ice shelves are the Ross Ice Shelf and the Ronne Ice Shelf, both separated by glacier ice that is grounded below sea level. Large tabular icebergs periodically calve from ice shelves.
ELEVATION OF THE ICE SHEET
Many mountaintops rise higher than Antarctica's highest point—Vinson Massif, 16,067 feet—but with an average elevation of 8,000 feet, the continent ranks as Earth's highest. Asia, its closest competitor, averages 3,000 feet. Roughly dome shaped, the ice sheet conceals much of the bedrock relief below. The 1,800-mile-long Transantarctic Mountains rival the Rockies in height, but only the peaks break through the ice.
THE BOTTOM OF THE WORLD
The South Pole, elevation 9,301 feet, is unlike any other place on Earth. Here the sun rises once each year, around September 21, and sets once each year around March 21. Thermometer readings drop below minus 50° F on more than 250 days. Precipitation falls from a clear sky almost daily; ice crystals from clouds too diffuse to be seen.
CLIMATE
The southern polar region is substantially colder than its northern counterpart. The lofty ice sheet reflects as much as 90 percent of solar radiation back to space, whereas in the Arctic Ocean ice partly melts in summer and the dark waters absorb heat. The temperature difference between the equatorial and polar regions drives atmospheric circulation. Because the South Pole is colder than the North, winds are stronger in the Southern Hemisphere. The ice sheet contains a climate record that extends back at least 200,000 years at some locations. Ice cores preserve a record of past atmospheric composition, volcanic eruptions, and other environmental information.
KATABATIC WINDS
Upper-level air circulates toward Antarctica from the tropics. By the time it reaches the continent, most moisture has been lost. Intensely chilled, the air descends over the central polar plateau, where winds are typically light. Then, like cold air spilling out of an open refrigerator, the air pours downhill with increasing speed until it blasts the coast at as much as 300 km (180 mi) an hour.
METEORITES
More than 16,000 meteorite fragments have been recovered from blue-ice areas of the Antarctic ice sheet. Found in almost pristine condition and representing most classes of meteorites described previously from finds in Earth's other continents, they yield information about the origin and evolution of the solar system. Some meteorites found are thought to have their origin on Mars or the Earth's moon because of their unique geochemical composition.
VOLCANOES
Mt. Erebus, the Earth's southernmost volcano, and Deception Island have remained active throughout the past century. Because it contains areas of volcanically-heated ground, Mt. Melbourne is considered to be a dormant volcano. Several other volcanoes in Marie Byrd Land (Mt. Takahe, Mt. Waesche, and Mt. Berlin) are known to have erupted tephra, now preserved within Antarctic ice, within the last few thousand years.
Azimuthal Equidistant Projection
SCALE 1:13,759,000
1 CENTIMETER = 138 KILOMETERS; 1 INCH = 217 MILES
KILOMETERS
STATUTE MILES
Year-round research station
Blue figures on the continent indicate thickness of the ice in meters.
WEDDELL SEA
BELLINGSHAUSEN SEA
AMUNDSEN SEA
ROSS SEA
ANTARCTIC PENINSULA
WEST ANTARCTICA
MARIE BYRD LAND
ELLSWORTH LAND
PALMER LAND
GRAHAM LAND
QUEEN MAUD LAND
NEW SCHWABENLAND
POLAR PLATEAU
TRANSANTARCTIC MOUNTAINS
RONNE ICE SHELF
ROSS ICE SHELF
LARSEN ICE SHELF
FIMBUL ICE SHELF
S. ORKNEY ISLANDS
SOUTH SHETLAND ISLANDS
Vinson Massif (16067 ft) 4897
Amundsen-Scott South Pole United States
South Pole 2835 (9301 ft)
BRITISH COMMONWEALTH TRANS-ANTARCTIC EXPEDITION 1958
Bentley Subglacial Trench
Lowest known point in Antarctica -2555 m (Ice covered)
HOLLICK-KENYON PLATEAU
ROCKEFELLER PLATEAU
HERCULES DOME
TITAN DOME
Mt. Erebus 3794
Mt. Takahe 3398
Mt. Waeshe 3292
Mt. Berlin 3498
Mt. Siple 3110
Mt. Fridtjof Nansen 4069
Mt. Markham 4351
Mt. Melbourne 2732
Mt. Minto 4165
Cape Adare
Longitude West 170° of Greenwich
Longitude East 170° of Gr.

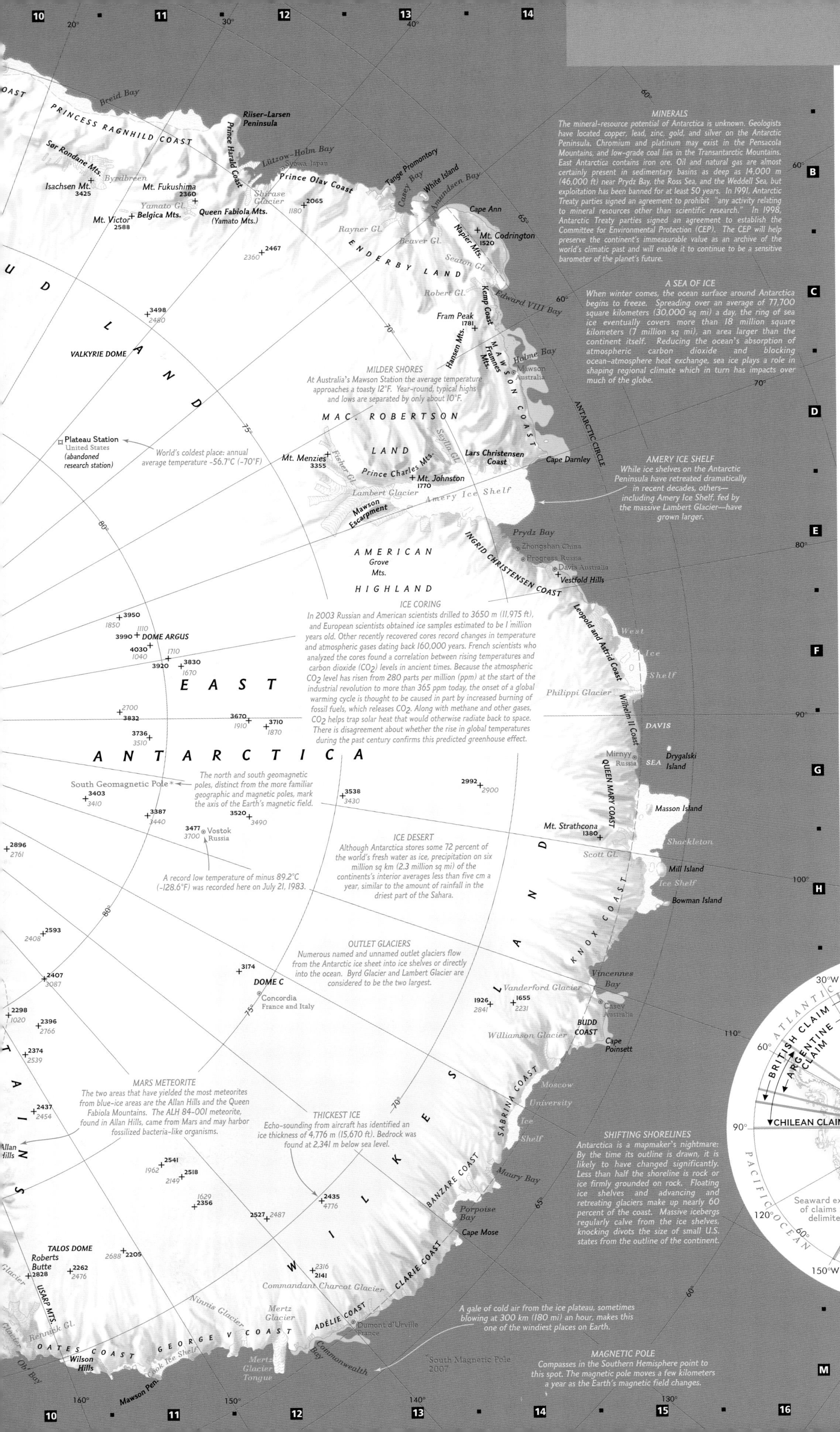

MINERALS
The mineral-resource potential of Antarctica is unknown. Geologists have located copper, lead, zinc, gold, and silver on the Antarctic Peninsula. Chromium and platinum may exist in the Pensacola Mountains, and low-grade coal lies in the Transantarctic Mountains. East Antarctica contains iron ore. Oil and natural gas are almost certainly present in sedimentary basins as deep as 14,000 m (46,000 ft) near Prydz Bay, the Ross Sea, and the Weddell Sea, but exploitation has been banned for at least 50 years. In 1991, Antarctic Treaty parties signed an agreement to prohibit "any activity relating to mineral resources other than scientific research." In 1998, Antarctic Treaty parties signed an agreement to establish the Committee for Environmental Protection (CEP). The CEP will help preserve the continent's immeasurable value as an archive of the world's climatic past and will enable it to continue to be a sensitive barometer of the planet's future.
A SEA OF ICE
When winter comes, the ocean surface around Antarctica begins to freeze. Spreading over an average of 77,700 square kilometers (30,000 sq mi) a day, the ring of sea ice eventually covers more than 18 million square kilometers (7 million sq mi), an area larger than the continent itself. Reducing the ocean's absorption of atmospheric carbon dioxide and blocking ocean-atmosphere heat exchange, sea ice plays a role in shaping regional climate which in turn has impacts over much of the globe.
MILDER SHORES
At Australia's Mawson Station the average temperature approaches a toasty 12°F. Year-round, typical highs and lows are separated by only about 10°F.
AMERY ICE SHELF
While ice shelves on the Antarctic Peninsula have retreated dramatically in recent decades, others—including Amery Ice Shelf, fed by the massive Lambert Glacier—have grown larger.
Plateau Station
United States
(abandoned research station)
World's coldest place: annual average temperature -56.7°C (-70°F)
ICE CORING
In 2003 Russian and American scientists drilled to 3650 m (11,975 ft), and European scientists obtained ice samples estimated to be 1 million years old. Other recently recovered cores record changes in temperature and atmospheric gases dating back 160,000 years. French scientists who analyzed the cores found a correlation between rising temperatures and carbon dioxide (CO2) levels in ancient times. Because the atmospheric CO2 level has risen from 280 parts per million (ppm) at the start of the industrial revolution to more than 365 ppm today, the onset of a global warming cycle is thought to be caused in part by increased burning of fossil fuels, which releases CO2. Along with methane and other gases, CO2 helps trap solar heat that would otherwise radiate back to space. There is disagreement about whether the rise in global temperatures during the past century confirms this predicted greenhouse effect.
South Geomagnetic Pole
The north and south geomagnetic poles, distinct from the more familiar geographic and magnetic poles, mark the axis of the Earth's magnetic field.
Vostok
Russia
A record low temperature of minus 89.2°C (-128.6°F) was recorded here on July 21, 1983.
ICE DESERT
Although Antarctica stores some 72 percent of the world's fresh water as ice, precipitation on six million sq km (2.3 million sq mi) of the continent's interior averages less than five cm a year, similar to the amount of rainfall in the driest part of the Sahara.
OUTLET GLACIERS
Numerous named and unnamed outlet glaciers flow from the Antarctic ice sheet into ice shelves or directly into the ocean. Byrd Glacier and Lambert Glacier are considered to be the two largest.
MARS METEORITE
The two areas that have yielded the most meteorites from blue-ice areas are the Allan Hills and the Queen Fabiola Mountains. The ALH 84-001 meteorite, found in Allan Hills, came from Mars and may harbor fossilized bacteria-like organisms.
THICKEST ICE
Echo-sounding from aircraft has identified an ice thickness of 4,776 m (15,670 ft). Bedrock was found at 2,341 m below sea level.
SHIFTING SHORELINES
Antarctica is a mapmaker's nightmare: By the time its outline is drawn, it is likely to have changed significantly. Less than half the shoreline is rock or ice firmly grounded on rock. Floating ice shelves and advancing and retreating glaciers make up nearly 60 percent of the coast. Massive icebergs regularly calve from the ice shelves, knocking divots the size of small U.S. states from the outline of the continent.
A gale of cold air from the ice plateau, sometimes blowing at 300 km (180 mi) an hour, makes this one of the windiest places on Earth.
MAGNETIC POLE
Compasses in the Southern Hemisphere point to this spot. The magnetic pole moves a few kilometers a year as the Earth's magnetic field changes.
South Magnetic Pole 2007
Princess Ragnhild Coast
Breid Bay
Riiser-Larsen Peninsula
Prince Harald Coast
Lützow-Holm Bay
Syowa Japan
Prince Olav Coast
Tange Promontory
Casey Bay
White Island
Amundsen Bay
Sør Rondane Mts.
Byrdbreen
Isachsen Mt. 3425
Mt. Fukushima 2360
Yamato Gl.
Belgica Mts.
Mt. Victor 2588
Queen Fabiola Mts. (Yamato Mts.)
Shirase Glacier
Cape Ann
Mt. Codrington 1520
Napier Mts.
Rayner Gl.
Beaver Gl.
Seaton Gl.
Enderby Land
Robert Gl.
Kemp Coast
Edward VIII Bay
Fram Peak 1781
Hansen Mts.
Framnes Mts.
Mawson Coast
Holme Bay
Mawson Australia
Valkyrie Dome
Mac. Robertson Land
Antarctic Circle
Mt. Menzies 3355
Fisher Gl.
Scylla Gl.
Prince Charles Mts.
Mt. Johnston 1770
Lars Christensen Coast
Cape Darnley
Lambert Glacier
Amery Ice Shelf
Mawson Escarpment
Prydz Bay
Zhongshan China
Progress Russia
Davis Australia
Vestfold Hills
Ingrid Christensen Coast
American Highland
Grove Mts.
Dome Argus
Leopold and Astrid Coast
West Ice Shelf
Philippi Glacier
Wilhelm II Coast
Davis Sea
Mirnyy Russia
Drygalski Island
Queen Mary Coast
Masson Island
Mt. Strathcona 1380
Shackleton Ice Shelf
Scott Gl.
Mill Island
Bowman Island
Knox Coast
East Antarctica
Dome C
Concordia France and Italy
Vincennes Bay
Vanderford Glacier
Casey Australia
Budd Coast
Cape Poinsett
Williamson Glacier
Wilkes Land
Sabrina Coast
Moscow University Ice Shelf
Maury Bay
Banzare Coast
Porpoise Bay
Cape Mose
Talos Dome
Roberts Butte
USARP Mts.
Clarie Coast
Commandant Charcot Glacier
Ninnis Glacier
Mertz Glacier
Mertz Glacier Tongue
Adélie Coast
Dumont d'Urville France
Commonwealth Bay
George V Coast
Oates Coast
Cook Ice Shelf
Wilson Hills
Rennick Gl.
Mawson Pen.
Allan Hills

CONTINENTAL DATA

AREA:
13,209,000 sq km
(5,100,000 sq mi)

GREATEST EXTENT:
5,500 km (3,400 mi), from Trinity Peninsula to Cape Poinsett

HIGHEST POINT:
Vinson Massif 4,897 m (16,067 ft)

LOWEST POINT:
Bentley Subglacial Trench
-2,555 m (-8,383 ft), ice covered

LOWEST RECORDED TEMPERATURE:
Vostok -89.2°C (-128.6°F),
July 21, 1983

HIGHEST RECORDED TEMPERATURE:
Vanda Station, Scott Coast
15°C (59°F), January 5, 1974

EARTH'S EXTREMES LOCATED IN ANTARCTICA:

- **Coldest Place on Earth:** Plateau Station, annual average temperature -56.7°C (-70°F)
- **Coldest Recorded Temperature on Earth:** Vostok -89.2°C (-128.6°F), July 21, 1983

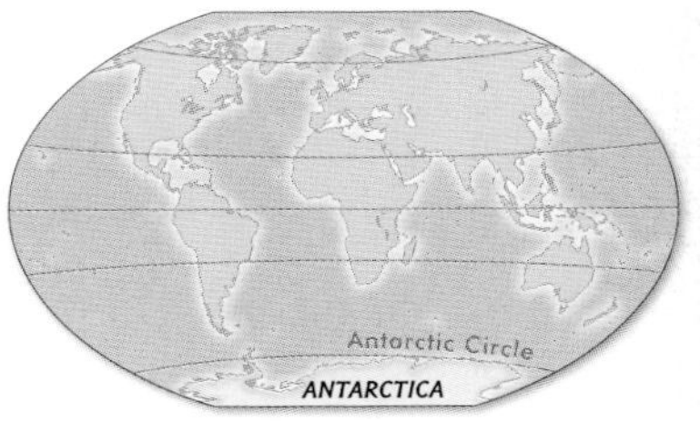

Antarctic Circle
ANTARCTICA

TERRITORIAL CLAIMS

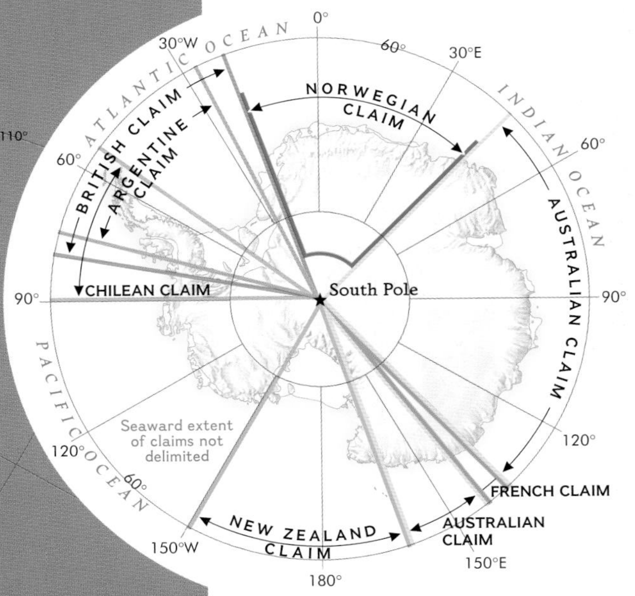

Atlantic Ocean
Indian Ocean
Pacific Ocean
Norwegian Claim
British Claim
Argentine Claim
Chilean Claim
South Pole
Australian Claim
French Claim
New Zealand Claim
Seaward extent of claims not delimited

The Antarctic Treaty of 1959 preserves Antarctica for scientific research by all nations. The treaty made static all claims and prohibits any new claims.

Appendix

Airline Distances in Kilometers

	BEIJING	CAIRO	CAPE TOWN	CARACAS	HONG KONG	HONOLULU	LONDON	MELBOURNE	MÉXICO	MONTRÉAL	MOSCOW	NEW DELHI	NEW YORK	PARIS	RIO DE JANEIRO	ROME	SAN FRANCISCO	SINGAPORE	STOCKHOLM	TOKYO
BEIJING		7557	12947	14411	1972	8171	8160	9093	12478	10490	5809	3788	11012	8236	17325	8144	9524	4465	6725	2104
CAIRO	7557		7208	10209	8158	14239	3513	13966	12392	8733	2899	4436	9042	3215	9882	2135	12015	8270	3404	9587
CAPE TOWN	12947	7208		10232	11867	18562	9635	10338	13703	12744	10101	9284	12551	9307	6075	8417	16487	9671	10334	14737
CARACAS	14411	10209	10232		16380	9694	7500	15624	3598	3932	9940	14221	3419	7621	4508	8363	6286	18361	8724	14179
HONG KONG	1972	8158	11867	16380		8945	9646	7392	14155	12462	7158	3770	12984	9650	17710	9300	11121	2575	8243	2893
HONOLULU	8171	14239	18562	9694	8945		11653	8862	6098	7915	11342	11930	7996	11988	13343	12936	3857	10824	11059	6208
LONDON	8160	3513	9635	7500	9646	11653		16902	8947	5240	2506	6724	5586	341	9254	1434	8640	10860	1436	9585
MELBOURNE	9093	13966	10338	15624	7392	8862	16902		13557	16730	14418	10192	16671	16793	13227	15987	12644	6050	15593	8159
MÉXICO	12478	12392	13703	3598	14155	6098	8947	13557		3728	10740	14679	3362	9213	7669	10260	3038	16623	9603	11319
MONTRÉAL	10490	8733	12744	3932	12462	7915	5240	16730	3728		7077	11286	533	5522	8175	6601	4092	14816	5900	10409
MOSCOW	5809	2899	10101	9940	7158	11342	2506	14418	10740	7077		4349	7530	2492	11529	2378	9469	8426	1231	7502
NEW DELHI	3788	4436	9284	14221	3770	11930	6724	10192	14679	11286	4349		11779	6601	14080	5929	12380	4142	5579	5857
NEW YORK	11012	9042	12551	3419	12984	7996	5586	16671	3362	533	7530	11779		5851	7729	6907	4140	15349	6336	10870
PARIS	8236	3215	9307	7621	9650	11988	341	16793	9213	5522	2492	6601	5851		9146	1108	8975	10743	1546	9738
RIO DE JANEIRO	17325	9882	6075	4508	17710	13343	9254	13227	7669	8175	11529	14080	7729	9146		9181	10647	15740	10682	18557
ROME	8144	2135	8417	8363	9300	12936	1434	15987	10260	6601	2378	5929	6907	1108	9181		10071	10030	1977	9881
SAN FRANCISCO	9524	12015	16487	6286	11121	3857	8640	12644	3038	4092	9469	12380	4140	8975	10647	10071		13598	8644	8284
SINGAPORE	4465	8270	9671	18361	2575	10824	10860	6050	16623	14816	8426	4142	15349	10743	15740	10030	13598		9646	5317
STOCKHOLM	6725	3404	10334	8724	8243	11059	1436	15593	9603	5900	1231	5579	6336	1546	10682	1977	8644	9646		8193
TOKYO	2104	9587	14737	14179	2893	6208	9585	8159	11319	10409	7502	5857	10870	9738	18557	9881	8284	5317	8193	

Abbreviations

Adm. *Administrative*
Af. *Africa*
Afghan. *Afghanistan*
Agr. *Agriculture*
Ala. *Alabama*
Alas. *Alaska*
Alban. *Albania*
Alg. *Algeria*
Alta. *Alberta*
Arch. *Archipelago, Archipiélago*
Arg. *Argentina*
Ariz. *Arizona*
Ark. *Arkansas*
Arm. *Armenia*
Atl. Oc. *Atlantic Ocean*
Aust. *Austria*
Austral. *Australia*
Azerb. *Azerbaijan*
B. *Baai, Baía, Baie, Bahía, Bay, Buḩayrat*
B.C. *British Columbia*
Belg. *Belgium*
Bol. *Bolivia*
Bosn. & Herzg. *Bosnia and Herzegovina*
Braz. *Brazil*
Bulg. *Bulgaria*
C. *Cabo, Cap, Cape, Capo*
Calif. *California*
Can. *Canada*
Cen. Af. Rep. *Central African Republic*
C.H. *Court House*
Chan. *Channel*
Chap. *Chapada*
CIS *Commonwealth of Independent States*
Cmte. *Comandante*
Cnel. *Coronel*
Co.-s. *Cerro-s*
Col. *Colombia*
Colo. *Colorado*
Conn. *Connecticut*
Cord. *Cordillera*
C.R. *Costa Rica*
Cr. *Creek, Crique*
C.S.I. Terr. *Coral Sea Islands Territory*
D.C. *District of Columbia*
Del. *Delaware*
Den. *Denmark*
Dom. Rep. *Dominican Republic*
D.R.C. *Democratic Republic of the Congo*
E. *East-ern*
Ecua. *Ecuador*
El Salv. *El Salvador*
Eng. *England*
Ens. *Ensenada*
Eq. *Equatorial*
Est. *Estonia*
Eth. *Ethiopia*
Exp. *Exports*
Falk. Is. *Falkland Islands*
Fd. *Fiord, Fiordo, Fjord*
Fin. *Finland*
Fk. *Fork*
Fla. *Florida*
Fn. *Fortín*
Fr. *France, French*
F.S.M. *Federated States of Micronesia*
ft *feet*
Ft. *Fort*
G. *Golfe, Golfo, Gulf*
Ga. *Georgia*
Ger. *Germany*
Gl. *Glacier*
Gr. *Greece*
Gral. *General*
Hbr. *Harbor, Harbour*
Hist. *Historic, -al*
Hond. *Honduras*
Hts. *Heights*
Hung. *Hungary*
Hwy. *Highway*
I.-s. *Île-s, Ilha-s, Isla-s, Island-s, Isle, Isol-a, -e*
Ice. *Iceland*
I.H.S. *International Historic Site*
Ill. *Illinois*
Ind. *Indiana*
Ind. *Industry*
Ind. Oc. *Indian Ocean*
Intl. *International*
Ire. *Ireland*
It. *Italy*
Jap. *Japan*
Jct. *Jonction, Junction*
Kans. *Kansas*
Kaz. *Kazakhstan*
Kep. *Kepulauan*
Ky. *Kentucky*
Kyrg. *Kyrgyzstan*
L. *Lac, Lago, Lake, Límni Loch, Lough*
La. *Louisiana*
Lab. *Labrador*
Lag. *Laguna*
Latv. *Latvia*
Leb. *Lebanon*
Lib. *Libya*
Liech. *Liechtenstein*
Lith. *Lithuania*
Lux. *Luxembourg*
m *meters*
Maced. *Macedonia*
Madag. *Madagascar*
Maurit. *Mauritius*
Mass. *Massachusetts*
Md. *Maryland*
Me. *Maine*
Medit. Sea *Mediterranean Sea*
Mex. *Mexico*
Mgne. *Montagne*
Mich. *Michigan*
Minn. *Minnesota*
Miss. *Mississippi*
Mo. *Missouri*
Mon. *Monument*
Mont. *Montana*
Mor. *Morocco*
Mt.-s. *Mont-s, Mount-ain-s*
N. *North-ern*
NA *Not Available*
Nat. *National*
Nat. Mem. *National Memorial*
Nat. Mon. *National Monument*
N.B. *National Battlefield*
N.B. *New Brunswick*
N.C. *North Carolina*
N. Dak. *North Dakota*
N.E. *Northeast*
Nebr. *Nebraska*
Neth. *Netherlands*
Nev. *Nevada*
Nfld. *Newfoundland*
N.H. *New Hampshire*
Nicar. *Nicaragua*
Nig. *Nigeria*
N. Ire. *Northern Ireland*
N.J. *New Jersey*
N. Mex. *New Mexico*
N.M.P. *National Military Park*
N.M.S. *National Marine Sanctuary*
Nor. *Norway*
N.P. *National Park*
N.S. *Nova Scotia*
N.S.W. *New South Wales*
N.V.M. *National Volcanic Monument*
N.W.T. *Northwest Territories*
N.Y. *New York*
N.Z. *New Zealand*
O. *Ostrov, Oued*
Oc. *Ocean*
Okla. *Oklahoma*
Ont. *Ontario*
Oreg. *Oregon*
Oz. *Ozero*
Pa. *Pennsylvania*
Pac. Oc. *Pacific Ocean*
Pak. *Pakistan*
Pan. *Panama*
Para. *Paraguay*
Pass. *Passage*
Peg. *Pegunungan*
P.E.I. *Prince Edward Island*
Pen. *Peninsula, Péninsule*
Pk. *Peak*
P.N.G. *Papua New Guinea*
Pol. *Poland*
Pol. *Poluostrov*
Port. *Portugal, Portuguese*
P.R. *Puerto Rico*
Prov. *Province, Provincial*
Pt.-e. *Point-e*
Pta. *Ponta, Punta*
Qnsld. *Queensland*
Que. *Quebec*
R. *Río, River, Rivière*
Ra.-s. *Range-s*
Rec. *Recreation*
Rep. *Republic*
Res. *Reservoir, Reserve, Reservatório*
R.I. *Rhode Island*
Rom. *Romania*
Russ. *Russia*
S. *South-ern*
Sa.-s. *Serra, Sierra-s*
S. Af. *South Africa*
Sask. *Saskatchewan*
S.C. *South Carolina*
Scot. *Scotland*
Sd. *Sound*
S. Dak. *South Dakota*
Sev. *Severn-yy, -aya, -oye*
Sk. *Shankou*
Slov. *Slovenia*
Sp. *Spain, Spanish*
Spr.-s. *Spring-s*
Sta. *Santa*
St.-e. *Saint-e, Sankt, Sint*
Str.-s. *Straat, Strait-s*
Switz. *Switzerland*
Syr. *Syria*
Taj. *Tajikistan*
Tas. *Tasmania*
Tenn. *Tennessee*
Terr. *Territory*
Tex. *Texas*
Tg. *Tanjung*
Thai. *Thailand*
Trin. *Trinidad*
Tun. *Tunisia*
Turk. *Turkey*
Turkm. *Turkmenistan*
U.A.E. *United Arab Emirates*
U.K. *United Kingdom*
Ukr. *Ukraine*
U.N. *United Nations*
Uru. *Uruguay*
U.S. *United States*
Uzb. *Uzbekistan*
Va. *Virginia*
Vdkhr. *Vodokhranilishche*
Vdskh. *Vodoskhovyshche*
Venez. *Venezuela*
V.I. *Virgin Islands*
Vic. *Victoria*
Viet. *Vietnam*
Vol. *Volcán, Volcano*
Vt. *Vermont*
W. *Wadi, Wādī, Webi*
W. *West-ern*
Wash. *Washington*
Wis. *Wisconsin*
W. Va. *West Virginia*
Wyo. *Wyoming*
Yug. *Yugoslavia*
Zakh. *Zakhod-ni, -nyaya, -nye*
Zimb. *Zimbabwe*

QUICK REFERENCE CHART FOR METRIC TO ENGLISH CONVERSION

1 METER	1 METER = 100 CENTIMETERS
1 FOOT	1 FOOT = 12 INCHES
1 KILOMETER	1 KILOMETER = 1,000 METERS
1 MILE	1 MILE = 5,280 FEET

METERS	1	10	20	50	100	200	500	1,000	2,000	5,000	10,000
FEET	3.28	32.8	65.6	164	328	656	1,640	3,280	6,560	16,400	32,800

KILOMETERS	1	10	20	50	100	200	500	1,000	2,000	5,000	10,000
MILES	0.62	6.2	12.4	31	62	124	310	620	1,240	3,100	6,200

CONVERSION FROM METRIC MEASURES

SYMBOL	WHEN YOU KNOW	MULTIPLY BY	TO FIND	SYMBOL
		LENGTH		
cm	centimeters	0.39	inches	in
m	meters	3.28	feet	ft
m	meters	1.09	yards	yd
km	kilometers	0.62	miles	mi
		AREA		
cm^2	square centimeters	0.16	square inches	in^2
m^2	square meters	10.76	square feet	ft^2
m^2	square meters	1.20	square yards	yd^2
km^2	square kilometers	0.39	square miles	mi^2
ha	hectares	2.47	acres	—
		MASS		
g	grams	0.04	ounces	oz
kg	kilograms	2.20	pounds	lb
t	metric tons	1.10	short tons	—
		VOLUME		
mL	milliliters	0.06	cubic inches	in^3
mL	milliliters	0.03	liquid ounces	liq oz
L	liters	2.11	pints	pt
L	liters	1.06	quarts	qt
L	liters	0.26	gallons	gal
m^3	cubic meters	35.31	cubic feet	ft^3
m^3	cubic meters	1.31	cubic yards	yd^3
		TEMPERATURE		
°C	degrees Celsius (centigrade)	9/5 then add 32	degrees Fahrenheit	°F

CONVERSION TO METRIC MEASURES

SYMBOL	WHEN YOU KNOW	MULTIPLY BY	TO FIND	SYMBOL
		LENGTH		
in	inches	2.54	centimeters	cm
ft	feet	0.30	meters	m
yd	yards	0.91	meters	m
mi	miles	1.61	kilometers	km
		AREA		
in^2	square inches	6.45	square centimeters	cm^2
ft^2	square feet	0.09	square meters	m^2
yd^2	square yards	0.84	square meters	m^2
mi^2	square miles	2.59	square kilometers	km^2
—	acres	0.40	hectares	ha
		MASS		
oz	ounces	28.35	grams	g
lb	pounds	0.45	kilograms	kg
—	short tons	0.91	metric tons	t
		VOLUME		
in^3	cubic inches	16.39	milliliters	mL
liq oz	liquid ounces	29.57	milliliters	mL
pt	pints	0.47	liters	L
qt	quarts	0.95	liters	L
gal	gallons	3.79	liters	L
ft^3	cubic feet	0.03	cubic meters	m^3
yd^3	cubic yards	0.76	cubic meters	m^3
		TEMPERATURE		
°F	degrees Fahrenheit	5/9 after subtracting 32	degrees Celsius (centigrade)	°C

World Temperature and Rainfall

Average daily high and low temperatures and monthly rainfall for selected world locations:

	JAN.			FEB.			MARCH			APRIL			MAY			JUNE			JULY			AUG.			SEPT.			OCT.			NOV.			DEC.		
CANADA																																				
CALGARY, *Alberta*	-4	-16	14	-2	-14	15	3	-9	20	11	-3	27	17	3	54	20	7	82	24	9	65	23	8	57	18	3	40	12	-1	18	3	-9	16	-2	-13	14
CHARLOTTETOWN, *P.E.I.*	-3	-11	100	-3	-12	83	1	-7	83	7	-1	77	14	4	79	20	10	75	24	14	78	23	14	86	18	10	91	13	5	106	6	0	106	0	-7	111
CHURCHILL, *Manitoba*	-23	-31	15	-22	-30	12	-15	-25	18	-6	-15	23	2	-5	27	11	1	43	17	7	55	16	7	62	9	2	53	2	-4	44	-9	-16	31	-18	-26	18
EDMONTON, *Alberta*	-9	-18	23	-5	-15	18	0	-9	19	10	-1	24	17	5	45	21	9	79	23	12	87	22	10	64	17	5	36	11	0	20	0	-8	18	-6	-15	22
FORT NELSON, *B.C.*	-18	-27	23	-11	-23	21	-2	-15	21	8	-4	20	16	3	44	21	8	65	23	10	76	21	8	58	15	3	39	6	-4	28	-9	-17	26	-16	-24	23
GOOSE BAY, *Nfld.*	-12	-22	1	-10	-21	4	-4	-15	4	3	-7	15	10	0	46	17	5	97	21	10	119	19	9	98	14	4	87	6	-2	58	0	-8	21	-9	-18	7
HALIFAX, *Nova Scotia*	0	-8	139	0	-9	121	3	-5	123	8	0	109	14	5	110	18	9	96	22	13	93	22	14	103	19	10	93	13	5	127	8	1	142	2	-5	141
MONTRÉAL, *Quebec*	-6	-15	71	-4	-13	66	2	-7	71	11	1	74	18	8	69	24	13	84	26	16	87	25	14	91	20	10	84	13	4	76	5	-2	90	-3	-11	85
MOOSONEE, *Ontario*	-14	-27	39	-12	-25	32	-5	-19	37	3	-8	36	11	0	55	18	5	72	22	9	79	20	8	78	15	5	77	8	0	66	-1	-9	53	-11	-21	41
OTTAWA, *Ontario*	-6	-16	67	-5	-15	59	1	-8	67	11	0	60	19	7	72	24	12	82	27	15	86	25	13	80	20	9	77	13	3	69	4	-3	70	-4	-12	74
PRINCE RUPERT, *B.C.*	4	-3	237	6	-1	198	7	0	202	9	2	179	12	5	133	14	8	110	16	10	115	16	10	149	15	8	218	11	5	345	7	1	297	5	-1	275
QUÉBEC, *Quebec*	-7	-17	85	-6	-16	75	0	-9	79	8	-1	76	17	5	93	22	10	108	25	13	112	23	12	109	18	7	113	11	2	89	3	-4	100	-5	-13	104
REGINA, *Saskatchewan*	-12	-23	17	-9	-21	13	-2	-13	18	10	-3	20	18	3	45	23	9	77	26	11	59	25	10	44	19	4	35	11	-2	20	0	-11	16	-8	-19	14
SAINT JOHN, *N.B.*	-3	-14	141	-2	-14	115	3	-7	111	10	-1	111	17	4	116	22	9	103	25	12	100	24	11	100	19	7	108	14	2	118	6	-3	149	-1	-10	157
ST. JOHN'S, *Nfld.*	-1	-8	69	-1	-9	69	1	-6	74	5	-2	80	10	1	91	16	6	95	20	11	78	20	11	122	16	8	125	11	3	147	6	0	122	2	-5	91
TORONTO, *Ontario*	-1	-8	68	-1	-9	60	3	-4	66	11	2	65	17	7	71	23	13	68	26	16	77	25	15	70	21	11	73	14	5	62	7	0	70	1	-6	67
VANCOUVER, *B.C.*	5	0	146	8	1	121	10	2	102	13	5	69	17	8	56	19	11	47	22	13	31	22	13	37	19	10	60	14	6	116	9	3	155	6	1	172
WHITEHORSE, *Yukon*	-14	-23	17	-9	-18	13	-2	-13	13	5	-5	9	13	1	14	18	5	30	20	8	37	18	6	39	12	3	31	4	-3	21	-6	-13	20	-12	-20	19
WINNIPEG, *Manitoba*	-13	-23	21	-10	-21	19	-2	-13	26	9	-2	34	18	5	55	23	10	81	26	14	74	25	12	66	19	6	55	12	1	35	-1	-9	26	-9	-18	22
YELLOWKNIFE, *N.W.T.*	-24	-32	14	-20	-30	12	-12	-24	11	-1	-13	10	10	0	16	18	8	20	21	12	35	18	10	39	10	4	29	1	-4	32	-10	-18	23	-20	-28	17
UNITED STATES																																				
ALBANY, *New York*	-1	-12	61	1	-10	59	7	-4	76	14	2	77	21	7	86	26	13	83	29	15	80	27	14	87	23	10	78	17	4	77	9	-1	80	2	-8	74
AMARILLO, *Texas*	9	-6	13	12	-4	14	16	0	23	22	6	28	26	11	71	31	16	88	33	19	70	32	18	74	28	14	50	23	7	35	15	0	15	10	-5	15
ANCHORAGE, *Alaska*	-6	-13	20	-3	-11	21	1	-8	17	6	-2	15	12	4	17	16	8	26	18	11	47	17	10	62	13	5	66	5	-2	47	-3	-9	29	-5	-12	28
ASPEN, *Colorado*	0	-18	32	2	-16	26	5	-11	35	10	-6	28	16	-2	39	22	1	34	26	5	44	25	4	45	21	0	34	15	-5	36	6	-10	31	1	-15	32
ATLANTA, *Georgia*	10	0	117	13	1	117	18	6	139	23	10	103	26	15	100	30	19	92	31	21	134	31	21	93	28	18	91	23	11	77	17	6	95	12	2	105
ATLANTIC CITY, *N.J.*	5	-6	83	6	-5	78	11	0	98	16	4	86	22	10	82	27	15	63	29	18	103	29	18	103	25	13	78	19	7	72	13	2	84	7	-3	81
AUGUSTA, *Maine*	-2	-11	76	0	-10	71	4	-5	84	11	1	92	19	7	95	23	12	85	26	16	85	25	15	84	20	10	80	14	4	92	7	-1	114	0	-8	93
BIRMINGHAM, *Alabama*	11	0	128	14	1	114	19	6	150	24	10	114	27	14	112	31	18	97	32	21	132	32	20	95	29	17	105	24	10	75	18	5	103	13	2	120
BISMARCK, *N. Dak.*	-7	-19	12	-3	-15	11	4	-8	20	13	-1	37	20	6	56	25	11	74	29	14	59	28	12	44	22	6	38	15	0	21	4	-8	14	-4	-16	12
BOISE, *Idaho*	2	-6	38	7	-3	28	12	0	32	16	3	31	22	7	31	27	11	22	32	14	8	31	14	9	25	9	16	18	4	18	9	-1	35	3	-5	35
BOSTON, *Massachusetts*	2	-6	95	3	-5	91	8	0	100	13	5	93	19	10	84	25	15	79	28	18	73	27	18	92	23	14	82	17	8	87	11	4	110	5	-3	105
BROWNSVILLE, *Texas*	21	10	37	22	11	36	26	15	16	29	19	41	31	22	64	33	24	74	34	24	39	34	24	69	32	23	134	30	19	89	26	15	41	22	11	30
BURLINGTON, *Vermont*	-4	-14	46	-3	-13	44	4	-6	55	12	1	71	20	7	78	24	13	85	27	15	90	26	14	101	21	9	85	14	4	77	7	-1	76	-1	-9	59
CHARLESTON, *S.C.*	14	3	88	16	4	80	20	9	114	24	12	71	28	17	97	31	21	155	32	23	180	32	22	176	29	20	135	25	14	77	21	8	63	16	5	82
CHARLESTON, *W. Va.*	5	-5	87	7	-4	82	14	2	100	19	6	85	24	11	99	28	15	92	30	18	126	29	17	102	26	14	81	20	7	67	14	2	85	8	-2	85
CHEYENNE, *Wyoming*	3	-9	10	5	-8	11	7	-6	26	13	-1	35	18	4	64	24	9	56	28	13	51	27	12	42	22	7	31	16	1	19	8	-5	15	4	-9	10
CHICAGO, *Illinois*	-1	-10	48	1	-7	42	8	-1	67	15	5	97	22	10	83	27	16	103	29	19	103	28	18	89	24	14	79	18	7	70	9	1	73	2	-6	65
CINCINNATI, *Ohio*	3	-6	89	5	-4	67	12	1	97	18	7	94	24	12	101	28	17	99	30	19	102	30	18	86	26	14	75	19	8	62	12	3	81	5	-3	75
CLEVELAND, *Ohio*	1	-7	62	2	-6	58	8	-2	78	15	4	85	21	9	90	26	14	89	28	17	88	27	16	86	23	12	80	17	7	65	10	2	80	3	-4	70
DALLAS, *Texas*	13	1	47	15	4	58	20	8	74	25	13	105	29	18	125	33	22	86	35	24	56	35	24	60	31	20	82	26	14	100	19	8	64	14	3	60
DENVER, *Colorado*	6	-9	14	8	-7	16	11	-3	34	17	1	45	22	6	63	27	11	43	31	15	47	30	14	38	25	9	28	19	2	26	11	-4	23	7	-8	15
DES MOINES, *Iowa*	-2	-12	26	1	-9	30	8	-2	57	17	4	85	23	11	103	28	16	108	30	19	97	29	18	105	24	13	80	18	6	58	9	-1	46	0	-9	31
DETROIT, *Michigan*	-1	-7	42	1	-7	43	7	-2	62	14	4	75	21	10	69	26	15	85	29	18	86	27	18	87	23	14	78	16	7	55	9	2	67	2	-4	67
DULUTH, *Minnesota*	-9	-19	31	-6	-16	21	1	-9	44	9	-2	59	17	4	84	22	9	105	25	13	102	23	12	101	18	7	95	11	2	62	2	-6	48	-6	-15	32
EL PASO, *Texas*	13	-1	11	17	1	11	21	5	8	26	9	7	31	14	9	36	18	17	36	20	38	34	19	39	31	16	34	26	10	20	19	4	11	14	-1	14
FAIRBANKS, *Alaska*	-19	-28	14	-14	-26	11	-5	-19	9	5	-6	7	15	3	15	21	10	35	22	11	45	19	8	46	13	2	28	0	-8	21	-12	-21	18	-17	-26	19
HARTFORD, *Connecticut*	1	-9	83	2	-7	79	8	-2	97	16	3	97	22	9	95	27	14	85	29	17	86	28	16	104	24	11	101	18	5	96	11	0	105	3	-6	99
HELENA, *Montana*	-1	-12	15	3	-9	12	7	-5	18	13	-1	24	19	4	45	24	9	53	29	12	28	28	11	27	21	5	28	15	0	19	6	-6	14	0	-12	16
HONOLULU, *Hawai'i*	27	19	80	27	19	68	28	20	72	28	20	32	29	21	25	30	22	10	31	23	15	32	23	14	31	23	18	31	22	53	29	21	67	27	19	89
HOUSTON, *Texas*	16	4	98	19	6	75	22	10	88	26	15	91	29	18	142	32	21	133	34	22	85	34	22	95	31	20	106	28	14	120	22	10	97	18	6	91
INDIANAPOLIS, *Indiana*	1	-8	69	4	-6	61	11	0	92	17	5	94	23	11	98	28	16	98	30	18	111	29	17	88	25	13	74	19	6	69	11	1	89	4	-5	77
JACKSONVILLE, *Florida*	18	5	83	19	6	89	23	10	100	26	13	77	29	17	92	32	21	140	33	22	164	33	22	186	31	21	199	27	15	99	23	10	52	19	6	65
JUNEAU, *Alaska*	-1	-7	139	1	-5	116	4	-3	113	8	0	105	13	4	109	16	7	88	18	9	120	17	8	160	13	6	217	8	3	255	3	-2	186	0	-5	153
KANSAS CITY, *Missouri*	2	-9	30	5	-6	32	12	0	67	18	7	88	24	12	138	29	17	102	32	20	115	30	19	99	26	14	120	20	8	83	11	1	56	4	-6	43
LAS VEGAS, *Nevada*	14	0	14	17	4	12	20	7	13	25	10	5	31	16	5	38	21	3	41	25	9	40	23	13	35	19	7	28	12	6	20	6	11	14	1	10
LITTLE ROCK, *Arkansas*	9	-1	85	12	1	88	17	6	120	23	11	134	26	15	141	31	20	84	33	22	83	32	21	80	28	18	85	23	11	102	16	6	153	10	1	123
LOS ANGELES, *California*	19	9	70	19	10	61	19	10	51	20	12	20	21	14	3	22	15	1	24	17	1	25	18	2	25	17	5	24	15	7	21	12	38	19	9	43
LOUISVILLE, *Kentucky*	5	-5	85	7	-3	88	14	2	113	20	7	101	24	13	114	29	17	90	31	20	106	30	19	84	27	15	76	21	8	68	14	3	92	7	-2	89
MEMPHIS, *Tennessee*	9	-1	118	12	2	112	17	6	136	23	11	142	27	16	126	32	21	98	34	23	101	33	22	87	29	18	83	24	11	74	17	6	124	11	2	135
MIAMI, *Florida*	24	15	52	25	16	53	26	18	63	28	20	82	30	22	150	31	24	227	32	25	152	32	25	198	31	24	215	29	22	178	27	19	80	25	16	47
MILWAUKEE, *Wisconsin*	-3	-11	32	-1	-8	31	5	-3	54	12	2	87	18	7	73	24	13	87	27	17	85	26	16	94	22	12	95	15	6	66	7	-1	65	0	-7	53
MINNEAPOLIS, *Minnesota*	-6	-16	21	-3	-13	22	4	-5	45	14	2	58	21	9	80	26	14	103	29	17	97	27	16	95	22	10	70	15	4	49	5	-4	37	-4	-12	24
NASHVILLE, *Tennessee*	8	-3	108	10	-1	100	16	4	127	22	9	104	26	14	118	30	18	99	32	21	99	31	20	85	28	16	89	23	9	67	16	4	101	10	-1	112
NEW ORLEANS, *Louisiana*	16	5	136	18	7	147	22	11	124	26	15	119	29	18	135	32	22	147	33	23	167	32	23	157	30	21	138	26	15	76	22	11	101	18	7	132
NEW YORK, *New York*	3	-4	80	4	-3	76	9	1	99	15	7	94	21	12	93	26	17	80	29	21	101	28	20	107	24	16	85	18	10	81	12	5	96	6	-1	90
OKLAHOMA CITY, *Okla.*	8	-4	28	11	-1	36	17	4	61	22	9	76	26	14	145	31	19	107	34	21	74	34	21	65	29	17	97	23	10	80	16	4	43	10	-2	37
OMAHA, *Nebraska*	-1	-12	18	2	-9	21	9	-2	61	17	5	73	23	11	118	28	16	105	30	19	96	29	18	95	24	13	90	18	6	60	9	-1	35	1	-9	23
PENSACOLA, *Florida*	15	5	109	17	7	126	21	11	150	25	15	112	28	19	105	32	22	168	32	23	187	32	23	176	30	21	166	26	15	102	21	11	91	17	7	105
PHILADELPHIA, *Pa.*	3	-5	82	5	-4	70	11	1	95	17	6	88	23	12	94	28	17	87	30	20	108	29	19	97	25	15	86	19	8	67	13	3	85	6	-2	86
PHOENIX, *Arizona*	19	3	21	22	5	21	25	7	30	29	9	7	33	13	5	38	18	3	39	23	21	38	22	30	36	18	23	30	12	14	23	7	18	19	3	28
PITTSBURGH, *Pa.*	1	-8	66	3	-7	60	9	-1	85	16	4	80	21	9	92	26	14	91	28	16	98	27	16	83	24	12	74	17	6	61	10	1	69	4	-4	71
PORTLAND, *Oregon*	7	1	133	11	2	105	13	4	92	16	5	61	20	8	53	23	12	38	27	14	15	27	14	23	24	11	41	18	7	76	11	4	135	8	2	149
PROVIDENCE, *R.I.*	3	-7	101	4	-6	91	8	-2	111	14	3	102	20	9	89	25	14	77	28	17	77	27	17	102	24	12	88	18	6	93	12	2	117	5	-4	110
RALEIGH, *N.C.*	9	-2	89	11	0	88	17	4	94	22	8	70	26	13	96	29	18	91	31	20	111	30	20	110	27	16	79	22	9	77	17	4	76	12	0	79
RAPID CITY, *S. Dak.*	2	-12	10	4	-10	12	8	-6	26	14	0	52	20	6	84	25	12	89	30	15	63	29	13	43	23	7	32	17	1	26	8	-5	12	3	-11	10
RENO, *Nevada*	7	-6	28	11	-4	24	14	-2	20	18	1	11	23	5	17	28	8	11	33	11	7	32	10	6	26	5	9	20	1	10	12	-3	19	8	-7	27
ST. LOUIS, *Missouri*	3	-6	50	6	-4	54	13	2	84	19	8	97	25	13	100	30	19	103	32	21	92	31	20	76	27	16	73	20	9	70	13	3	78	5	-3	64
SALT LAKE CITY, *Utah*	2	-7	32	6	-4	30	11	0	45	16	3	52	22	8	46	28	13	23	33	18	18	32	17	21	26	11	27	19	5	34	10	-1	34	3	-6	34
SAN DIEGO, *California*	19	9	56	19	10	41	19	12	50	20	13	20	21	15	5	22	17	2	25	19	1	25	20	2	25	19	5	24	16	9	21	12	30	19	9	35
SAN FRANCISCO, *Calif.*	14	8	112	16	9	77	16	9	78	17	10	34	17	10	10	18	11	4	18	12	1	19	13	2	20	13	7	20	13	28	17	11	73	14	8	91

RED FIGURES: Average daily high temperature (°C) **BLUE FIGURES:** Average daily low temperature (°C) **BLACK FIGURES:** Average monthly rainfall (mm)
1 millimeter = 0.039 inches

	JAN.	FEB.	MARCH	APRIL	MAY	JUNE	JULY	AUG.	SEPT.	OCT.	NOV.	DEC.
UNITED STATES												
SANTA FE, *New Mexico*	6 -10 11	9 -7 9	13 -5 12	18 -1 13	24 4 23	29 9 31	31 12 52	29 11 64	25 7 38	20 1 32	13 -5 14	7 -9 12
SEATTLE, *Washington*	7 2 141	10 3 107	12 4 94	14 5 64	18 8 42	21 11 38	24 13 20	24 13 27	21 11 47	15 8 89	10 5 149	7 2 149
SPOKANE, *Washington*	1 -6 52	5 -3 39	9 -1 37	14 2 28	19 6 35	24 10 33	28 12 15	28 12 16	22 8 20	15 2 31	5 -2 51	1 -6 57
TAMPA, *Florida*	21 10 54	22 11 73	25 14 90	28 16 44	31 20 76	32 23 143	32 24 189	32 24 196	32 23 160	29 18 60	25 14 46	22 11 54
VICKSBURG, *Mississippi*	14 2 155	16 3 131	21 8 160	25 12 147	29 16 130	32 20 88	33 22 106	33 21 80	30 18 85	26 12 106	20 8 126	16 4 168
WASHINGTON, *D.C.*	6 -3 71	8 -2 66	14 3 90	19 8 72	25 14 94	29 19 80	31 22 97	31 21 104	27 17 84	21 10 78	15 5 76	8 0 79
WICHITA, *Kansas*	4 -7 19	8 -5 23	14 1 57	20 7 57	25 12 99	30 18 105	34 21 82	33 20 78	27 15 85	21 8 62	13 1 37	6 -5 29
MIDDLE AMERICA												
ACAPULCO, *Mexico*	29 21 8	31 21 1	31 21 0	31 22 1	32 23 36	32 24 325	32 24 231	32 24 236	31 24 353	31 23 170	31 22 30	31 21 10
BALBOA, *Panama*	31 22 34	32 22 16	32 22 14	32 23 73	31 23 198	30 23 203	31 23 176	31 23 200	30 23 197	29 23 271	29 23 260	31 23 133
CHARLOTTE AMALIE, *V.I.*	28 23 50	27 22 41	28 23 49	28 23 63	29 24 105	30 25 67	31 26 71	31 26 112	31 26 132	31 25 139	29 24 131	28 23 69
GUATEMALA, *Guatemala*	23 12 4	25 12 5	27 14 10	28 14 32	29 16 110	27 16 257	26 16 197	26 16 193	26 16 235	24 16 98	23 14 33	22 13 13
GUAYMAS, *Mexico*	23 13 17	24 14 6	26 16 5	29 18 1	31 21 2	34 24 1	34 27 46	35 27 71	35 26 28	32 22 17	28 18 8	23 13 18
HAVANA, *Cuba*	26 18 71	26 18 46	27 19 46	29 21 58	30 22 119	31 23 165	32 24 124	32 24 135	31 24 150	29 23 173	27 21 79	26 19 58
KINGSTON, *Jamaica*	30 19 29	30 19 24	30 20 23	31 21 39	31 22 104	32 23 96	32 23 46	32 23 107	32 23 127	31 23 181	31 22 95	31 21 41
MANAGUA, *Nicaragua*	33 21 2	33 21 3	35 22 4	36 23 3	35 24 136	32 23 237	32 23 132	32 23 121	33 23 213	32 23 315	32 22 42	32 22 10
MÉRIDA, *Mexico*	28 17 30	29 17 23	32 19 18	33 21 20	34 22 81	33 23 142	33 23 132	33 23 142	32 23 173	31 22 97	29 19 33	28 18 33
MÉXICO, *Mexico*	19 6 8	21 6 5	24 8 11	25 11 19	26 12 49	24 13 106	23 12 129	23 12 121	23 12 110	21 10 44	20 8 15	19 6 7
MONTERREY, *Mexico*	20 9 18	22 11 23	24 14 16	29 17 29	31 20 40	33 22 68	32 22 62	33 22 76	30 21 151	27 18 78	22 13 26	18 10 20
NASSAU, *Bahamas*	25 18 48	25 18 43	26 19 41	27 21 65	29 22 132	31 23 178	31 24 153	32 24 170	31 24 180	29 23 171	27 21 71	26 19 43
PORT-AU-PRINCE, *Haiti*	31 20 32	31 20 50	32 21 79	32 22 156	32 22 218	33 23 96	34 23 73	34 23 139	33 23 166	32 22 164	31 22 84	31 21 35
PORT-OF-SPAIN, *Trinidad*	29 19 69	30 19 41	31 19 46	31 21 53	32 21 94	31 22 193	31 21 218	31 22 246	31 22 193	31 22 170	31 21 183	30 21 124
SAN JOSÉ, *Costa Rica*	24 14 11	24 14 5	26 15 14	26 17 46	27 17 224	26 17 276	25 17 215	26 16 243	26 16 326	25 16 323	25 16 148	24 14 42
SAN JUAN, *Puerto Rico*	27 21 75	27 21 56	27 21 59	28 22 95	29 23 156	29 24 112	29 24 115	29 24 133	30 24 136	29 24 140	29 23 148	27 22 118
SAN SALVADOR, *El Salv.*	32 16 7	33 16 7	34 17 13	34 18 53	33 19 179	31 19 315	32 18 312	32 19 307	31 19 317	31 18 230	31 17 40	32 16 12
SANTO DOMINGO, *Dom. Rep.*	29 19 57	29 19 43	29 19 49	29 21 77	30 22 179	31 22 154	31 22 155	31 23 162	31 22 173	31 22 164	30 21 111	29 19 63
TEGUCIGALPA, *Honduras*	25 13 9	27 14 4	29 14 8	30 17 32	29 18 151	28 18 159	28 17 82	28 17 87	28 17 185	27 17 135	26 16 38	25 15 12
SOUTH AMERICA												
ANTOFAGASTA, *Chile*	24 17 0	24 17 0	23 16 0	21 14 0	19 13 0	18 11 1	17 11 1	17 11 1	18 12 0	19 13 0	21 14 0	22 16 0
ASUNCIÓN, *Paraguay*	35 22 150	34 22 133	33 21 142	29 18 145	25 14 120	22 12 73	23 12 51	26 14 48	28 16 83	30 17 136	32 18 144	34 21 142
BELÉM, *Brazil*	31 22 351	30 22 412	31 23 441	31 23 370	31 23 282	31 22 164	31 22 154	31 22 122	32 22 129	32 22 105	32 22 101	32 22 202
BOGOTÁ, *Colombia*	19 9 48	20 9 52	19 10 81	19 11 119	19 11 103	18 11 61	18 10 47	18 10 48	19 9 58	19 10 142	19 10 115	19 9 67
BRASÍLIA, *Brazil*	27 18 262	27 18 213	28 18 202	28 17 103	26 13 20	25 11 4	26 11 4	28 13 6	31 16 35	28 18 140	28 19 238	26 18 329
BUENOS AIRES, *Arg.*	29 17 93	28 17 81	26 16 117	22 12 90	18 8 77	14 5 64	14 6 59	16 6 65	18 8 78	21 10 97	24 13 89	28 16 96
CARACAS, *Venezuela*	24 13 41	25 13 27	26 14 22	27 16 20	27 17 36	26 17 52	26 16 53	26 16 53	27 16 48	26 16 47	25 16 50	26 14 58
COM. RIVADAVIA, *Arg.*	26 13 16	25 13 11	22 11 21	18 8 21	13 6 34	11 3 21	11 3 25	12 3 22	14 5 13	19 9 13	22 10 13	24 12 15
CÓRDOBA, *Argentina*	31 16 110	30 16 102	28 14 96	24 11 45	21 7 25	18 3 10	18 3 10	21 4 13	23 7 27	25 11 69	28 13 97	30 16 118
GUAYAQUIL, *Ecuador*	31 21 224	31 22 278	31 22 287	32 22 180	31 20 53	31 20 17	29 19 2	30 18 0	31 19 2	30 20 3	31 20 3	31 21 30
LA PAZ, *Bolivia*	17 6 130	17 6 105	18 6 72	18 4 47	18 3 13	17 1 6	17 1 9	17 2 14	18 3 29	19 4 40	19 6 50	18 6 93
LIMA, *Peru*	28 19 1	28 19 1	28 19 1	27 17 0	23 16 1	20 14 2	19 14 4	19 13 3	20 14 3	22 14 2	23 16 1	26 17 1
MANAUS, *Brazil*	31 24 264	31 24 262	31 24 298	31 24 283	31 24 204	31 24 103	32 24 67	33 24 46	33 24 63	33 24 111	33 24 161	32 24 220
MARACAIBO, *Venezuela*	32 23 5	32 23 5	33 23 6	33 24 39	33 25 65	34 25 55	34 24 25	34 25 53	34 25 76	33 24 119	33 24 55	33 24 22
MONTEVIDEO, *Uruguay*	28 17 95	28 16 100	26 15 111	22 12 83	18 9 76	15 6 74	14 6 86	15 6 84	17 8 90	20 9 98	23 12 78	26 15 84
PARAMARIBO, *Suriname*	29 22 209	29 22 149	29 22 168	30 23 219	30 23 307	30 23 302	31 23 227	32 23 163	33 23 80	33 23 82	32 23 117	30 22 204
PUNTA ARENAS, *Chile*	14 7 35	14 7 28	12 5 39	10 4 41	7 2 42	5 1 32	4 -1 34	6 1 33	8 2 28	11 3 24	12 4 29	14 6 32
QUITO, *Ecuador*	22 8 113	22 8 128	22 8 154	21 8 176	21 8 124	22 7 48	22 7 20	23 7 24	23 7 78	22 8 127	22 7 109	22 8 103
RECIFE, *Brazil*	30 25 62	30 25 102	30 24 197	29 24 252	28 23 301	28 23 302	27 22 254	27 22 156	28 23 78	29 24 36	29 24 29	29 25 40
RIO DE JANEIRO, *Brazil*	29 23 135	29 23 124	28 22 134	27 21 109	25 19 78	24 18 52	24 17 45	24 18 46	24 18 62	25 19 82	26 20 100	28 22 137
SANTIAGO, *Chile*	29 12 3	29 11 3	27 9 5	23 7 13	18 5 64	14 3 84	15 3 76	17 4 56	19 6 30	22 7 15	26 9 8	28 11 5
SÃO PAULO, *Brazil*	27 17 225	28 18 208	27 17 160	26 14 71	23 12 67	22 11 54	22 9 35	23 11 48	23 12 77	24 14 117	26 15 139	27 16 185
VALPARAÍSO, *Chile*	22 13 0	22 13 0	21 12 0	19 11 22	17 10 38	16 9 100	16 8 111	16 8 42	17 9 27	18 10 15	21 11 15	22 12 1
EUROPE												
AJACCIO, *Corsica*	13 3 76	14 4 58	16 5 66	18 7 56	21 10 41	25 14 23	27 16 71	28 16 18	26 15 43	22 11 97	18 7 112	15 4 79
AMSTERDAM, *Neth.*	4 1 79	5 1 44	8 3 89	11 6 39	16 10 50	18 13 60	21 15 73	20 15 60	18 13 80	13 9 104	8 5 76	5 2 72
ATHENS, *Greece*	13 6 48	14 7 41	16 8 41	20 11 23	25 16 18	30 20 7	33 23 5	33 23 8	29 19 10	24 15 53	19 12 55	15 8 62
BARCELONA, *Spain*	13 6 38	14 7 38	16 9 47	18 11 47	21 14 44	25 18 38	28 21 28	28 21 44	25 19 76	21 15 96	16 11 51	13 8 44
BELFAST, *N. Ireland*	6 2 83	7 2 55	9 3 59	12 4 51	15 6 56	18 9 65	18 11 79	18 11 78	16 9 82	13 7 85	9 4 75	7 3 84
BELGRADE, *Serbia*	3 -3 42	5 -2 39	11 2 43	18 7 57	23 12 73	26 15 84	28 17 63	28 17 53	24 13 47	18 8 50	11 4 55	5 0 52
BERLIN, *Germany*	2 -3 43	3 -3 38	8 0 38	13 4 41	19 8 49	22 12 64	24 14 71	23 13 62	20 10 44	13 6 44	7 2 46	3 -1 48
BIARRITZ, *France*	11 4 106	12 4 93	15 6 92	16 8 95	18 11 97	22 14 93	23 16 64	24 16 74	22 15 102	19 11 129	15 7 135	12 5 134
BORDEAUX, *France*	9 2 76	11 2 65	15 4 66	17 6 65	20 9 71	24 12 65	25 14 52	26 14 59	23 12 70	18 8 87	13 5 88	9 3 86
BRINDISI, *Italy*	12 6 57	13 7 61	15 8 67	18 11 35	22 14 26	26 18 20	29 21 9	29 21 25	26 18 47	22 15 71	18 11 72	14 8 65
BRUSSELS, *Belgium*	4 -1 82	7 0 51	10 2 81	14 5 53	18 8 74	22 11 74	23 12 58	22 12 42	21 11 69	15 7 85	9 3 61	6 0 68
BUCHAREST, *Romania*	1 -7 44	4 -5 37	10 -1 35	18 5 46	23 10 65	27 14 86	30 16 56	30 15 56	25 11 35	18 6 28	10 2 45	4 -3 42
BUDAPEST, *Hungary*	1 -4 41	4 -2 36	10 2 41	17 7 49	22 11 69	26 15 71	28 16 53	27 16 53	23 12 45	16 7 52	8 3 58	4 -1 49
CAGLIARI, *Sardinia*	14 7 53	15 7 52	17 9 45	19 11 35	23 14 27	27 18 10	30 21 3	30 21 10	27 19 29	23 15 57	19 11 56	16 9 55
CANDIA, *Crete*	16 9 94	16 9 76	17 10 41	20 12 23	23 15 18	27 19 3	29 21 1	29 22 3	27 19 18	24 17 43	21 14 69	18 11 102
COPENHAGEN, *Denmark*	2 -2 42	2 -3 25	5 -1 35	10 3 40	16 8 42	19 11 52	22 14 67	21 14 75	18 11 51	12 7 53	7 3 52	4 1 51
DUBLIN, *Ireland*	7 2 64	8 2 51	10 3 52	12 5 49	14 7 56	18 9 55	19 11 65	19 11 77	17 10 62	14 7 73	10 4 69	8 3 69
DURAZZO, *Albania*	11 6 76	12 6 84	13 8 99	17 13 56	22 17 41	25 21 48	28 23 13	28 22 48	24 18 43	20 14 180	14 11 216	12 8 185
EDINBURGH, *Scotland*	6 1 55	6 1 41	8 2 47	11 4 39	14 6 50	17 9 50	18 11 64	18 11 69	16 9 63	12 7 62	9 4 63	7 2 61
FLORENCE, *Italy*	9 2 64	11 3 62	14 5 69	19 8 71	23 12 73	27 15 56	30 18 34	30 17 47	26 15 83	20 11 99	14 7 103	11 4 79
GENEVA, *Switzerland*	4 -2 55	6 -1 53	10 2 60	15 5 63	19 9 76	23 13 81	25 15 72	24 14 90	21 12 90	14 7 91	8 3 81	4 0 66
HAMBURG, *Germany*	2 -2 61	3 -2 40	7 -1 52	13 3 47	18 7 55	21 11 74	22 13 81	22 12 79	19 10 68	13 6 62	7 3 65	4 0 71
HELSINKI, *Finland*	-3 -9 46	-4 -9 37	0 -7 35	6 -1 37	14 4 42	19 9 46	22 13 62	20 12 75	15 8 67	8 3 69	3 -1 66	-1 -5 55
LISBON, *Portugal*	14 8 95	15 8 87	17 10 85	20 12 60	21 13 44	25 15 18	27 17 4	28 17 5	26 17 33	22 14 75	17 11 100	15 9 97
LIVERPOOL, *England*	7 2 69	7 2 48	9 3 38	11 5 41	14 8 56	17 11 51	19 13 71	18 13 79	16 11 66	13 8 76	9 5 76	7 3 64
LONDON, *England*	7 2 62	7 2 36	11 8 50	13 4 43	17 7 45	21 11 46	23 13 46	22 12 44	19 11 43	14 7 73	9 4 45	7 2 59
LUXEMBOURG, *Lux.*	3 -1 66	4 -1 54	10 1 55	14 4 53	18 8 66	21 11 65	23 13 70	22 12 69	19 10 62	13 6 70	7 3 71	4 0 74
MADRID, *Spain*	9 2 45	11 2 43	15 5 37	18 7 45	21 10 40	27 15 25	31 17 9	30 17 10	25 14 29	19 10 46	13 5 64	9 2 47
MARSEILLE, *France*	10 2 49	12 2 40	15 5 45	18 8 46	22 11 46	26 15 26	29 17 15	28 17 24	25 15 63	20 10 94	15 6 76	11 3 59

World Temperature and Rainfall

Average daily high and low temperatures and monthly rainfall for selected world locations:

	JAN.			FEB.			MARCH			APRIL			MAY			JUNE			JULY			AUG.			SEPT.			OCT.			NOV.			DEC.		
EUROPE																																				
MILAN, *Italy*	5	0	61	8	2	58	13	6	72	18	10	85	23	14	98	27	17	81	29	20	68	28	19	81	24	16	82	17	11	116	10	6	106	6	2	75
MUNICH, *Germany*	1	-5	49	3	-5	43	9	-1	52	14	3	70	18	7	101	21	11	123	23	13	127	23	12	112	20	9	83	13	4	62	7	0	54	2	-4	51
NANTES, *France*	8	2	79	9	2	62	13	4	62	15	6	54	19	9	61	22	12	55	24	14	50	24	13	54	21	12	70	16	8	89	11	5	91	8	3	86
NAPLES, *Italy*	12	4	94	13	5	81	15	6	76	18	9	66	22	12	46	26	16	46	29	18	15	29	18	18	26	16	71	22	12	130	17	9	114	14	6	137
NICE, *France*	13	4	77	13	5	73	15	7	73	17	9	64	20	13	49	24	16	37	27	18	19	27	18	32	25	16	65	21	12	111	17	8	117	13	5	88
OSLO, *Norway*	-2	-7	41	-1	-7	31	4	-4	34	10	1	36	16	6	45	20	10	59	22	13	75	21	12	86	16	8	72	9	3	71	3	-1	57	0	-4	49
PALERMO, *Italy*	16	8	44	16	8	35	17	9	30	20	11	29	24	14	14	27	18	9	30	21	2	30	21	8	28	19	28	25	16	59	21	12	66	18	10	68
PALMA DE MALLORCA, *Spain*	14	6	39	15	6	35	17	8	37	19	10	35	22	13	34	26	17	20	29	20	8	29	20	18	27	18	52	23	14	77	18	10	54	15	8	54
PARIS, *France*	6	1	46	7	1	39	12	4	41	16	6	44	20	10	56	23	13	57	25	15	57	24	14	55	21	12	53	16	8	57	10	5	54	7	2	49
PRAGUE, *Czech. Rep.*	1	-4	21	3	-2	19	7	1	26	13	4	36	18	9	59	22	13	68	23	14	67	23	14	62	18	11	41	12	7	30	5	2	27	1	-2	23
RIGA, *Latvia*	-4	-10	32	-3	-10	24	2	-7	26	10	1	35	16	6	42	21	9	58	22	11	72	21	11	68	17	8	66	11	4	54	4	-1	52	-2	-7	39
ROME, *Italy*	11	5	80	13	5	71	15	7	69	19	10	67	23	13	52	28	17	34	30	20	16	30	19	24	26	17	69	22	13	113	16	9	111	13	6	97
SEVILLE, *Spain*	15	6	56	17	7	74	20	9	84	24	11	58	27	13	33	32	17	23	36	20	3	36	20	3	32	18	28	26	14	66	20	10	94	16	7	71
SOFIA, *Bulgaria*	2	-4	34	4	-3	34	10	1	38	16	5	54	21	10	69	24	14	78	27	16	56	26	15	43	22	11	40	17	8	35	9	3	52	4	-2	44
SPLIT, *Croatia*	10	5	80	11	5	65	14	7	65	18	11	62	23	16	62	27	19	48	30	22	28	30	22	43	26	19	66	20	14	87	15	10	111	12	7	113
STOCKHOLM, *Sweden*	-1	-5	31	-1	-5	25	3	-4	26	8	1	29	14	6	34	19	11	44	22	14	64	20	13	66	15	9	49	9	5	51	5	1	44	2	-2	39
VALENCIA, *Spain*	15	6	23	16	6	38	18	8	23	20	10	30	23	13	28	26	17	33	29	20	10	29	20	13	27	18	56	23	13	41	19	10	64	16	7	33
VALETTA, *Malta*	14	10	84	15	10	58	16	11	38	18	13	20	22	16	10	26	19	3	29	22	1	29	23	5	27	22	33	24	19	69	20	16	91	16	12	99
VENICE, *Italy*	6	1	51	8	2	53	12	5	61	17	10	71	21	14	81	25	17	84	27	19	66	27	18	66	24	16	66	19	11	94	12	7	89	8	3	66
VIENNA, *Austria*	1	-4	38	3	-3	36	8	1	46	15	6	51	19	10	71	23	14	69	25	15	76	24	15	69	20	11	51	14	7	25	7	3	48	3	-1	46
WARSAW, *Poland*	0	-6	28	0	-6	26	6	-2	31	12	3	37	20	9	50	23	12	66	24	15	77	23	14	72	19	10	47	13	5	41	6	1	38	2	-3	35
ZÜRICH, *Switzerland*	2	-3	61	5	-2	61	10	1	68	15	4	85	19	8	101	23	12	127	25	14	128	24	13	124	20	11	98	14	6	83	7	2	71	3	-2	72
ASIA																																				
ADEN, *Yemen*	27	23	8	27	23	7	29	24	8	31	26	4	34	28	3	35	29	1	34	28	2	33	27	3	34	28	4	32	26	2	29	24	2	27	23	4
ALMATY, *Kazakhstan*	-5	-14	33	-3	13	23	4	-6	56	13	3	102	20	10	94	24	14	66	27	16	36	27	14	30	22	8	25	13	2	51	4	-5	48	-2	-9	33
ANKARA, *Turkey*	4	-4	49	6	-3	52	11	-1	45	17	4	44	23	9	56	26	12	37	30	15	13	31	15	8	26	11	28	21	7	21	14	3	28	6	-2	63
ARKHANGEL'SK, *Russia*	-12	-20	30	-10	-18	28	-4	-13	28	5	-4	18	12	2	33	17	6	48	20	10	66	19	10	69	12	5	56	4	-1	48	-2	-7	41	-8	-15	33
BAGHDAD, *Iraq*	16	4	27	18	6	28	22	9	27	29	14	19	36	19	7	41	23	0	43	24	0	43	24	0	40	21	0	33	16	3	25	11	20	18	6	26
BALIKPAPAN, *Indonesia*	29	23	243	30	23	221	30	23	249	29	23	226	29	23	258	29	23	252	28	23	259	29	23	257	29	23	201	29	23	186	29	23	176	29	23	245
BANGKOK, *Thailand*	32	20	11	33	22	28	34	24	31	35	25	72	34	25	189	33	24	152	32	24	158	32	24	187	32	24	320	31	24	231	31	22	57	31	20	9
BEIJING, *China*	2	-9	4	5	-7	5	12	-1	8	20	7	18	27	13	33	31	18	78	32	22	224	31	21	170	27	14	58	21	7	18	10	-1	9	3	-7	3
BEIRUT, *Lebanon*	17	11	187	17	11	151	19	12	96	22	14	51	26	18	19	28	21	2	31	23	0	32	23	0	30	23	6	27	21	48	23	16	119	18	13	176
BRUNEI	30	24	371	30	24	193	31	24	198	32	24	249	32	24	277	31	24	241	31	25	229	31	24	185	31	24	300	31	24	368	31	24	386	30	24	330
CHENNAI (MADRAS), *India*	29	19	29	31	20	9	33	22	9	35	26	17	38	28	44	38	27	52	36	26	99	35	26	124	34	25	125	32	24	285	29	22	345	29	21	138
CHONGQING, *China*	9	5	18	13	7	21	18	11	38	23	16	94	27	19	148	29	22	174	34	24	151	35	25	128	28	22	144	22	16	103	16	12	49	13	8	23
COLOMBO, *Sri Lanka*	30	22	84	31	22	64	31	23	114	31	24	255	31	26	335	29	25	190	29	25	129	29	25	96	29	25	158	29	24	353	29	23	308	29	22	152
DAMASCUS, *Syria*	12	2	39	14	4	32	18	6	23	24	9	13	29	13	5	33	16	1	36	18	0	37	18	0	33	16	0	27	12	9	19	8	26	13	4	42
DAVAO, *Philippines*	31	22	117	32	22	110	32	22	109	33	22	149	32	23	223	31	23	205	31	22	171	31	22	161	32	22	177	32	22	184	32	22	139	31	22	139
DHAKA, *Bangladesh*	26	13	8	28	15	21	32	20	58	33	23	116	33	24	267	32	26	358	31	26	399	31	26	317	32	26	256	31	24	164	29	19	30	26	14	6
HANOI, *Vietnam*	20	13	20	21	14	30	23	17	64	28	21	91	32	23	104	33	26	284	33	26	302	32	26	386	31	24	254	29	22	89	26	18	66	22	15	71
HO CHI MINH CITY, *Viet.*	32	21	14	33	22	4	34	23	9	35	24	51	33	24	213	32	24	309	31	24	295	31	24	271	31	23	342	31	23	261	31	23	119	31	22	47
HONG KONG, *China*	18	13	27	17	13	44	19	16	75	24	19	140	28	23	298	29	26	399	31	26	371	31	26	377	29	25	297	27	23	119	23	18	38	20	15	25
IRKUTSK, *Russia*	-16	-26	13	-12	-25	10	-4	-17	8	6	-7	15	13	1	33	20	7	56	21	10	79	20	9	71	14	2	43	5	-6	18	-7	-17	15	-16	-24	15
ISTANBUL, *Turkey*	8	3	91	9	2	69	11	3	62	16	7	42	21	12	30	25	16	28	28	18	24	28	19	31	24	16	48	20	13	66	15	9	92	11	5	114
JAKARTA, *Indonesia*	29	23	342	29	23	302	30	23	210	31	24	135	31	24	108	31	23	90	31	23	59	31	23	48	31	23	69	31	23	106	30	23	139	29	23	208
JEDDAH, *Saudi Arabia*	29	19	5	29	18	1	29	19	1	33	21	1	35	23	1	36	24	0	37	23	1	37	27	1	36	25	1	35	23	1	33	22	25	30	19	30
JERUSALEM, *Israel*	13	5	140	13	6	111	18	8	116	23	10	17	27	14	6	29	16	0	31	17	0	31	18	0	29	17	0	27	15	11	21	12	68	15	7	129
KABUL, *Afghanistan*	2	-8	33	4	-6	54	12	1	70	19	6	66	26	11	21	31	13	1	33	16	5	33	15	1	29	11	2	23	6	4	17	1	11	8	-3	21
KARACHI, *Pakistan*	25	13	7	26	14	10	29	19	10	32	23	3	34	26	0	34	28	10	33	27	90	31	26	58	31	25	27	33	22	3	31	18	3	27	14	5
KATHMANDU, *Nepal*	18	2	17	19	4	15	25	7	30	28	12	37	30	16	102	29	19	201	29	20	375	28	20	325	28	19	189	27	13	56	23	7	2	19	3	10
KOLKATA (CALCUTTA), *India*	27	13	12	29	15	25	34	21	32	36	24	53	36	25	129	33	26	291	32	26	329	32	26	338	32	26	266	32	23	131	29	18	21	26	13	7
KUNMING, *China*	16	3	11	18	4	14	21	7	17	24	11	20	26	14	90	25	17	175	25	17	205	25	17	203	24	15	126	21	12	78	18	7	40	17	3	13
LAHORE, *Pakistan*	21	4	25	22	7	24	28	12	27	35	17	15	40	22	17	41	26	39	38	27	155	36	26	135	36	23	63	35	15	10	28	8	3	23	4	14
LHASA, *China*	7	-10	0	9	-7	3	12	-2	4	16	1	6	19	5	24	24	9	72	23	9	132	22	9	128	21	7	58	17	1	9	13	-5	1	9	-9	1
MANAMA, *Bahrain*	30	14	14	21	15	16	24	17	11	29	21	8	33	26	1	36	28	0	37	29	0	38	29	0	36	27	0	32	24	0	28	21	7	22	16	17
MANDALAY, *Myanmar*	28	13	2	31	15	13	36	19	7	38	25	35	37	26	142	34	26	124	34	26	83	33	25	113	33	24	155	32	23	125	29	19	45	27	14	10
MANILA, *Philippines*	30	21	21	31	21	10	33	22	15	34	23	30	34	24	123	33	24	262	31	24	423	31	24	421	31	24	353	31	23	197	31	22	135	30	21	65
MOSCOW, *Russia*	-9	-16	38	-6	-14	36	0	-8	28	10	1	46	19	8	56	21	11	74	23	13	76	22	12	74	16	7	48	9	3	69	2	-3	43	-5	-10	41
MUMBAI (BOMBAY), *India*	28	19	3	28	19	1	30	22	1	32	24	2	33	27	14	32	26	518	29	25	647	29	24	384	29	24	276	32	24	55	32	23	15	31	21	2
MUSCAT, *Oman*	25	19	28	25	19	18	28	22	10	32	26	10	37	30	1	38	31	3	36	31	1	33	29	1	34	28	0	34	27	3	30	23	10	26	20	18
NAGASAKI, *Japan*	9	2	75	10	2	87	14	5	124	19	10	190	23	14	191	26	18	326	29	23	284	31	23	187	27	20	236	22	14	108	17	9	89	12	4	80
NEW DELHI, *India*	21	7	23	24	9	20	31	14	15	36	20	10	41	26	15	39	28	68	36	27	200	34	26	200	34	24	123	34	18	19	29	11	3	23	8	10
NICOSIA, *Cyprus*	15	5	70	16	5	50	19	7	35	24	10	21	29	14	26	34	18	9	37	21	1	37	21	2	33	18	6	28	14	23	22	10	41	17	7	74
ODESA, *Ukraine*	0	-6	25	2	-4	18	5	-1	18	12	6	28	19	12	28	23	16	48	26	18	41	26	18	36	21	14	28	16	9	36	10	4	28	4	-2	28
PHNOM PENH, *Cambodia*	31	21	7	32	22	9	34	23	32	34	24	73	33	24	149	33	24	149	32	24	151	32	24	157	31	24	231	31	24	259	30	23	129	30	22	38
PONTIANAK, *Indonesia*	31	23	275	32	23	213	32	23	242	33	23	280	33	23	279	32	23	228	32	23	178	32	23	206	32	23	245	32	23	356	31	23	385	31	23	321
RIYADH, *Saudi Arabia*	21	8	14	23	9	10	28	13	30	32	18	30	38	22	13	42	25	0	42	26	0	42	24	0	39	22	0	34	16	1	29	13	5	21	9	11
ST. PETERSBURG, *Russia*	-7	-13	25	-5	-12	23	0	-8	23	8	4	25	15	6	41	20	11	51	21	13	64	20	13	71	15	9	53	9	4	46	2	-2	36	-3	-8	30
SANDAKAN, *Malaysia*	29	23	454	29	23	271	30	23	200	31	23	118	32	23	153	32	23	196	32	23	185	32	23	205	32	23	240	31	23	263	31	23	356	30	23	470
SAPPORO, *Japan*	-2	-12	100	-1	-11	79	2	-7	70	11	0	61	16	4	59	21	10	65	24	14	86	26	16	117	22	11	136	16	4	114	8	-2	106	1	-8	102
SEOUL, *South Korea*	0	-9	21	3	-7	28	8	-2	49	17	5	105	22	11	88	27	16	151	29	21	384	31	22	263	26	15	160	19	7	49	11	0	43	3	-7	24
SHANGHAI, *China*	8	1	47	8	1	61	13	4	85	19	10	95	25	15	104	28	19	174	32	23	145	32	23	137	28	19	138	23	14	69	17	7	52	12	2	37
SINGAPORE, *Singapore*	30	23	239	31	23	165	31	24	174	31	24	166	32	24	171	31	24	163	31	24	150	31	24	171	31	24	164	31	23	191	31	23	250	31	23	269
TAIPEI, *China*	19	12	95	18	12	141	21	14	162	25	17	167	28	21	209	32	23	280	33	24	248	33	24	277	31	23	201	27	19	112	24	17	76	21	14	76
T'BILISI, *Georgia*	6	-2	16	7	-1	21	12	2	30	18	7	52	23	12	83	27	16	73	31	19	49	31	19	40	26	15	44	20	9	39	13	4	32	8	0	21
TEHRAN, *Iran*	7	-3	42	10	0	37	15	4	39	22	9	33	28	14	15	34	19	3	37	22	2	36	22	2	32	18	2	24	12	9	17	6	24	11	1	32
TEL AVIV-YAFO, *Israel*	17	9	165	18	9	64	19	10	58	23	12	13	27	16	3	29	18	0	31	21	0	31	21	0	30	20	1	29	18	14	25	15	85	19	11	144
TOKYO, *Japan*	8	-2	50	9	-1	72	12	2	106	17	8	129	22	12	144	24	17	176	28	21	136	30	22	149	26	19	216	21	13	194	16	6	96	11	1	54
ULAANBAATAR, *Mongolia*	-19	-32	1	-13	-29	1	-4	-22	3	7	-8	5	13	-2	8	21	7	25	22	11	74	21	8	48	14	2	20	6	-8	5	-6	-20	5	-16	-28	3
VIENTIANE, *Laos*	28	14	7	30	17	18	33	19	41	34	23	88	32	23	212	32	24	216	31	24	209	31	24	254	31	24	244	31	21	81	29	18	16	28	16	5
VLADIVOSTOK, *Russia*	-11	-18	8	-6	-14	10	1	-7	18	8	1	30	13	6	53	17	11	74	22	16	84	24	18	119	20	13	109	13	5	48	2	-4	30	-7	-13	15

RED FIGURES: Average daily high temperature (°C) **BLUE FIGURES:** Average daily low temperature (°C) **BLACK FIGURES:** Average monthly rainfall (mm)
1 millimeter = 0.039 inches

	JAN.			FEB.			MARCH			APRIL			MAY			JUNE			JULY			AUG.			SEPT.			OCT.			NOV.			DEC.		
ASIA																																				
WUHAN, *China*	8	1	41	9	2	57	14	6	92	21	13	136	26	18	165	31	23	212	34	26	165	34	26	114	29	21	73	23	16	74	17	9	49	11	3	30
YAKUTSK, *Russia*	-43	-47	8	-33	-40	5	-18	-29	3	-3	-14	8	9	-1	10	19	9	28	23	12	41	19	9	33	10	1	28	-5	-12	13	-26	-31	10	-39	-43	8
YANGON (RANGOON), *Myanmar*	32	18	4	33	19	4	36	22	17	36	24	47	33	25	307	30	24	478	29	24	535	29	24	511	30	24	368	31	24	183	31	23	62	31	19	11
YEKATERINBURG, *Russia*	-14	-21	8	-10	-17	10	-4	-12	5	6	-3	8	14	4	15	18	9	48	21	12	38	18	10	53	12	5	46	3	-2	23	-7	-12	10	-12	-18	8
AFRICA																																				
ABIDJAN, *Côte d'Ivoire*	31	23	22	32	24	47	32	24	110	32	24	142	31	24	309	29	23	543	28	23	238	28	22	36	28	23	74	29	23	172	31	23	168	31	23	85
ACCRA, *Ghana*	31	23	15	31	24	29	31	24	57	31	24	90	31	24	136	29	23	199	27	23	50	27	22	19	27	23	43	29	23	64	31	24	34	31	24	20
ADDIS ABABA, *Ethiopia*	24	6	17	24	8	38	25	9	68	25	10	86	25	10	86	23	9	132	21	10	268	21	10	281	22	9	186	24	7	28	23	6	11	23	5	10
ALEXANDRIA, *Egypt*	18	11	52	19	11	28	21	13	13	23	15	4	26	18	1	28	21	0	29	23	0	31	23	0	30	23	1	28	20	8	25	17	35	21	13	55
ALGIERS, *Algeria*	15	9	93	16	9	73	17	11	67	20	13	52	23	15	34	26	18	14	28	21	2	29	22	5	27	21	33	23	17	77	19	13	96	16	11	114
ANTANANARIVO, *Madag.*	26	16	287	26	16	262	26	16	194	24	14	57	23	12	18	21	10	9	20	9	8	21	9	10	23	11	16	27	12	61	27	14	153	27	16	290
ASMARA, *Eritrea*	23	7	0	24	8	0	25	9	1	26	11	7	26	12	23	26	12	48	22	12	114	22	12	123	23	13	49	22	12	4	22	10	3	22	9	0
BAMAKO, *Mali*	33	16	0	36	19	0	39	22	3	39	24	19	39	24	59	34	23	131	32	22	229	31	22	307	32	22	198	34	22	63	34	18	7	33	17	0
BANGUI, *Cen. Af. Rep.*	32	20	20	34	21	39	33	22	107	33	22	133	32	21	163	31	21	143	29	21	181	29	21	225	31	21	190	31	21	202	31	20	93	32	19	29
BEIRA, *Mozambique*	32	24	267	32	24	259	31	23	263	30	22	117	28	18	67	26	16	40	25	16	34	26	17	33	28	18	25	31	22	34	31	22	121	31	23	243
BENGHAZI, *Libya*	17	10	66	18	11	41	21	12	20	23	14	5	26	17	3	28	20	1	29	22	1	29	22	1	28	21	3	27	19	18	23	16	46	19	12	66
BUJUMBURA, *Burundi*	29	20	97	29	20	97	29	20	126	29	20	129	29	20	64	29	19	11	30	19	3	30	19	17	31	20	43	31	20	62	29	20	98	29	20	100
CAIRO, *Egypt*	18	8	5	21	9	4	24	11	4	28	14	2	33	17	1	35	20	0	36	21	0	35	22	0	32	20	0	30	18	1	26	14	3	20	10	6
CAPE TOWN, *S. Africa*	26	16	15	26	16	15	25	14	22	22	12	50	19	9	92	18	8	105	17	7	91	18	8	83	18	9	54	21	11	40	23	13	24	24	14	19
CASABLANCA, *Morocco*	17	7	57	18	8	53	19	9	51	21	11	38	22	13	21	24	16	6	26	18	0	27	19	1	26	17	6	24	14	34	21	11	65	18	8	73
CONAKRY, *Guinea*	31	22	1	31	23	1	32	23	6	32	23	21	32	24	141	30	23	503	28	22	1210	28	22	1016	29	23	664	31	23	318	31	24	106	31	23	14
DAKAR, *Senegal*	26	18	1	27	17	1	27	18	0	27	18	0	29	20	1	31	23	15	31	24	75	31	24	215	32	24	146	32	24	42	30	23	3	27	19	4
DAR ES SALAAM, *Tanzania*	31	25	66	31	25	66	31	24	130	30	23	290	29	22	188	29	20	33	28	19	31	28	19	30	28	19	30	29	21	41	30	22	74	31	24	91
DURBAN, *S. Africa*	27	21	119	27	21	126	27	20	132	26	18	84	24	14	56	23	12	34	22	11	35	22	13	49	23	15	73	24	17	110	25	18	118	26	19	120
HARARE, *Zimbabwe*	26	16	190	26	16	177	26	14	107	26	13	33	23	9	10	21	7	3	21	7	1	23	8	2	26	12	7	28	14	32	27	16	93	26	16	173
JOHANNESBURG, *S. Africa*	26	14	150	25	14	129	24	13	110	22	10	48	19	6	24	17	4	6	17	4	10	20	6	10	23	9	25	25	12	65	25	13	126	26	14	141
KAMPALA, *Uganda*	28	18	58	28	18	68	27	18	128	26	18	185	26	17	134	25	17	71	25	17	55	26	16	87	27	17	100	27	17	119	27	17	142	27	17	95
KHARTOUM, *Sudan*	32	15	0	34	16	0	38	19	0	41	22	0	42	25	4	41	26	7	38	25	49	37	24	69	39	25	21	40	24	5	36	20	0	33	17	0
KINSHASA, *D.R.C.*	31	21	138	31	22	148	32	22	184	32	22	220	31	22	145	29	19	5	27	18	3	29	18	4	31	20	40	31	21	133	31	22	235	30	21	156
KISANGANI, *D.R.C.*	31	21	97	31	21	107	31	21	172	31	21	190	31	21	162	30	21	128	29	19	114	28	20	178	29	20	164	30	20	233	29	20	207	30	20	105
LAGOS, *Nigeria*	31	23	27	32	25	44	32	26	98	32	25	146	31	24	252	29	23	414	28	23	253	28	23	69	28	23	153	29	23	197	31	24	66	31	24	25
LIBREVILLE, *Gabon*	31	23	164	31	22	137	32	23	248	32	23	232	31	22	181	29	21	24	28	20	3	29	21	6	29	22	69	30	22	332	30	22	378	31	22	197
LIVINGSTONE, *Zambia*	29	19	175	29	19	160	29	18	95	30	15	25	28	11	5	25	7	1	25	7	0	28	10	0	32	15	2	34	19	26	33	19	78	31	19	176
LUANDA, *Angola*	28	23	34	29	24	35	30	24	90	29	24	127	28	23	18	25	20	0	23	18	0	23	18	1	24	19	2	26	22	6	28	23	32	28	23	23
LUBUMBASHI, *D.R.C.*	28	16	253	28	17	256	28	16	210	28	14	51	27	10	4	26	7	1	26	6	0	28	8	0	32	11	6	33	14	31	31	16	150	28	17	272
LUSAKA, *Zambia*	26	17	213	26	17	172	26	17	104	26	15	22	25	12	3	23	10	0	23	9	0	25	12	0	29	15	1	31	18	14	29	18	86	27	17	200
LUXOR, *Egypt*	23	6	0	26	7	0	30	10	0	35	15	0	40	21	0	41	21	0	42	23	0	41	23	0	39	22	0	37	18	1	31	12	0	26	7	0
MAPUTO, *Mozambique*	30	22	153	31	22	134	29	21	99	28	19	52	27	16	29	25	13	18	24	13	15	26	14	13	27	16	32	28	18	51	28	19	78	29	21	94
MARRAKECH, *Morocco*	18	4	27	20	6	31	23	9	36	26	11	32	29	14	17	33	17	7	38	19	2	38	20	3	33	17	7	28	14	20	23	9	37	19	6	28
MOGADISHU, *Somalia*	30	23	0	30	23	0	31	24	8	32	26	58	32	25	59	29	23	78	28	23	67	28	23	42	29	23	21	30	24	30	31	24	40	30	24	9
MONROVIA, *Liberia*	30	23	5	29	23	3	31	23	112	31	23	297	30	22	340	27	23	917	27	22	615	27	23	472	27	22	759	28	22	640	29	23	208	30	23	74
NAIROBI, *Kenya*	25	12	45	26	13	43	25	14	73	24	14	160	22	13	119	21	12	30	21	11	13	21	11	13	24	11	26	24	13	42	23	13	121	23	13	77
N'DJAMENA, *Chad*	34	14	0	37	16	0	40	21	0	42	23	8	40	25	31	38	24	62	33	22	150	31	22	215	33	22	91	36	21	22	36	17	0	33	14	0
NIAMEY, *Niger*	34	14	0	37	18	0	41	22	3	42	25	6	41	27	35	38	25	75	34	23	143	32	23	187	34	23	90	38	23	16	38	18	1	34	15	0
NOUAKCHOTT, *Maurit.*	29	14	1	31	15	3	32	17	1	32	18	1	34	21	1	33	23	3	32	23	13	32	24	104	34	24	23	33	22	10	32	18	3	28	13	1
TIMBUKTU, *Mali*	31	13	0	34	14	0	38	19	0	42	22	1	43	26	4	43	27	19	39	25	62	36	24	79	39	24	33	40	23	3	37	18	0	32	13	0
TRIPOLI, *Libya*	16	8	69	17	9	40	19	11	27	22	14	13	24	16	5	27	19	1	29	22	0	30	22	1	29	22	11	27	18	38	23	14	60	18	9	81
TUNIS, *Tunisia*	14	6	62	16	7	52	18	8	46	21	11	38	24	13	22	29	17	10	32	20	3	33	21	7	31	19	32	25	15	55	20	11	54	16	7	63
WADI HALFA, *Sudan*	24	9	0	27	10	0	31	14	0	36	18	0	40	22	1	41	24	0	41	25	1	41	25	0	40	24	0	37	21	0	30	15	0	25	11	0
YAOUNDÉ, *Cameroon*	29	19	26	29	19	55	29	19	140	29	19	193	28	19	216	27	19	163	27	19	62	27	18	80	27	19	216	27	18	292	28	19	120	28	19	28
ZANZIBAR, *Tanzania*	32	24	75	33	24	61	33	25	150	30	25	350	29	24	251	28	23	54	28	22	44	28	22	39	29	22	48	30	23	86	32	24	201	32	24	145
ZOMBA, *Malawi*	27	18	299	27	18	269	26	18	230	26	17	85	24	14	23	22	12	13	22	12	8	24	13	8	27	15	8	29	18	29	29	19	124	27	18	281
ATLANTIC ISLANDS																																				
ASCENSION ISLAND	29	23	4	31	23	8	31	24	23	31	24	27	31	23	10	29	23	14	29	22	12	28	22	10	28	22	8	28	22	7	28	22	4	29	22	3
FALKLAND ISLANDS	13	6	71	13	5	58	12	4	64	9	3	66	7	1	66	5	-1	53	4	-1	51	5	-1	51	7	1	38	9	2	41	11	3	51	12	4	71
FUNCHAL, *Madeira Is.*	19	13	87	18	13	88	19	13	79	19	14	43	21	16	22	22	17	9	24	19	2	24	19	3	24	19	27	23	18	85	22	16	106	19	14	87
HAMILTON, *Bermuda Is.*	20	14	112	20	14	119	20	14	122	22	15	104	24	18	117	27	21	112	29	23	114	30	23	137	29	22	132	26	21	147	23	17	127	21	16	119
LAS PALMAS, *Canary Is.*	21	14	28	22	14	21	22	15	15	22	16	10	23	17	3	24	18	1	25	19	1	26	21	0	26	21	6	26	19	18	24	18	37	22	16	32
NUUK, *Greenland*	-7	-12	36	-7	-13	43	-4	-11	41	-1	-7	30	4	-2	43	8	1	36	11	3	56	11	3	79	6	1	84	2	-3	64	-2	-7	48	-5	-10	38
PONTA DELGADA, *Azores*	17	12	105	17	11	91	17	12	87	18	12	62	20	13	57	22	15	36	25	17	25	26	18	34	25	17	75	22	16	97	20	14	108	18	12	98
PRAIA, *Cape Verde*	25	20	1	25	19	2	26	20	0	26	21	0	27	21	0	28	22	0	28	24	7	29	24	63	29	25	88	29	24	44	28	23	15	26	22	5
REYKJAVÍK, *Iceland*	2	-2	86	3	-2	75	4	-1	76	6	1	56	10	4	42	12	7	45	14	9	51	14	8	62	11	6	71	7	3	88	4	0	83	2	-2	84
THULE, *Greenland*	-17	-27	7	-20	-29	8	-19	-28	4	-13	-23	4	-2	-9	5	5	-1	6	8	2	14	6	1	17	1	-6	13	-5	-13	11	-11	-19	11	-18	-27	5
TRISTAN DA CUNHA	19	15	103	20	16	110	19	14	133	18	14	137	16	12	153	14	11	153	14	10	54	13	9	162	13	9	157	15	11	148	16	12	124	18	14	131
PACIFIC ISLANDS																																				
APIA, *Samoa*	30	24	437	29	24	360	30	23	356	30	24	236	29	23	174	29	23	135	29	23	100	29	24	111	29	23	144	29	24	206	30	23	259	29	23	374
AUCKLAND, *New Zealand*	23	16	70	23	16	86	22	15	77	19	13	96	17	11	115	14	9	126	13	8	131	14	8	112	16	9	94	17	11	93	19	12	82	21	14	78
DARWIN, *Australia*	32	25	396	32	25	331	33	25	282	33	24	97	33	23	18	31	21	3	31	19	1	32	21	4	33	23	15	34	25	60	34	26	130	33	26	239
DUNEDIN, *New Zealand*	19	10	81	19	10	70	17	9	78	15	7	75	12	5	78	9	4	78	9	3	70	11	3	61	13	5	61	15	6	70	17	7	79	18	9	81
GALÁPAGOS IS., *Ecuador*	30	22	20	30	24	36	31	24	28	31	24	18	30	23	1	28	22	1	27	21	1	27	19	1	27	19	1	27	19	1	27	20	1	28	21	1
GUAM, *Mariana Is.*	29	24	138	29	23	116	29	24	121	31	24	108	31	25	164	31	25	150	30	24	274	30	24	368	30	24	374	30	24	334	30	25	231	29	24	160
HOBART, *Tasmania*	22	12	51	22	12	38	20	11	46	17	9	51	14	7	46	12	5	51	11	4	51	13	5	49	15	6	47	17	8	60	19	9	52	21	11	57
MELBOURNE, *Australia*	26	14	48	26	14	47	24	13	52	20	11	57	17	8	58	14	7	49	13	6	49	15	6	50	17	8	59	19	9	67	22	11	60	24	12	59
NAHA, *Okinawa*	19	13	125	19	13	126	21	15	159	24	18	165	27	20	252	29	24	280	32	25	178	31	25	270	31	24	175	27	21	165	24	18	133	21	14	111
NOUMÉA, *N. Caledonia*	30	22	111	29	23	130	29	22	155	28	21	121	26	19	106	25	18	107	24	17	91	24	16	73	26	17	56	27	18	53	28	20	55	30	21	77
PAPEETE, *Tahiti*	32	22	335	32	22	292	32	22	165	32	22	173	31	21	124	30	21	81	30	20	66	30	20	48	30	21	58	31	21	86	31	22	165	31	22	302
PERTH, *Australia*	29	17	9	29	17	13	27	16	19	24	14	45	21	12	122	18	10	182	17	9	174	18	9	136	19	10	80	21	12	53	24	14	21	27	16	13
PORT MORESBY, *P.N.G.*	32	24	179	31	24	196	31	24	190	31	24	120	30	24	65	29	23	39	28	23	27	28	23	26	29	23	33	30	24	35	31	24	56	32	24	121
SUVA, *Fiji Islands*	30	23	305	30	23	293	30	23	367	29	23	342	28	22	261	27	21	166	26	20	142	26	20	184	27	21	200	27	21	217	28	22	266	29	23	296
SYDNEY, *Australia*	26	18	103	26	18	111	24	17	131	22	14	130	19	11	123	16	9	129	16	8	103	17	9	80	19	11	69	22	13	83	23	16	81	25	17	78
WELLINGTON, *N.Z.*	21	13	79	21	13	80	19	12	85	17	11	98	14	8	121	13	7	124	12	6	139	12	6	121	14	8	99	16	9	105	17	10	88	19	12	90

Aaglet *well*
Aain *spring*
Aauinat *spring*
Āb *river, water*
Ache *stream*
Açude *reservoir*
Ada,-si *island*
Adrar *mountain-s, plateau*
Aguada *dry lake bed*
Aguelt *water hole, well*
'Ain, Aïn *spring, well*
Aïoun-et *spring-s, well*
Aivi *mountain*
Ákra, Akrotírion *cape, promontory*
Alb *mountain, ridge*
Alföld *plain*
Alin' *mountain range*
Alpe-n *mountain-s*
Altiplanicie *high-plain, plateau*
Alto *hill-s, mountain-s, ridge*
Älv-en *river*
Āmba *hill, mountain*
Anou *well*
Anse *bay, inlet*
Ao *bay, cove, estuary*
Ap *cape, point*
Archipel, Archipiélago *archipelago*
Arcipelago, Arkhipelag *archipelago*
Arquipélago *archipelago*
Arrecife-s *reef-s*
Arroio, Arroyo *brook, gully, rivulet, stream*
Ås *ridge*
Ava *channel*
Aylagy *gulf*
'Ayn *spring, well*

Ba *intermittent stream, river*
Baai *bay, cove, lagoon*
Bāb *gate, strait*
Badia *bay*
Bælt *strait*
Bagh *bay*
Bahar *drainage basin*
Bahía *bay*
Bahr, Baḩr *bay, lake, river, sea, wadi*
Baía, Baie *bay*
Bajo-s *shoal-s*
Ban *village*
Bañado-s *flooded area, swamp-s*
Banc, Banco-s *bank-s, sandbank-s, shoal-s*
Band *lake*
Bandao *peninsula*
Baño-s *hot spring-s, spa*
Baraj-ı *dam, reservoir*
Barra *bar, sandbank*
Barrage, Barragem *dam, lake, reservoir*
Barranca *gorge, ravine*
Bazar *marketplace*
Ben, Benin *mountain*
Belt *strait*
Bereg *bank, coast, shore*
Berg-e *mountain-s*
Bil *lake*
Biq'at *plain, valley*
Bir, Bîr, Bi'r *spring, well*
Birket *lake, pool, swamp*
Bjerg-e *mountain-s, range*
Boca, Bocca *channel, river, mouth*
Bocht *bay*
Bodden *bay*
Boğaz, -i *strait*
Bögeni *reservoir*
Boka *gulf, mouth*
Bol'sh-oy, -aya, -oye *big*
Bolsón *inland basin*
Boubairet *lagoon, lake*
Bras *arm, branch of a stream*
Braţ, -ul *arm, branch of a stream*
Bre, -en *glacier, ice cap*
Bredning *bay, broad water*
Bruch *marsh*
Bucht *bay*
Bugt-en *bay*
Buḩayrat, Buheirat *lagoon, lake, marsh*
Bukhta, Bukta, Bukt-en *bay*
Bulak, Bulaq *spring*
Bum *hill, mountain*
Burnu, Burun *cape, point*
Busen *gulf*
Buuraha *hill-s, mountain-s*
Buyuk *big, large*

Cabeza-s *head-s, summit-s*
Cabo *cape*
Cachoeira *rapids, waterfall*
Cal *hill, peak*
Caleta *cove, inlet*
Campo-s *field-s, flat country*
Canal *canal, channel, strait*
Caño *channel, stream*
Cao Nguyen *mountain, plateau*
Cap, Capo *cape*
Capitán *captain*
Càrn *mountain*
Castillo *castle, fort*
Catarata-s *cataract-s, waterfall-s*
Causse *upland*
Çay *brook, stream*
Cay-s, Cayo-s *island-s, key-s, shoal-s*
Cerro-s *hill-s, peak-s*
Chaîne, Chaînons *mountain chain, range*
Chapada-s *plateau, upland-s*
Chedo *archipelago*
Chenal *river channel*
Chersónisos *peninsula*
Chhung *bay*
Chi *lake*
Chiang *bay*
Chiao *cape, point, rock*
Ch'ih *lake*
Chink *escarpment*
Chott *intermittent salt lake, salt marsh*
Chou *island*
Ch'ü *canal*
Ch'üntao *archipelago, islands*
Chute-s *cataract-s, waterfall-s*
Chyrvony *red*
Cima *mountain, peak, summit*
Ciudad *city*
Co *lake*
Col *pass*
Collina, Colline *hill, mountains*
Con *island*
Cordillera *mountain chain*
Corno *mountain, peak*
Coronel *colonel*
Corredeira *cascade, rapids*
Costa *coast*
Côte *coast, slope*
Coxilha, Cuchilla *range of low hills*
Crique *creek, stream*
Csatorna *canal, channel*
Cul de Sac *bay, inlet*

Da *great, greater*
Daban *pass*
Dağ, -ı, Dagh *mountain*
Dağlar, -ı *mountains*
Dahr *cliff, mesa*
Dake *mountain, peak*
Dal-en *valley*
Dala *steppe*
Dan *cape, point*
Danau *lake*
Dao *island*
Dar'ya *lake, river*
Daryācheh *lake, marshy lake*
Dasht *desert, plain*
Dawan *pass*
Dawḩat *bay, cove, inlet*
Deniz, -i *sea*
Dent-s *peak-s*
Deo *pass*
Desēt *hummock, island, land-tied island*
Desierto *desert*
Détroit *channel, strait*
Dhar *hills, ridge, tableland*
Ding *mountain*
Distrito *district*
Djebel *mountain, range*
Do *island-s, rock-s*
Doi *hill, mountain*
Dome *ice dome*
Dong *village*
Dooxo *floodplain*
Dzong *castle, fortress*

Eiland-en *island-s*
Eilean *island*
Ejland *island*
Elv *river*
Embalse *lake, reservoir*
Emi *mountain, rock*
Enseada, Ensenada *bay, cove*
Ér *rivulet, stream*
Erg *sand dune region*
Est *east*
Estación *railroad station*
Estany *lagoon, lake*
Estero *estuary, inlet, lagoon, marsh*
Estrecho *strait*
Étang *lake, pond*
Eylandt *island*
Ežeras *lake*
Ezers *lake*

Falaise *cliff, escarpment*
Farvand-et *channel, sound*
Fell *mountain*
Feng *mount, peak*
Fiord-o *inlet, sound*
Fiume *river*
Fjäll-et *mountain*
Fjällen *mountains*
Fjärd-en *fjord*
Fjardar, Fjörður *fjord*
Fjeld *mountain*
Fjell-ene *mountain-s*
Fjöll *mountain-s*
Fjord-en *inlet, fjord*
Fleuve *river*
Fljót *large river*
Flói *bay, marshland*
Foci *river mouths*
Főcsatorna *principal canal*
Förde *fjord, gulf, inlet*
Forsen *rapids, waterfall*
Fortaleza *fort, fortress*
Fortín *fortified post*
Foss-en *waterfall*
Foum *pass, passage*
Foz *mouth of a river*
Fuerte *fort, fortress*
Fwafwate *waterfalls*

Gacan-ka *hill, peak*
Gal *pond, spring, waterhole, well*
Gang *harbor*
Gangri *peak, range*
Gaoyuan *plateau*
Garaet, Gara'et *lake, lake bed, salt lake*
Gardaneh *pass*
Garet *hill, mountain*
Gat *channel*
Gata *bay, inlet, lake*
Gattet *channel, strait*
Gaud *depression, saline tract*
Gave *mountain stream*
Gebel *mountain-s, range*
Gebergte *mountain range*
Gebirge *mountains, range*
Geçidi *mountain pass, passage*
Geçit *mountain pass, passage*
Gezâir *islands*
Gezîra-t, Gezîret *island, peninsula*
Ghats *mountain range*
Ghubb-at, -et *bay, gulf*
Giri *mountain*
Gletscher *glacier*
Gobernador *governor*
Gobi *desert*
Gol *river, stream*
Göl, -ü *lake*
Golets *mountain, peak*
Golf, -e, -o *gulf*
Gor-a, -y, Gór-a, -y *mountain,-s*
Got *point*
Gowd *depression*
Goz *sand ridge*
Gran, -de *great, large*
Gryada *mountains, ridge*
Guan *pass*
Guba *bay, gulf*
Guelta *well*
Gum *desert*
Guntō *archipelago*
Gunung *mountain*
Gura *mouth, passage*
Guyot *table mount*

Haḍabat *plateau*
Haehyŏp *strait*
Haff *lagoon*
Hai *lake, sea*
Haihsia *strait*
Haixia *channel, strait*
Hakau *reef, rock*
Hakuchi *anchorage*
Halvø, Halvøy-a *peninsula*
Hama *beach*
Hamada, Ḩammādah *rocky desert*
Hamn *harbor, port*
Hāmūn, Hamun *depression, lake*
Hana *cape, point*
Hantō *peninsula*
Har *hill, mound, mountain*
Ḩarrat *lava field*
Hasi, Hassi *spring, well*
Hauteur *elevation, height*
Hav-et *sea*
Havn, Havre *harbor, port*
Hawr *lake, marsh*
Häyk' *lake, reservoir*
Hegy, -ség *mountain, -s, range*
Heiau *temple*
Ho *canal, lake, river*
Hoek *hook, point*
Hög-en *high, hill*
Höhe, -n *height, high*
Høj *height, hill*
Holm, -e, Holmene *island-s, islet -s*
Ḩolot *dunes*
Hon *island-s*
Hor-a, -y *mountain, -s*
Horn *horn, peak*
Houma *point*
Hoved *headland, peninsula, point*
Hraun *lava field*
Hsü *island*
Hu *lake, reservoir*
Huk *cape, point*
Hüyük *hill, mound*

Idehan *sand dunes*
Île-s, Ilha-s, Illa-s, Îlot-s *island-s, islet-s*
Îlet, Ilhéu-s *islet, -s*
Irhil *mountain-s*
'Irq *sand dune-s*
Isblink *glacier, ice field*
Is-en *glacier*
Isla-s, Islote *island-s, islet*
Isol-a, -e *island, -s*
Istmo *isthmus*
Iwa *island, islet, rock*

Jabal, Jebel *mountain-s, range*
Järv, -i, Jaure, Javrre *lake*
Jazā'ir, Jazīrat, Jazīreh *island-s*
Jehīl *lake*
Jezero, Jezioro *lake*
Jiang *river, stream*
Jiao *cape*
Jibāl *hill, mountain, ridge*
Jima *island-s, rock-s*
Jøkel, Jökull *glacier, ice cap*
Joki, Jokka *river*
Jökulsá *river from a glacier*
Jūn *bay*

Kaap *cape*
Kafr *village*
Kaikyō *channel, strait*
Kaise *mountain*
Kaiwan *bay, gulf, sea*
Kanal *canal, channel*
Kangri *mountain, peak*
Kap, Kapp *cape*
Kavīr *salt desert*
Kefar *village*
Kënet' *lagoon, lake*
Kep *cape, point*
Kepulauan *archipelago, islands*
Khalīg, Khalīj *bay, gulf*
Khirb-at, -et *ancient site, ruins*
Khrebet *mountain range*
Kinh *canal*
Klint *bluff, cliff*
Kō *bay, cove, harbor*
Ko *island, lake*
Koh *island, mountain, range*
Köl-i *lake*
Kólpos *gulf*
Kong *mountain*
Körfez, -i *bay, gulf*
Kosa *spit of land*
Kou *estuary, river mouth*
Kowtal-e *pass*
Krasn-yy, -aya, -oye *red*
Kryazh *mountain range, ridge*
Kuala *estuary, river mouth*
Kuan *mountain pass*
Kūh, Kūhhā *mountain-s, range*
Kul', Kuli *lake*
Kum *sandy desert*
Kundo *archipelago*
Kuppe *hill-s, mountain-s*
Kust *coast, shore*
Kyst *coast*
Kyun *island*

La *pass*
Lac, Lac-ul, -us *lake*
Lae *cape, point*
Lago, -a *lagoon, lake*
Lagoen, Lagune *lagoon*
Laguna-s *lagoon-s, lake-s*
Laht *bay, gulf, harbor*
Laje *reef, rock ledge*
Laut *sea*
Lednik *glacier*
Leida *channel*
Lhari *mountain*
Li *village*
Liedao *archipelago, islands*
Liehtao *archipelago, islands*
Liman-ı *bay, estuary*
Límni *lake*
Ling *mountain-s, range*
Linn *pool, waterfall*
Lintasan *passage*
Liqen *lake*
Llano-s *plain-s*
Loch, Lough *lake, arm of the sea*
Loma-s *hill-s, knoll-s*

Mal *mountain, range*
Mal-yy, -aya, -oye *little, small*
Mamarr *pass, path*
Man *bay*
Mar, Mare *large lake, sea*
Marsa, Marsá *bay, inlet*
Masabb *mouth of river*
Massif *massif, mountain-s*
Mauna *mountain*
Mēda *plain*
Meer *lake, sea*
Melkosopochnik *undulating plain*
Mesa, Meseta *plateau, tableland*
Mierzeja *sandspit*
Minami *south*
Mios *island*
Misaki *cape, peninsula, point*
Mochun *passage*
Mong *town, village*
Mont-e, -i, -s *mount, -ain, -s*
Montagne, -s *mount, -ain, -s*
Montaña, -s *mountain, -s*
More *sea*
Morne *hill, peak*
Morro *bluff, headland, hill*
Motu, -s *islands*
Mouïet *well*
Mouillage *anchorage*
Muang *town, village*
Mui *cape, point*
Mull *headland, promontory*
Munkhafad *depression*
Munte *mountain*
Munţi-i *mountains*
Muong *town, village*
Mynydd *mountain*
Mys *cape*
Nacional *national*
Nada *gulf, sea*
Næs, Näs *cape, point*
Nafūd *area of dunes, desert*
Nagor'ye *mountain range, plateau*
Nahar, Nahr *river, stream*
Nakhon *town*
Namakzār *salt waste*
Ne *island, reef, rock-s*
Neem *cape, point, promontory*
Nes, Ness *peninsula, point*
Nevado-s *snow-capped mountain-s*
Nez *cape, promontory*
Ni *village*
Nísi, Nísia, Nisís, Nísoi *island-s, islet-s*
Nisídhes *islets*
Nizhn-iy, -yaya, -eye *lower*
Nizmennost' *low country*
Noord *north*
Nord-re *north-ern*
Nørre *north-ern*
Nos *cape, nose, point*
Nosy *island, reef, rock*
Nov-yy, -aya, -oye *new*
Nudo *mountain*
Numa *lake*
Nunatak, -s, -ker *peak-s surrounded by ice cap*
Nur *lake, salt lake*
Nuruu *mountain range, ridge*
Nut-en *peak*
Nuur *lake*
Ö-n, Ø-er *island-s*
Oblast' *administrative division, province, region*
Oceanus *ocean*
Odde-n *cape, point*
Øer-ne *islands*
Oglat *group of wells*
Oguilet *well*
Ór-os, -i *mountain, -s*
Órmos *bay, port*
Ort *place, point*
Øst-er *east*
Ostrov, -a, Ostrv-o, -a *island, -s*
Otoci, Otok *islands, island*
Ouadi, Oued *river, watercourse*
Øy-a *island*
Øyane *islands*
Ozer-o, -a *lake, -s*
Pää *mountain, point*
Palus *marsh*
Pampa-s *grassy plain-s*
Pantà *lake, reservoir*
Pantanal *marsh, swamp*
Pao, P'ao *lake*
Parbat *mountain*
Parque *park*
Pas, -ul *pass*
Paso, Passo *pass*
Passe *channel, pass*
Pasul *pass*
Pedra *rock*
Pegunungan *mountain range*
Pellg *bay, bight*
Peña *cliff, rock*
Pendi *basin*
Penedo-s *rock-s*
Péninsule *peninsula*
Peñón *point, rock*
Pereval *mountain pass*
Pertuis *strait*
Peski *sands, sandy region*
Phnom *hill, mountain, range*
Phou *mountain range*
Phu *mountain*
Piana-o *plain*
Pic, Pik, Piz *peak*
Picacho *mountain, peak*
Pico-s *peak-s*
Pistyll *waterfall*
Piton-s *peak-s*
Pivdennyy *southern*
Plaja, Playa *beach, inlet, shore*
Planalto, Plato *plateau*
Planina *mountain, plateau*
Plassen *lake*
Ploskogor'ye *plateau, upland*
Pointe *point*
Polder *reclaimed land*
Poluostrov *peninsula*
Pongo *water gap*
Ponta, -l *cape, point*
Ponte *bridge*
Poolsaar *peninsula*
Portezuelo *pass*
Porto *port*
Poulo *island*
Praia *beach, seashore*
Presa *reservoir*
Presidente *president*
Presqu'île *peninsula*
Prokhod *pass*
Proliv *strait*
Promontorio *promontory*
Průsmyk *mountain pass*
Przylądek *cape*
Puerto *bay, pass, port*
Pulao *island-s*
Pulau, Pulo *island*
Pun *peak*
Puncak *peak, summit, top*
Punt, Punta, -n *point, -s*
Puu *hill, mountain*
Puy *peak*
Qā' *depression, marsh, mud flat*
Qal'at *fort*
Qal'eh *castle, fort*
Qanâ *canal*
Qārat *hill-s, mountain-s*
Qaşr *castle, fort, hill*
Qila *fort*
Qiryat *settlement, suburb*
Qolleh *peak*
Qooriga *anchorage, bay*
Qoz *dunes, sand ridge*
Qu *canal*
Quebrada *ravine, stream*
Qullai *peak, summit*
Qum *desert, sand*
Qundao *archipelago, islands*
Qurayyāt *hills*
Raas *cape, point*
Rabt *hill*
Rada *roadstead*
Rade *anchorage, roadstead*
Rags *point*
Ramat *hill, mountain*
Rand *ridge of hills*
Rann *swamp*
Raqaba *wadi, watercourse*
Ras, Râs, Ra's *cape*
Ravnina *plain*
Récif-s *reef-s*
Regreg *marsh*
Represa *reservoir*
Reservatório *reservoir*
Restinga *barrier, sand area*
Rettō *chain of islands*
Ri *mountain range, village*
Ría *estuary*
Ribeirão *stream*
Río, Rio *river*
Rivière *river*
Roca-s *cliff, rock-s*
Roche-r, -s *rock-s*
Rosh *mountain, point*
Rt *cape, point*
Rubha *headland*
Rupes *scarp*
Saar *island*
Saari, Sar *island*
Sabkha-t, Sabkhet *lagoon, marsh, salt lake*
Sagar *lake, sea*
Sahara, Şaḩrā' *desert*
Sahl *plain*
Saki *cape, point*
Salar *salt flat*
Salina *salt pan*
Salin-as, -es *salt flat-s, salt marsh-es*
Salto *waterfall*
Sammyaku *mountain range*
San *hill, mountain*
San, -ta, -to *saint*
Sandur *sandy area*
Sankt *saint*
Sanmaek *mountain range*
São *saint*
Sarīr *gravel desert*
Sasso *mountain, stone*
Savane *savanna*
Scoglio *reef, rock*
Se *reef, rock-s, shoal-s*
Sebjet *salt lake, salt marsh*
Sebkha *salt lake, salt marsh*
Sebkhet *lagoon, salt lake*
See *lake, sea*
Selat *strait*
Selkä *lake, ridge*
Semenanjung *peninsula*
Sen *mountain*
Seno *bay, gulf*
Serra, Serranía *range of hills or mountains*
Severn-yy, -aya, -oye *northern*
Sgùrr *peak*
Sha *island, shoal*
Sha'ib *ravine, watercourse*
Shamo *desert*
Shan *island-s, mountain-s, range*
Shankou *mountain pass*
Shanmo *mountain range*
Sharm *cove, creek, harbor*
Shaţţ *large river*
Shi *administrative division, municipality*
Shima *island-s, rock-s*
Shō *island, reef, rock*
Shotō *archipelago*
Shott *intermittent salt lake*
Shuiku *reservoir*
Shuitao *channel*
Shyghanaghy *bay, gulf*
Sierra *mountain range*
Silsilesi *mountain chain, ridge*
Sint *saint*
Sinus *bay, sea*
Sjö-n *lake*
Skarv-et *barren mountain*
Skerry *rock*
Slieve *mountain*
Sø *lake*
Sønder, Søndre *south-ern*
Sopka *conical mountain, volcano*
Sor *lake, salt lake*
Sør, Sör *south-ern*
Sory *salt lake, salt marsh*
Spitz-e *peak, point, top*
Sredn-iy, -yaya, -eye *central, middle*
Stagno *lake, pond*
Stantsiya *station*
Stausee *reservoir*
Stenón *channel, strait*
Step'-i *steppe-s*
Štít *summit, top*
Stor-e *big, great*
Straat *strait*
Straum-en *current-s*
Strelka *spit of land*
Stretet, Stretto *strait*
Su *reef, river, rock, stream*
Sud *south*
Sudo *channel, strait*
Suidō *channel, strait*
Şummān *rocky desert*
Sund *sound, strait*
Sunden *channel, inlet, sound*
Svyat-oy, -aya, -oye *holy, saint*
Sziget *island*
Tagh *mountain-s*
Tall *hill, mound*
T'an *lake*
Tanezrouft *desert*
Tang *plain, steppe*
Tangi *peninsula, point*
Tanjong, Tanjung *cape, point*
Tao *island-s*
Tarso *hill-s, mountain-s*
Tassili *plateau, upland*
Tau *mountain-s, range*
Taūy *hills, mountains*
Tchabal *mountain-s*
Te Ava *tidal flat*
Tel-l *hill, mound*
Telok, Teluk *bay*
Tepe, -si *hill, peak*
Tepuí *mesa, mountain*
Terara *hill, mountain, peak*
Testa *bluff, head*
Thale *lake*
Thang *plain, steppe*
Tien *lake*
Tierra *land, region*
Ting *hill, mountain*
Tir'at *canal*
Tó *lake, pool*
To, Tō *island-s, rock-s*
Tonle *lake*
Tope *hill, mountain, peak*
Top-pen *peak-s*
Träsk *bog, lake*
Tso *lake*
Tsui *cape, point*
Tübegi *peninsula*
Tulu *hill, mountain*
Tunturi-t *hill-s, mountain-s*
Uad *wadi, watercourse*
Udde-m *point*
Ujong, Ujung *cape, point*
Umi *bay, lagoon, lake*
Ura *bay, inlet, lake*
'Urūq *dune area*
Uul, Uula *mountain, range*
'Uyûn *springs*
Vaara *mountain*
Vaart *canal*
Vær *fishing station*
Vaïn *channel, strait*
Valle, Vallée *valley, wadi*
Vallen *waterfall*
Valli *lagoon, lake*
Vallis *valley*
Vanua *land*
Varre *mountain*
Vatn, Vatten, Vatnet *lake, water*
Veld *grassland, plain*
Verkhn-iy, -yaya, -eye *higher, upper*
Vesi *lake, water*
Vest-er *west*
Via *road*
Vidda *plateau*
Vig, Vík, Vik, -en *bay, cove*
Vinh *bay, gulf*
Vodokhranilishche *reservoir*
Vodoskhovyshche *reservoir*
Volcan, Volcán *volcano*
Vostochn-yy, -aya, -oye *eastern*
Vötn *stream*
Vozvyshennost' *plateau, upland*
Vozyera *lake-s*
Vrchovina *mountains*
Vrch-y *mountain-s*
Vrh *hill, mountain*
Vrŭkh *mountain*
Vyaliki *big, large*
Vysočina *highland*
Wabē *stream*
Wadi, Wâdi, Wādī *valley, watercourse*
Wâhât, Wāḩat *oasis*
Wald *forest, wood*
Wan *bay, gulf*
Water *harbor*
Webi *stream*
Wiek *cove, inlet*
Xia *gorge, strait*
Xiao *lesser, little*
Yanchi *salt lake*
Yang *ocean*
Yarymadasy *peninsula*
Yazovir *reservoir*
Yŏlto *island group*
Yoma *mountain range*
Yü *island*
Yumco *lake*
Yunhe *canal*
Yuzhn-yy, -aya, -oye *southern*
Zaki *cape, point*
Zaliv *bay, gulf*
Zan *mountain, ridge*
Zangbo *river, stream*
Zapadn-yy, -aya, -oye *western*
Zatoka *bay, gulf*
Zee *bay, sea*
Zemlya *land*

The following system is used to locate a place on a map in the *National Geographic Concise Atlas of the World.* The boldface type after an entry refers to the plate on which the map is found. The letter-number combination refers to the grid on which the particular place-name is located. The edge of each map is marked horizontally with numbers and vertically with letters. In between, at equally spaced intervals, are index squares (■). If these ticks were connected with lines, each page would be divided into a grid. Take Cartagena, Colombia, for example. The index entry reads "Cartagena, *Col.* **68** A2." On page 68, Cartagena is located within the grid square where row A and column 2 intersect (see below).

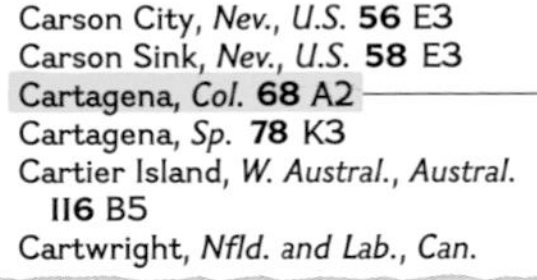
Carson City, *Nev., U.S.* **56** E3
Carson Sink, *Nev., U.S.* **58** E3
Cartagena, *Col.* **68** A2
Cartagena, *Sp.* **78** K3
Cartier Island, *W. Austral., Austral.* **116** B5
Cartwright, *Nfld. and Lab., Can.*

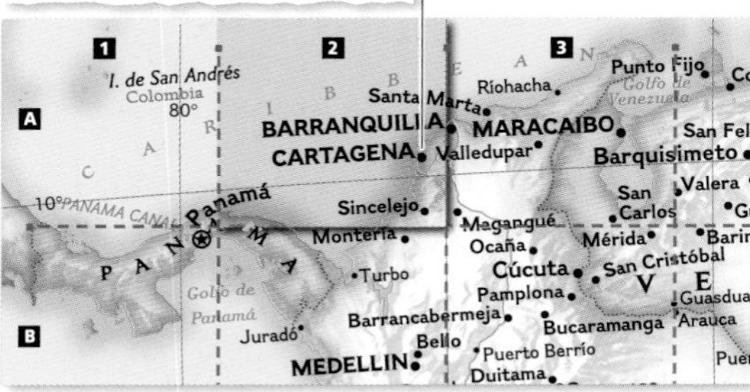

A place-name may appear on several maps, but the index lists only the best presentation. Usually, this means that a feature is indexed to the largest-scale map on which it appears in its entirety. (Note: Rivers are often labeled multiple times even on a single map. In such cases, the rivers are indexed to labels that are closest to their mouths.) The name of the country or continent in which a feature lies is shown in italic type and is usually abbreviated. (A full list of abbreviations appears on page 130.)

The index lists more than proper names. Some entries include a description, as in "Elba, *island, It.* **78** J6" and "Amazon, *river, Braz.-Peru* **70** D8." In languages other than English, the description of a physical feature may be part of the name; e.g., the "'Erg" in "Chech, 'Erg, *Alg.-Mali* **104** E4," means "sand dune region." The glossary of Foreign Terms on pages 136–137 translates such terms into English.

When a feature or place can be referred to by more than one name, both may appear in the index with cross-references. For example, the entry for Cairo, Egypt reads "Cairo *see* El Qâhira, *Egypt* **102** D9." That entry is "El Qâhira (Cairo), *Egypt* **102** D9."

Acknowledgments

WORLD THEMATIC SECTION

Structure of the Earth
pp. 22–23

CONSULTANTS
Laurel M. Bybell
U.S. Geological Survey (USGS)
Robert I. Tilling
U.S. Geological Survey (USGS)

GRAPHICS
CONTINENTS ADRIFT IN TIME: Christopher R. Scotese/PALEOMAP Project

CUTAWAY OF THE EARTH: Tibor G. Tóth

TECTONIC BLOCK DIAGRAMS: Susan Sanford

PLATE TECTONICS AND GEOLOGIC TIME: *National Geographic Atlas of the World*, 8th ed. Washington, D.C.: The National Geographic Society, 2005.

Climate
pp. 24–27

CONSULTANTS
William Burroughs
H. Michael Mogil
Certified Consulting Meteorologist (CCM)
Vladimir Ryabinin
World Climate Research Programme

GRAPHICS
TOPOGRAPHY: Chapel Design & Marketing and XNR Productions

GLOBAL AIR TEMPERATURE CHANGES, 1850–2000: Reproduced by kind permission of the Climatic Research Unit.

SATELLITE IMAGES
Images originally created for the GLOBE program by NOAA's National Geophysical Data Center, Boulder, Colorado, U.S.A.

CLOUD COVER: International Satellite Cloud Climatology Project (ISCCP); National Aeronautics and Space Administration (NASA); Goddard Institute for Space Studies (GISS). PRECIPITATION: Global Precipitation Climatology Project (GPCP); International Satellite Land Surface Climatology Project (ISLSCP). SOLAR ENERGY: Earth Radiation Budget Experiment (ERBE); Greenhouse Effect Detection Experiment (GEDEX). TEMPERATURE: National Center for Environmental Prediction (NCEP); National Center for Atmospheric Research (NCAR); National Weather Service (NWS).

PHOTOGRAPHS
PAGE 25, Sharon G. Johnson

Population
pp. 28–31

CONSULTANTS
Carl Haub
Population Reference Bureau
Gregory Yetman
Center for International Earth Science Information Network (CIESIN), Columbia University

GENERAL REFERENCES
Center for International Earth Science Information Network (CIESIN), Columbia University: www.ciesin.org

International Migration, 2002. Population Division of the Department of Economic and Social Affairs of the United Nations Secretariat. New York: United Nations, 2002.

Population Reference Bureau: www.prb.org

United Nations World Population Prospects: The 2006 Revision Population Database: esa.un.org/unpp

World Urbanization Prospects: The 2005 Revision. Population Division of the Department of Economic and Social Affairs of the United Nations Secretariat. New York: United Nations, 2006.

GRAPHICS
POPULATION DENSITY: Center for International Earth Science Information Network (CIESIN), Columbia University, and Centro Internacional de Agricultura Tropical (CIAT), 2005. Gridded Population of the World Version 3 (GPWv3): Population Density Grids—World Population Density, 2005 [map]. Palisades, New York: Socioeconomic Data and Applications Center (SEDAC), Columbia University. Available at http://sedac.ciesin.columbia.edu/gpw. Accessed April 2006.

SATELLITE IMAGES
LIGHTS OF THE WORLD: Composite image: MODIS imagery; ETOPO-2 relief; NOAA/NGDC and DMSP lights at night data.

Religions
pp. 32–33

CONSULTANTS
William M. Bodiford
University of California—Los Angeles
Todd Johnson
Center for the Study of Global Christianity, Gordon-Conwell Theological Seminary

GENERAL REFERENCES
World Christian Database: Center for the Study of Global Christianity, Gordon-Conwell Theological Seminary (www.worldchristiandatabase.org)

GRAPHICS
MAJOR RELIGIONS: *National Geographic Atlas of the World*, 8th ed. Washington, D.C.: The National Geographic Society, 2005.

PHOTOGRAPHS
PAGE 32, (LE), Jodi Cobb, National Geographic Photographer
(RT), James L. Stanfield
PAGES 32–33, Tony Heiderer
PAGE 33, (LE), Thomas J. Abercrombie; (RT), Annie Griffiths Belt

Economy
pp. 34–35

CONSULTANTS
William Beyers
University of Washington
Michael Finger
World Trade Organization (WTO)
Richard R. Fix
World Bank
Susan Martin
Institute for the Study of International Migration

GENERAL REFERENCES
CIA *World Factbook*: www.cia.gov

International Monetary Fund: www.imf.org

International Telecommunication Union: www.itu.int

International Trade Statistics, 2006. Geneva, Switzerland: World Trade Organization.

UNESCO Institute for Statistics: www.uis.unesco.org

World Development Indicators, 2005. Washington, D.C.: World Bank.

Note: GDP and GDP (PPP) data on this spread are from the IMF.

GRAPHICS
LABOR MIGRATION: *National Geographic Atlas of the World*, 8th ed. Washington, D.C.: The National Geographic Society, 2005.

Trade
pp. 36–37

CONSULTANTS
Michael Finger and Peter Werner
World Trade Organization (WTO)
United Nations Conference on Trade and Development (UNCTAD)

GENERAL REFERENCES
International Trade Statistics, 2006. Geneva, Switzerland: World Trade Organization.

United Nations Conference on Trade and Development: www.unctad.org

World Trade Organization: www.wto.org

GRAPHICS
GROWTH OF WORLD TRADE: World Trade Organization

Health and Education
pp. 38–39

CONSULTANTS
Carlos Castillo-Salgado
Pan American Health Organization (PAHO)/ World Health Organization (WHO)
George Ingram and Annababette Wils
Education Policy and Data Center
Margaret Kruk
United Nations Millennium Project and University of Michigan School of Public Health
Ruth Levine
Center for Global Development

GENERAL REFERENCES
2006 Report on the Global AIDS Epidemic. World Health Organization and the Joint United Nations Programme on HIV/AIDS, 2006.

Education Policy and Data Center: www.epdc.org

Global Burden of Disease Estimates. Geneva: World Health Organization, 2004.

Human Development Report, 2006. New York: United Nations Development Programme (UNDP), 2006.

UN Millennium Development Goals: www.un.org/millenniumgoals

The State of the World's Children 2007. Table 5: Education. New York: UNICEF, 2007.

The World Health Report 2006. Annex table 5. Selected national health accounts indicators. Geneva: World Health Organization, 2006.

World Bank list of economies, 2005. Washington, D.C.: World Bank.

World Health Organization: www.who.int

Youth (15–24) and Adult (15+) Literacy Rates by Country and by Gender. New York: UNESCO Institute for Statistics, 2006.

GRAPHICS
ACCESS TO IMPROVED SANITATION: Adapted from *WHO Water Supply and Sanitation Monitoring Mid-Term Report, 2004.*

DEVELOPING HUMAN CAPITAL: Adapted from Human Capital Projections developed by Education Policy and Data Center.

Conflict and Terror
pp. 40–41

CONSULTANTS
Barbara Harff
U.S. Naval Academy
Monty G. Marshall
Center for Systemic Peace and Center for Global Policy, George Mason University
Christian Oxenboll
United Nations High Commissioner for Refugees (UNHCR)

GENERAL REFERENCES
Global Statistics. Internal Displacement Monitoring Centre (iDMC). 2006: www.internal-displacement.org

Marshall, Monty G., and Jack Goldstone. *Global Report on Conflict, Governance, and State Fragility 2007.* Foreign Policy Bulletin 17.1 (Winter 2007): 3-21. (Cambridge University Press Journals)

Proliferation News and Resources. Carnegie Endowment for International Peace. 2005: www.carnegieendowment.org/npp

United Nations High Commissioner for Refugees (UNHCR): www.unhcr.org

United Nations Peacekeeping: www.un.org/Depts/dpko

Environmental Stresses
pp. 42–43

CONSULTANT
Christian Lambrechts
Division of Early Warning and Assessment (DEWA), United Nations Environmental Program (UNEP)

GENERAL REFERENCES
Acidification and eutrophication of developing country ecosystems. Swedish University of Agricultural Sciences (SLU), 2002.

Centre of Documentation, Research and Experimentation on Accidental Water Pollution (Cedre): www.le-cedre.fr

EM-DAT: The OFDA/CRED International Disaster Database. Université Catholique de Louvain, Brussels, Belgium: www.em-dat.net

Energy Information Administration. U.S. Department of Energy: www.eia.doe.gov

Global Forest Resources Assessment. Forestry Department of the Food and Agriculture Organization of the United Nations, 2005.

United Nations Environment Programme-World Conservation and Monitoring Program (UNEP-WCMC): www.unep-wcmc.org

GRAPHICS
HUMAN FOOTPRINT: *National Geographic Atlas of the World*, 8th ed. Washington, D.C.: The National Geographic Society, 2005.

SATELLITE IMAGES
DEPLETION OF THE OZONE LAYER: Ozone Processing Team at NASA/Goddard Space Flight Center.

CONTINENTAL AND U.S. THEMATIC MAPS

North America, pages 54–55; South America, pages 72–73; Europe, pages 82–83; Asia, pages 94–95; Africa, pages 106–107; Australia and Oceania, pages 120–121

POPULATION DENSITY: LandScan, Oak Ridge National Laboratory, Department of Energy

DOMINANT ECONOMY: CIA, *The World Factbook*

ENERGY CONSUMPTION: Population Reference Bureau

CLIMATE ZONES: H. J. de Blij, P. O. Muller, and John Wiley & Sons, Inc.

NATURAL EVENTS: USGS Earthquake Hazard Program; Global Volcanism Program, Smithsonian Institution; DMSP lights at night data.

WATER AVAILABILITY: Aaron Wolf, Oregon State University

United States, pages 60–61;

POPULATION CHANGE: U.S. Census Bureau

RELIGIOUS GROUPS: Data for Major Religious Families by Counties of the United States, 2000 from *Religious Congregations and Membership in the United States 2000*, Dale E. Jones, et. al. Nashville, TN: Glenmary Research Center. © 2002 Association of Statisticians of American Religious Bodies. All rights reserved.

RISK TO PROPERTY: USGS Earthquake Hazard Program; Global Volcanism Program, Smithsonian Institution; DMSP lights at night data.

NATIONAL PARKS AND RESERVES: National Park Service, Bureau of Land Management; USDA Forest Service; U.S. Fish and Wildlife Service; Bureau of Indian Affairs; Department of Defense; Department of Energy; NOAA.

FLAGS AND FACTS

Carl Haub
Population Reference Bureau

Whitney Smith
Flag Research Center

DATES OF NATIONAL INDEPENDENCE

Harm J. de Blij
Michigan State University

Leo Dillon
Department of State, Office of the Geographer

Carl Haub
Population Reference Bureau

ART AND ILLUSTRATIONS

COVER ART AND GLOBE, PAGE 7: Tibor G. Tóth

PAGE 160: Tibor G. Tóth (The Living Earth, Inc. data)

SATELLITE IMAGES

WORLD AND CONTINENTAL LAND COVER SATELLITE IMAGES: Boston University Department of Geography and Environment Global Land Cover Project. Source data provided by NASA's Moderate Resolution Imaging Spectroradiometer.

PAGES 10–11: THE WORLD, NASA/JPL/CalTech/Cartographic Applications Group (CAG), NGS. Data derived from NOAA AVHRR 1km (2, 2, 1).

PAGES 20–21: ETOPO-2 relief; Digital Chart of the World

PAGE 24: *Images originally created for the GLOBE program by NOAA's National Geophysical Data Center, Boulder, Colorado, U.S.A. For more detail, see listings under Climate acknowledgments on page 158.*

PAGE 28: LIGHTS OF THE WORLD: Composite image: MODIS imagery; ETOPO-2 relief; NOAA/NGDC and DMSP lights at night data.

PAGE 42: DEPLETION OF THE OZONE LAYER: Ozone Processing Team at NASA/Goddard Space Flight Center.

PHOTOGRAPHS

PAGE 25, Sharon G. Johnson
PAGE 32, (LE), Jodi Cobb/National Geographic Photographer
PAGE 32, (RT), James L. Stanfield
PAGES 32–33, Tony Heiderer
PAGE 33, (LE), Thomas J. Abercrombie
PAGE 33, (RT), Annie Griffiths Belt

PHYSICAL AND POLITICAL MAPS

Bureau of the Census, U.S. Department of Commerce

Bureau of Land Management, U.S. Department of the Interior

Central Intelligence Agency (CIA)

National Geographic Maps

National Geospatial-Intelligence Agency (NGA)

National Park Service, U.S. Department of the Interior

Office of the Geographer, U.S. Department of State

U.S. Board on Geographic Names (BGN)

U.S. Geological Survey, U.S. Department of the Interior

PRINCIPAL REFERENCE SOURCES

Columbia Gazetteer of the World. Cohen, Saul B., ed. New York: Columbia University Press, 1998.

Encarta World English Dictionary. New York: St. Martin's Press and Microsoft Encarta, 1999.

Human Development Report, 2005. New York: United Nations Development Programme (UNDP), Oxford University Press, 2005.

International Trade Statistics, 2005. Geneva, Switzerland: World Trade Organization.

McKnight, Tom L. *Physical Geography: A Landscape Appreciation.* 5th ed. Upper Saddle River, New Jersey: Prentice Hall, 1996.

National Geographic Atlas of the World, 8th ed. Washington, D.C.: The National Geographic Society, 2005.

Strahler, Alan and Arthur Strahler. *Physical Geography: Science and Systems of the Human Environment.* 2nd ed. John Wiley & Sons, Inc, 2002.

Tarbuck, Edward J. and Frederick K. Lutgens. *Earth: An Introduction to Physical Geology.* 7th ed. Upper Saddle River, New Jersey: Prentice Hall, 2002.

World Development Indicators, 2005. Washington, D.C.: World Bank.

The World Factbook 2007. Washington, D.C.: Central Intelligence Agency, 2007.

The World Health Report 2006. Geneva: World Health Organization, 2006.

World Investment Report, 2005. New York and Geneva: United Nations Conference on Trade and Development, 2005.

PRINCIPAL ONLINE SOURCES

Cambridge Dictionaries Online
dictionary.cambridge.org

Central Intelligence Agency
www.cia.gov

CIESIN
www.ciesin.org

Conservation International
www.conservation.org

International Monetary Fund
www.imf.org

Merriam-Webster OnLine
www.m-w.com

National Aeronautics and Space Administration
www.nasa.gov

National Atmospheric and Oceanic Administration
www.noaa.gov

National Climatic Data Center
www.ncdc.noaa.gov

National Geophysical Data Center
www.ngdc.noaa.gov

National Park Service
www.nps.gov

National Renewable Energy Laboratory
www.nrel.gov

Population Reference Bureau
www.prb.org

United Nations
www.un.org

UN Conference on Trade and Development
www.unctad.org

UN Development Programme
www.undp.org

UN Educational, Cultural, and Scientific Organization
www.unesco.org

UNEP-WCMC
www.unep-wcmc.org

UN Millennium Development Goals
www.un.org/millenniumgoals

UN Population Division
www.unpopulation.org

UN Refugee Agency
www.unhcr.org

UN Statistics Division
unstats.un.org

U.S. Board on Geographic Names
geonames.usgs.gov

U.S. Geological Survey
www.usgs.gov

World Bank
www.worldbank.org

World Health Organization
www.who.int

World Trade Organization
www.wto.org

KEY TO FLAGS AND FACTS

The National Geographic Society, whose cartographic policy is to recognize de facto countries, counted 193 independent nations in mid-2007. At the end of each chapter of the *Concise Atlas of the World* there is a fact box for every independent nation and for most dependencies located on the continent or region covered in that chapter. Each box includes the flag of a political entity, as well as important statistical data. Boxes for some dependencies show two flags—a local one and the sovereign flag of the administering country. Dependencies are non-independent political entities associated in some way with a particular independent nation.

The statistical data provide highlights of geography, demography, and economy. These details offer a brief overview of each political entity; they present general characteristics and are not intended to be comprehensive studies. The structured nature of the text results in some generic collective or umbrella terms. The industry category, for instance, includes services in addition to traditional manufacturing sectors. Space limitations dictate the amount of information included. For example, the only languages listed for the U.S. are English and Spanish, although many others are spoken. The North America chapter also includes concise fact boxes for U.S. states, showing the state flag, population, and capital.

Fact boxes are arranged alphabetically by the conventional short forms of the country or dependency names. Country and dependency boxes are grouped separately. The conventional long forms of names appear in colored type below the conventional short form; if there are no long forms, the short forms are repeated. Except where otherwise noted below, all demographic data are derived from the CIA *World Factbook.*

AREA accounts for the total area of a country, or dependency, including all land and inland water delimited by international boundaries, intranational boundaries, or coastlines.

POPULATION figures for independent nations and dependencies are mid-2006 figures from the Population Reference Bureau in Washington, D.C. Next to CAPITAL is the name of the seat of government, followed by the city's population. Capital city populations for both independent nations and dependencies are from 2005 United Nations estimates and represent the populations of metropolitan areas. In the POPULATION category, the figures for U.S. state populations are from the U.S. Census Bureau's 2006 midyear estimates. POPULATION figures for countries, dependencies, and U.S. states are rounded to the nearest thousand.

Under RELIGION, the most widely practiced faith appears first. "Traditional" or "indigenous" connotes beliefs of important local sects, such as the Maya in Middle America. Under LANGUAGE, if a country has an official language, it is listed first. Often, a country may list more than one official language. Otherwise both RELIGION and LANGUAGE are in rank ordering.

LITERACY generally indicates the percentage of the population above the age of 15 who can read and write. There are no universal standards of literacy, so these estimates are based on the most common definition available for a nation.

LIFE EXPECTANCY represents the average number of years a group of infants born in the same year can be expected to live if the mortality rate at each age remains constant in the future. (Data from the Population Reference Bureau.)

GDP PER CAPITA is Gross Domestic Product divided by midyear population estimates. GDP estimates for independent nations and dependencies use the purchasing power parity (PPP) conversion factor designed to equalize the purchasing powers of different currencies.

Individual income estimates such as GDP PER CAPITA are among the many indicators used to assess a nation's well-being. As statistical averages, they hide extremes of poverty and wealth. Furthermore, they take no account of factors that affect quality of life, such as environmental degradation, educational opportunities, and health care.

ECONOMY information for the independent nations and dependencies is divided into three general categories: Industry, Agriculture, and Exports. Because of structural limitations, only the primary industries (IND), agricultural commodities (AGR), and exports (EXP) are reported. Agriculture serves as an umbrella term for not only crops but also livestock, products, and fish. In the interest of conciseness, agriculture for the independent nations presents, when applicable, four major crops, followed respectively by leading entries for livestock, products, and fish.

NA indicates that data are not available.

Published by the National Geographic Society

John M. Fahey, Jr. — *President and Chief Executive Officer*

Gilbert M. Grosvenor — *Chairman of the Board*

Nina D. Hoffman — *Executive Vice President; President, Book Publishing Group*

Prepared by the Book Division

Kevin Mulroy — *Senior Vice President and Publisher*

Marianne R. Koszorus — *Design Director*

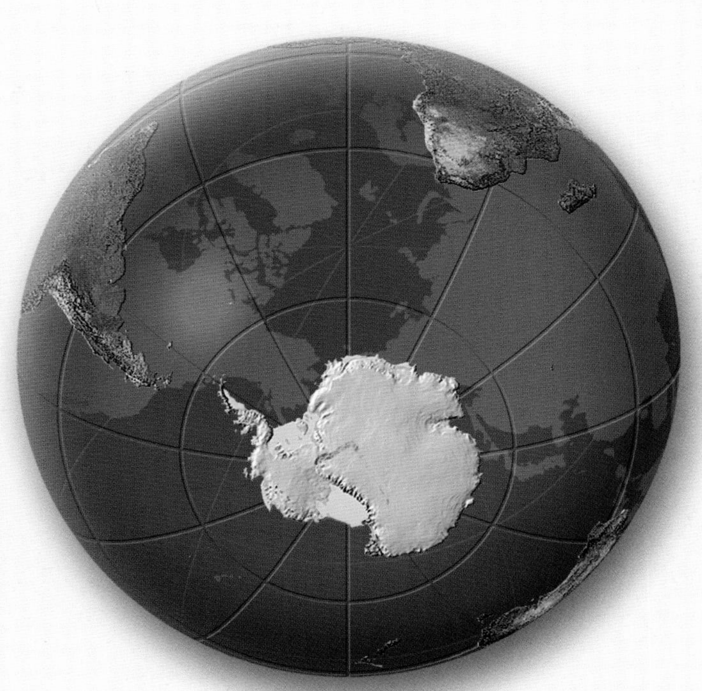

Staff for This Atlas

Carl Mehler — *Project Editor and Director of Maps*

Laura Exner, Thomas L. Gray, Joseph F. Ochlak, Nicholas P. Rosenbach — *Map Editors*

Nathan Eidem, Steven D. Gardner, NG Maps, and XNR Productions — *Map Research and Compilation*

Matt Chwastyk — *Map Production Manager*

Steven D. Gardner, James Huckenpahler, Michael McNey, Gregory Ugiansky, NG Maps, and XNR Productions — *Map Production*

Marty Ittner — *Book Design*

Rebecca Lescaze, Victoria Garrett Jones — *Text Editors*

Elisabeth B. Booz, Patrick Booz, William Burroughs, Carlos Castillo-Salgado, Michael Finger, Noel Grove, K.M. Kostyal, Monty G. Marshall, Antony Shugaar, Robert I. Tilling — *Contributing Writers*

Elisabeth B. Booz, Nathan Eidem, Steven D. Gardner, Joseph F. Ochlak, Nicholas P. Rosenbach — *Text Researchers*

Tibor G. Tóth — *Art and Illustrations*

R. Gary Colbert — *Production Director*

Manufacturing and Quality Control

Christopher A. Liedel — *Chief Financial Officer*

Phillip L. Schlosser — *Vice President*

John T. Dunn — *Technical Director*

Reproduction by Quad/Graphics, Alexandria, Virginia
Printed and Bound by Mondadori S.p.A., Verona, Italy

RUSSIA
Alaska
see United States
56–59
GREENLAND
ICELAND
CANADA
UNITED KINGDOM
IRELAND
NORTH
AMERICA
48–65
UNITED STATES
56–59
PORTUGAL
MOROCCO
WESTERN SAHARA
MAURITANIA
Hawai'i
see United States
56–59
MEXICO
CUBA
BAHAMAS
DOMINICAN REPUBLIC
HAITI
JAMAICA
BELIZE
HONDURAS
PUERTO RICO
ST. KITTS AND NEVIS
ANTIGUA AND BARBUDA
DOMINICA
ST. LUCIA
BARBADOS
GRENADA
ST. VINCENT AND THE GRENADINES
TRINIDAD AND TOBAGO
GUATEMALA
EL SALVADOR
NICARAGUA
COSTA RICA
PANAMA
CAPE VERDE
SENEGAL
GAMBIA
GUINEA-BISSAU
GUINEA
SIERRA LEONE
LIBERIA
VENEZUELA
GUYANA
SURINAME
FRENCH GUIANA
COLOMBIA
ECUADOR
BRAZIL
KIRIBATI
AUSTRALIA and
OCEANIA
112–125
AMERICAN SAMOA
SAMOA
FRENCH POLYNESIA
TONGA
SOUTH
AMERICA
66–75
PERU
BOLIVIA
PARAGUAY
CHILE
URUGUAY
ARGENTINA
FALKLAND ISLANDS